I'm a huge fan of a certain "magical kingdom" and all its movies. There's just nothing that can compare to that sense of joy, wonder and euphoria. Maybe someday they'll make a Dragon Ball Land too...

—Toyotarou, 2018

Toyotarou

Toyotarou created the manga adaptation for the *Dragon Ball Z* anime's 2015 film, *Dragon Ball Z: Resurrection F*. He is also the author of the spin-off series *Dragon Ball Heroes: Victory Mission*, which debuted in *V-Jump* in Japan in November 2012.

Akira Toriyama

Renowned worldwide for his playful, innovative storytelling and humorous, distinctive art style, Akira Toriyama burst onto the manga scene in 1980 with the wildly popular *Dr. Slump*. His hit series *Dragon Ball* (published in the U.S. as *Dragon Ball* and *Dragon Ball Z*) ran from 1984 to 1995 in Shueisha's *Weekly Shonen Jump* magazine. He is also known for his design work on video games such as *Dragon Quest*, *Chrono Trigger*, *Tobal No. 1* and *Blue Dragon*. His recent manga works include *COWA!*, *Kajika*, *Sand Land*, *Neko Majin*, *Jaco the Galactic Patrolman* and a children's book, *Toccio the Angel*. He lives with his family in Japan.

SHONEN JUMP Manga Edition

STORY BY **Akira Toriyama**
ART BY **Toyotarou**

TRANSLATION **Caleb Cook**
TOUCH-UP ART AND LETTERING **James Gaubatz**
DESIGN **Shawn Carrico**
EDITOR **Marlene First**

DRAGON BALL SUPER © 2015 BY BIRD STUDIO, Toyotarou
All rights reserved. First published in Japan in 2015 by SHUEISHA Inc., Tokyo.
English translation rights arranged by SHUEISHA Inc.

The stories, characters and incidents mentioned
in this publication are entirely fictional.

Printed in the U.S.A.

Published by VIZ Media, LLC
P.O. Box 77010
San Francisco, CA 94107

10 9 8 7 6 5 4 3 2 1
First printing, March 2020

viz.com

shonenjump.com

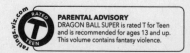

PARENTAL ADVISORY
DRAGON BALL SUPER is rated T for Teen
and is recommended for ages 13 and up.
This volume contains fantasy violence.

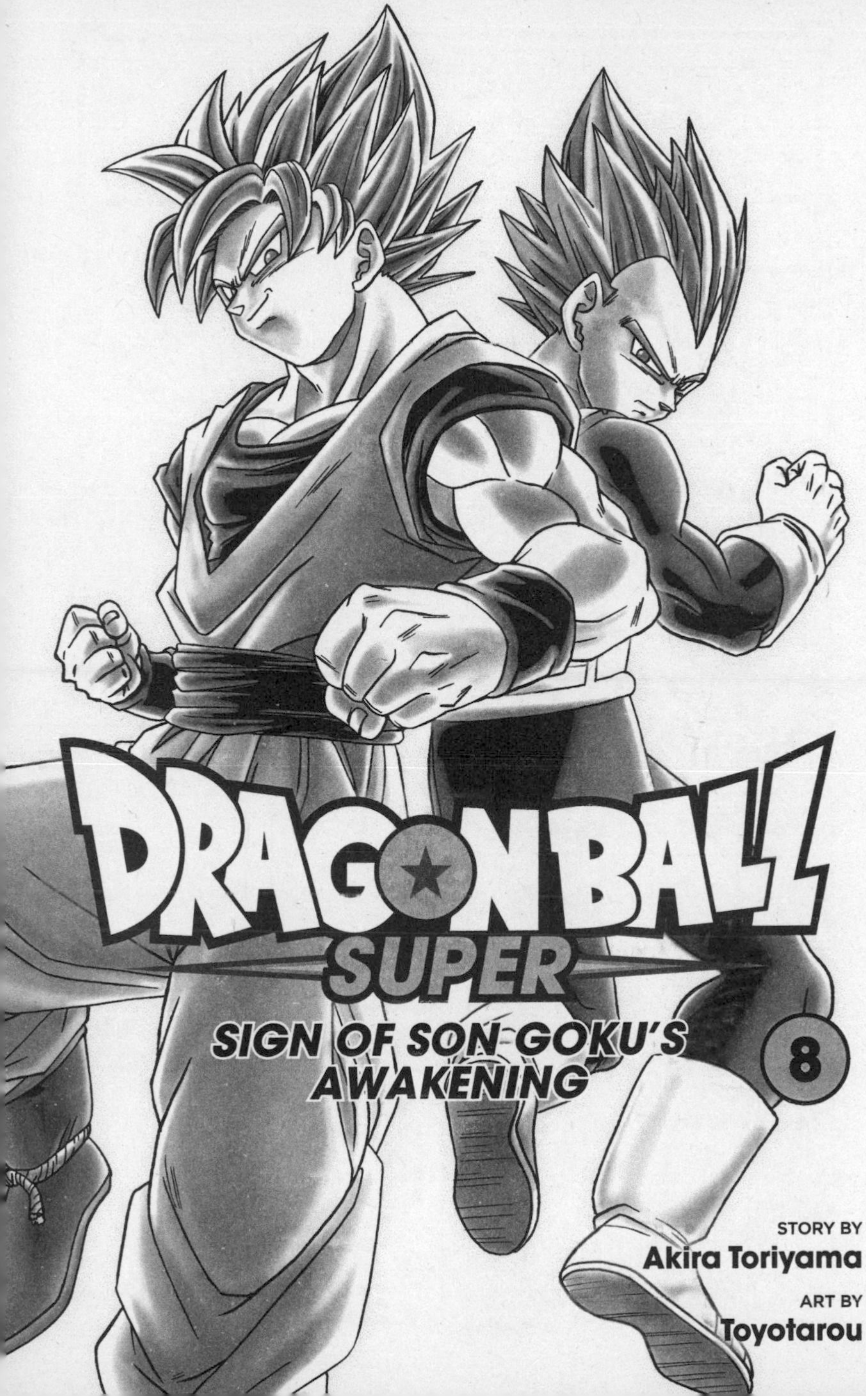

DRAGON BALL SUPER

SIGN OF SON GOKU'S AWAKENING

8

STORY BY
Akira Toriyama

ART BY
Toyotarou

CAST OF CHARACTERS

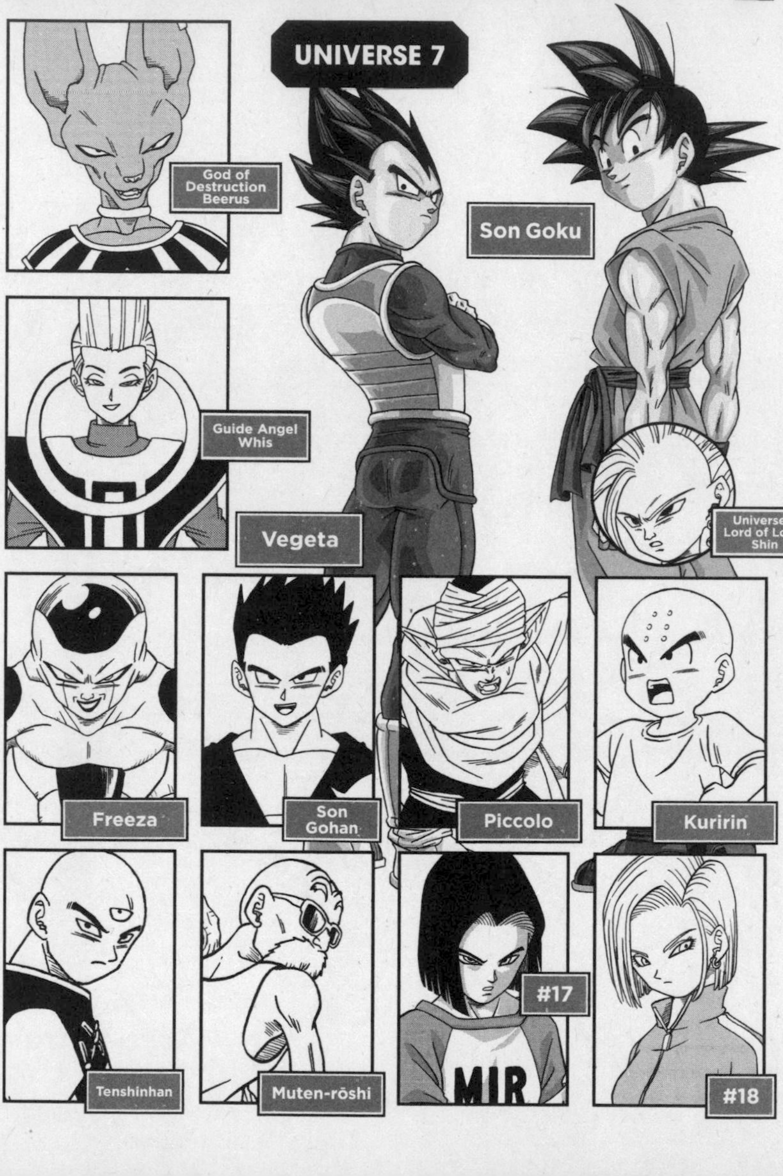
UNIVERSE 7
Son Goku
Vegeta
God of Destruction Beerus
Guide Angel Whis
Universe 7 Lord of Lords Shin
Kuririn
Piccolo
Son Gohan
Freeza
#18
#17
MIR
Muten-rōshi
Tenshinhan

From Other Universes

Grand Priest

Toppo (Universe 11)

Jiren (Universe 11)

Lords of Everything

Caulifla (Universe 6)

Kale (Universe 6)

STORY THUS FAR

A long, long time ago, Son Goku left on a journey in search of the legendary Dragon Balls—a set of seven balls that, when gathered, would summon the dragon Shenlong to grant any wish. After a great adventure, he collects them all. Later, he becomes the apprentice of Kame-Sen'nin, fights a number of vicious enemies, defeats the great Majin Boo and restores peace on Earth. Some time passes, and then Lord Beerus, the God of Destruction, suddenly awakens and sets out in search of the Super Saiyan God. Goku, by becoming the Super Saiyan God, manages to stop Beerus from destroying the Earth and starts training under him with Vegeta. One day, Trunks appears hoping to save the future. Goku and Vegeta travel to his future, but they soon find themselves struggling against Goku Black and Zamas from the parallel world. Things get even worse when Goku Black and Zamas perform Potara fusion to become the immortal God Zamas. With little hope remaining, Goku ends up asking for help from the Lord of Everything, who erases the entire future world, along with Zamas. After some time, the Lords of Everything decide to host a Tournament of Power, where all losing universes are to be obliterated. Goku's team from Universe 7 has already lost four fighters. Can the remaining six defeat some of the strongest warriors from neighboring universes?!

8

DRAGON BALL SUPER

TABLE OF CON-TENTS

DRAGON BALL SUPER

CHAPTER 37: AWAKEN, SUPER SAIYAN KALE

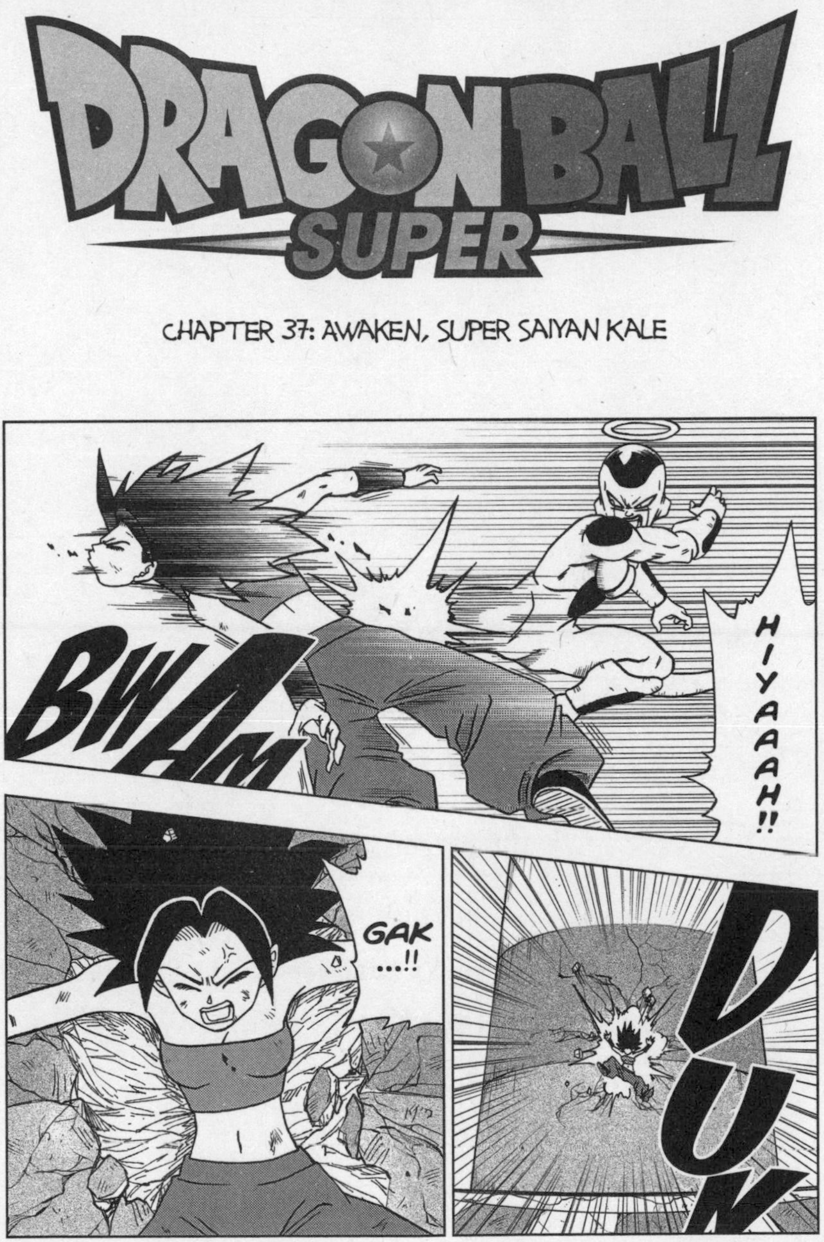
HIYAAAAH!!
BWAM
DU
GAK ...!!

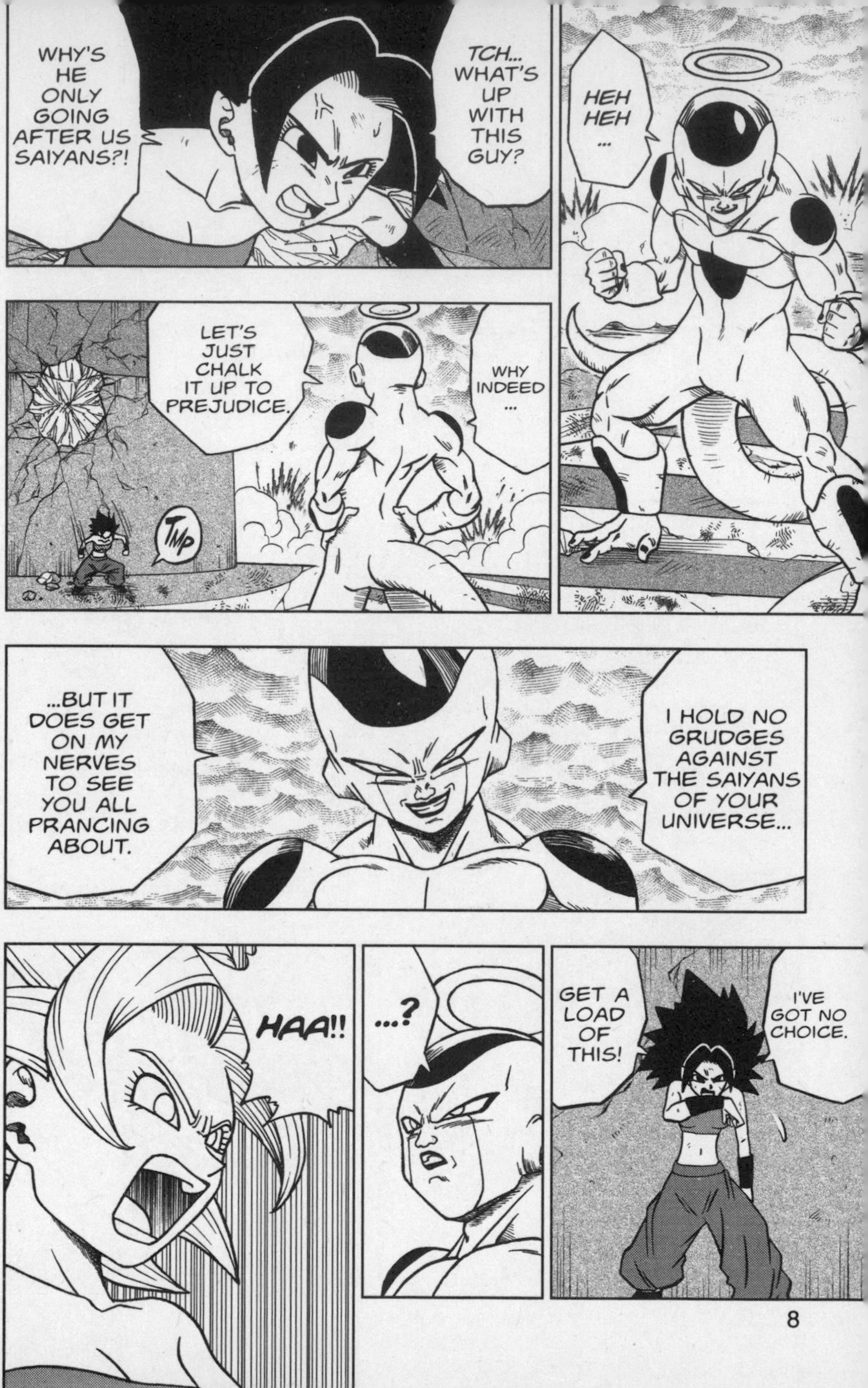
HEH HEH ...
TCH... WHAT'S UP WITH THIS GUY?
WHY'S HE ONLY GOING AFTER US SAIYANS?!
WHY INDEED ...
LET'S JUST CHALK IT UP TO PREJUDICE.
TMP
I HOLD NO GRUDGES AGAINST THE SAIYANS OF YOUR UNIVERSE...
...BUT IT DOES GET ON MY NERVES TO SEE YOU ALL PRANCING ABOUT.
I'VE GOT NO CHOICE.
GET A LOAD OF THIS!
...?
HAA!!

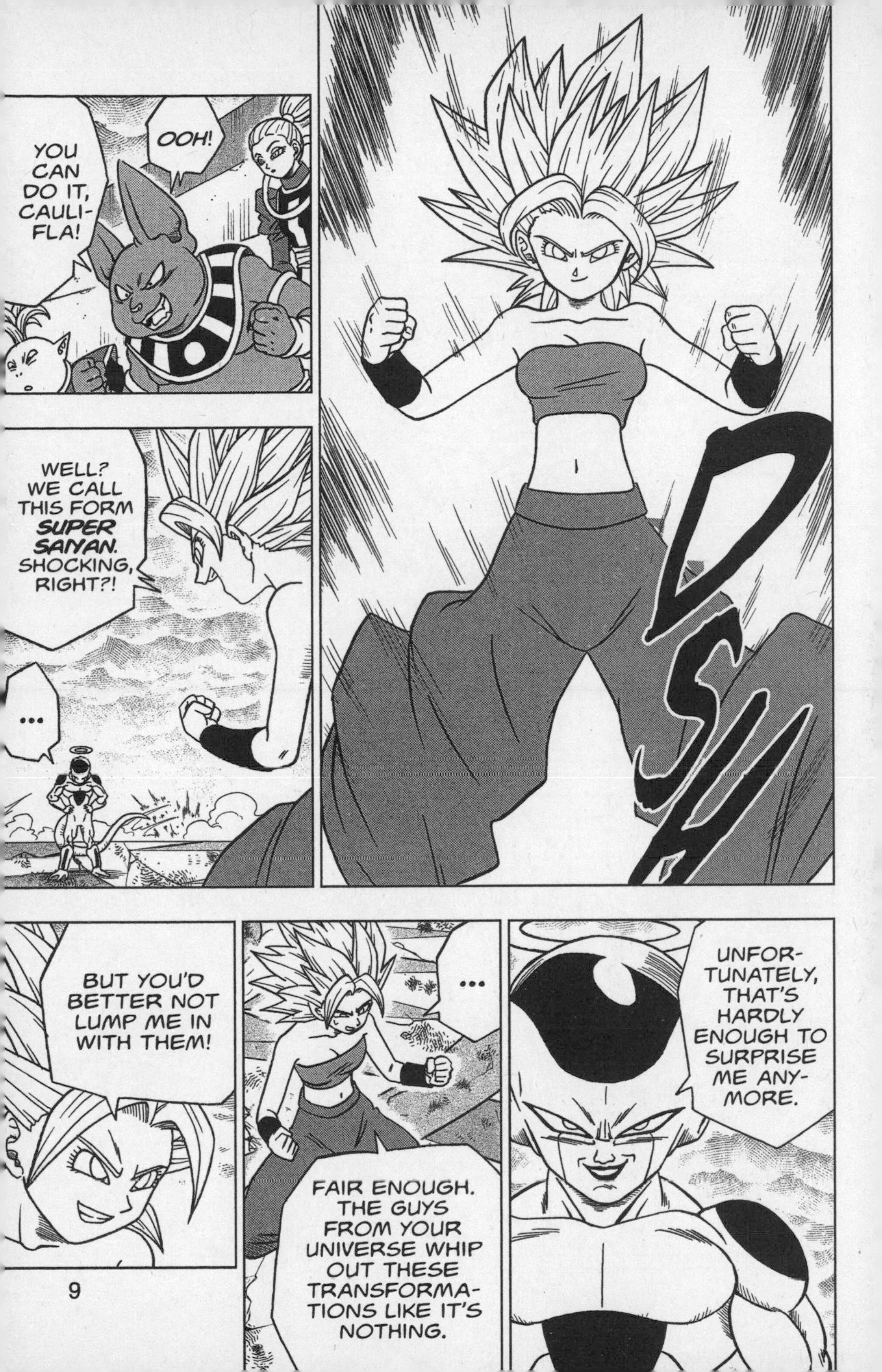
DSH
OOH!
YOU CAN DO IT, CAULI-FLA!
WELL? WE CALL THIS FORM **SUPER SAIYAN**. SHOCKING, RIGHT?!
...
UNFOR-TUNATELY, THAT'S HARDLY ENOUGH TO SURPRISE ME ANY-MORE.
...
FAIR ENOUGH. THE GUYS FROM YOUR UNIVERSE WHIP OUT THESE TRANSFORMA-TIONS LIKE IT'S NOTHING.
BUT YOU'D BETTER NOT LUMP ME IN WITH THEM!

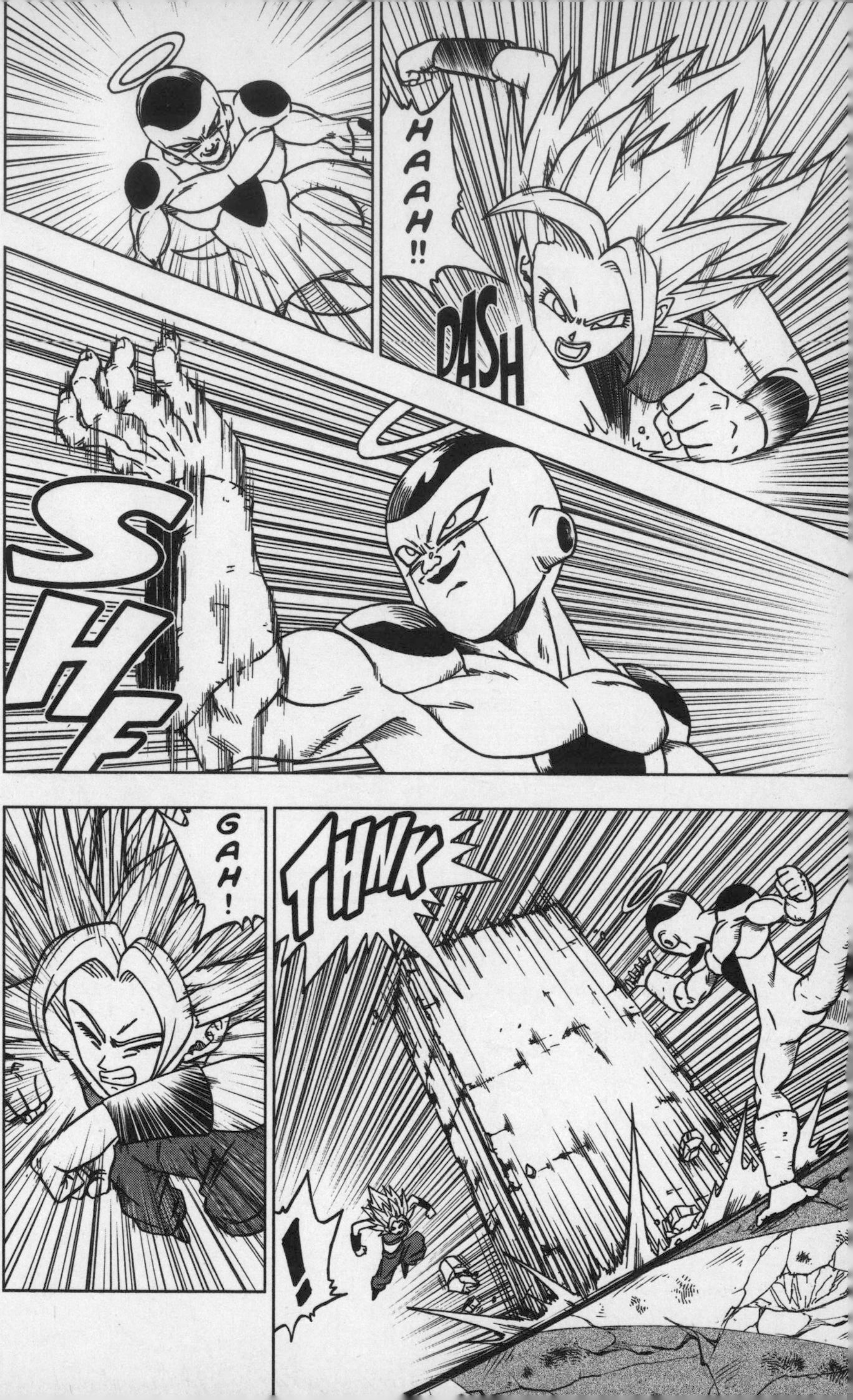
HAAAH!!
DASH
SHF
THNK
!
GAH!

HMPH!

DUN

!!

wUNCH

POW

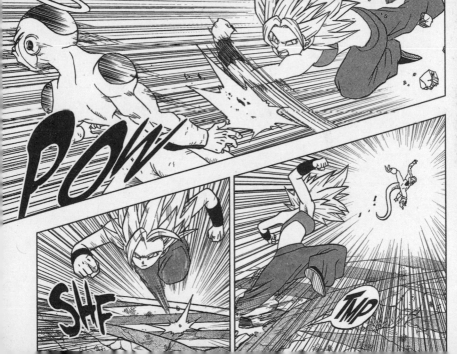

SHF

TMP

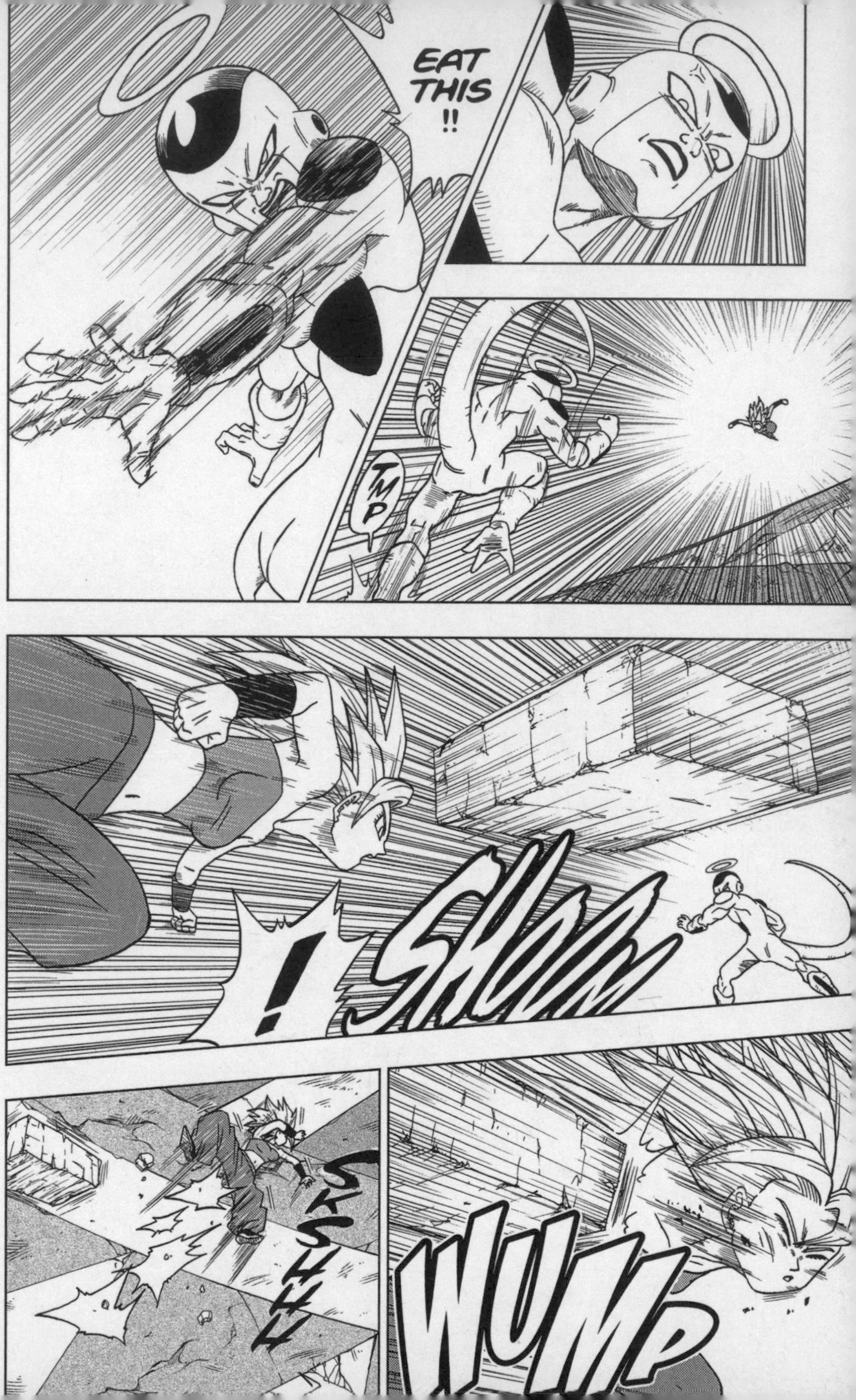
TMP
EAT THIS!!
!
SHOOM
WUMP
SKSHHH

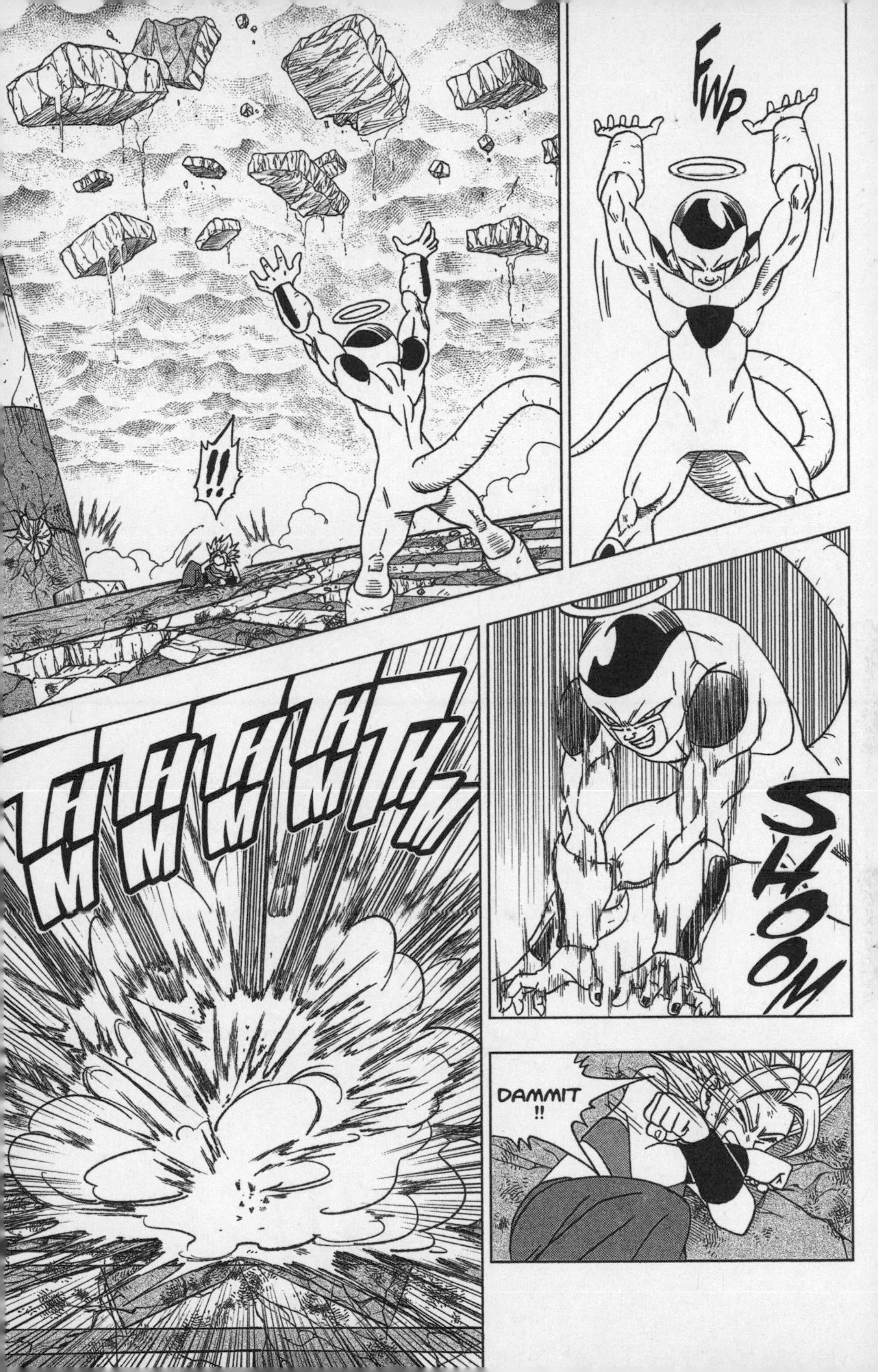
FWP
!!
SHOOM
DAMMIT !!

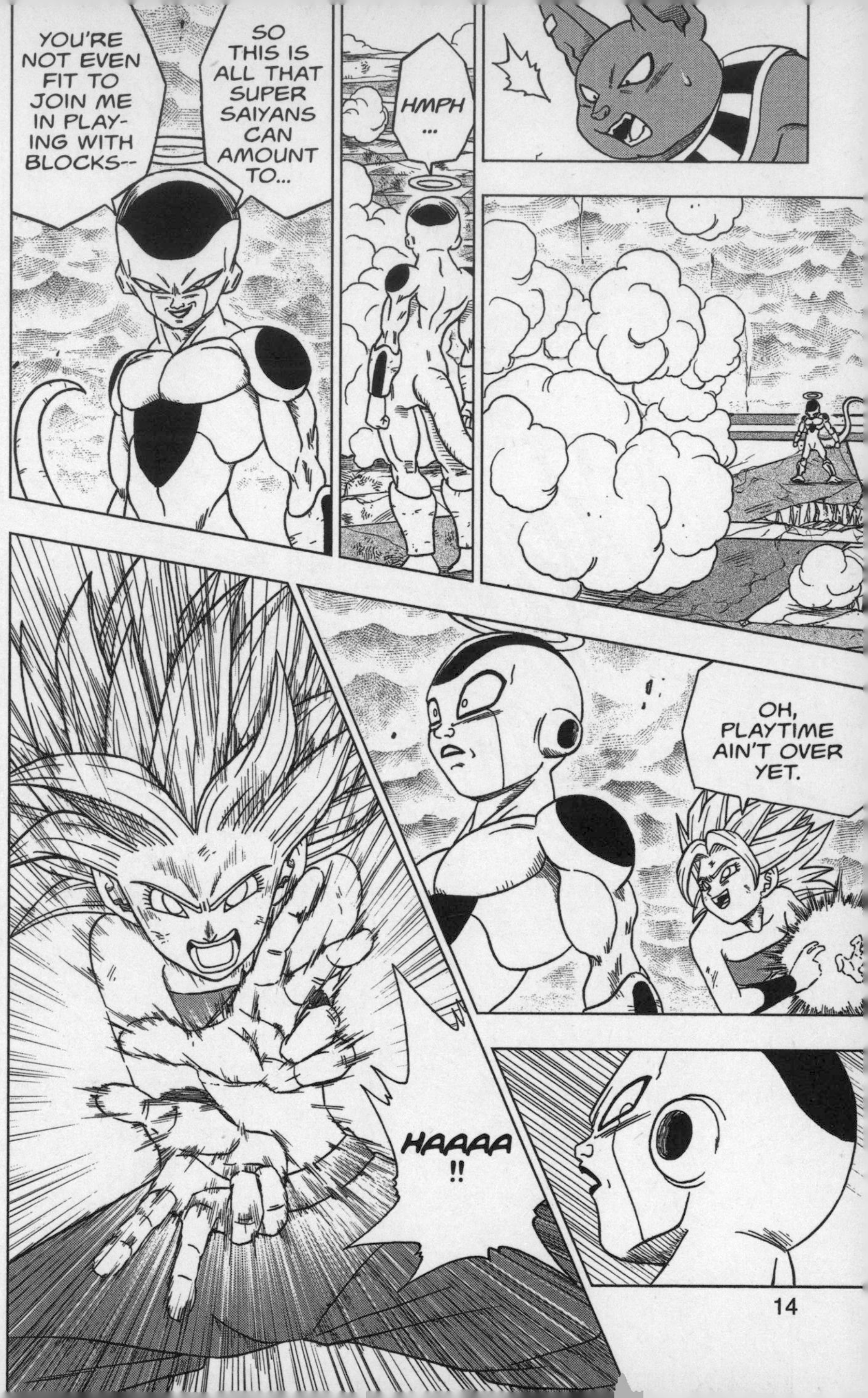
HMPH
...
SO THIS IS ALL THAT SUPER SAIYANS CAN AMOUNT TO...
YOU'RE NOT EVEN FIT TO JOIN ME IN PLAY-ING WITH BLOCKS--
OH, PLAYTIME AIN'T OVER YET.
HAAAA !!

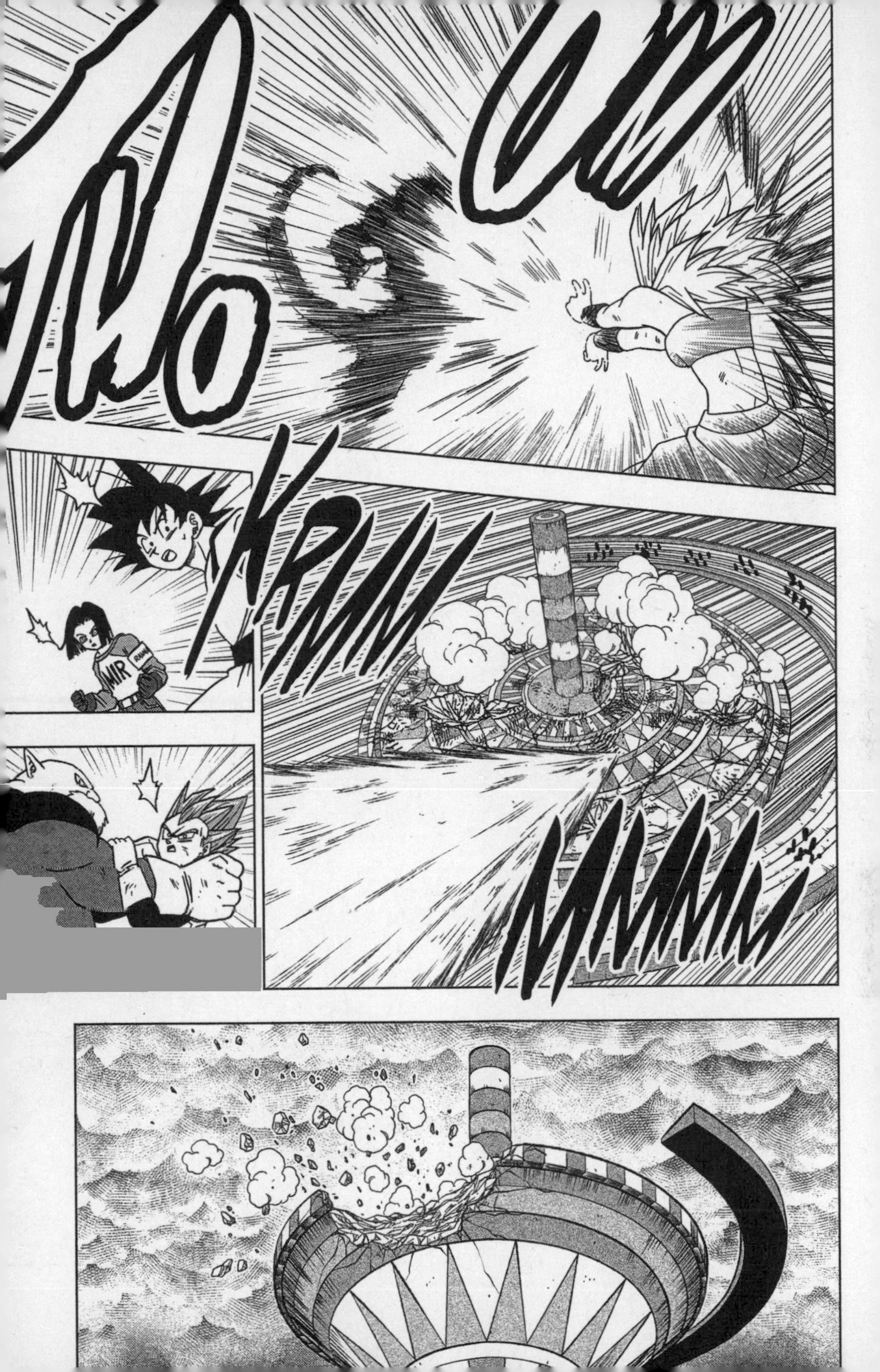
KRAM
MMMMM

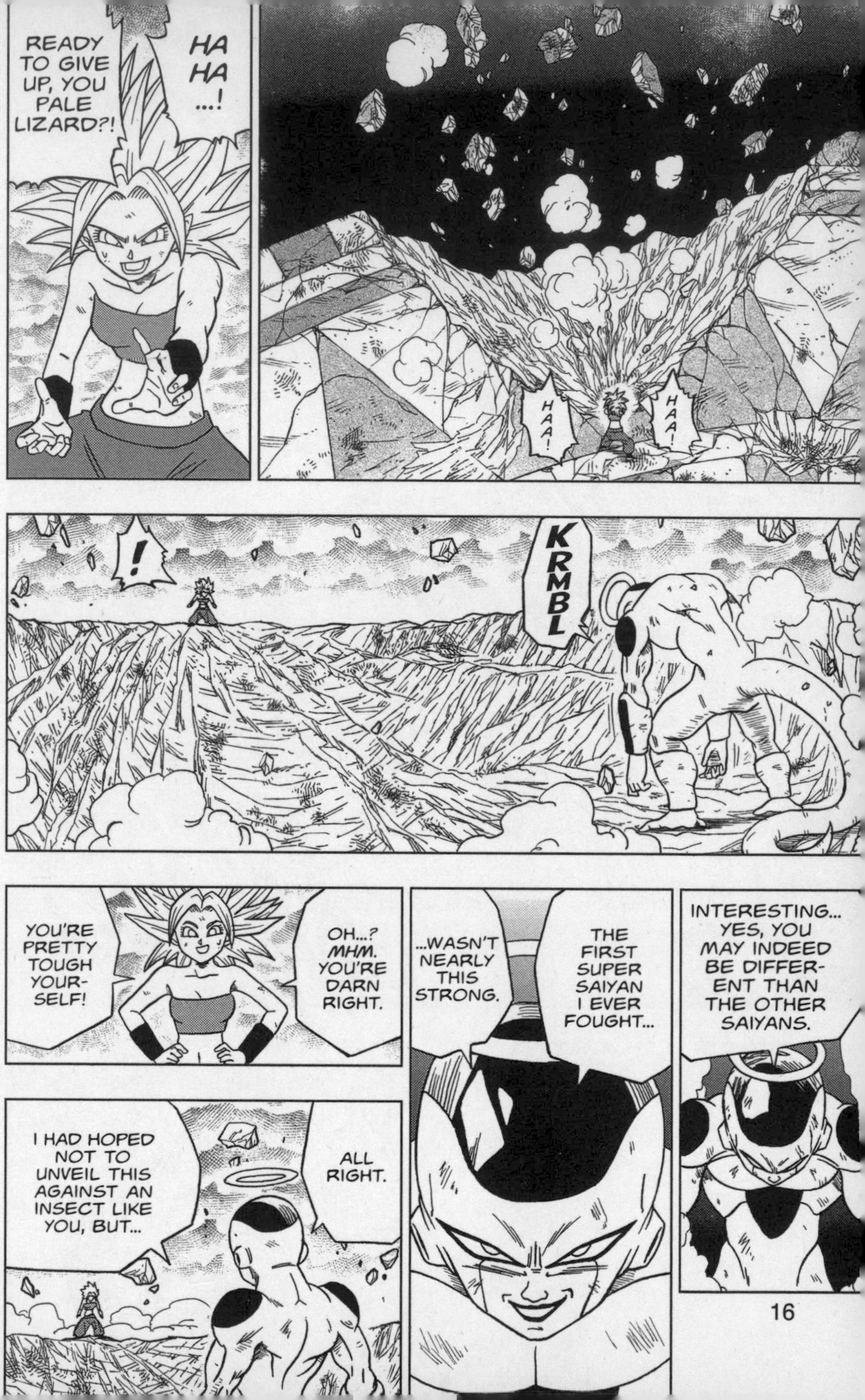
HAA!
HAA!
HA HA ...!
READY TO GIVE UP, YOU PALE LIZARD?!
KRMBL
!
INTERESTING... YES, YOU MAY INDEED BE DIFFERENT THAN THE OTHER SAIYANS.
THE FIRST SUPER SAIYAN I EVER FOUGHT...
...WASN'T NEARLY THIS STRONG.
OH...? MHM. YOU'RE DARN RIGHT.
YOU'RE PRETTY TOUGH YOURSELF!
ALL RIGHT.
I HAD HOPED NOT TO UNVEIL THIS AGAINST AN INSECT LIKE YOU, BUT...

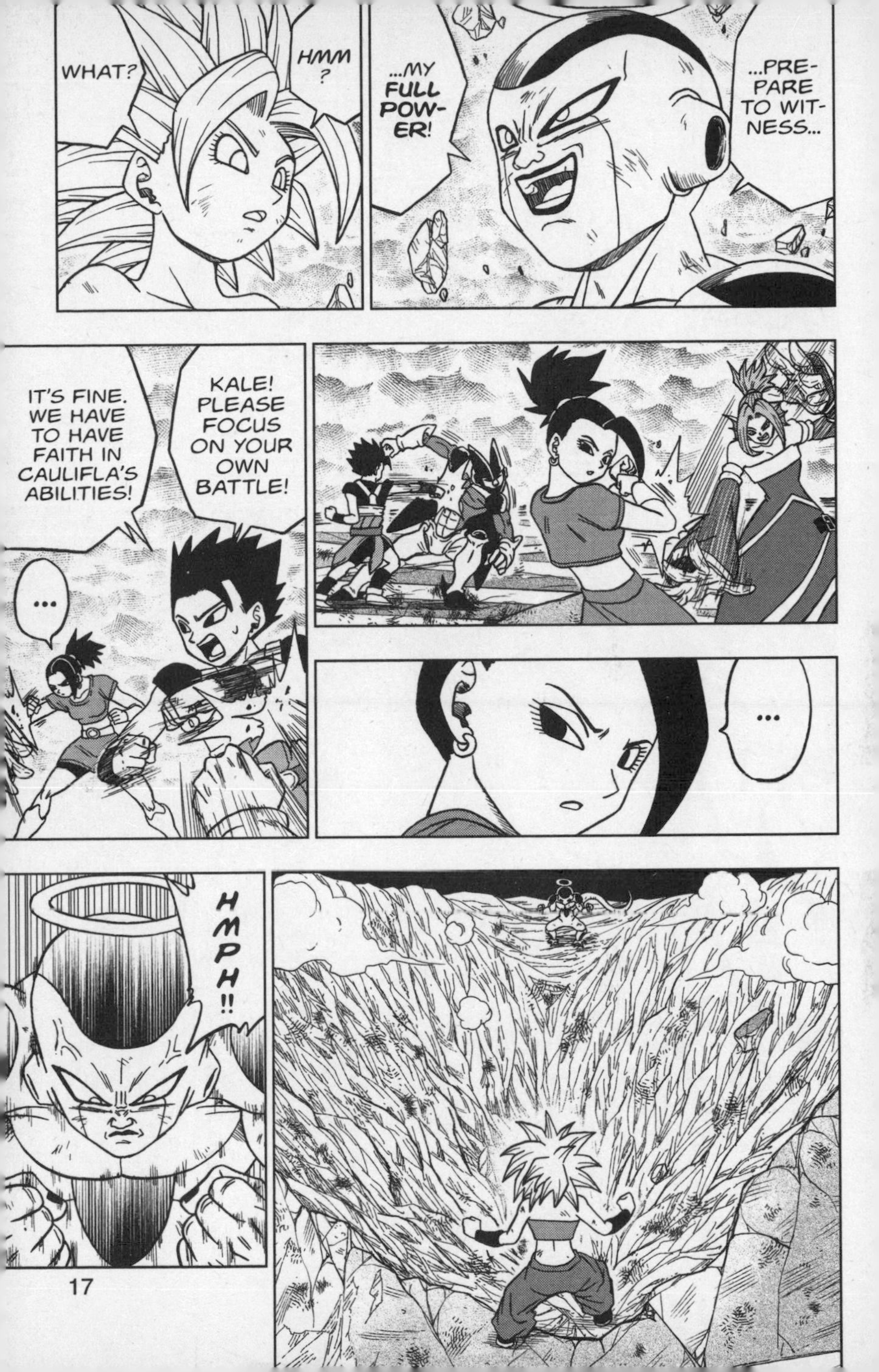
...PREPARE TO WITNESS...
...MY FULL POWER!
HMM?
WHAT?
...
KALE! PLEASE FOCUS ON YOUR OWN BATTLE!
IT'S FINE. WE HAVE TO HAVE FAITH IN CAULIFLA'S ABILITIES!
...
HMPH!!

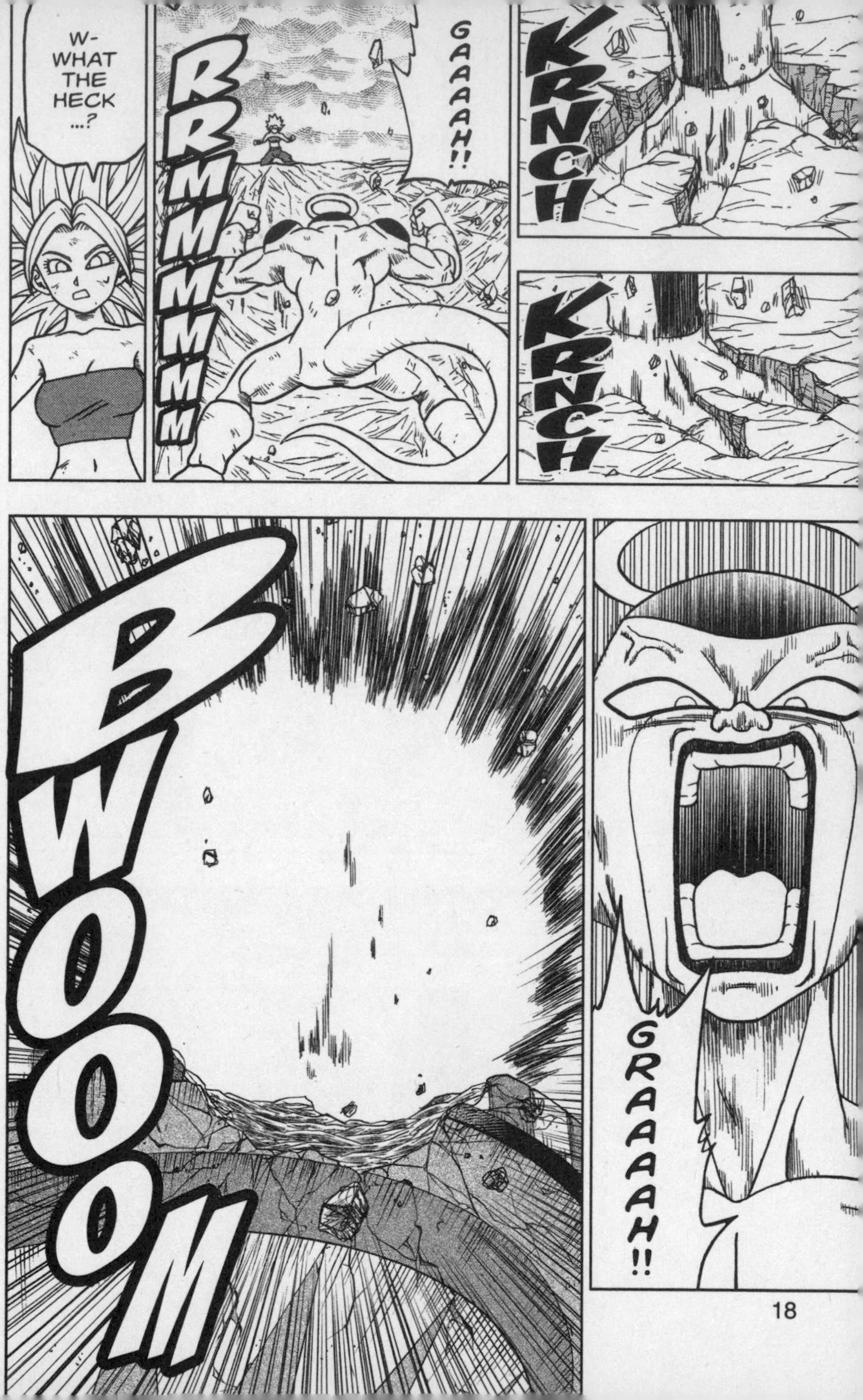
KRNCH
KRNCH
GAAAAAH!!
RRMMMMMMM
W-WHAT THE HECK ...?
GRAAAAAH!!
BWOOOM

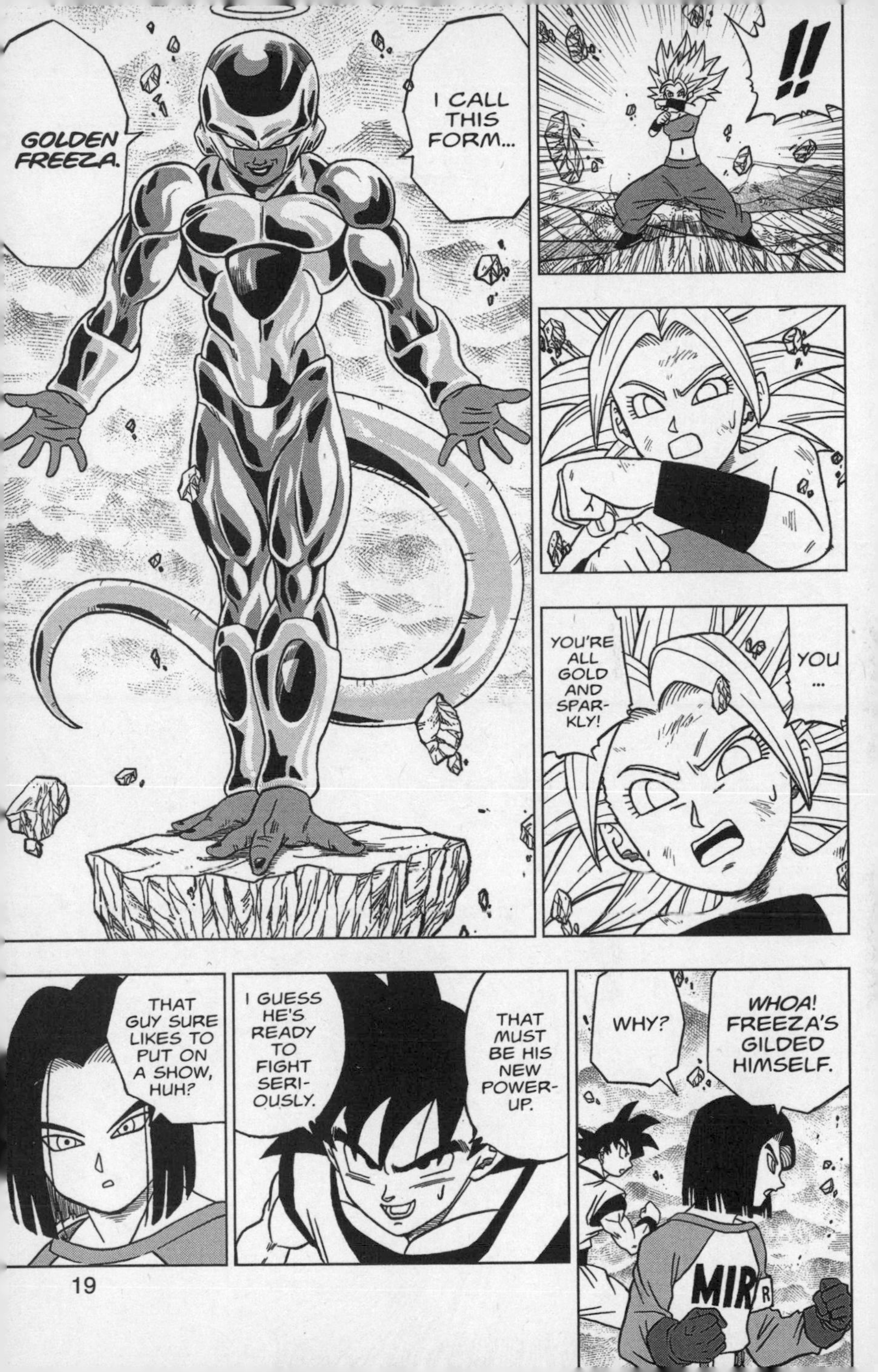
!!
YOU ...
YOU'RE ALL GOLD AND SPAR-KLY!
I CALL THIS FORM...
GOLDEN FREEZA.
WHOA! FREEZA'S GILDED HIMSELF.
WHY?
MIR
THAT MUST BE HIS NEW POWER-UP.
I GUESS HE'S READY TO FIGHT SERI-OUSLY.
THAT GUY SURE LIKES TO PUT ON A SHOW, HUH?

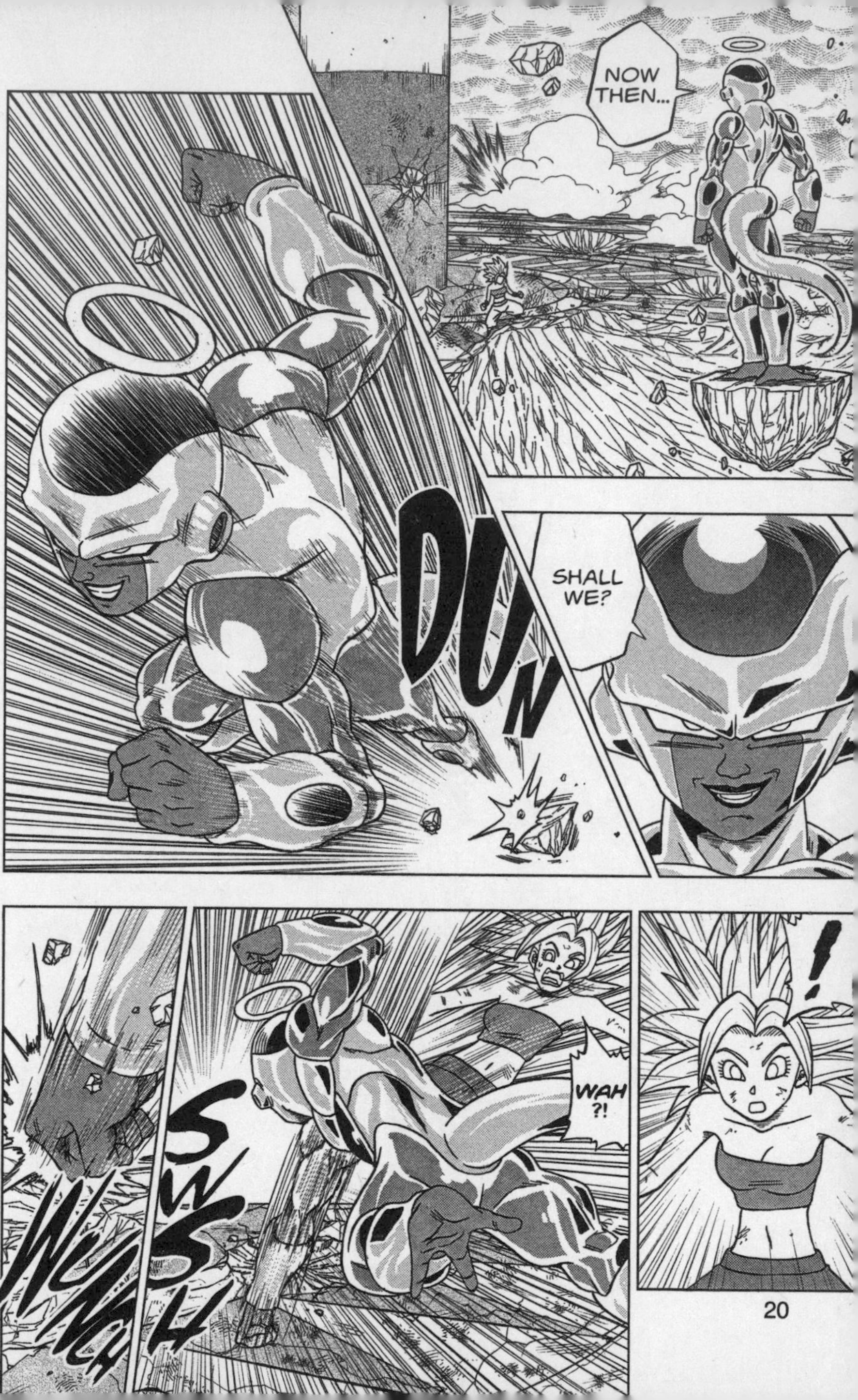
NOW THEN...
SHALL WE?
DUN
!
WAH ?!
SWSH
WUNCH

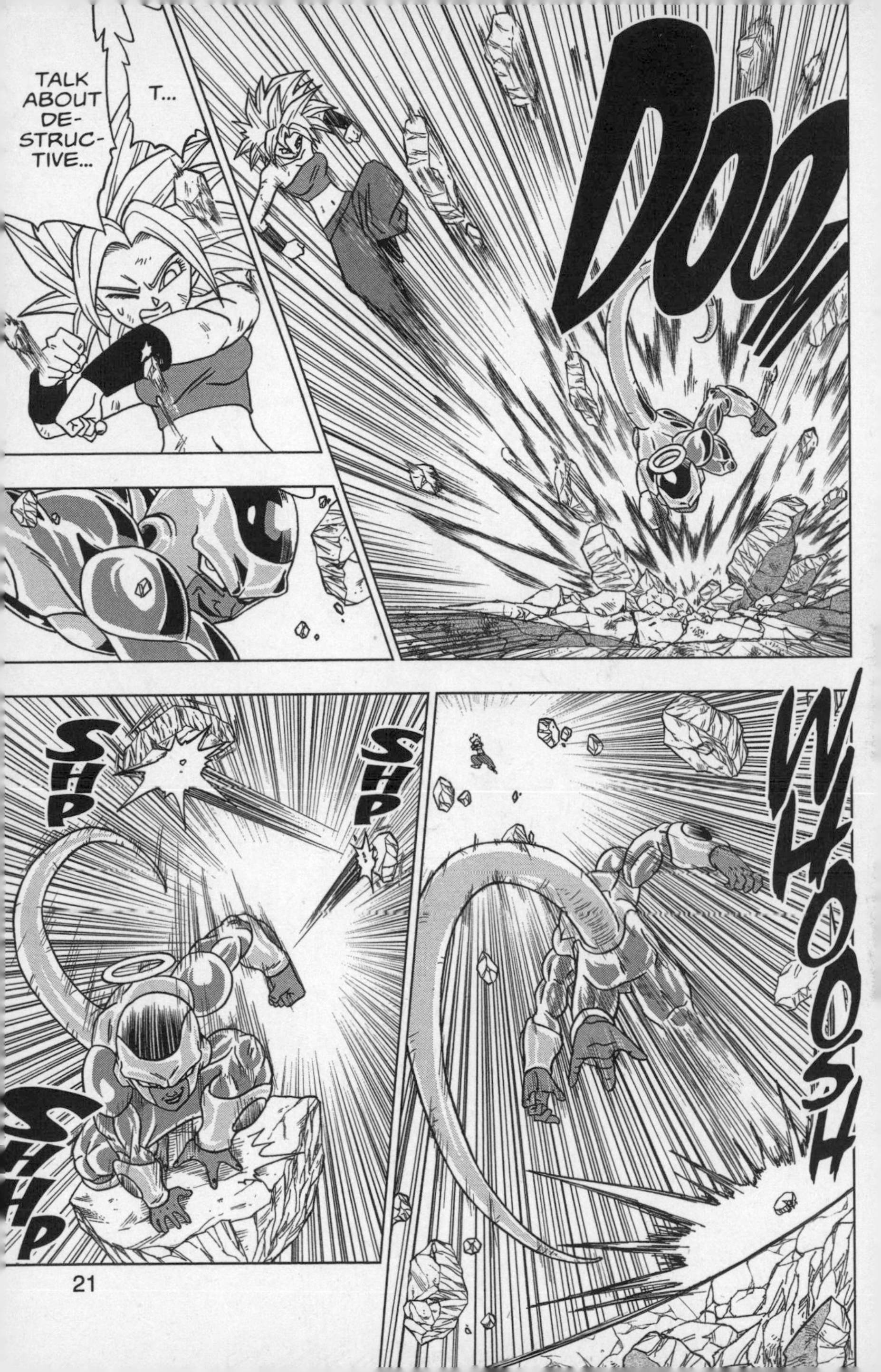
DOOOM
T...
TALK ABOUT DE-STRUCTIVE...
WHOOOSH
SHP
SHP
SHHP

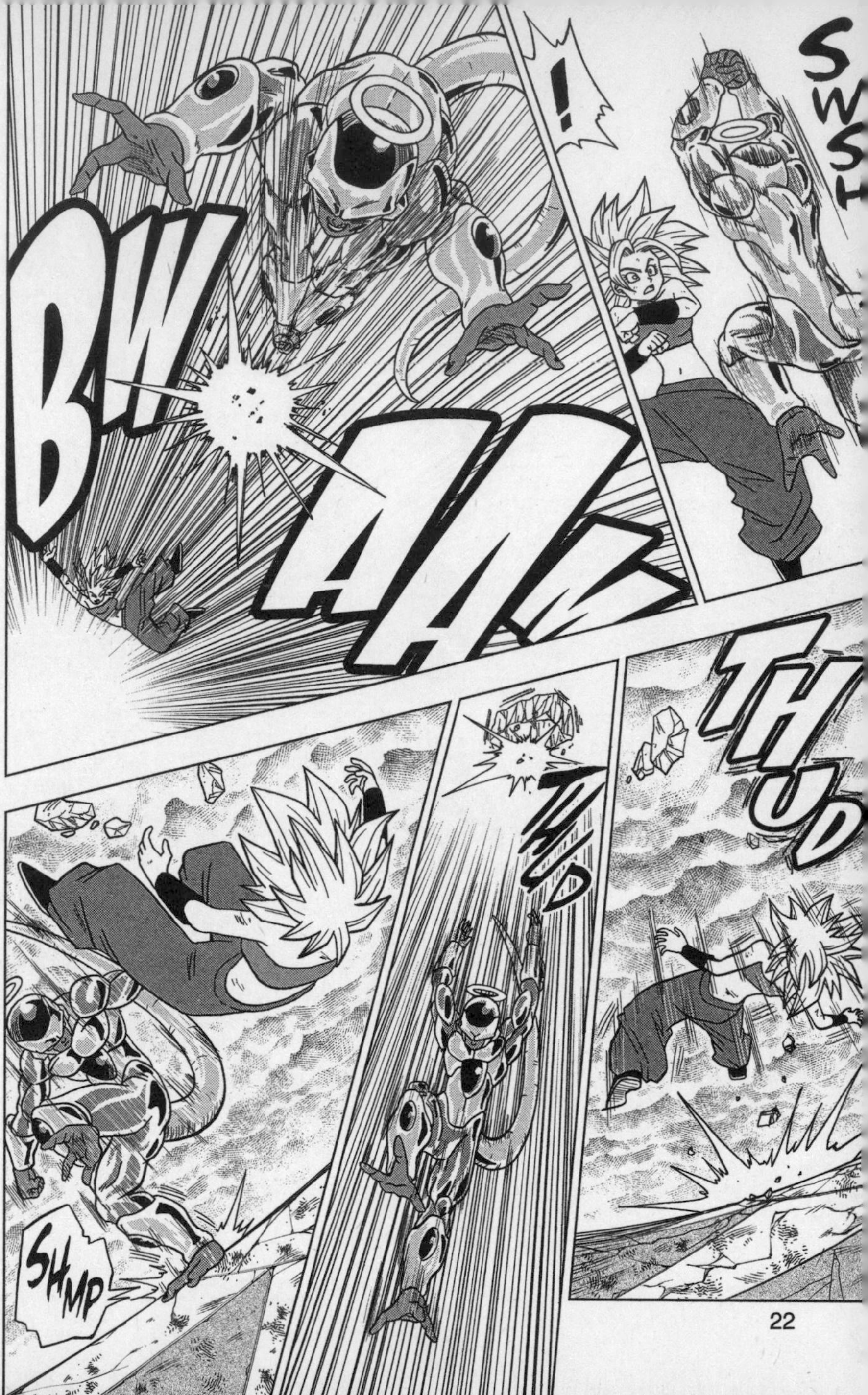
SWSH
!
BWAA
THUD
THUD
SHMP

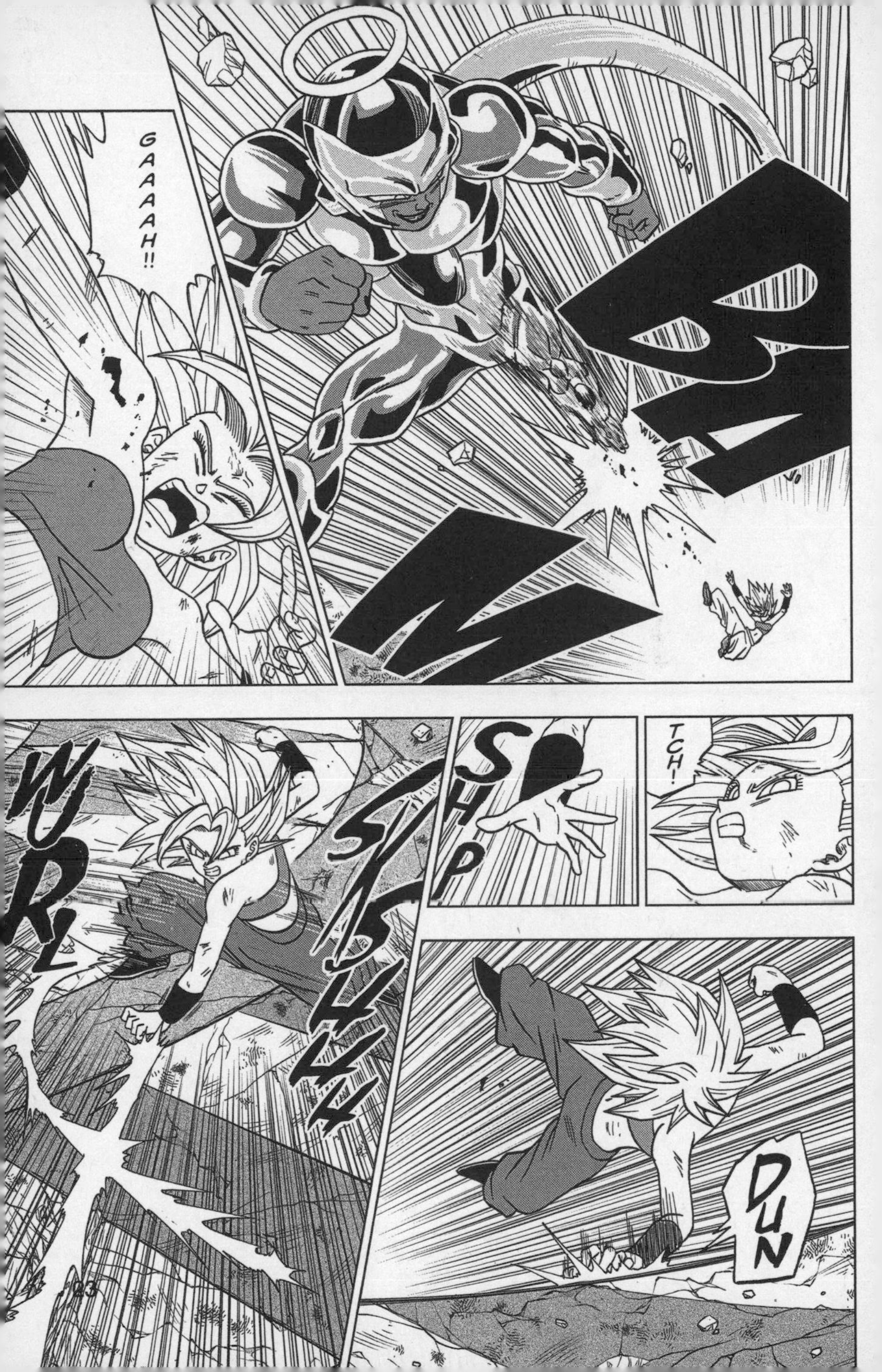
GAAAAAH!!
TCH!
SHP
DUN
WURL

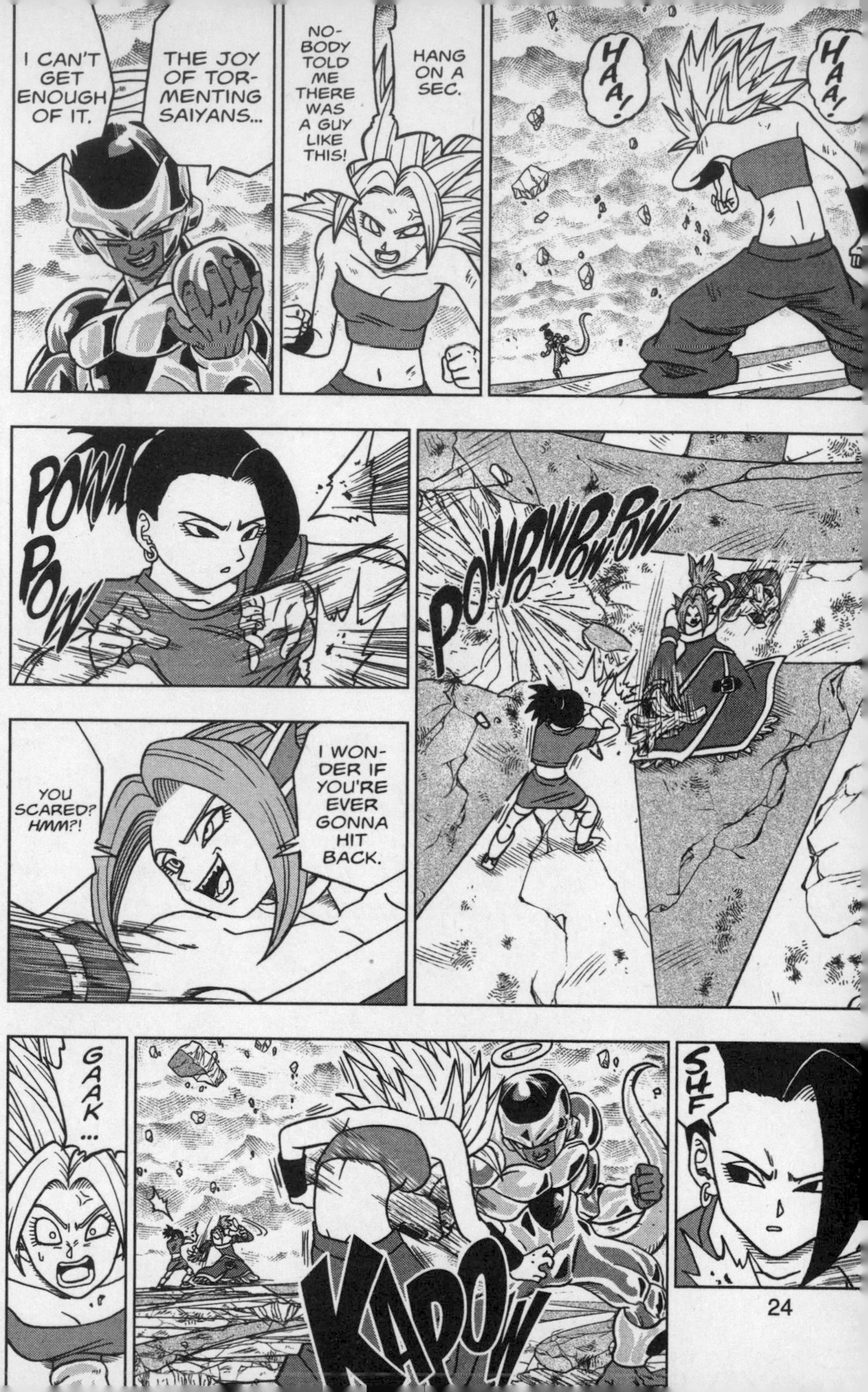
HAAA!
HAAA!
HANG ON A SEC.
NOBODY TOLD ME THERE WAS A GUY LIKE THIS!
THE JOY OF TORMENTING SAIYANS...
I CAN'T GET ENOUGH OF IT.
POWPOWPOWPOW
POW POW
I WONDER IF YOU'RE EVER GONNA HIT BACK.
YOU SCARED? HMM?!
SHF
KAPOW
GAAK...

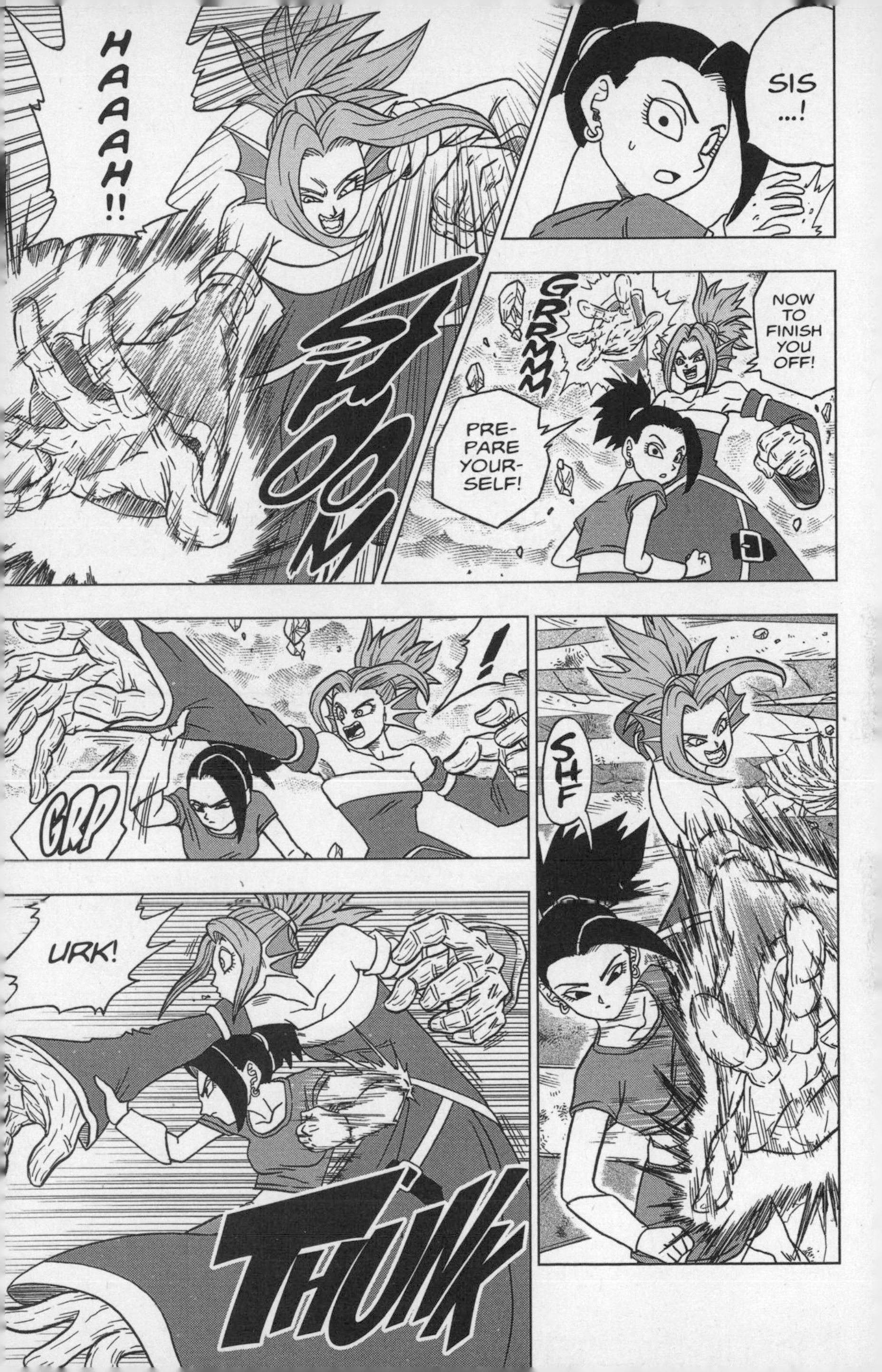
SIS ...!
NOW TO FINISH YOU OFF!
GRRMMM
PRE-PARE YOUR-SELF!
HAAAAH!!
SHF
!
GRP
URK!
THUNK

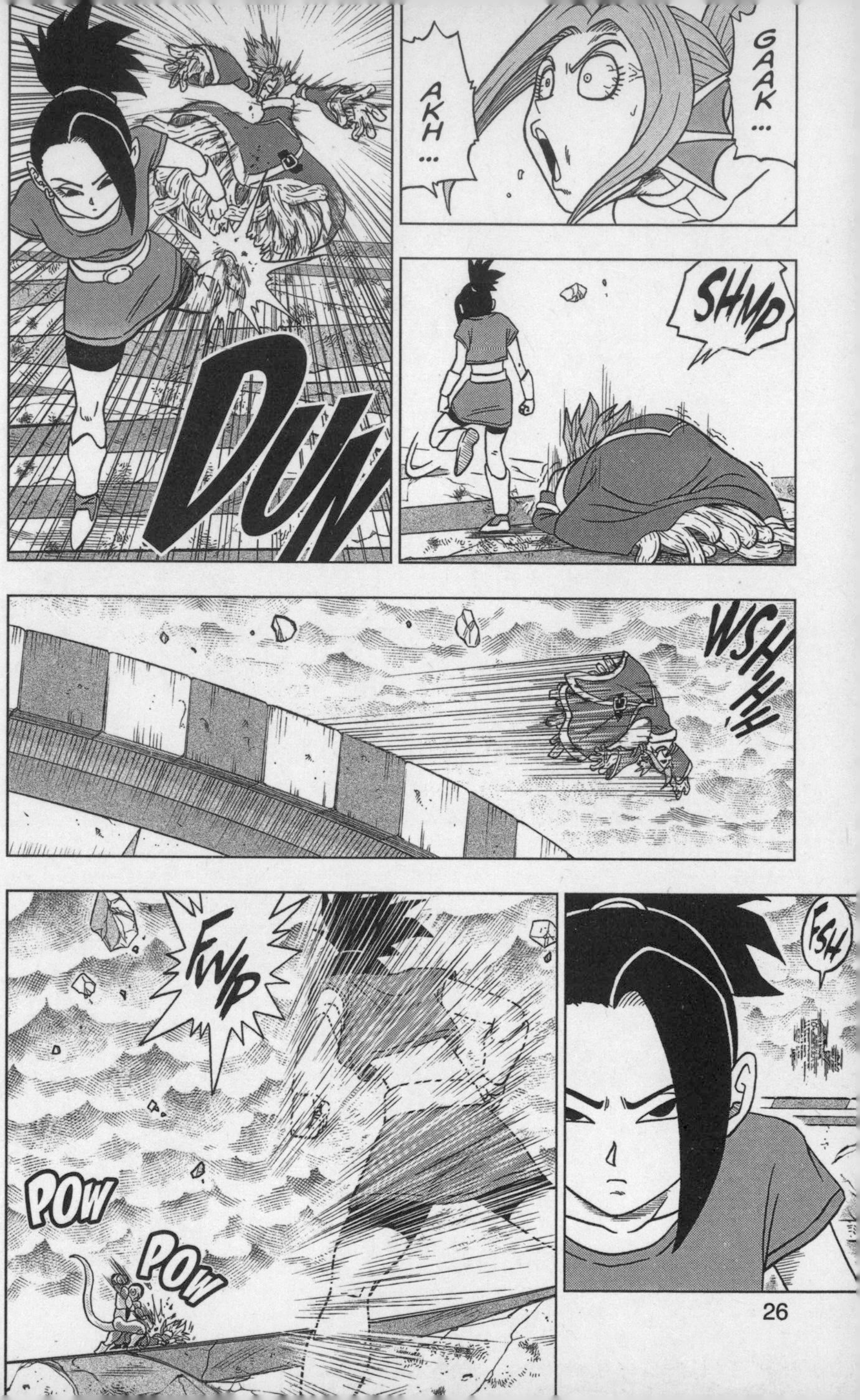
GAAK...
AKH...
SHMP
DUN
WSHHH!!
FSH
FWIP
POW
POW

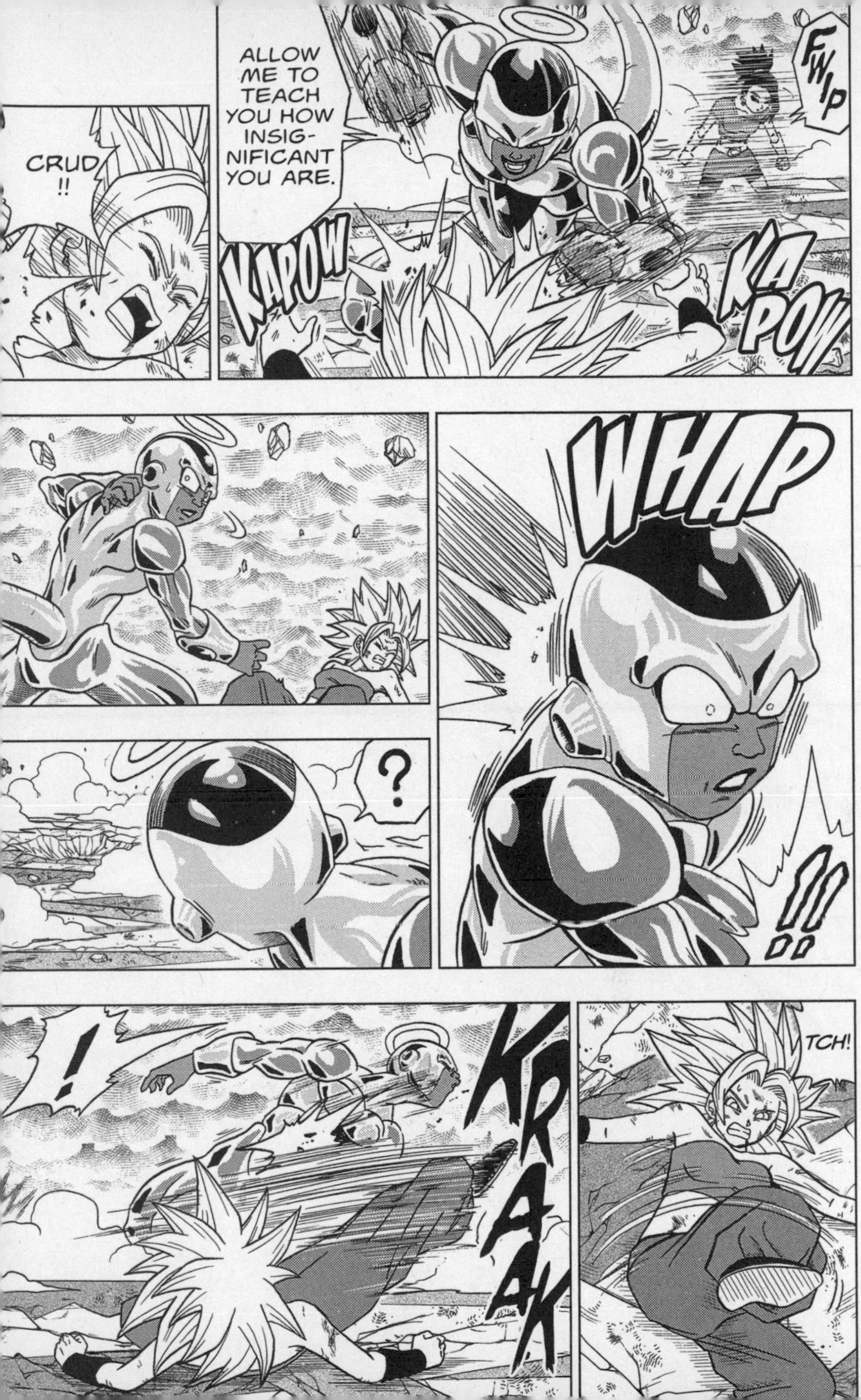
FWIP
ALLOW ME TO TEACH YOU HOW INSIG-NIFICANT YOU ARE.
KA POW
KAPOW
CRUD !!
WHAP
!!
?
TCH!
KRAAK
!

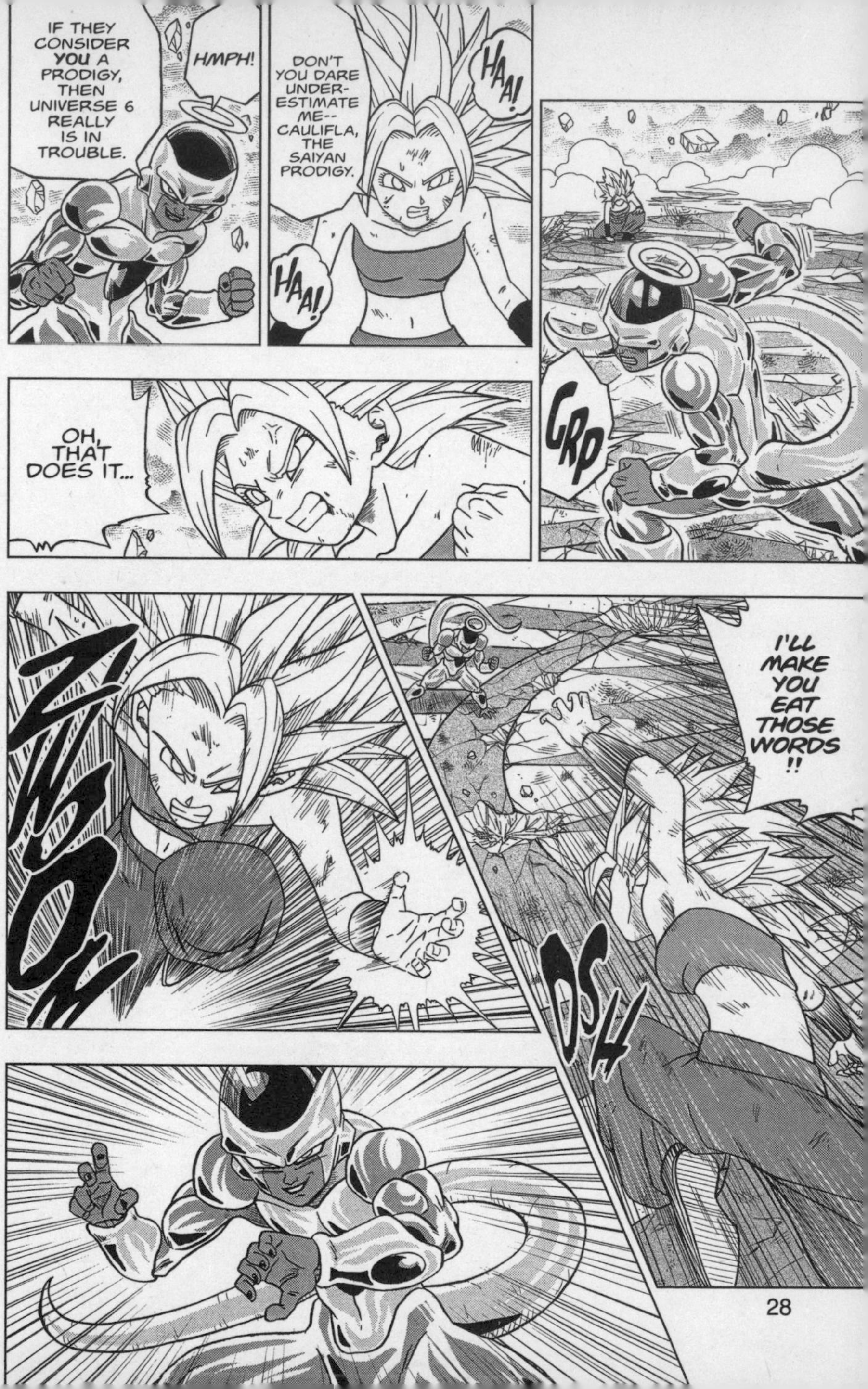
GRP
HAA!
DON'T YOU DARE UNDER-ESTIMATE ME-- CAULIFLA, THE SAIYAN PRODIGY.
HAA!
HMPH!
IF THEY CONSIDER YOU A PRODIGY, THEN UNIVERSE 6 REALLY IS IN TROUBLE.
OH, THAT DOES IT...
I'LL MAKE YOU EAT THOSE WORDS!!
DSH
ZWOM

WHAP

SSOOM

URK!

DRRIMMMM

HAAAAAAA!!

TCH!

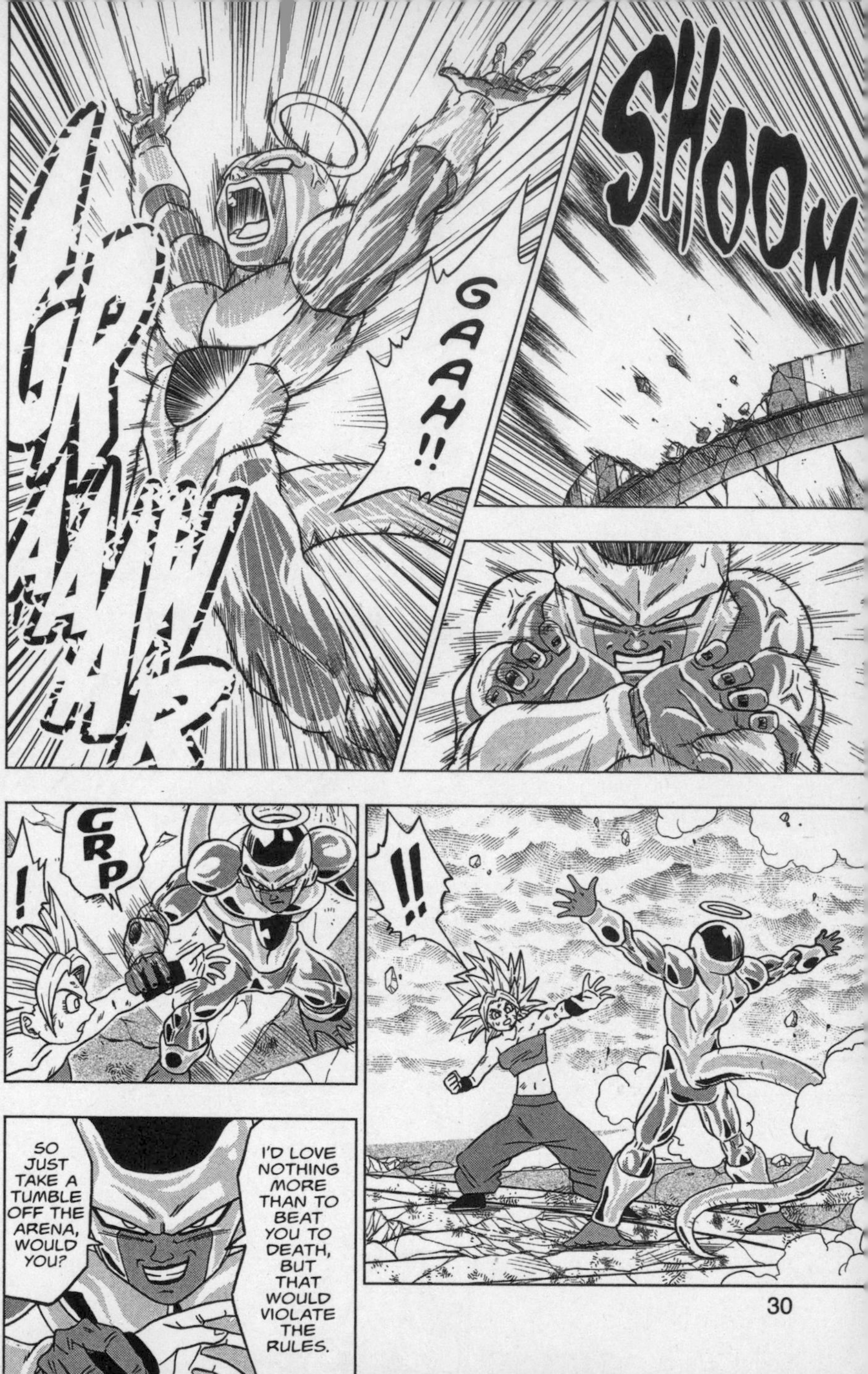
SHOOM
GAAAH!!
!!
GRP
!
I'D LOVE NOTHING MORE THAN TO BEAT YOU TO DEATH, BUT THAT WOULD VIOLATE THE RULES.
SO JUST TAKE A TUMBLE OFF THE ARENA, WOULD YOU?

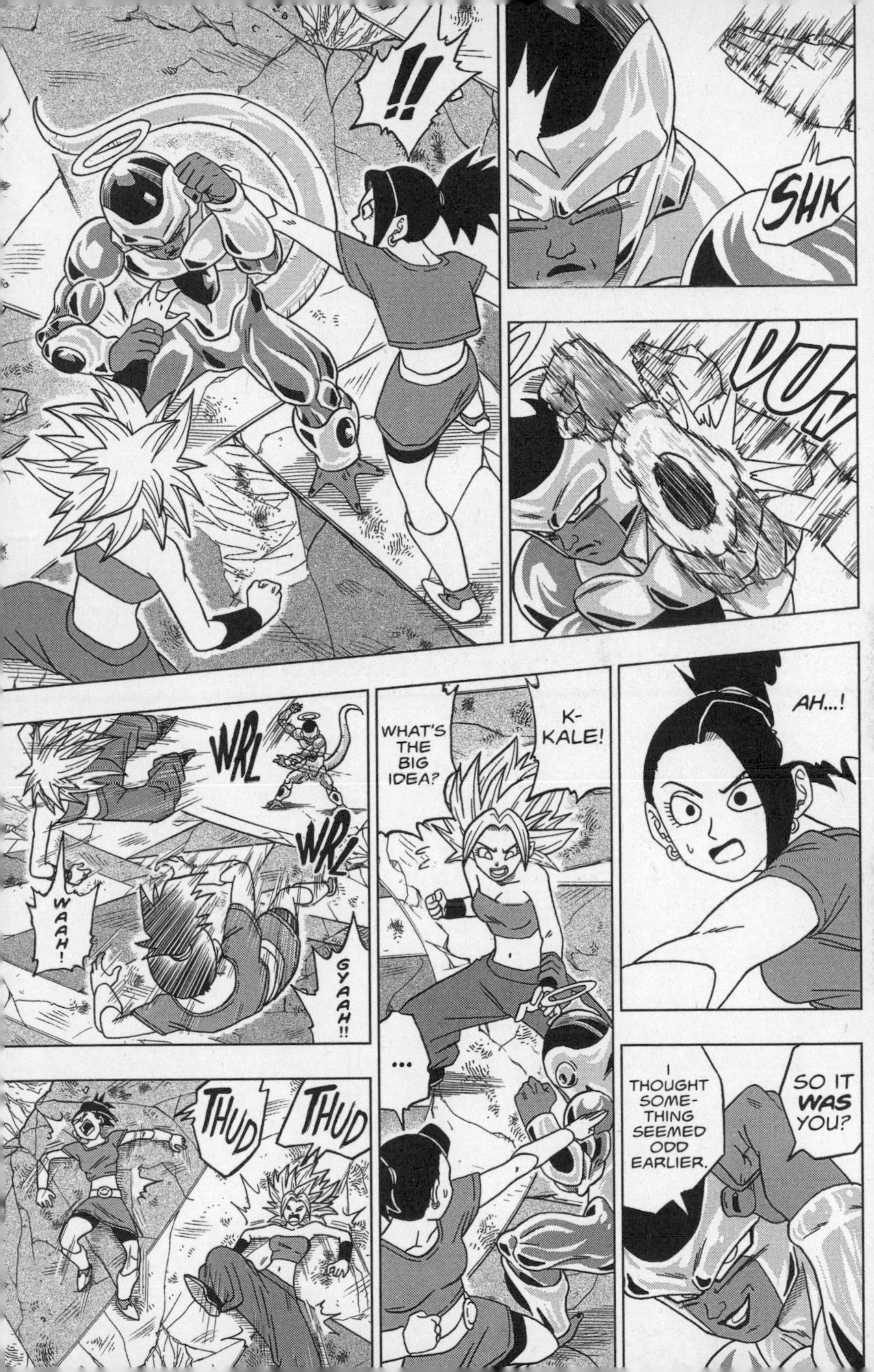
SHK
DUN
!!
AH...!
SO IT **WAS** YOU?
I THOUGHT SOME-THING SEEMED ODD EARLIER.
K-KALE!
WHAT'S THE BIG IDEA?
...
WRL
WRL
GYAAAH!!
WAAAH!
THUD
THUD

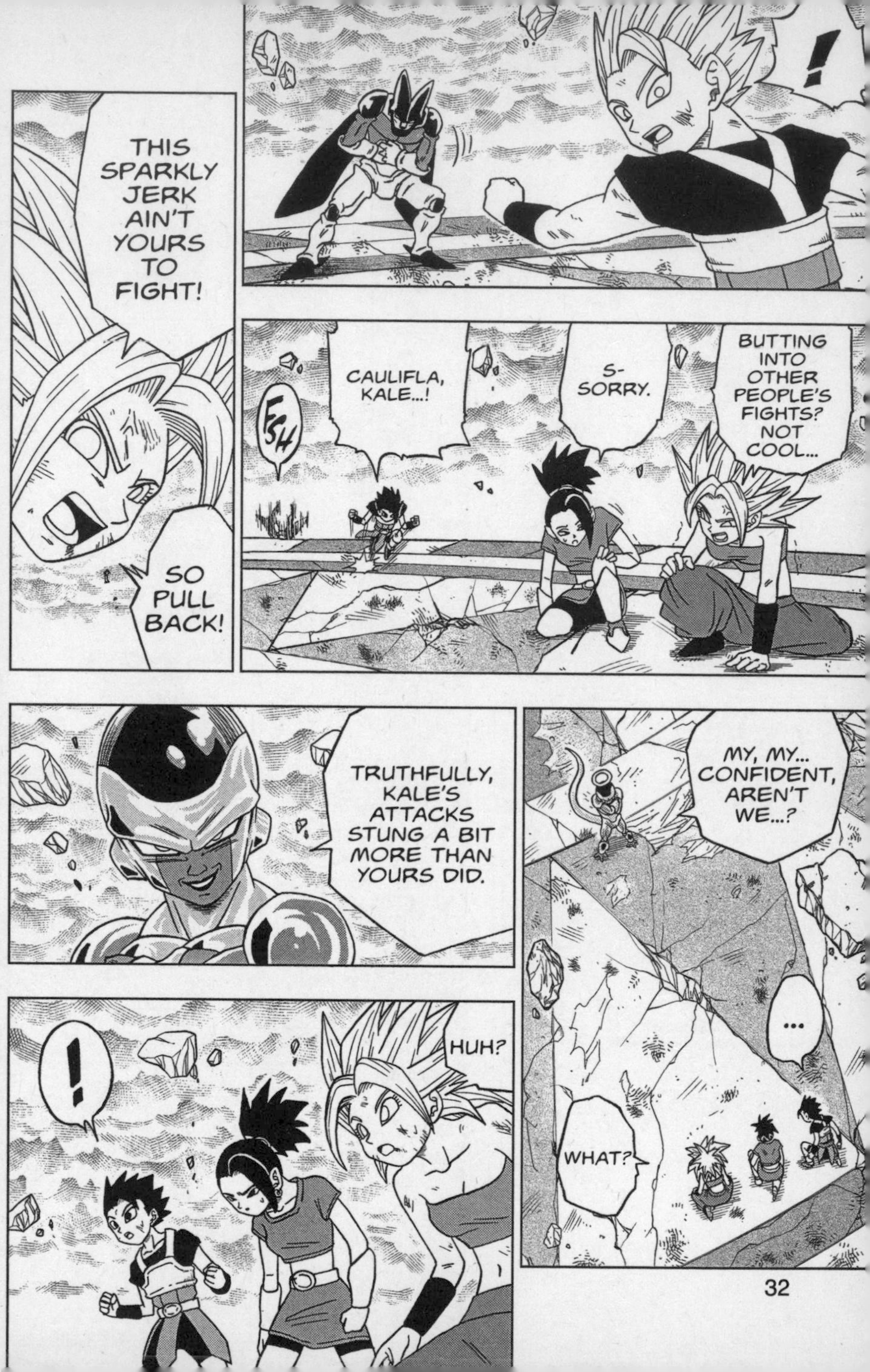
!
BUTTING INTO OTHER PEOPLE'S FIGHTS? NOT COOL...
S-SORRY.
CAULIFLA, KALE...!
FSH
THIS SPARKLY JERK AIN'T YOURS TO FIGHT!
SO PULL BACK!
MY, MY... CONFIDENT, AREN'T WE...?
...
WHAT?
TRUTHFULLY, KALE'S ATTACKS STUNG A BIT MORE THAN YOURS DID.
HUH?
!

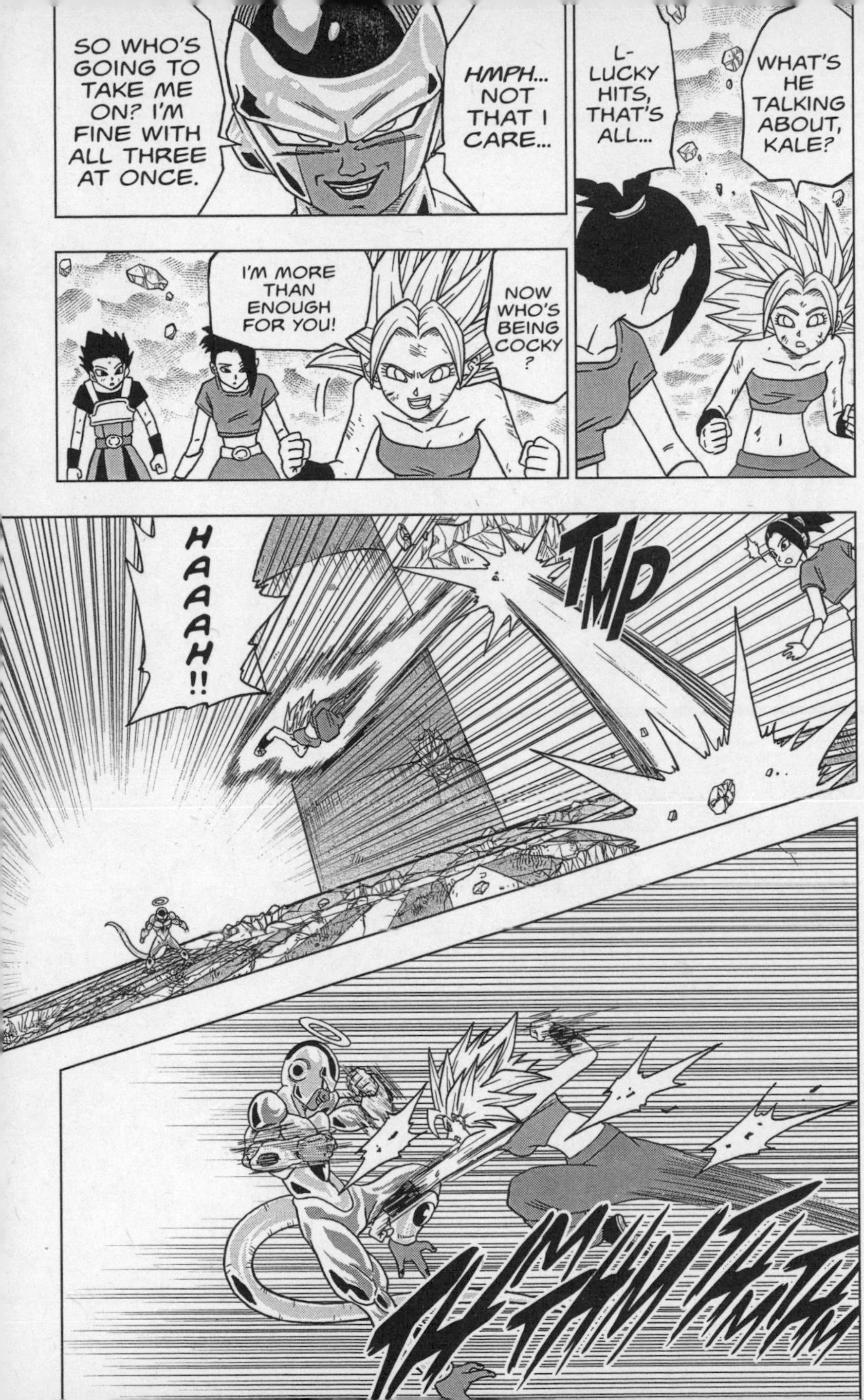
WHAT'S HE TALKING ABOUT, KALE?
L- LUCKY HITS, THAT'S ALL...
HMPH... NOT THAT I CARE...
SO WHO'S GOING TO TAKE ME ON? I'M FINE WITH ALL THREE AT ONCE.
NOW WHO'S BEING COCKY?
I'M MORE THAN ENOUGH FOR YOU!
TMP
HAAAAH!!

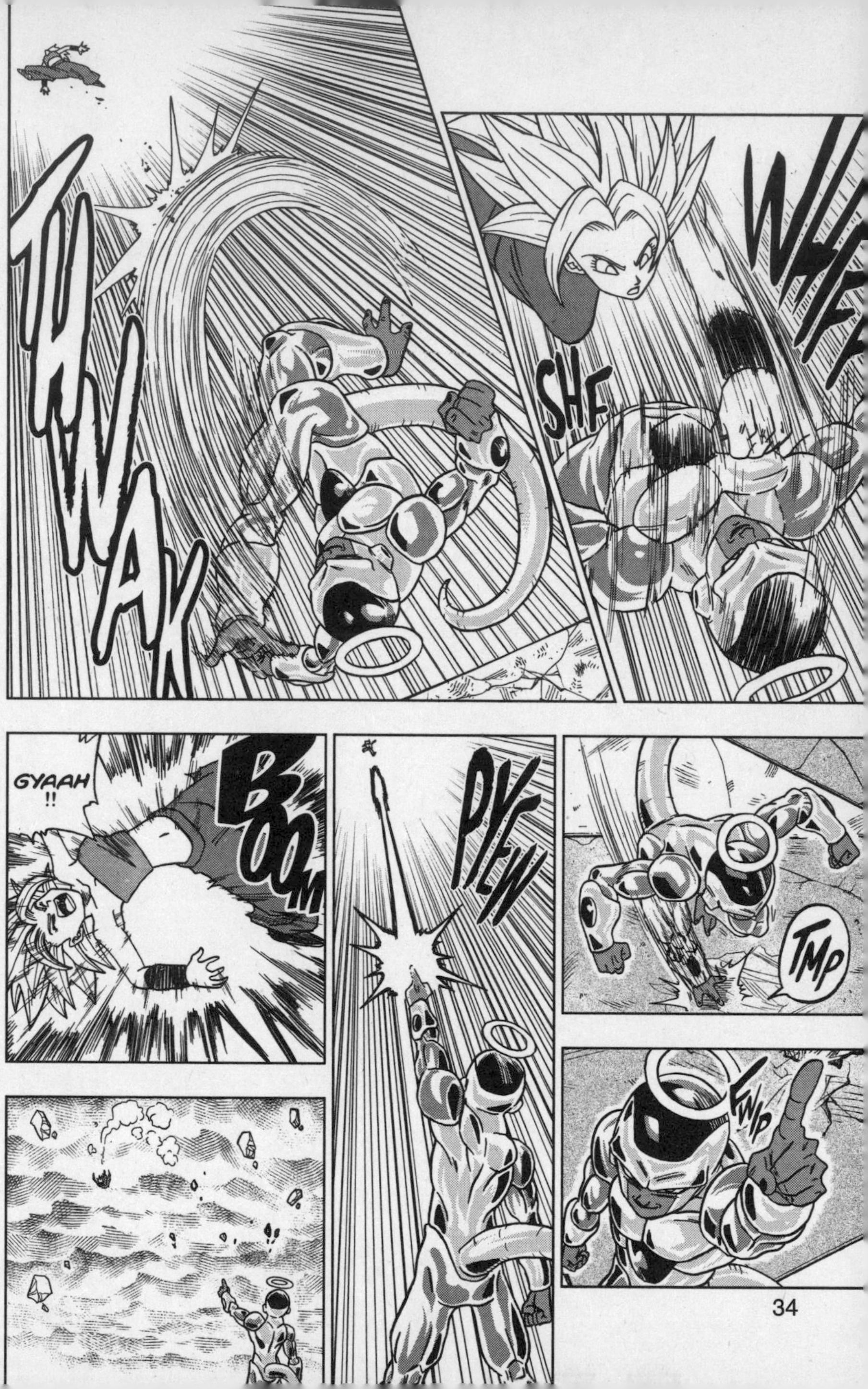
WHFF
SHF
THWAK
TMP
FWIP
PYEW
GYAAH!!
BOOM

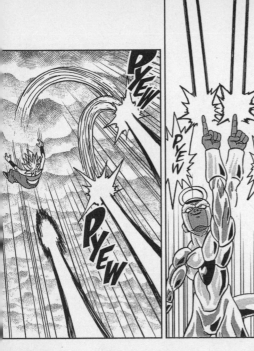

PYEW

PYEW

PYEW

PYEW

PYEW

PYEW

PYEW

GAAH!

GRP

S- SIS...!

AH ...

KALE ...

HA HA HA! STAY UP IN THE AIR AWHILE, WON'T YOU?

DON'T TELL ME YOU'VE BEEN HIDING YOUR TRUE STRENGTH?!

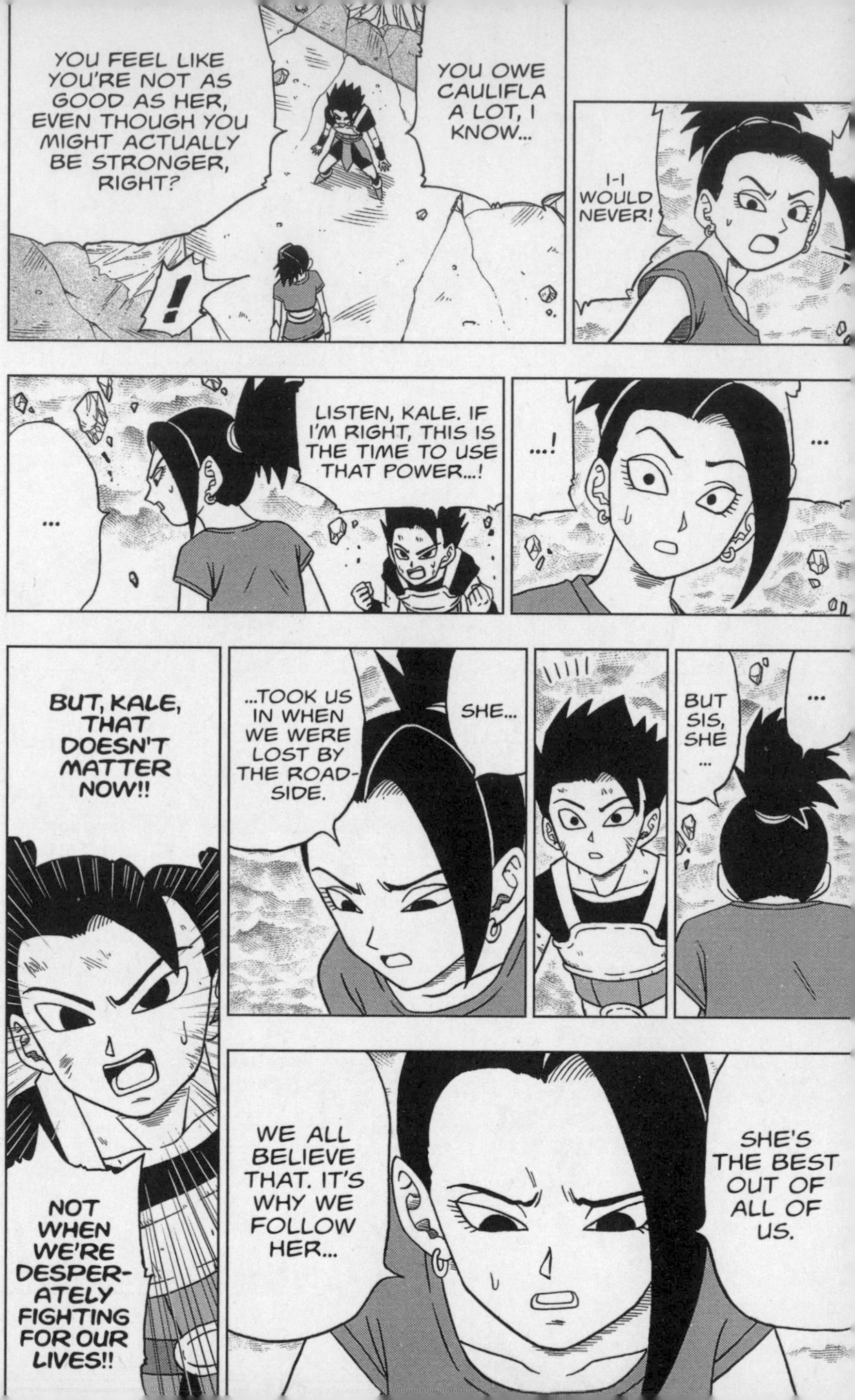
I-I WOULD NEVER!
YOU OWE CAULIFLA A LOT, I KNOW...
YOU FEEL LIKE YOU'RE NOT AS GOOD AS HER, EVEN THOUGH YOU MIGHT ACTUALLY BE STRONGER, RIGHT?
!
...
...!
LISTEN, KALE. IF I'M RIGHT, THIS IS THE TIME TO USE THAT POWER...!
...
...
BUT SIS, SHE ...
SHE...
...TOOK US IN WHEN WE WERE LOST BY THE ROAD-SIDE.
SHE'S THE BEST OUT OF ALL OF US.
WE ALL BELIEVE THAT. IT'S WHY WE FOLLOW HER...
BUT, KALE, THAT DOESN'T MATTER NOW!!
NOT WHEN WE'RE DESPER-ATELY FIGHTING FOR OUR LIVES!!

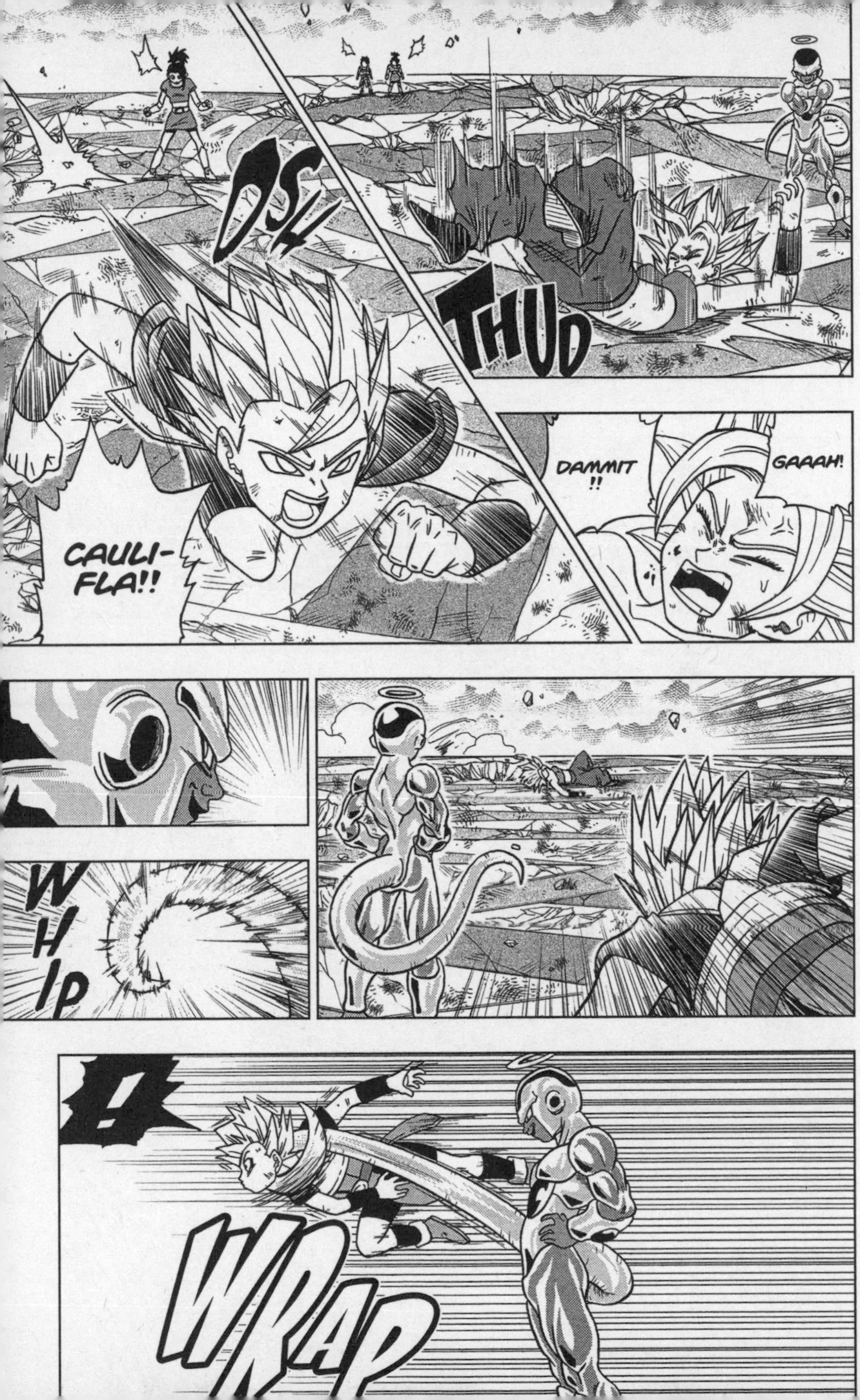
THUD
GAAAH!
DAMMIT!!
DSH
CAULI-FLA!!
WHIP
WRAP

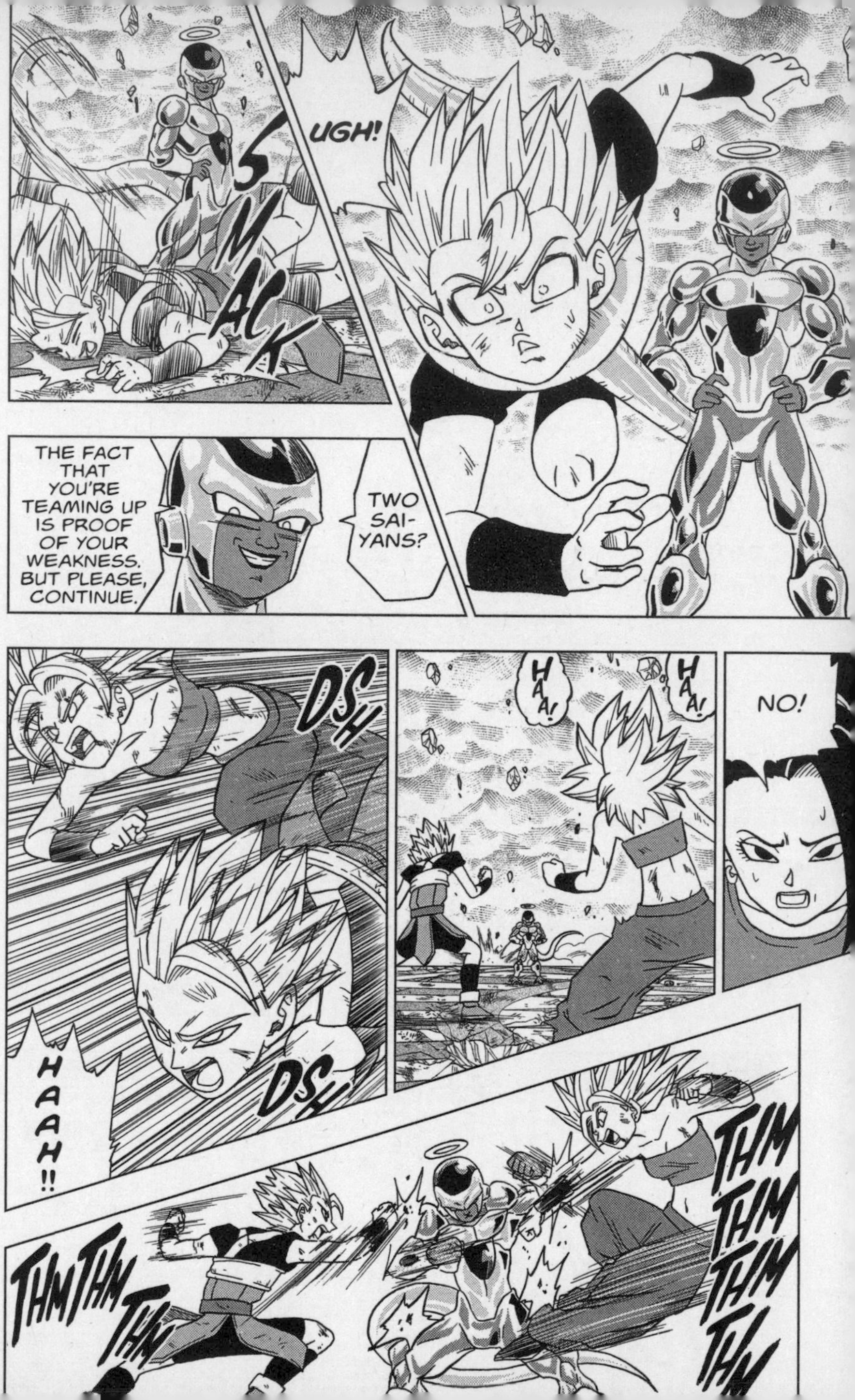
UGH!
SMACK
TWO SAI-YANS?
THE FACT THAT YOU'RE TEAMING UP IS PROOF OF YOUR WEAKNESS. BUT PLEASE, CONTINUE.
NO!
HAAA!
HAAA!
DSH
DSH
HAAAH!!
THM THM THM THM
THM THM THM

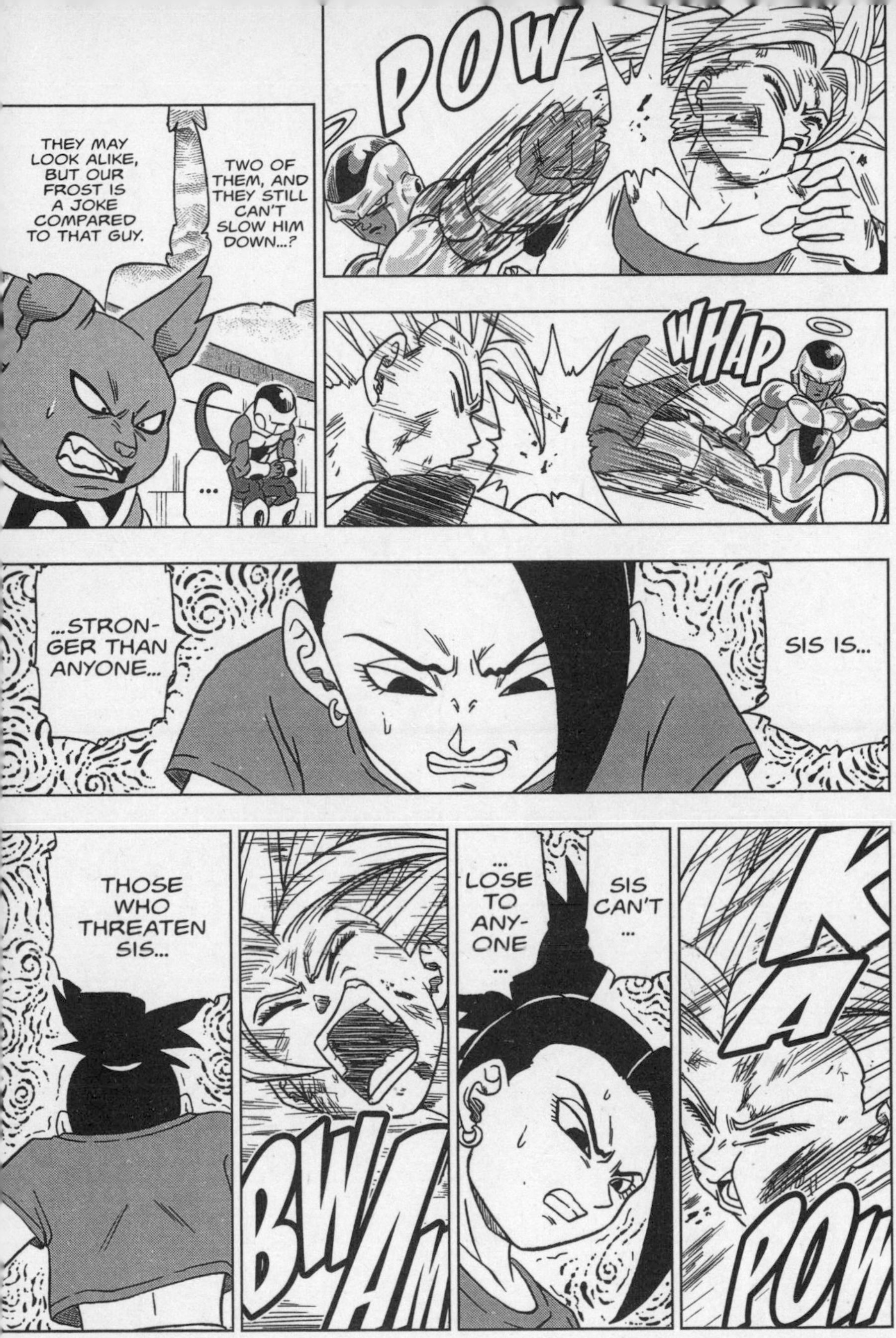
POW
WHAP
TWO OF THEM, AND THEY STILL CAN'T SLOW HIM DOWN...?
THEY MAY LOOK ALIKE, BUT OUR FROST IS A JOKE COMPARED TO THAT GUY.
...
SIS IS...
...STRONGER THAN ANYONE...
KA
POW
SIS CAN'T ...
... LOSE TO ANYONE ...
BWAM
THOSE WHO THREATEN SIS...

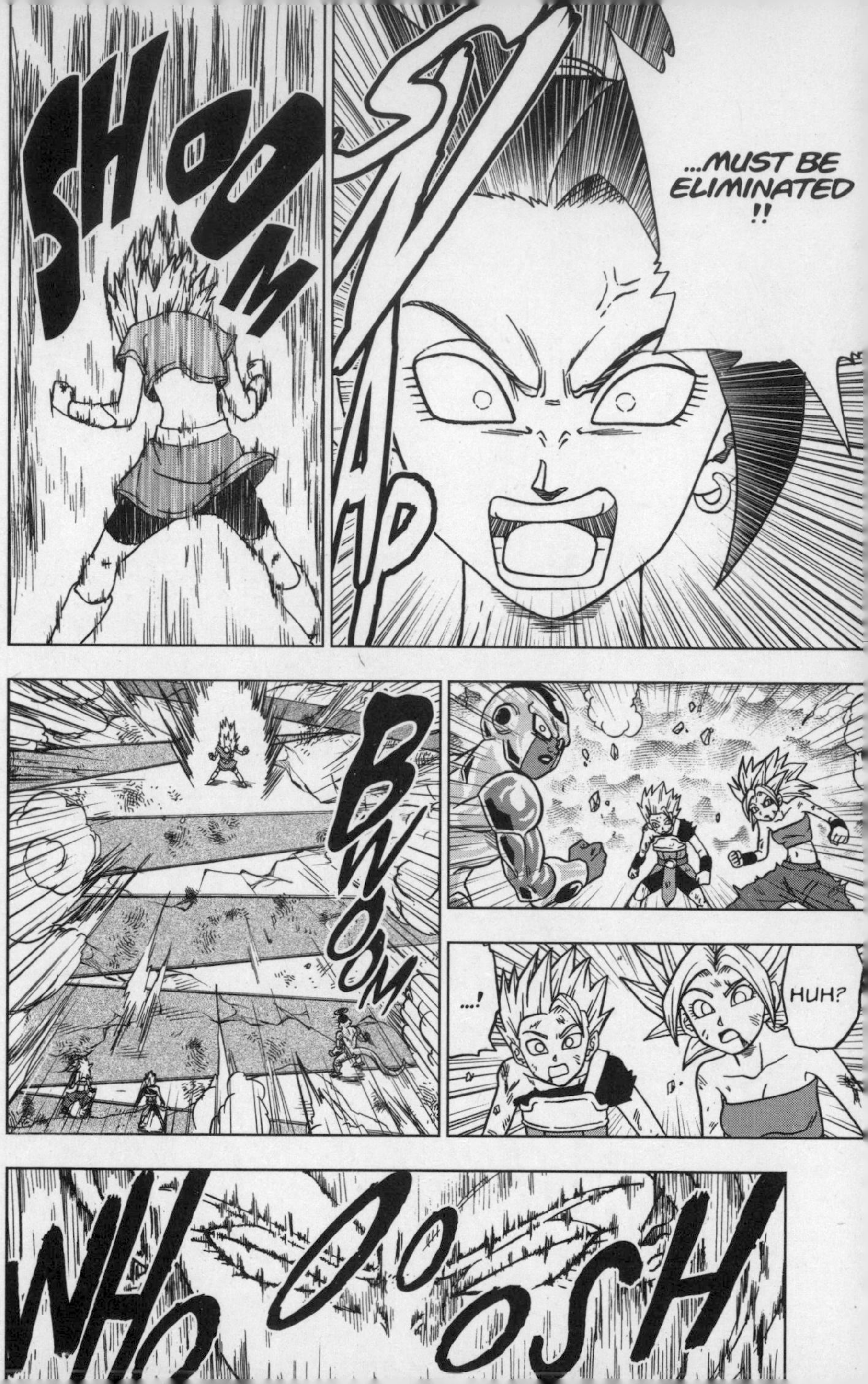
SNAP
...MUST BE ELIMINATED!!
SHOOM
HUH?
...!
BWOOOM
WHOOOOSH

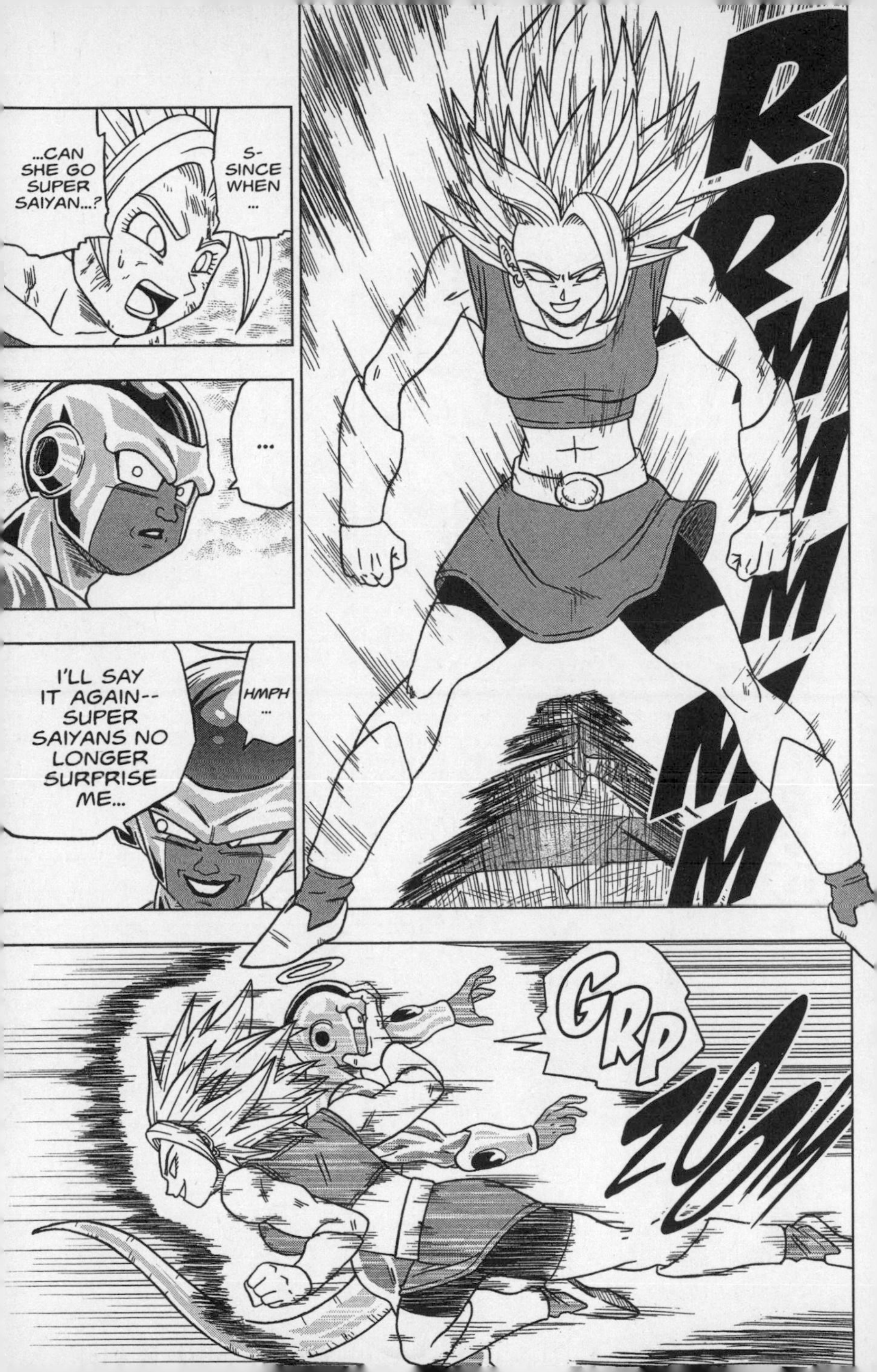
RRMMMMM
S-SINCE WHEN...
...CAN SHE GO SUPER SAIYAN...?
...
HMPH...
I'LL SAY IT AGAIN--SUPER SAIYANS NO LONGER SURPRISE ME...
GRP
ZOOM

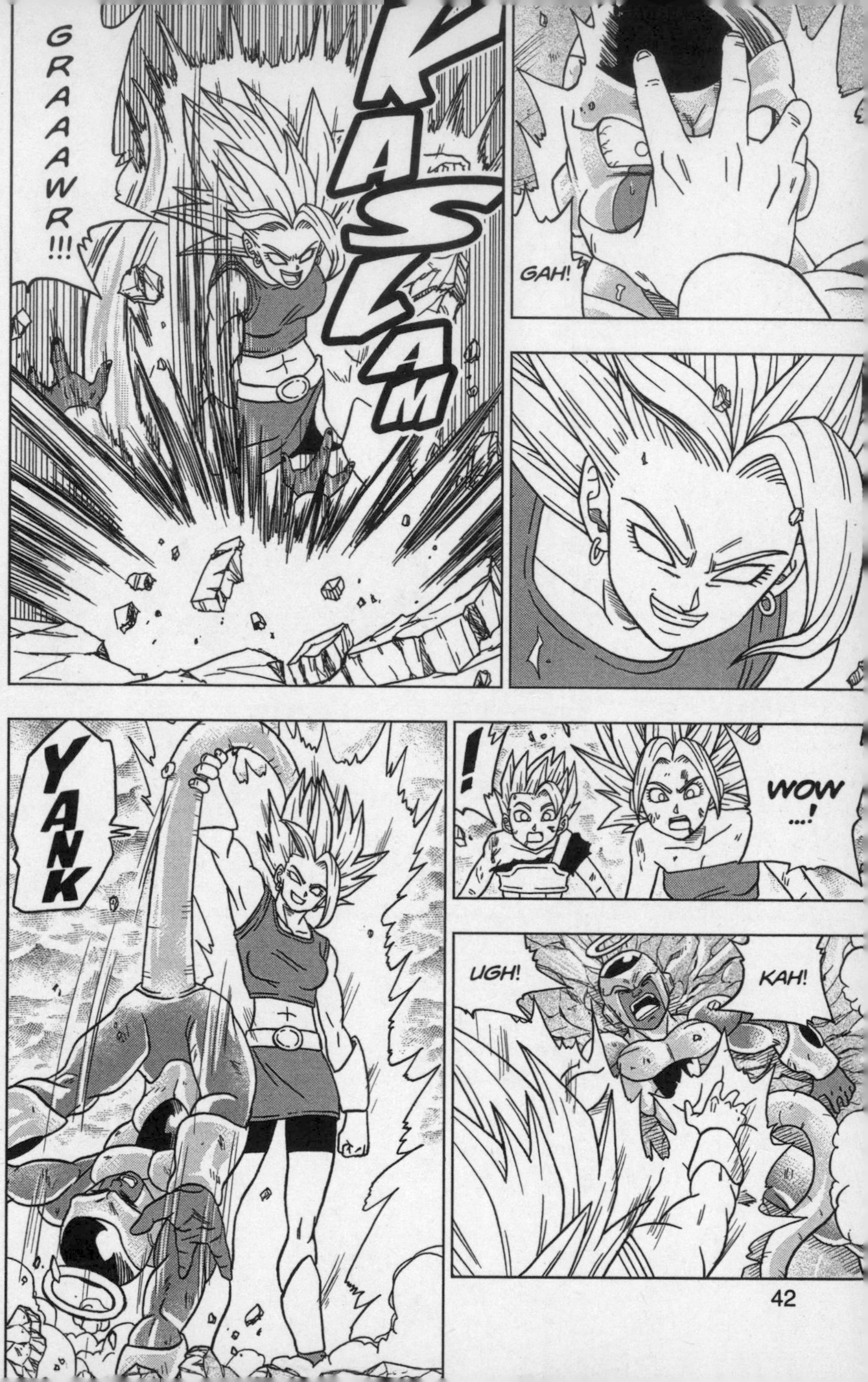
GAH!
KASLAM
GRAAAAWR!!!
WOW ...!
!
KAH!
UGH!
YANK

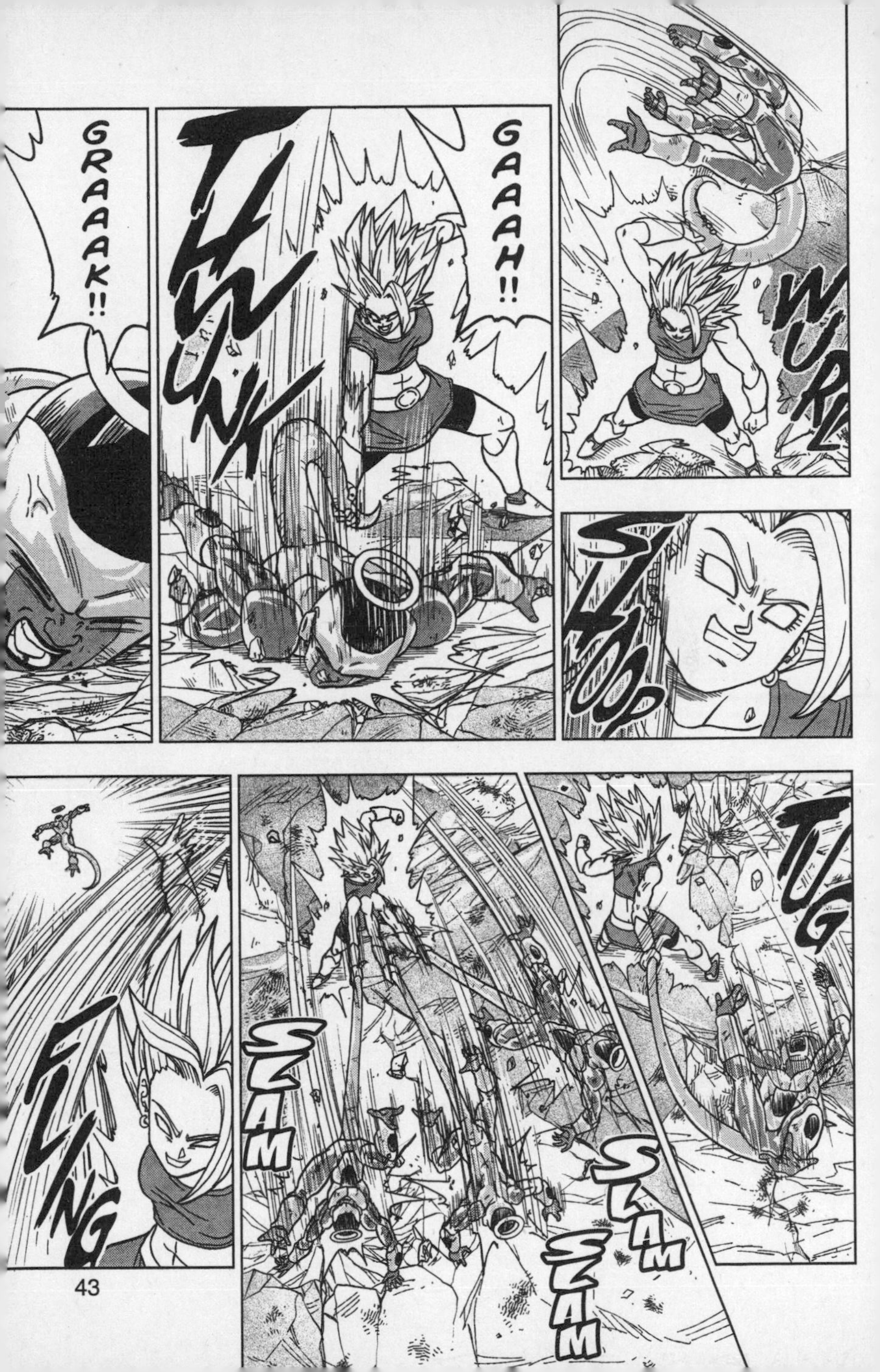

WURL
SHOOP
GAAAAH!!
THWUNK
GRAAAK!!
TUG
SLAM
SLAM
SLAM
SLAM
FLING

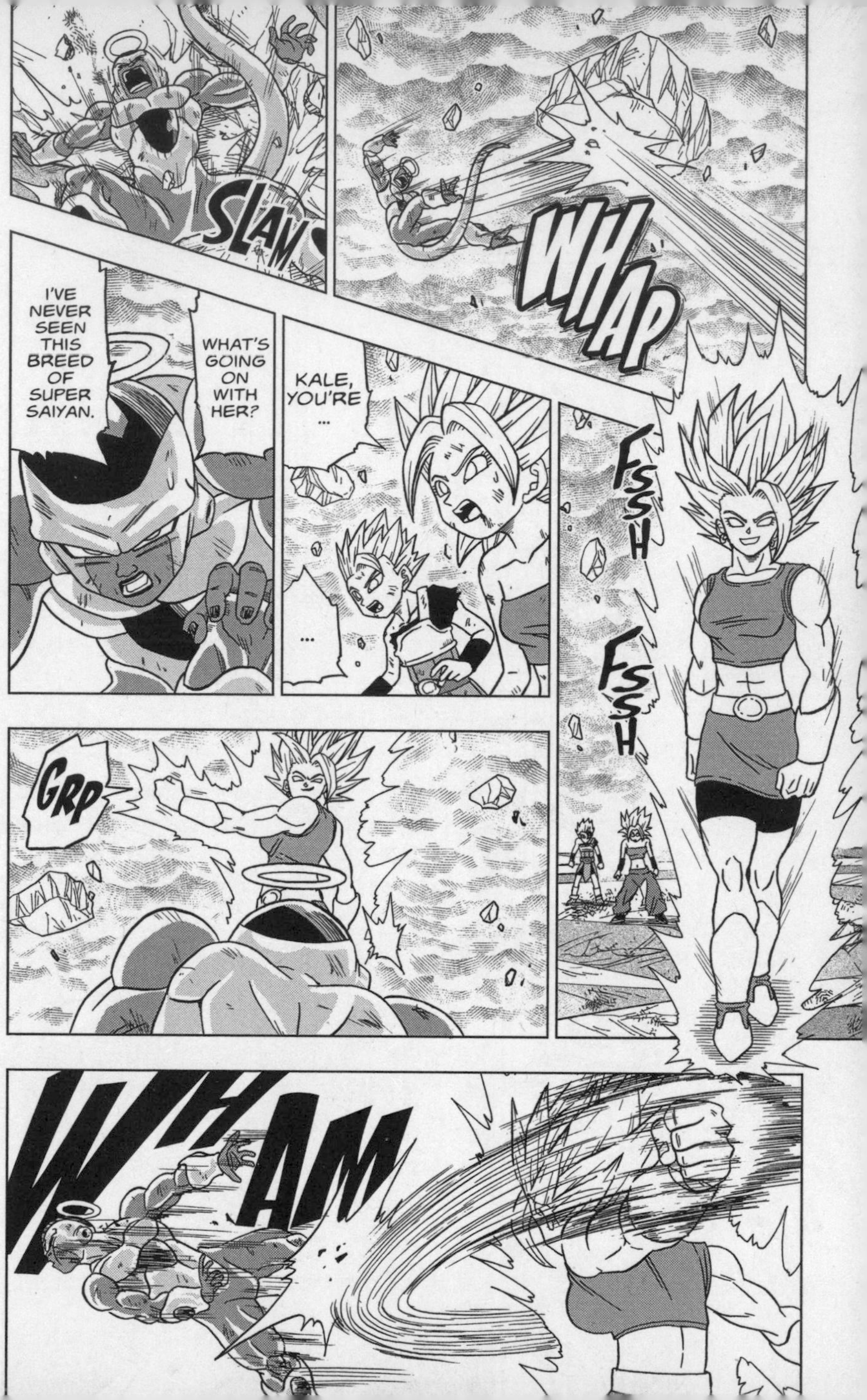
WHAP
SLAM
FSSH
FSSH
WHAT'S GOING ON WITH HER?
KALE, YOU'RE ...
...
I'VE NEVER SEEN THIS BREED OF SUPER SAIYAN.
GRP
WHAM

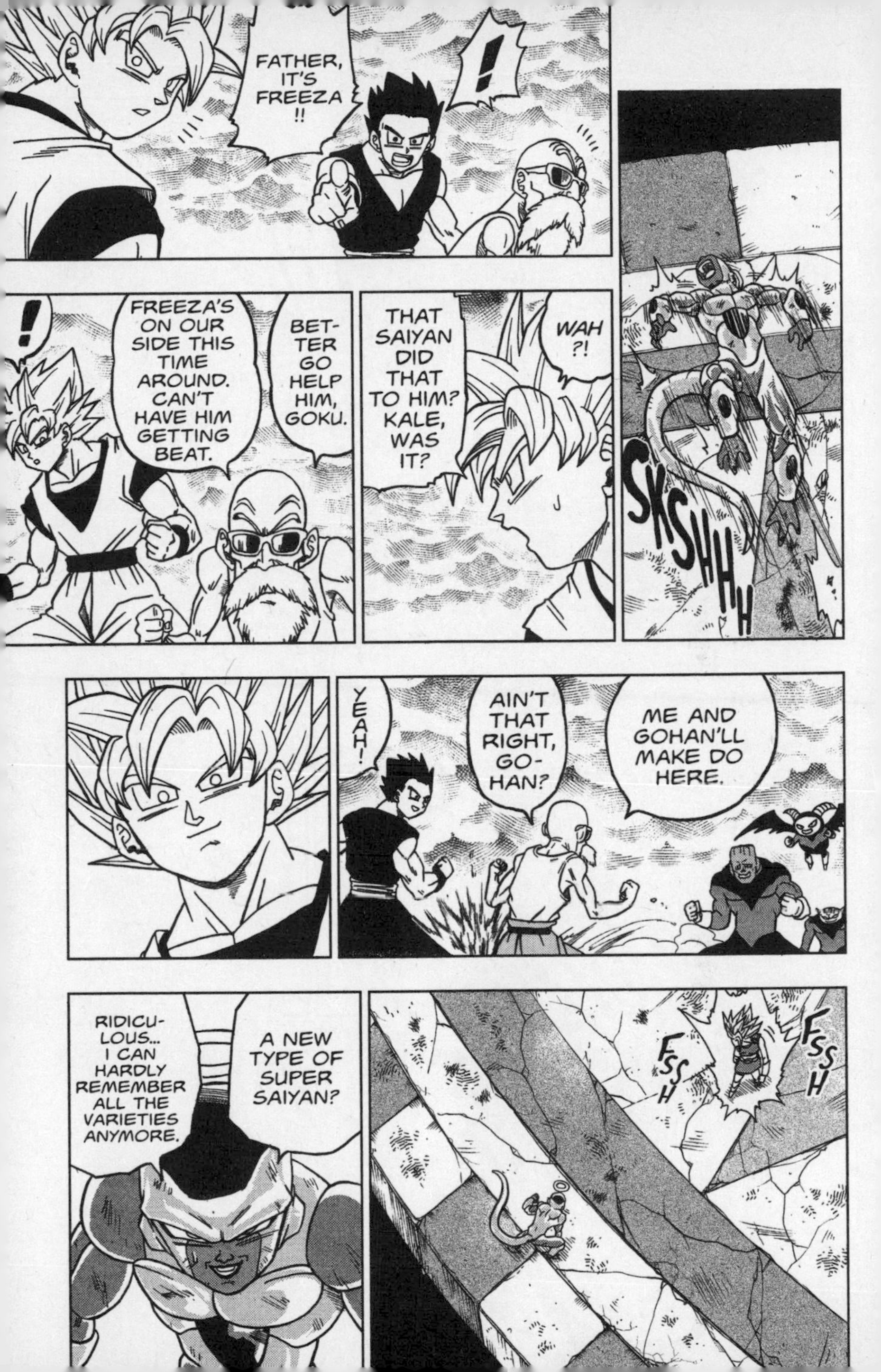
SKSHHHH
!
FATHER, IT'S FREEZA!!
WAH?!
THAT SAIYAN DID THAT TO HIM? KALE, WAS IT?
BETTER GO HELP HIM, GOKU.
FREEZA'S ON OUR SIDE THIS TIME AROUND. CAN'T HAVE HIM GETTING BEAT.
!
ME AND GOHAN'LL MAKE DO HERE.
AIN'T THAT RIGHT, GOHAN?
YEAH!
FSSH
FSSH
A NEW TYPE OF SUPER SAIYAN?
RIDICULOUS... I CAN HARDLY REMEMBER ALL THE VARIETIES ANYMORE.

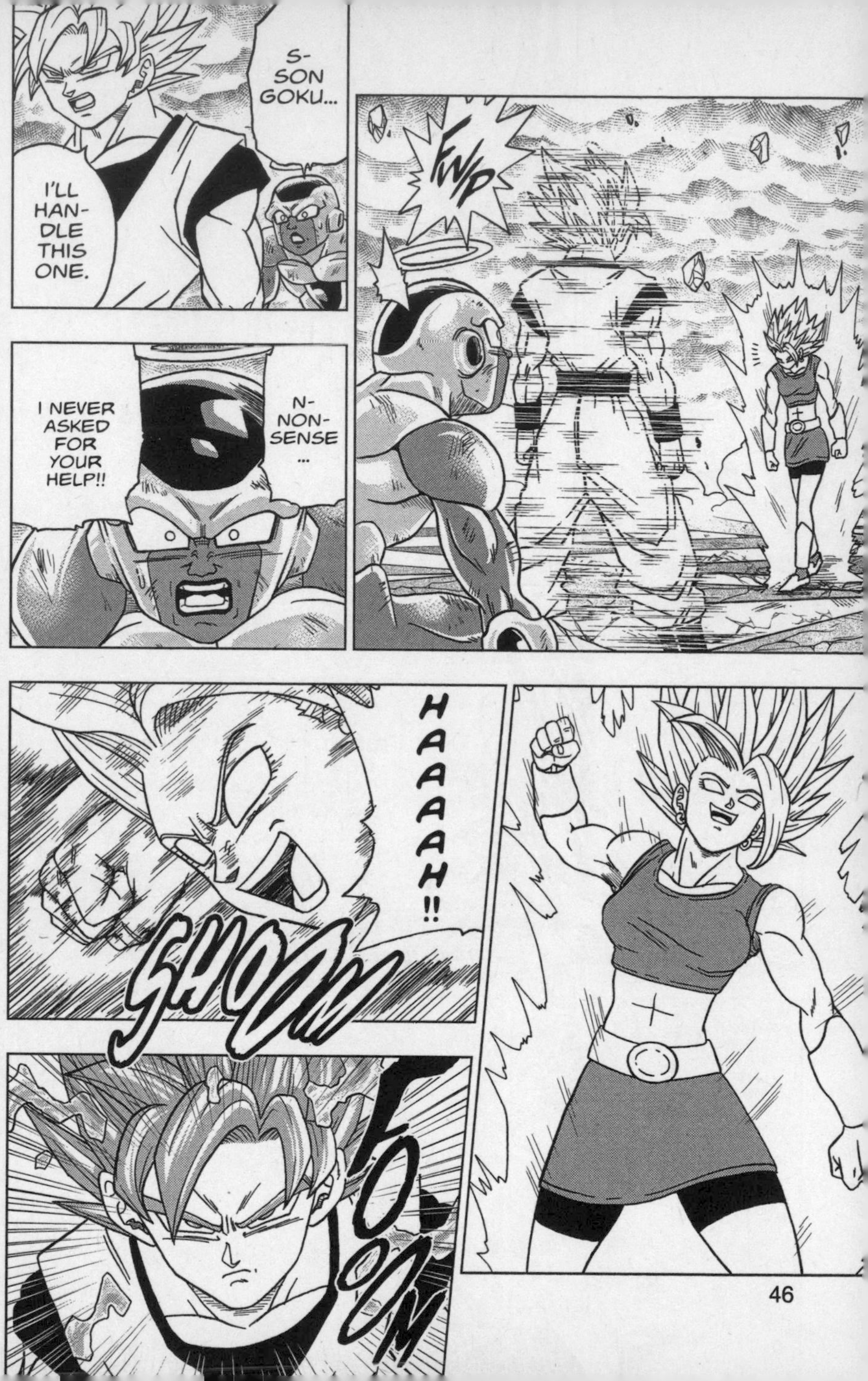
FWIP
S-SON GOKU...
I'LL HANDLE THIS ONE.
N-NONSENSE...
I NEVER ASKED FOR YOUR HELP!!
HAAAAAH!!
SHOOM
FOOOM

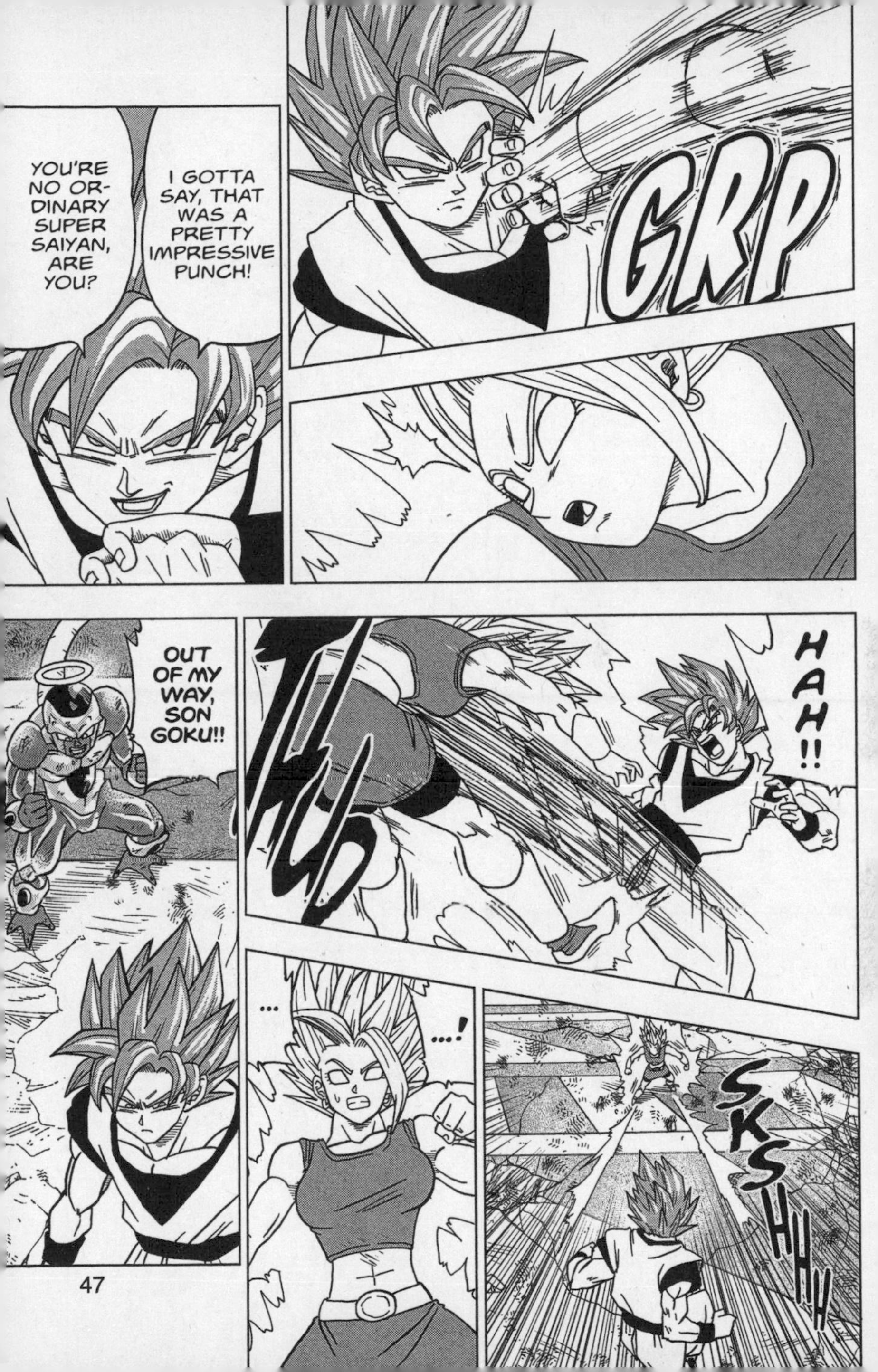
GRP
I GOTTA SAY, THAT WAS A PRETTY IMPRESSIVE PUNCH!
YOU'RE NO ORDINARY SUPER SAIYAN, ARE YOU?
HAH!!
OUT OF MY WAY, SON GOKU!!
SKSHHHH
...
...!

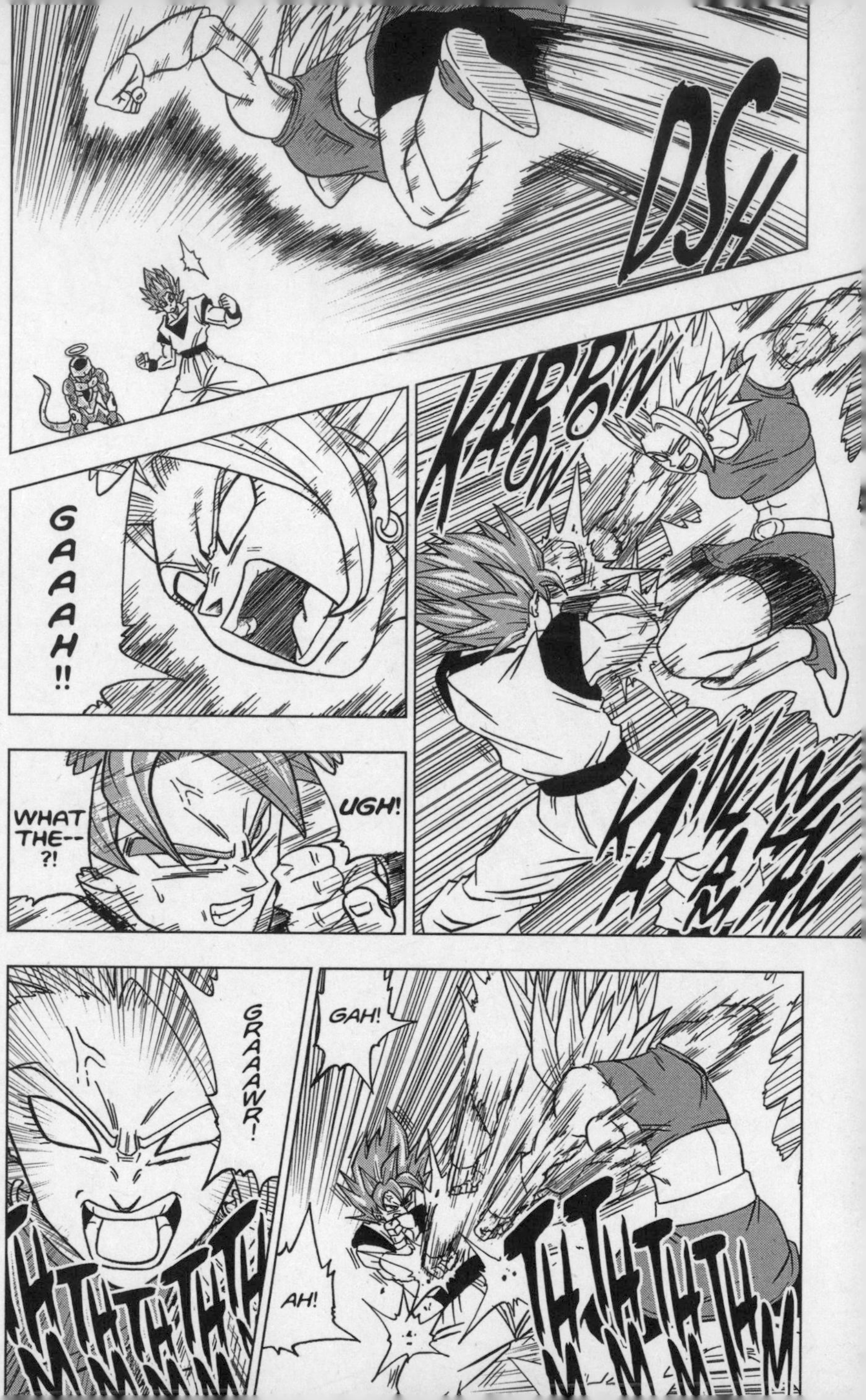
DSH
GAAAAH!!
UGH!
WHAT THE-- ?!
GAH!
AH!
GRAAAAWR!

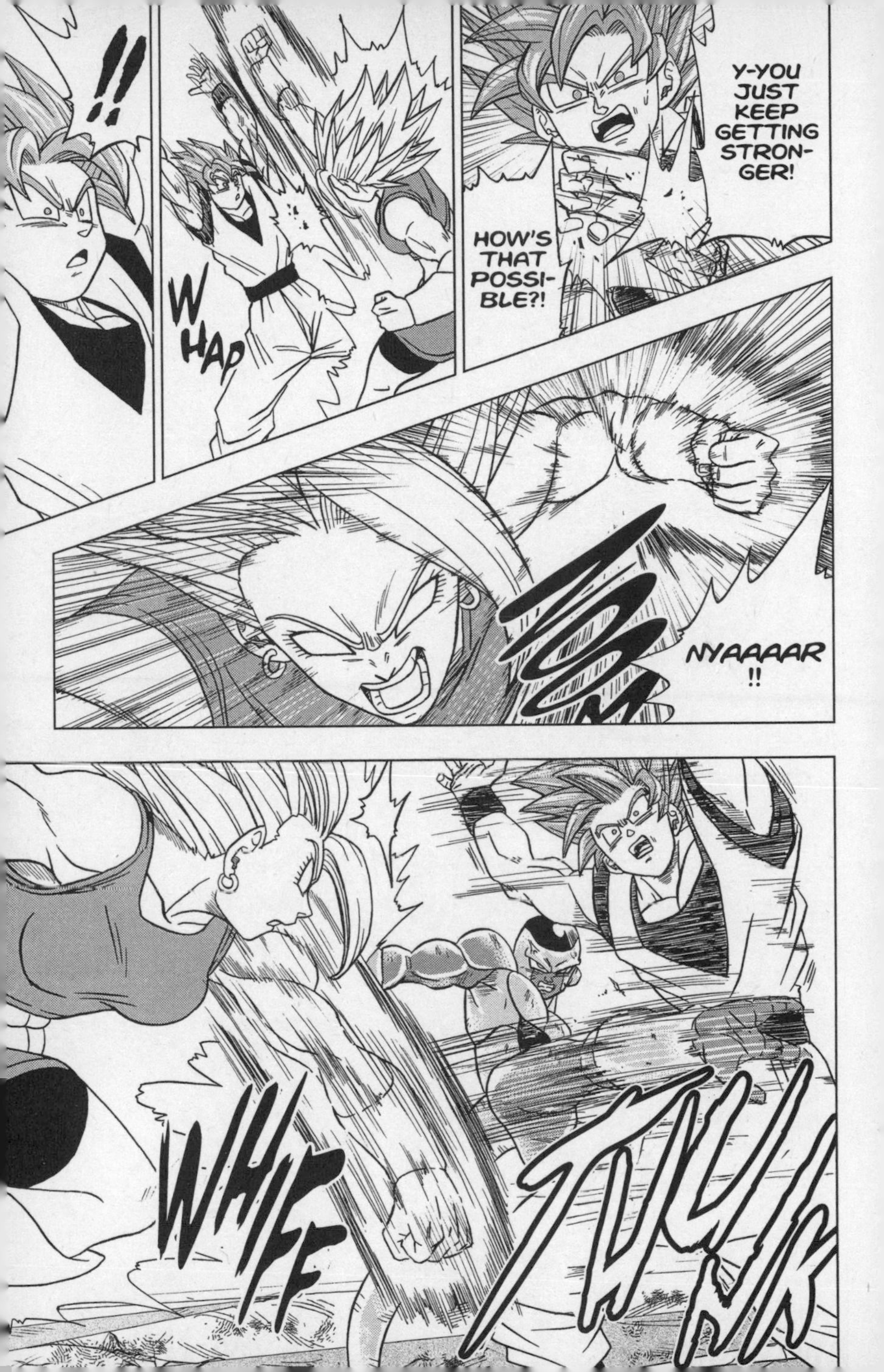
Y-YOU JUST KEEP GETTING STRONGER!
HOW'S THAT POSSIBLE?!
WHAP
!!
NYAAAAR!!
WHIFF

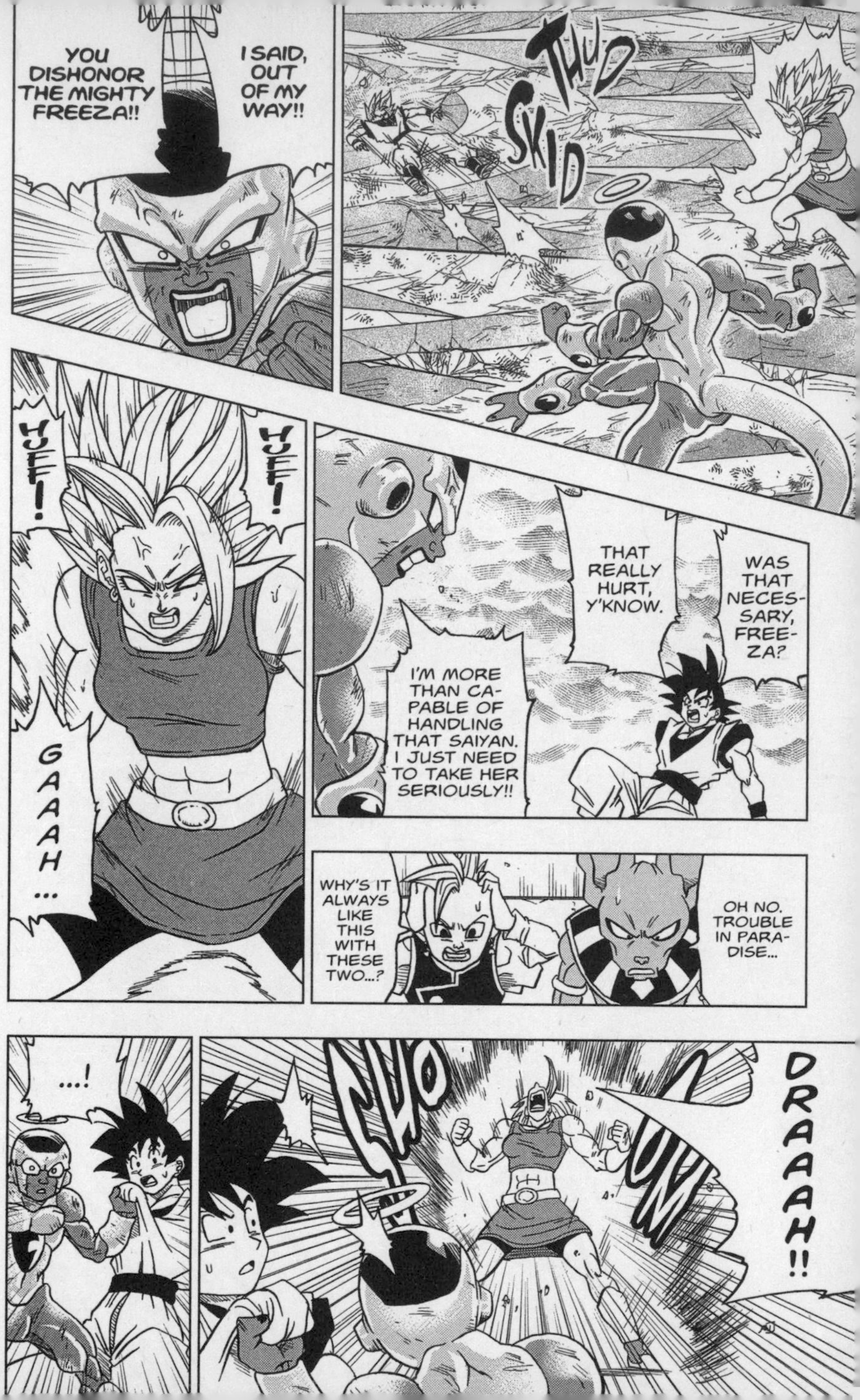
THUD
SKID
I SAID, OUT OF MY WAY!!
YOU DISHONOR THE MIGHTY FREEZA!!
WAS THAT NECES-SARY, FREE-ZA?
THAT REALLY HURT, Y'KNOW.
I'M MORE THAN CA-PABLE OF HANDLING THAT SAIYAN. I JUST NEED TO TAKE HER SERIOUSLY!!
OH NO. TROUBLE IN PARA-DISE...
WHY'S IT ALWAYS LIKE THIS WITH THESE TWO...?
HUFF!
HUFF!
GAAAAH...
DRAAAAH!!
...!

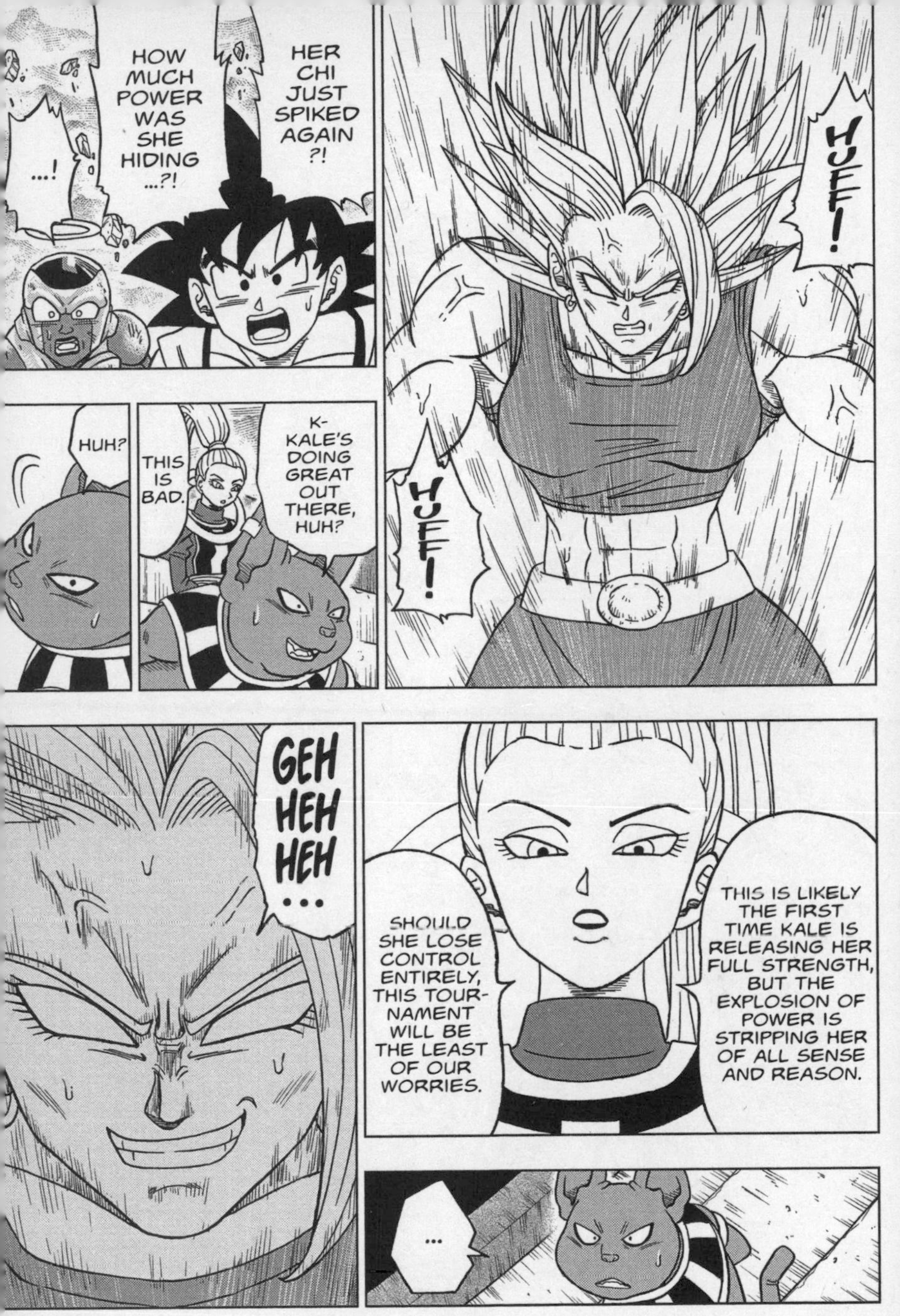
HUFF!
HUFF!
HER CHI JUST SPIKED AGAIN ?!
HOW MUCH POWER WAS SHE HIDING ...?!
...!
K-KALE'S DOING GREAT OUT THERE, HUH?
THIS IS BAD.
HUH?
THIS IS LIKELY THE FIRST TIME KALE IS RELEASING HER FULL STRENGTH, BUT THE EXPLOSION OF POWER IS STRIPPING HER OF ALL SENSE AND REASON.
SHOULD SHE LOSE CONTROL ENTIRELY, THIS TOURNAMENT WILL BE THE LEAST OF OUR WORRIES.
...
GEH HEH HEH ...

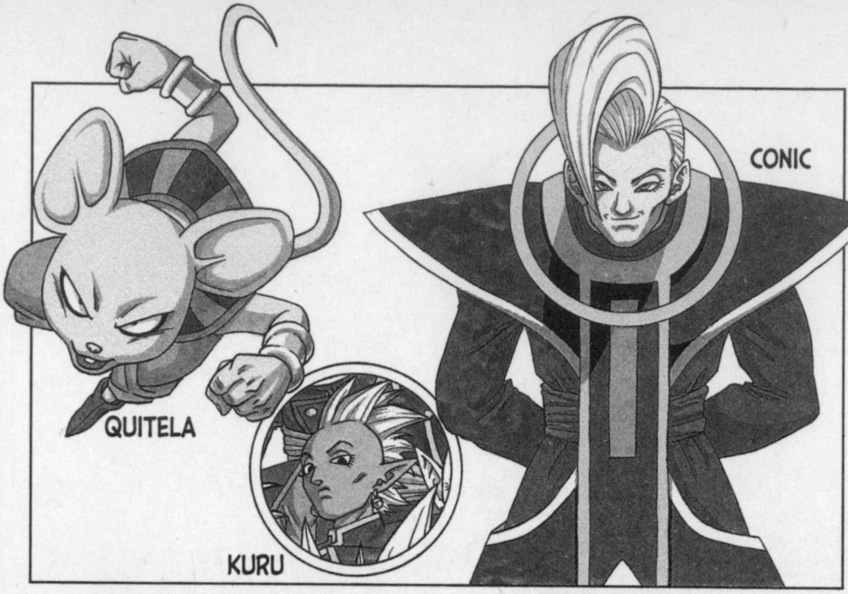
CONIC
QUITELA
KURU

UNIVERSE 4

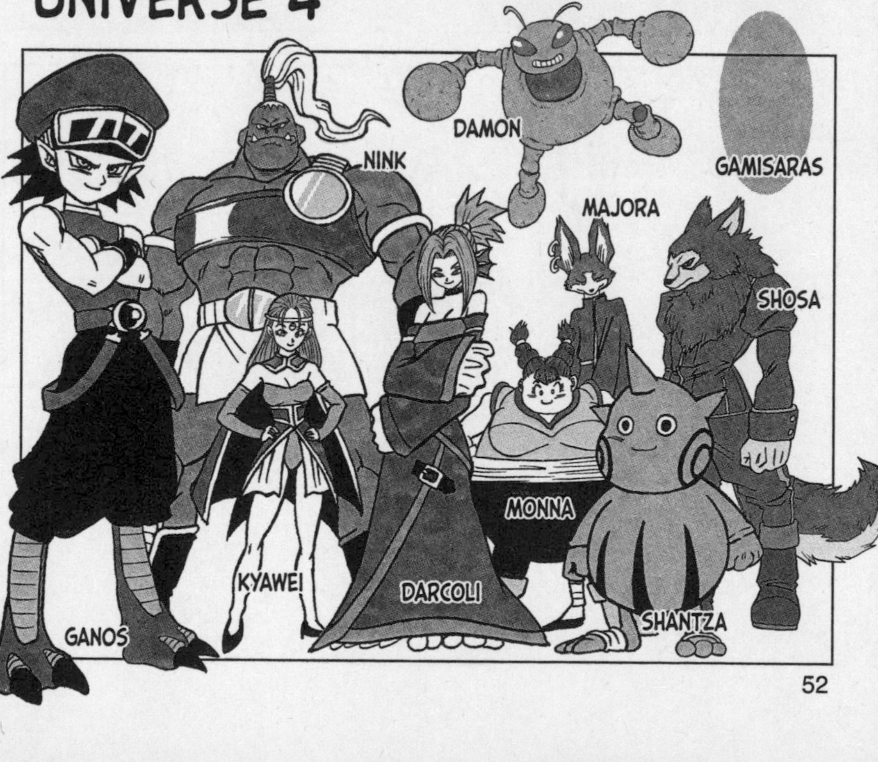
GAMISARAS
DAMON
NINK
MAJORA
SHOSA
MONNA
DARCOLI
KYAWEI
SHANTZA
GANOS

DRAGON BALL SUPER

CHAPTER 38: UNIVERSE 6'S LAST RESORT

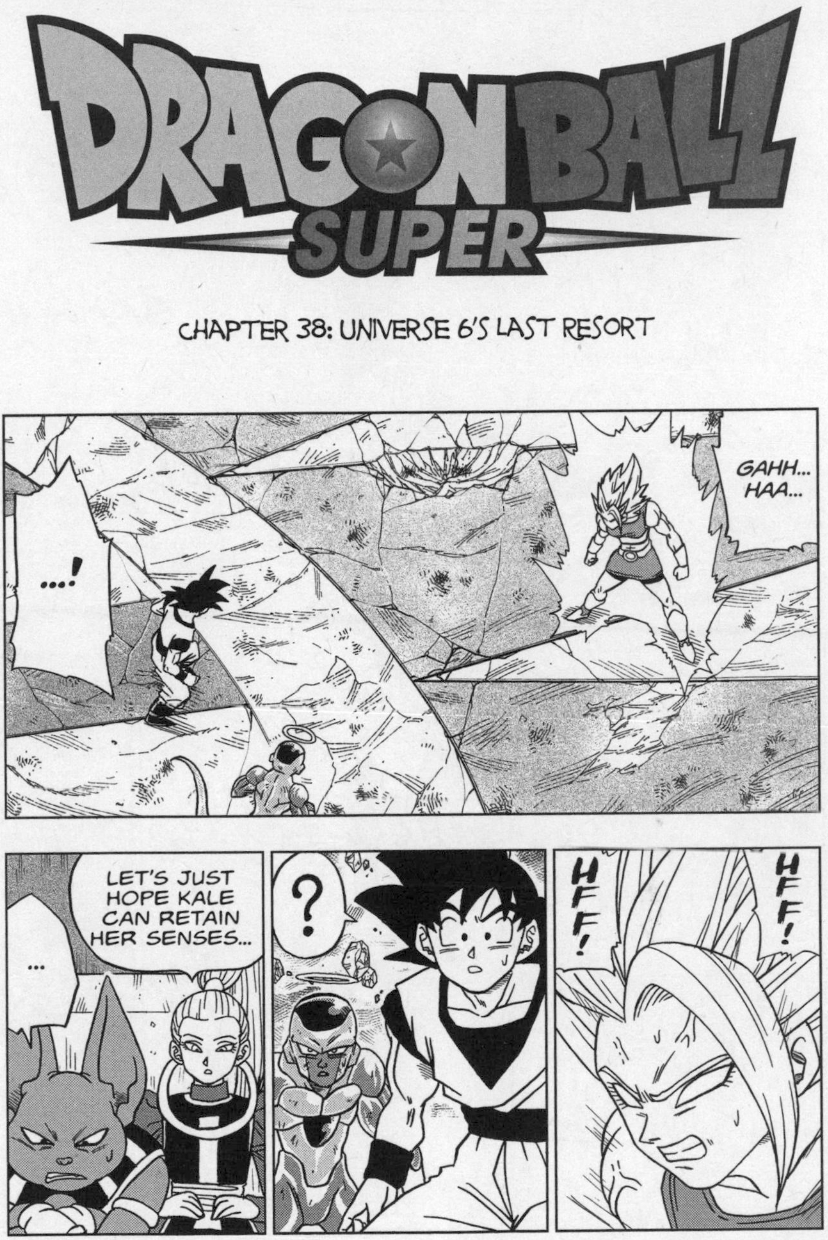
GAHH... HAA...
...!
HFF HFF!
?
LET'S JUST HOPE KALE CAN RETAIN HER SENSES...
...

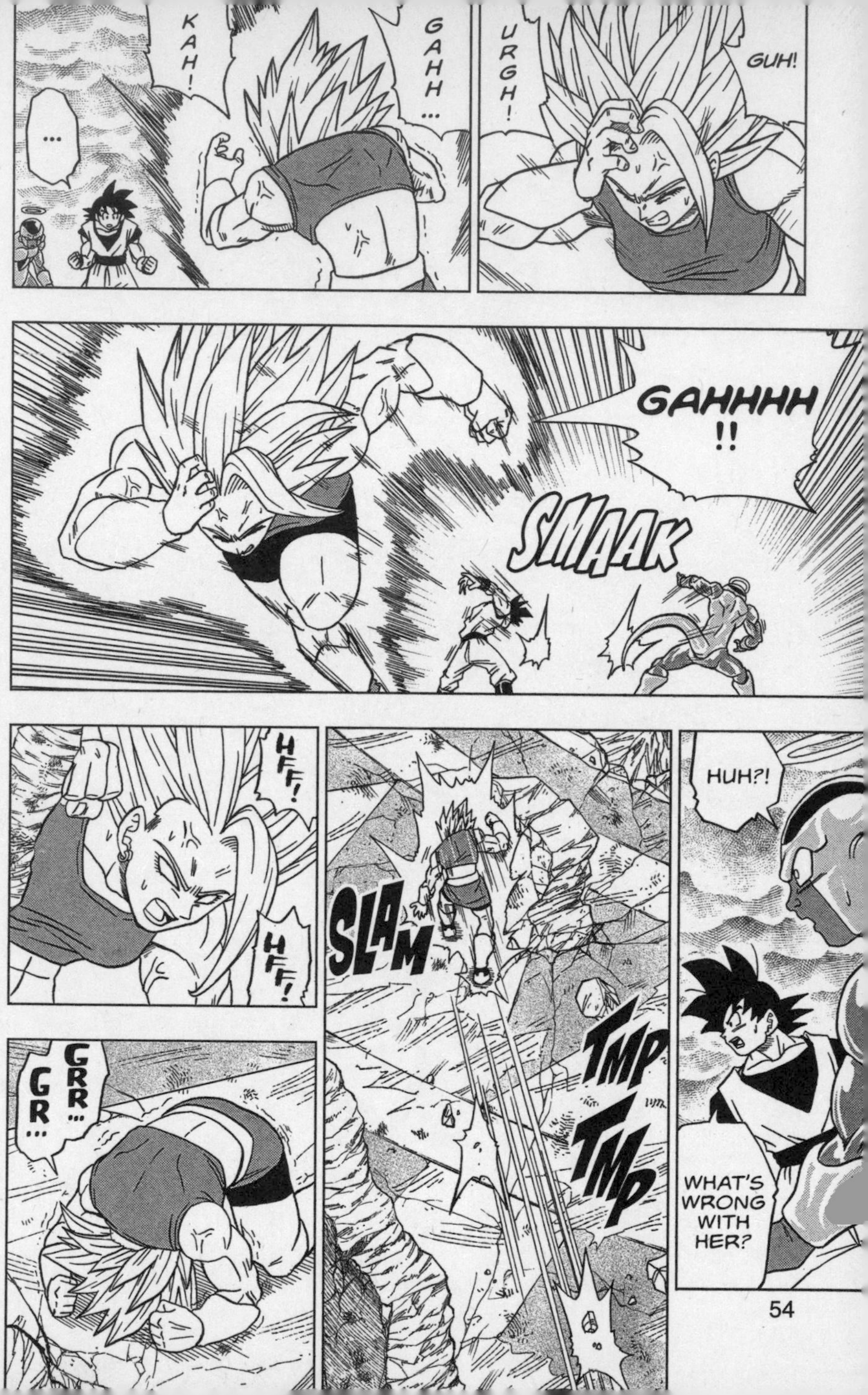
GUH!
URGH!
GAHH...
KAH!
...
GAHHHH !!
SMAAK
HUH?!
WHAT'S WRONG WITH HER?
SLAM
TMP
TMP
HFF!
HFF!
GRR...
GR...

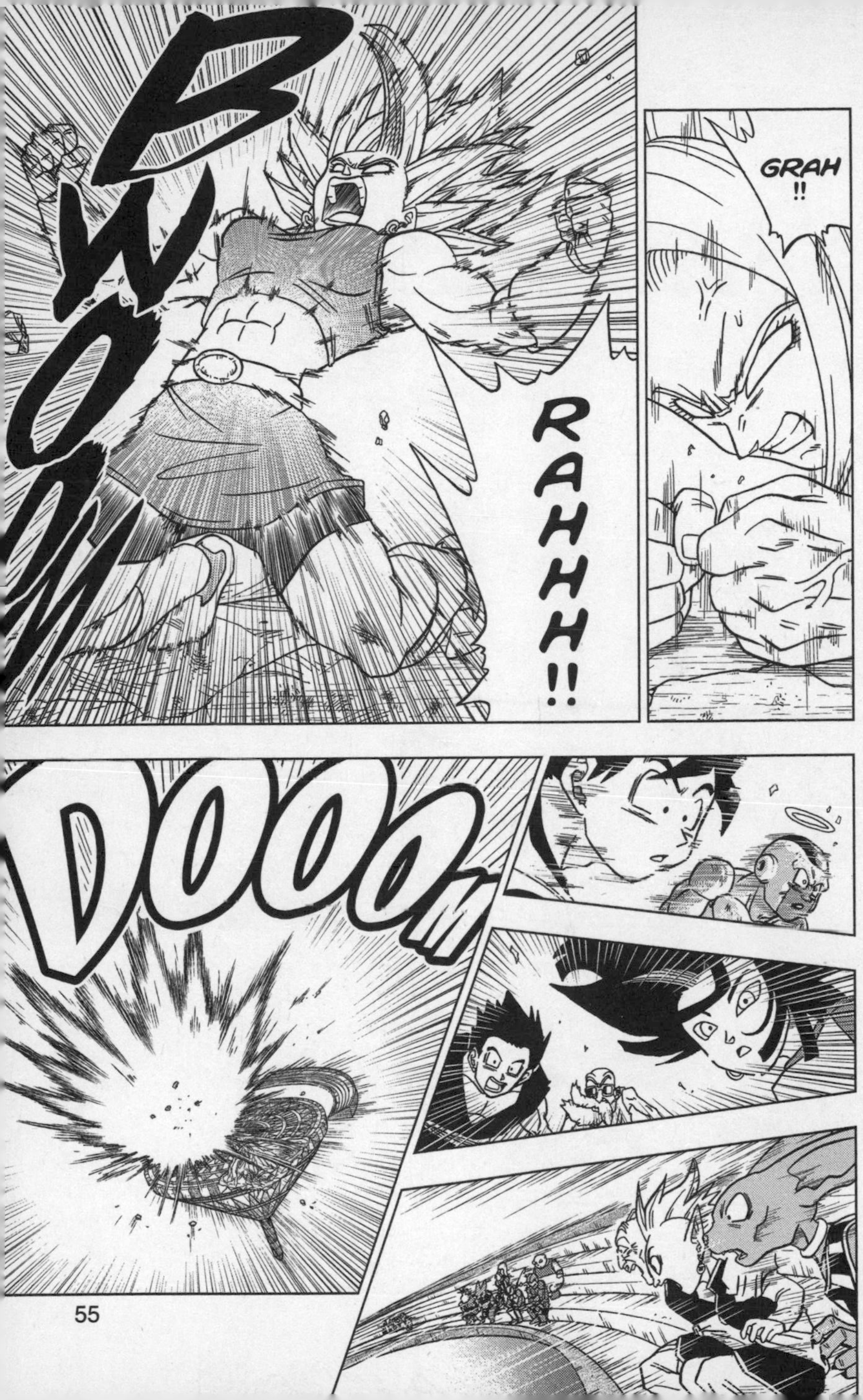
GRAH!!
BWOOM
RAHHHH!!
DOOOOM

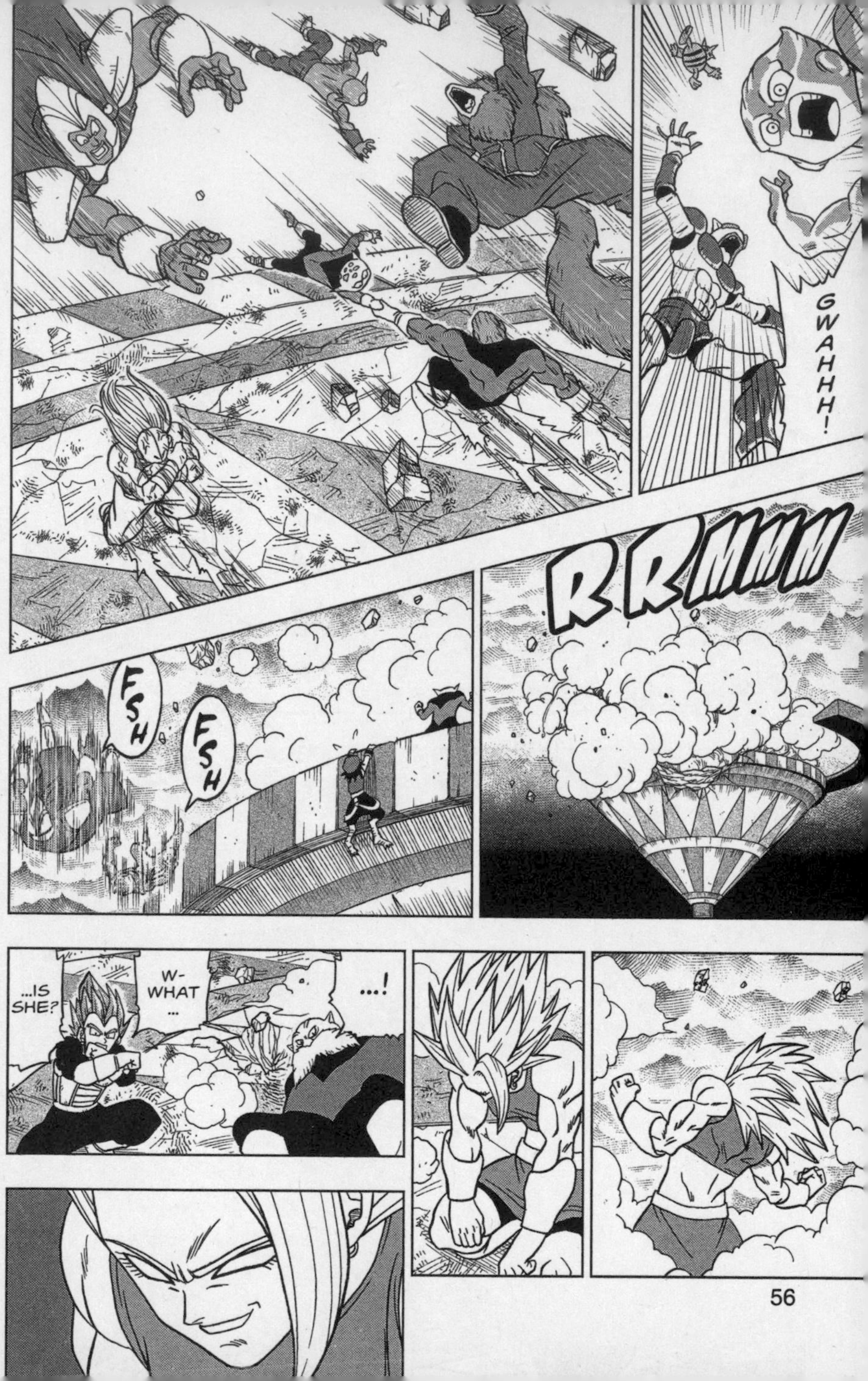
GWAHHH!
RRMMMM
FSH
FSH
...!
W-WHAT...
...IS SHE?

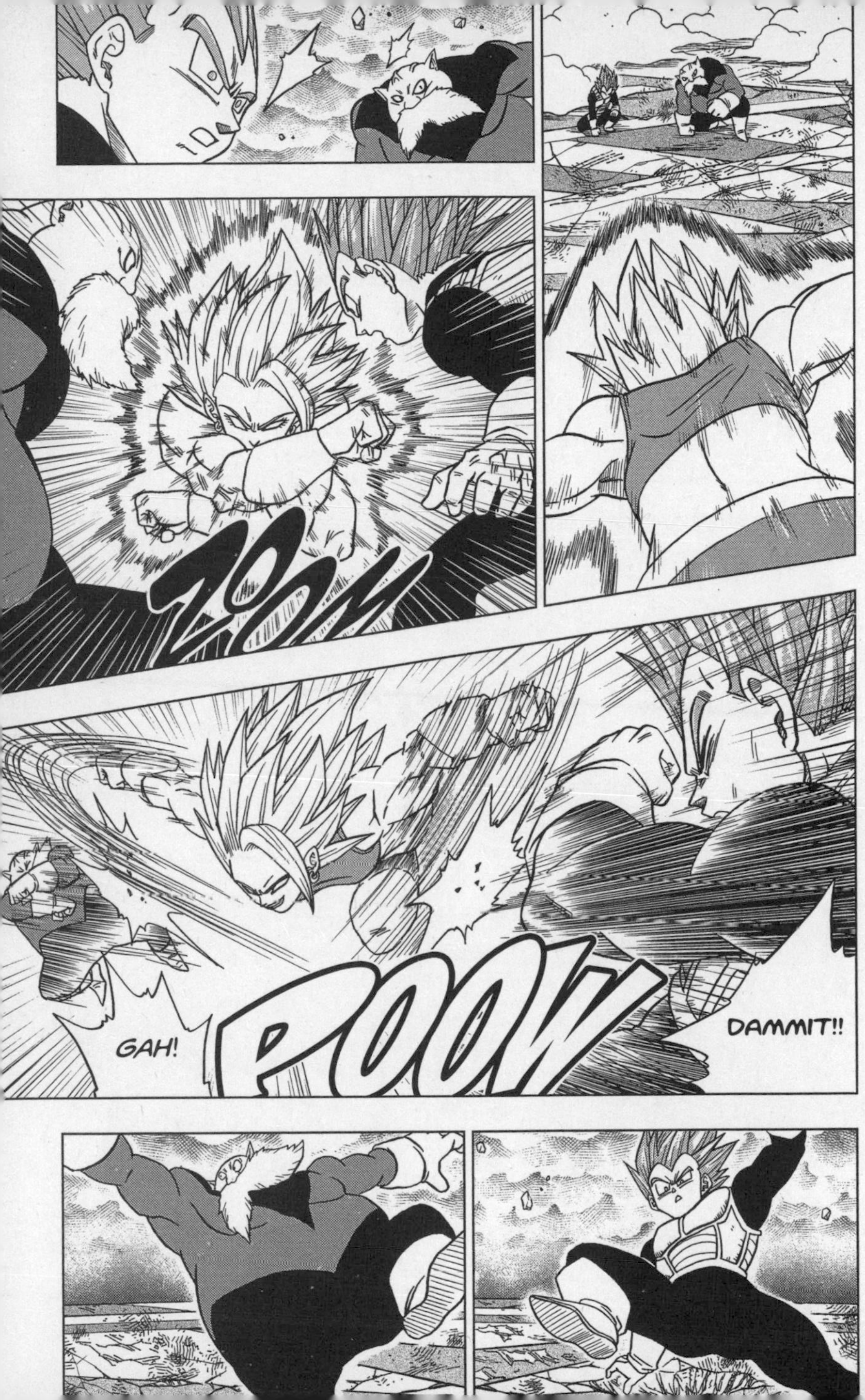
ZOOM
DAMMIT!!
POOW
GAH!

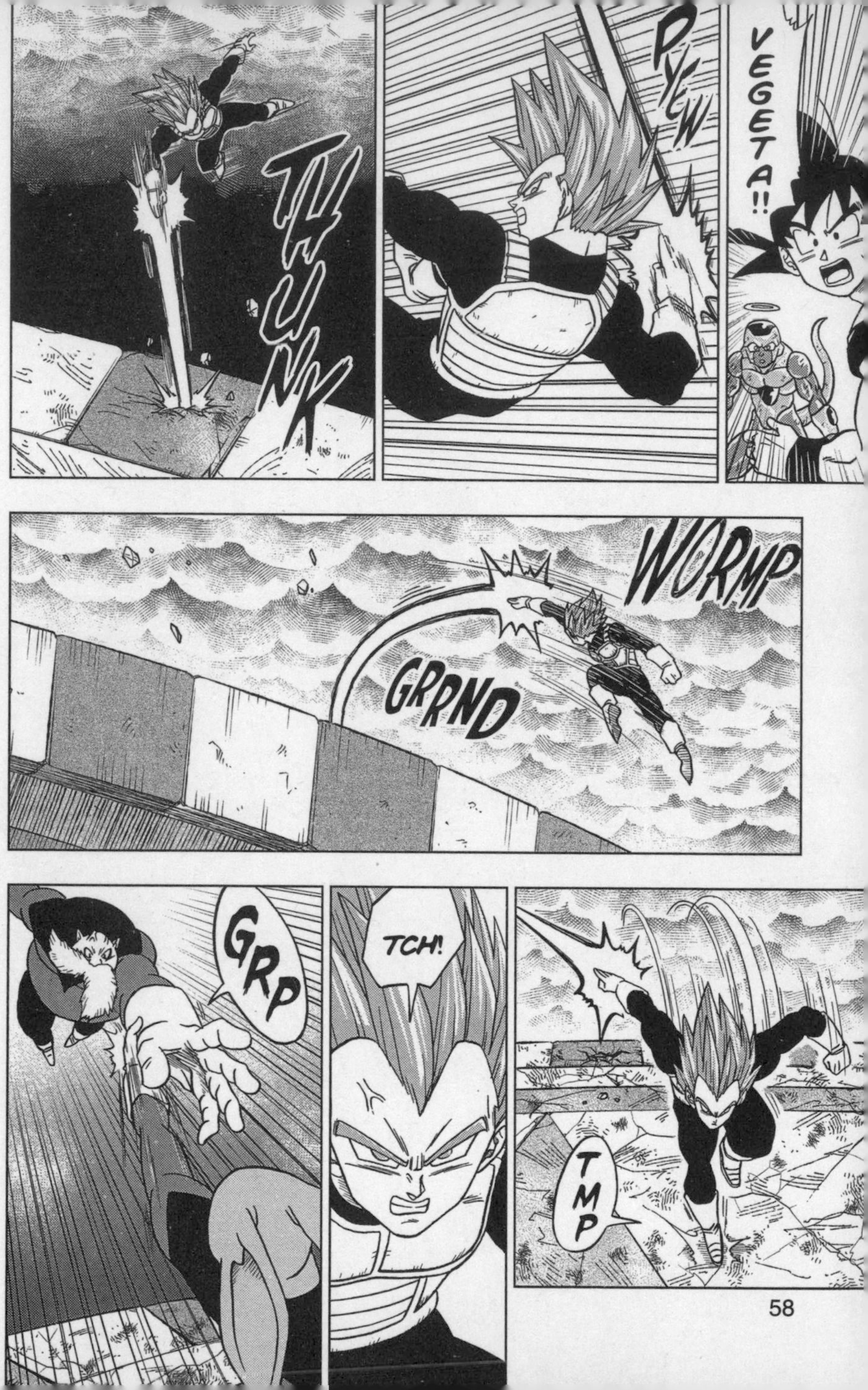
VEGETA!!
PYEW
THUNK
WORMP
GRRND
TMP
TCH!
GRP

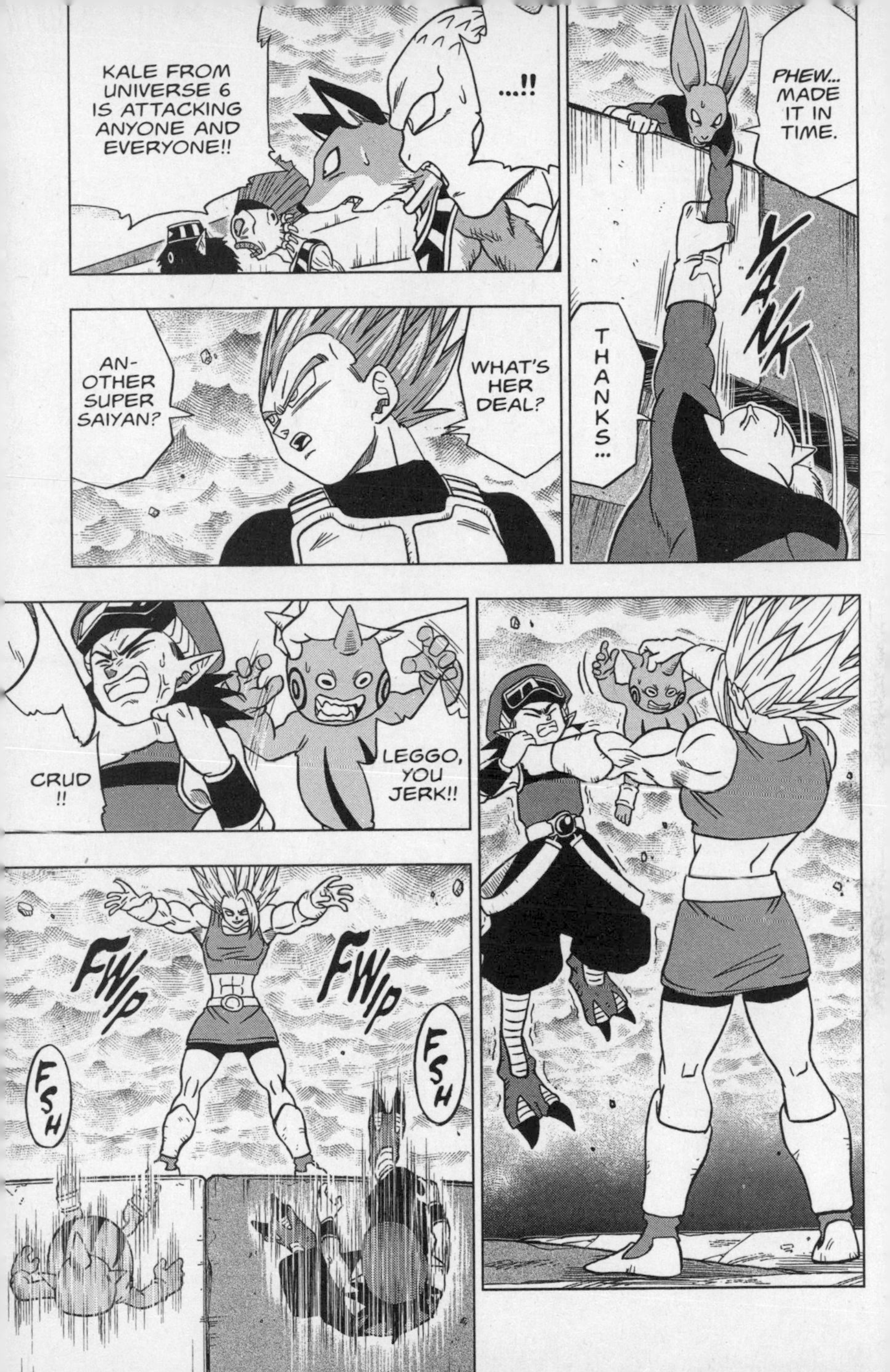
PHEW... MADE IT IN TIME.
YANK
THANKS...
...!!
KALE FROM UNIVERSE 6 IS ATTACKING ANYONE AND EVERYONE!!
WHAT'S HER DEAL?
AN-OTHER SUPER SAIYAN?
LEGGO, YOU JERK!!
CRUD!!
FWIP
FWIP
FSH
FSH

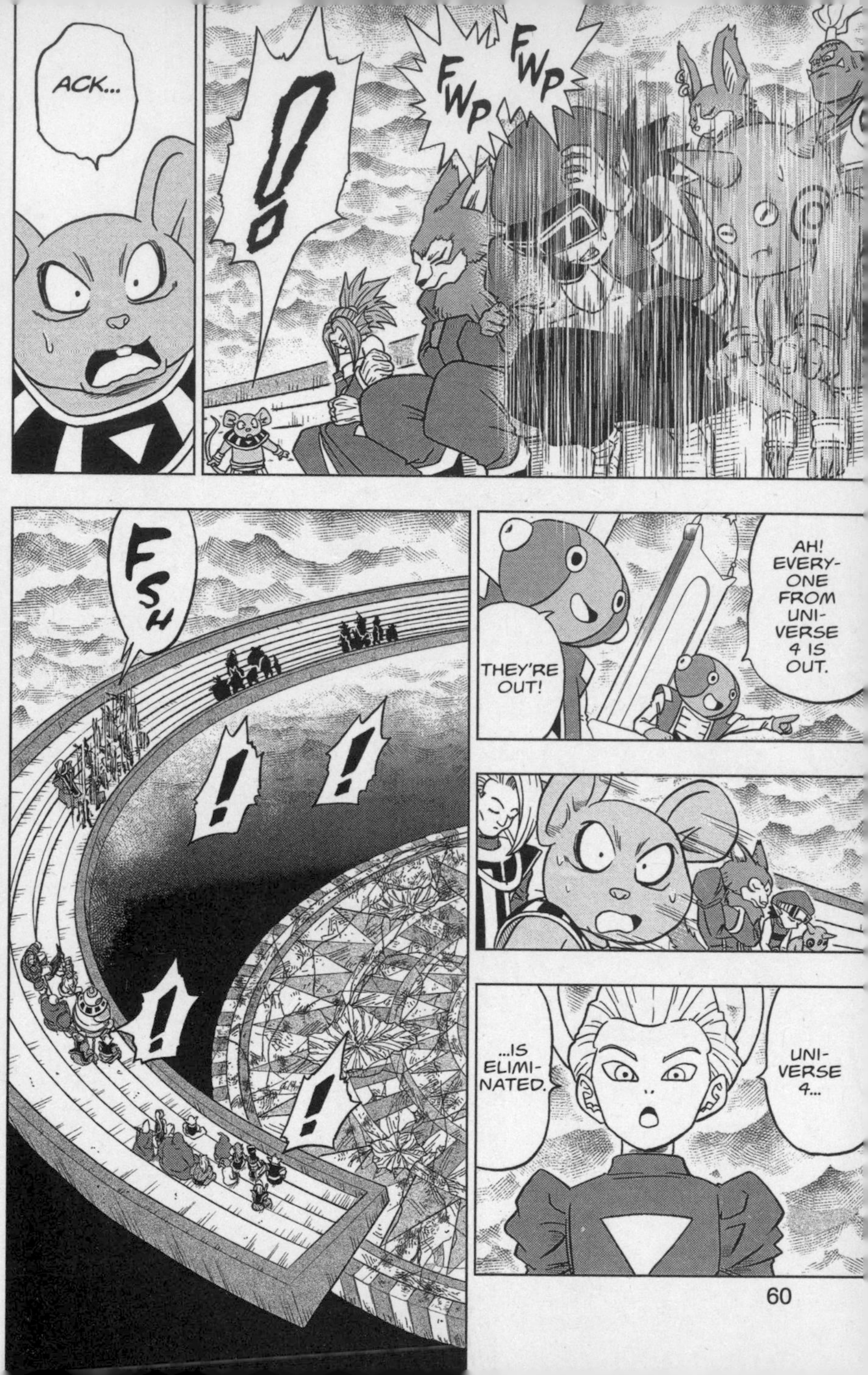
FWP
FWP
!
ACK...
AH! EVERYONE FROM UNIVERSE 4 IS OUT.
THEY'RE OUT!
UNIVERSE 4...
...IS ELIMINATED.
FSH
!
!
!
!

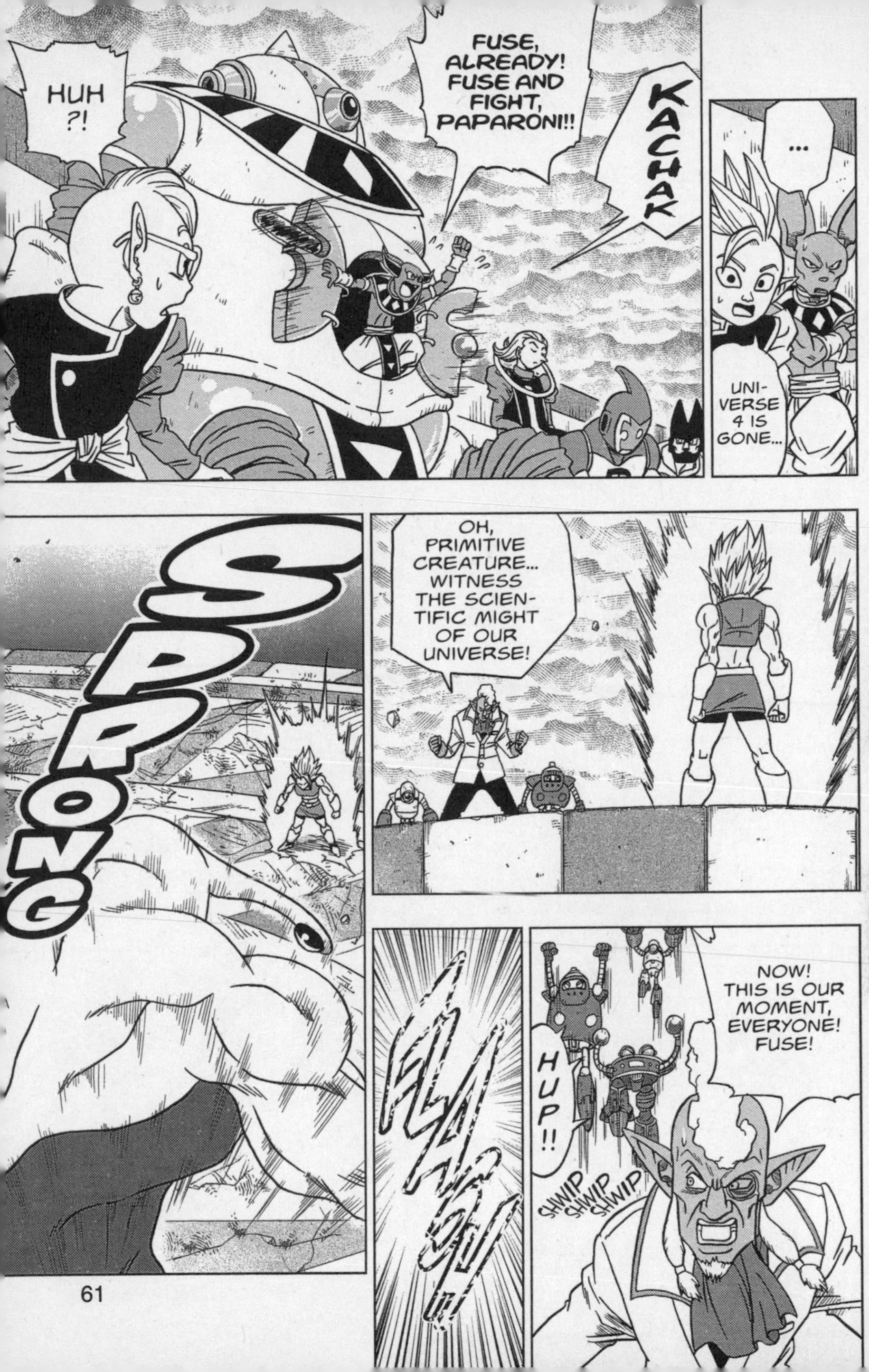
...
UNIVERSE 4 IS GONE...
FUSE, ALREADY! FUSE AND FIGHT, PAPARONI!!
KACHAK
HUH ?!
OH, PRIMITIVE CREATURE... WITNESS THE SCIENTIFIC MIGHT OF OUR UNIVERSE!
NOW! THIS IS OUR MOMENT, EVERYONE! FUSE!
HUP!!
SHWIP SHWIP SHWIP
SPRONG

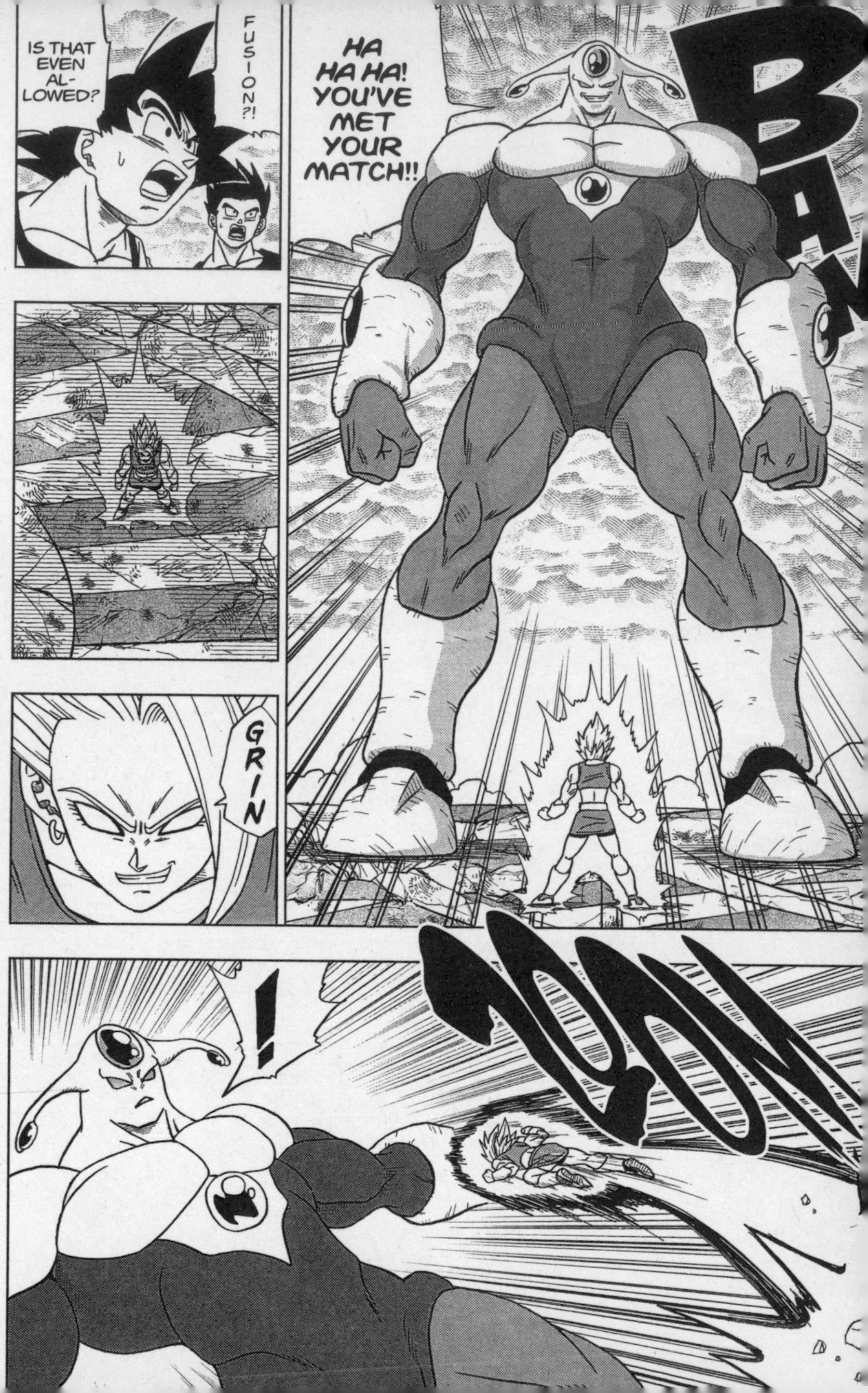

BAM
HA HA HA! YOU'VE MET YOUR MATCH!!
FUSION?!
IS THAT EVEN AL-LOWED?
GRIN
ZOOM
!

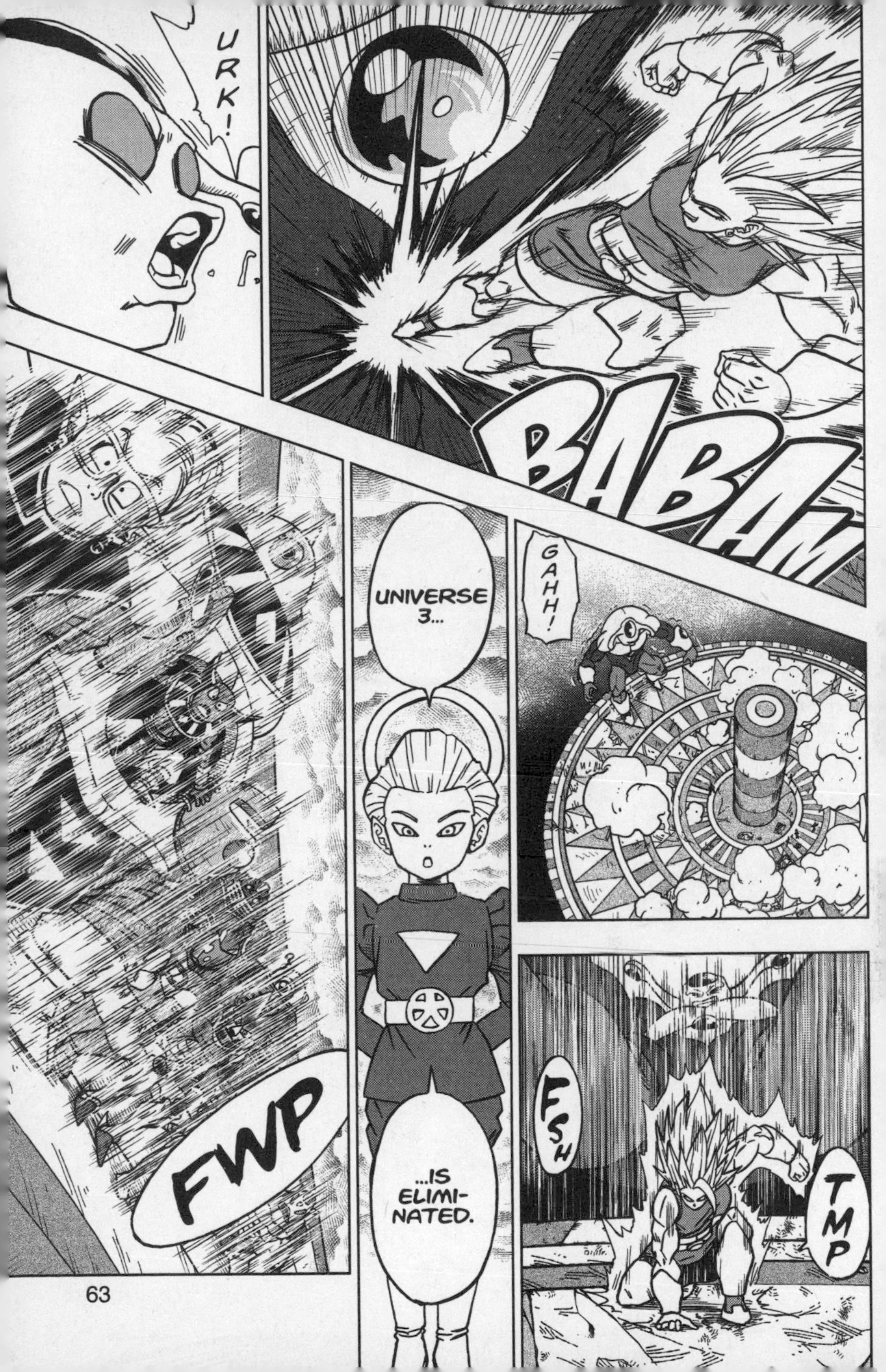
BABAM
URK!
GAHH!
FSH
TMP
UNIVERSE 3...
...IS ELIMINATED.
FWP

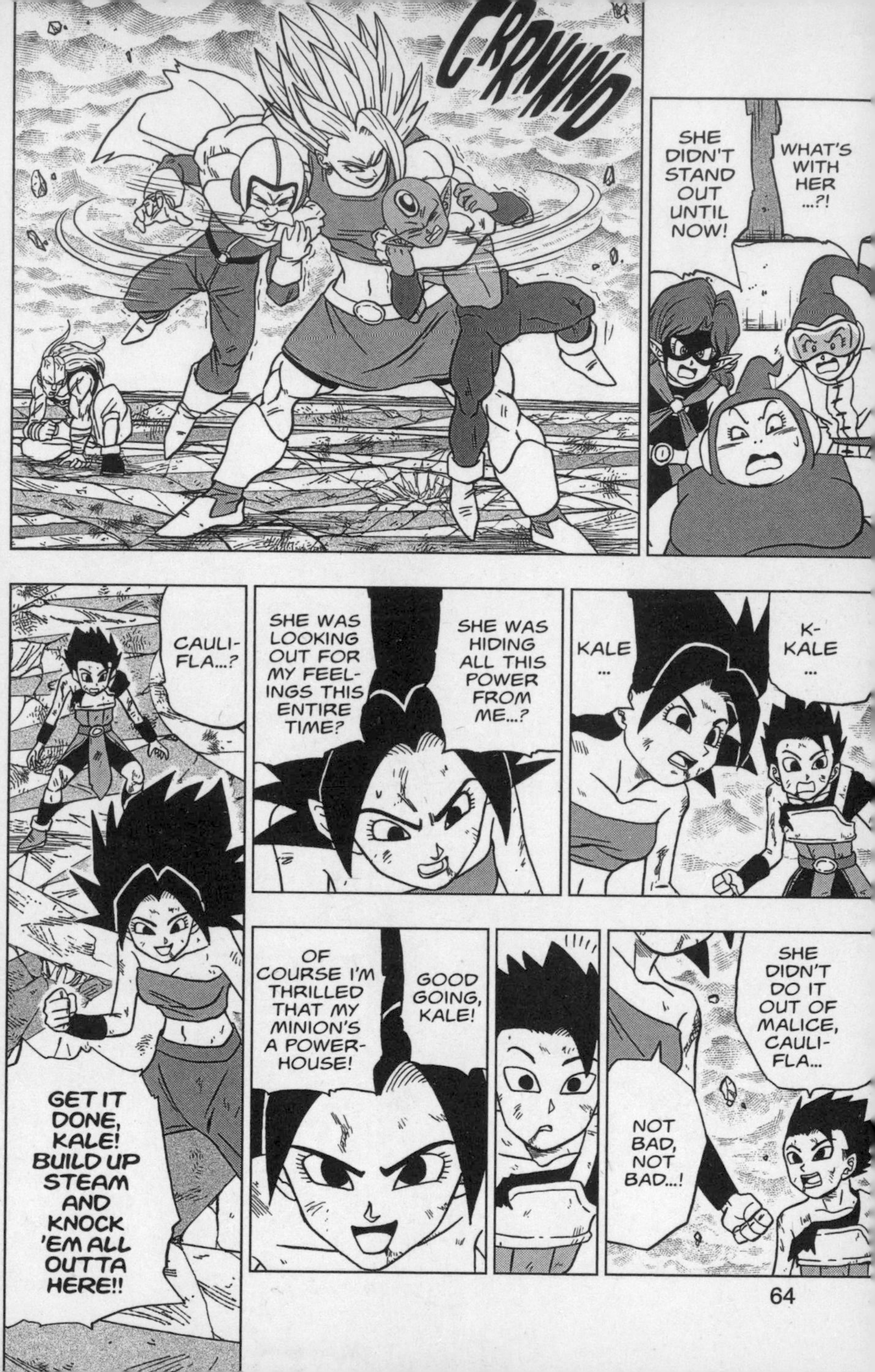
WHAT'S WITH HER ...?!
SHE DIDN'T STAND OUT UNTIL NOW!
CRRNNND
K-KALE ...
KALE ...
SHE WAS HIDING ALL THIS POWER FROM ME...?
SHE WAS LOOKING OUT FOR MY FEELINGS THIS ENTIRE TIME?
SHE DIDN'T DO IT OUT OF MALICE, CAULI-FLA...
NOT BAD, NOT BAD...!
GOOD GOING, KALE!
OF COURSE I'M THRILLED THAT MY MINION'S A POWER-HOUSE!
CAULI-FLA...?
GET IT DONE, KALE! BUILD UP STEAM AND KNOCK 'EM ALL OUTTA HERE!!

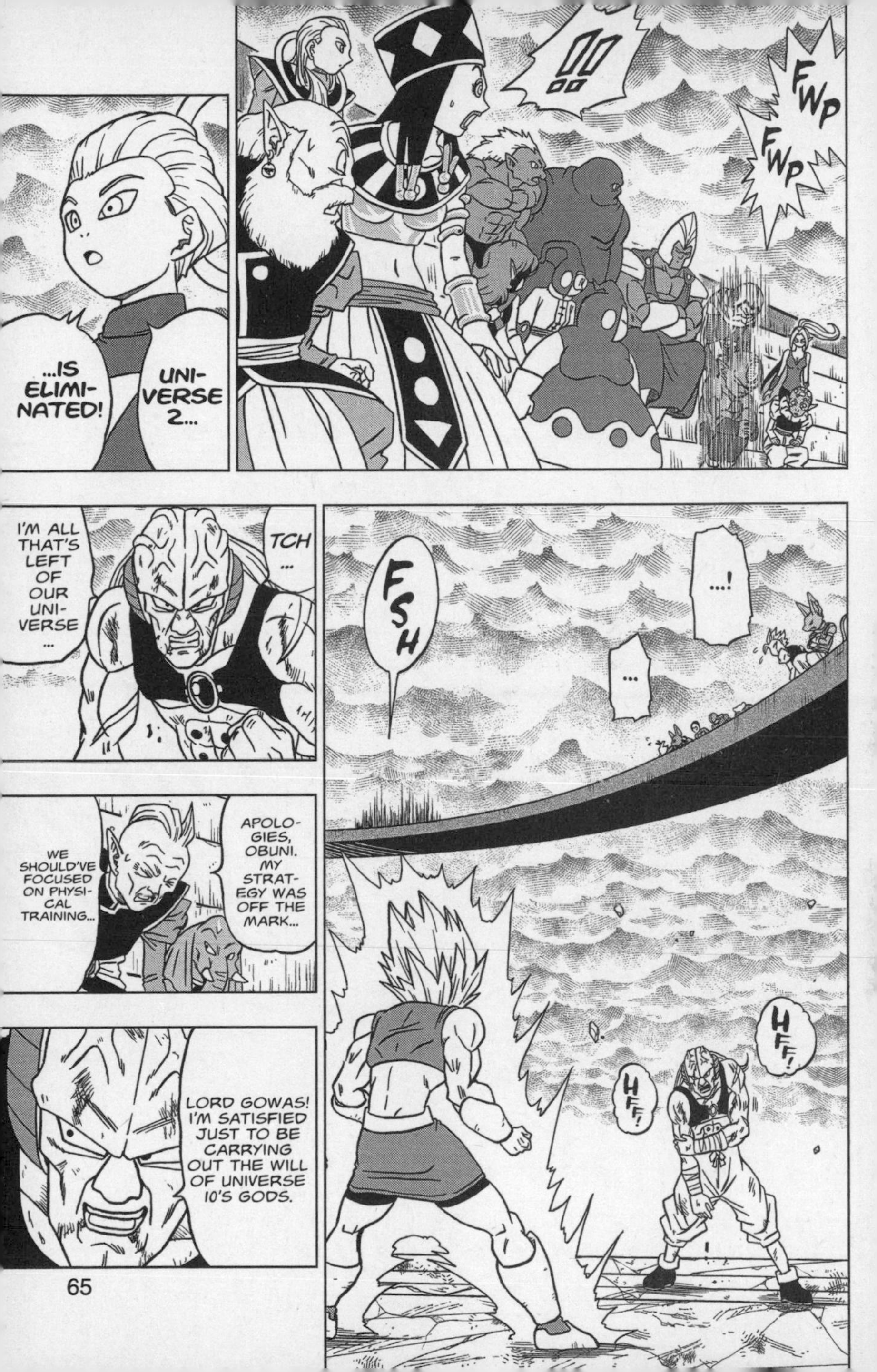
!!
FWP FWP
UNIVERSE 2...
...IS ELIMINATED!
...!
...
FSH
HFF!
HFF!
TCH...
I'M ALL THAT'S LEFT OF OUR UNIVERSE...
APOLOGIES, OBUNI. MY STRATEGY WAS OFF THE MARK...
WE SHOULD'VE FOCUSED ON PHYSICAL TRAINING...
LORD GOWAS! I'M SATISFIED JUST TO BE CARRYING OUT THE WILL OF UNIVERSE 10'S GODS.

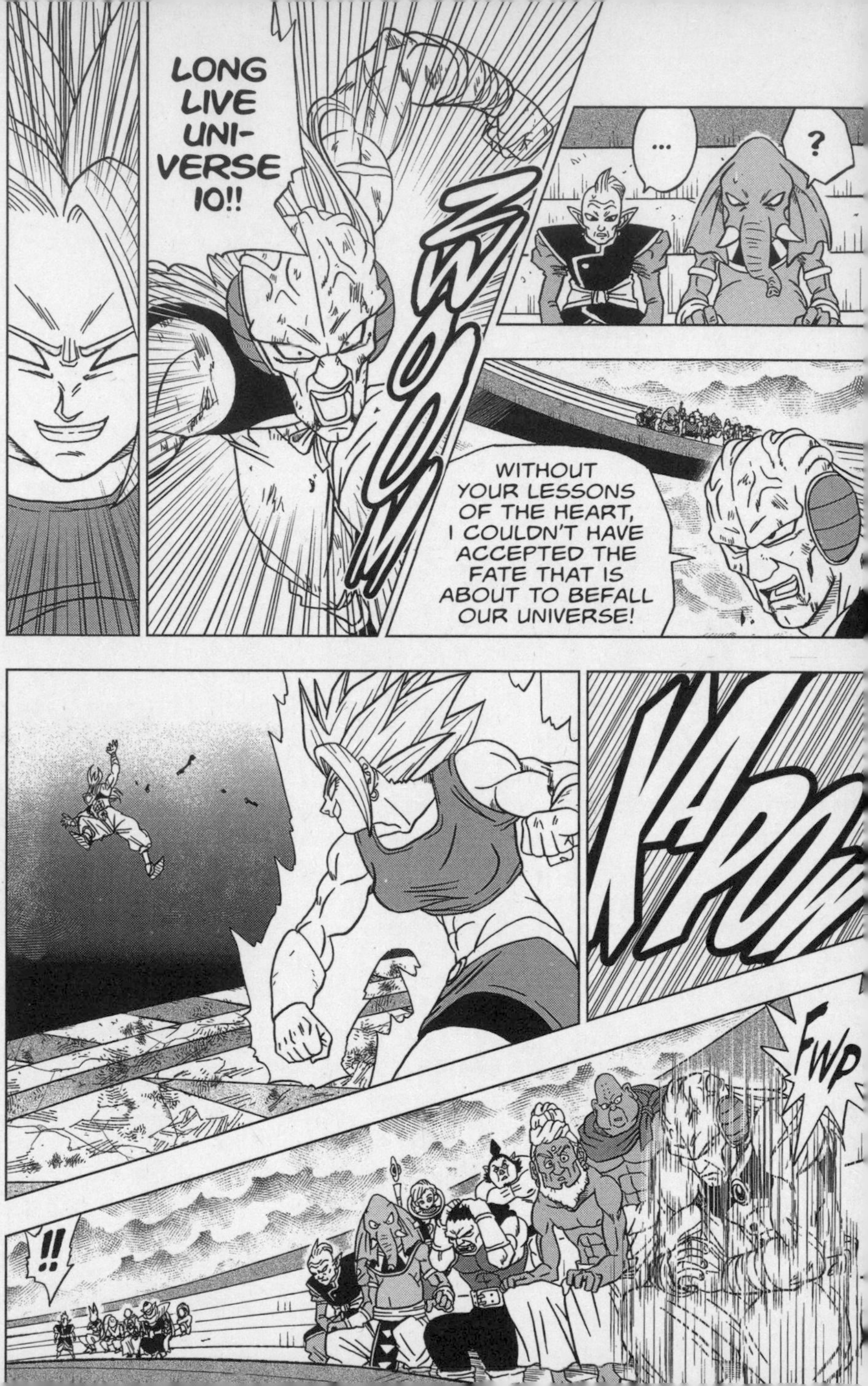
?
...
WITHOUT YOUR LESSONS OF THE HEART, I COULDN'T HAVE ACCEPTED THE FATE THAT IS ABOUT TO BEFALL OUR UNIVERSE!
LONG LIVE UNI-VERSE 10!!
FWP
!!

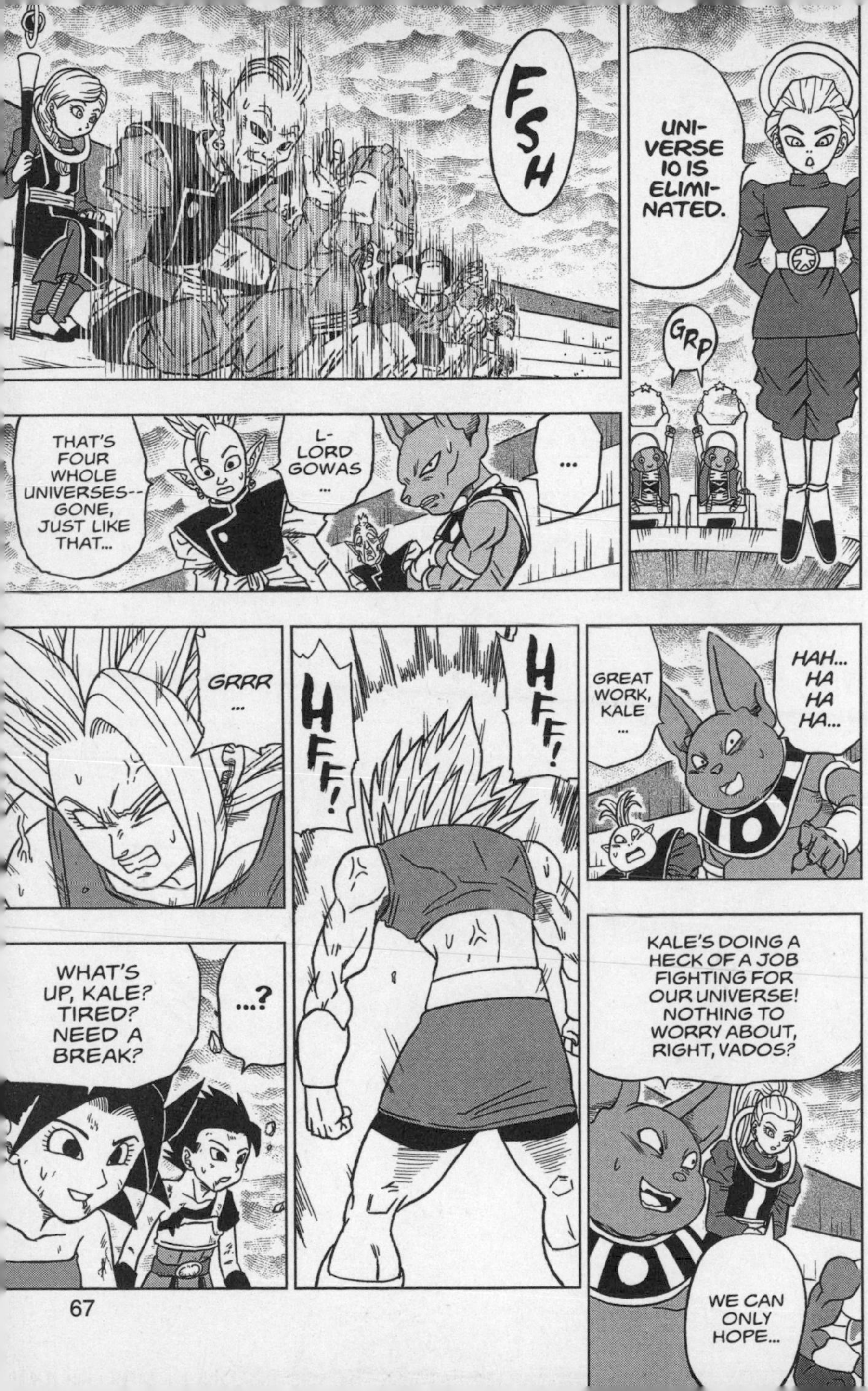
UNI-VERSE 10 IS ELIMI-NATED.
GRP
FSH
...
L-LORD GOWAS ...
THAT'S FOUR WHOLE UNIVERSES-- GONE, JUST LIKE THAT...
HAH... HA HA HA...
GREAT WORK, KALE ...
KALE'S DOING A HECK OF A JOB FIGHTING FOR OUR UNIVERSE! NOTHING TO WORRY ABOUT, RIGHT, VADOS?
WE CAN ONLY HOPE...
HFF!
HFF!
GRRR ...
...?
WHAT'S UP, KALE? TIRED? NEED A BREAK?

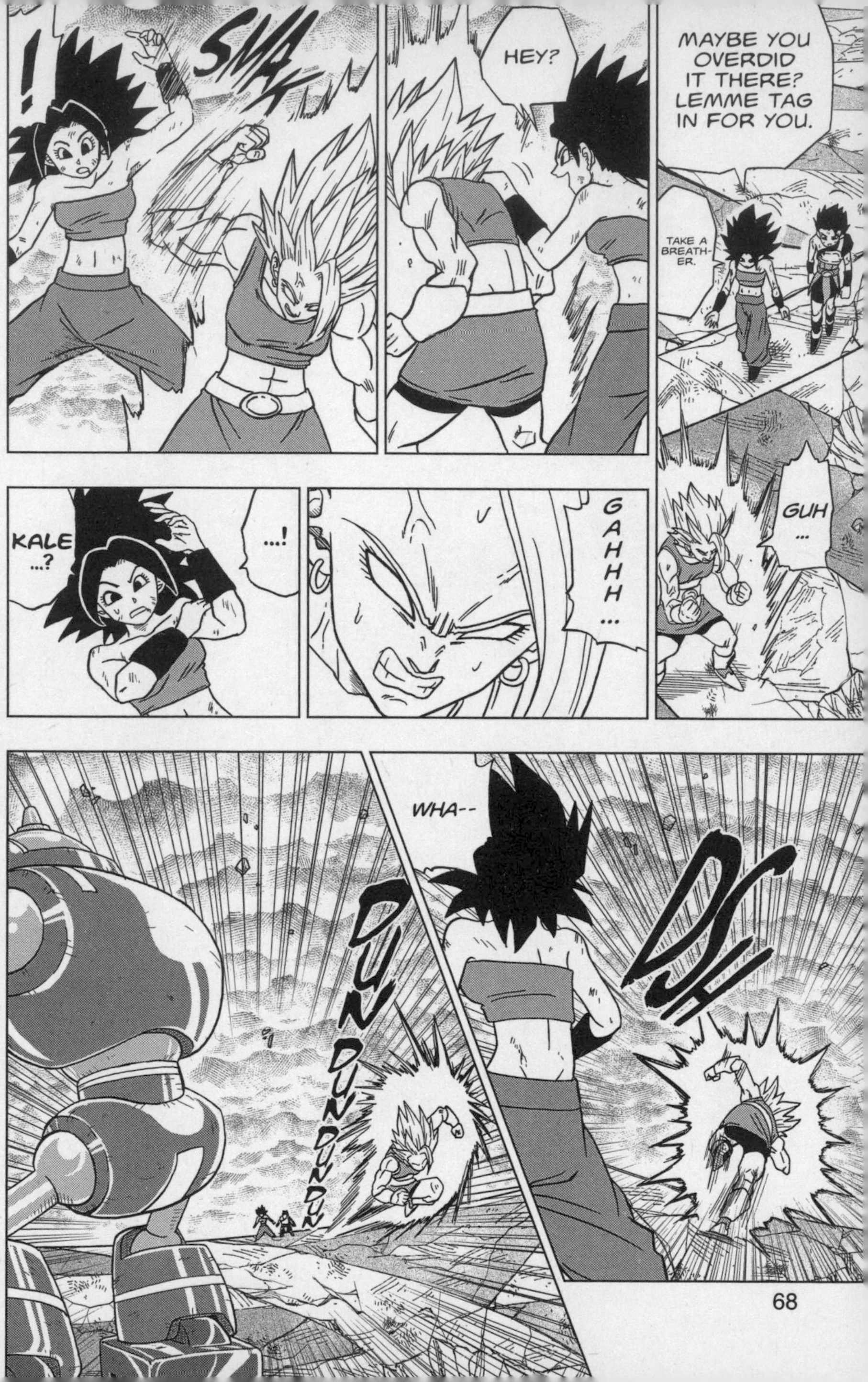

MAYBE YOU OVERDID IT THERE? LEMME TAG IN FOR YOU.
TAKE A BREATHER.
HEY?
SMAK
!
GUH ...
GAHHH ...
...!
KALE ...?
DSH
WHA--
DUNDUNDUNDUNDUN

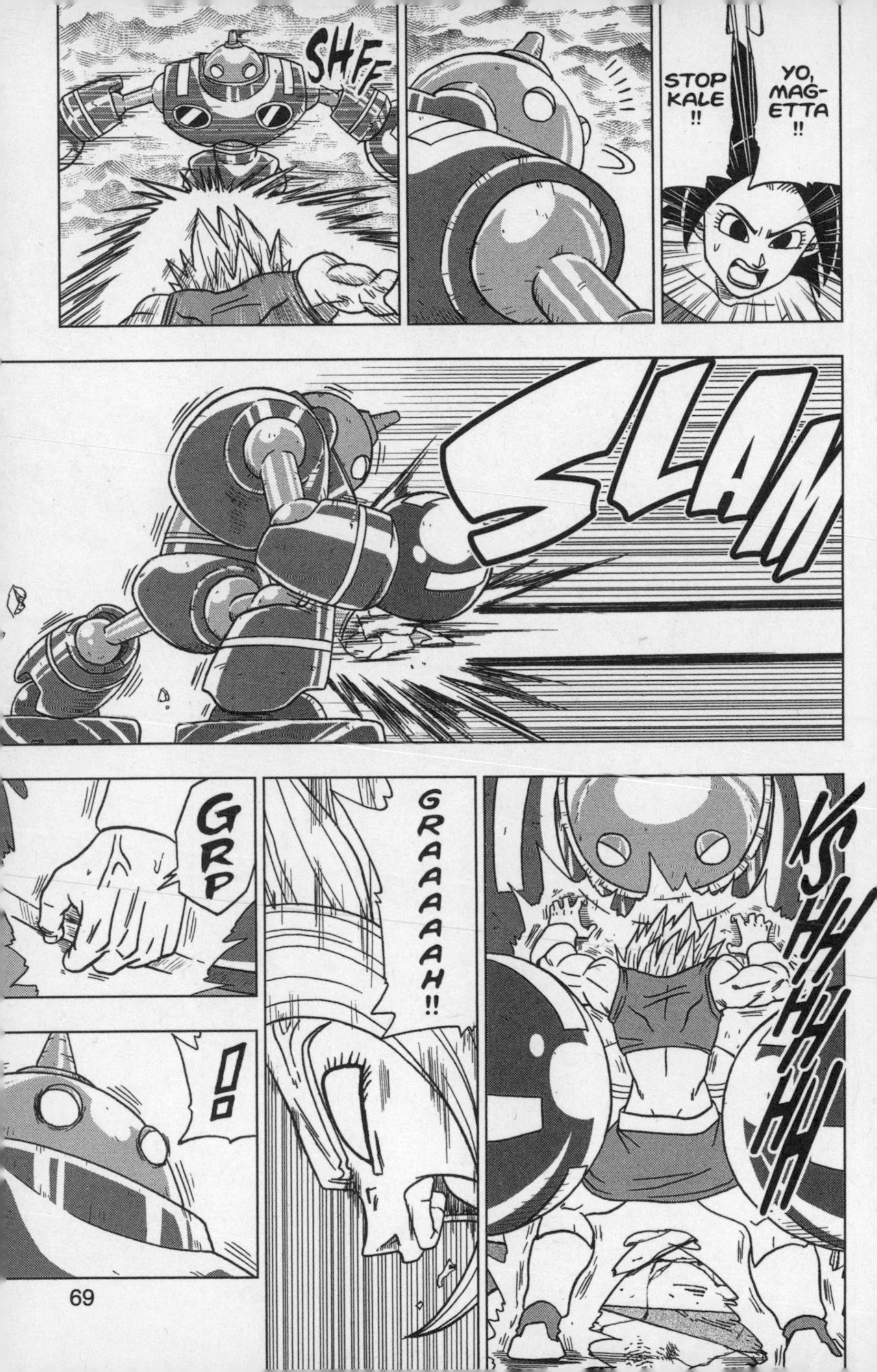
YO, MAG-ETTA!!
STOP KALE!!
SHFF
SLAM
KSHHHHHH
GRAAAAAH!!
GRP
!

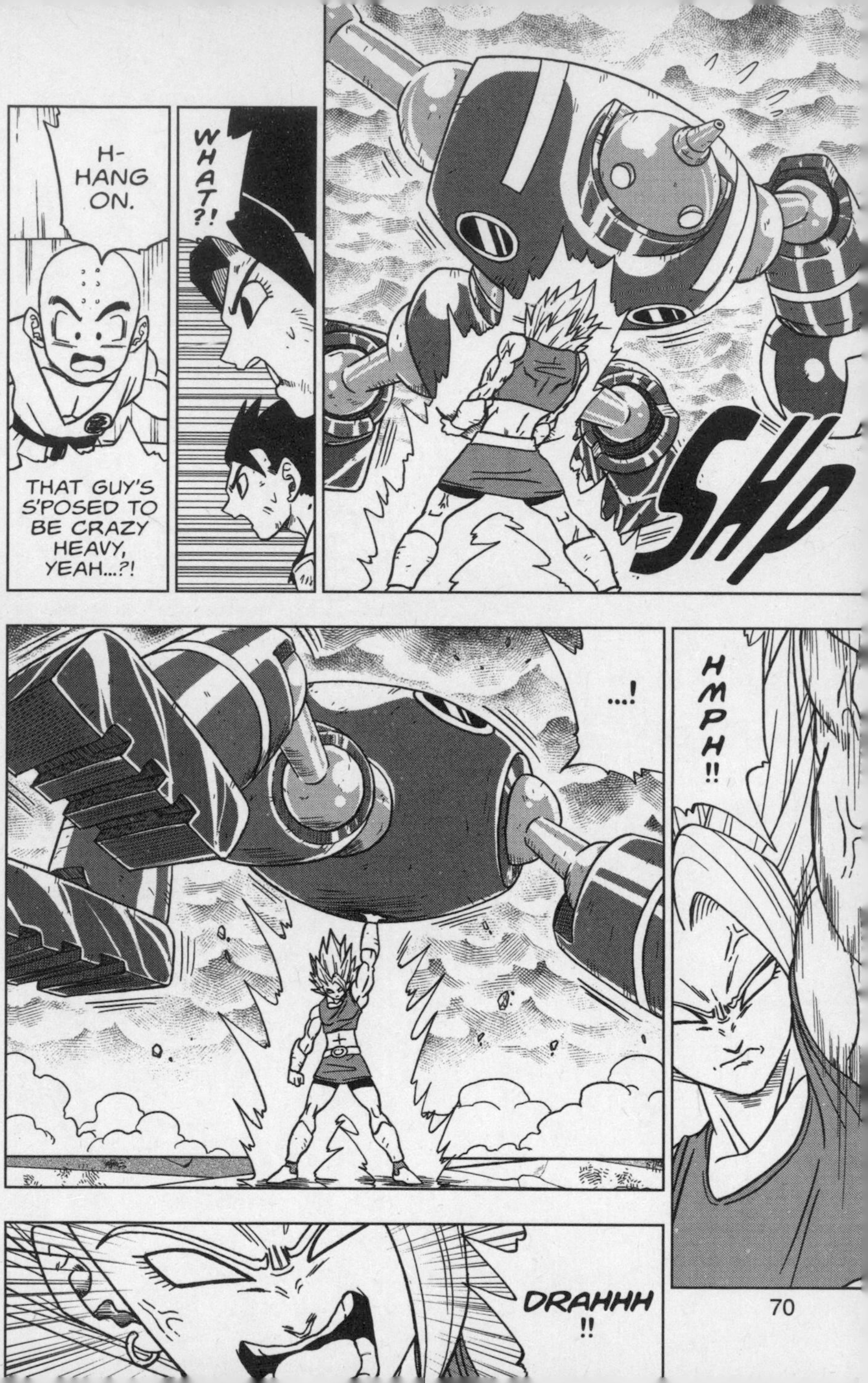
SHP
WHAT?!
H-HANG ON.
THAT GUY'S S'POSED TO BE CRAZY HEAVY, YEAH...?!
HMPH!!
...!
DRAHHH!!

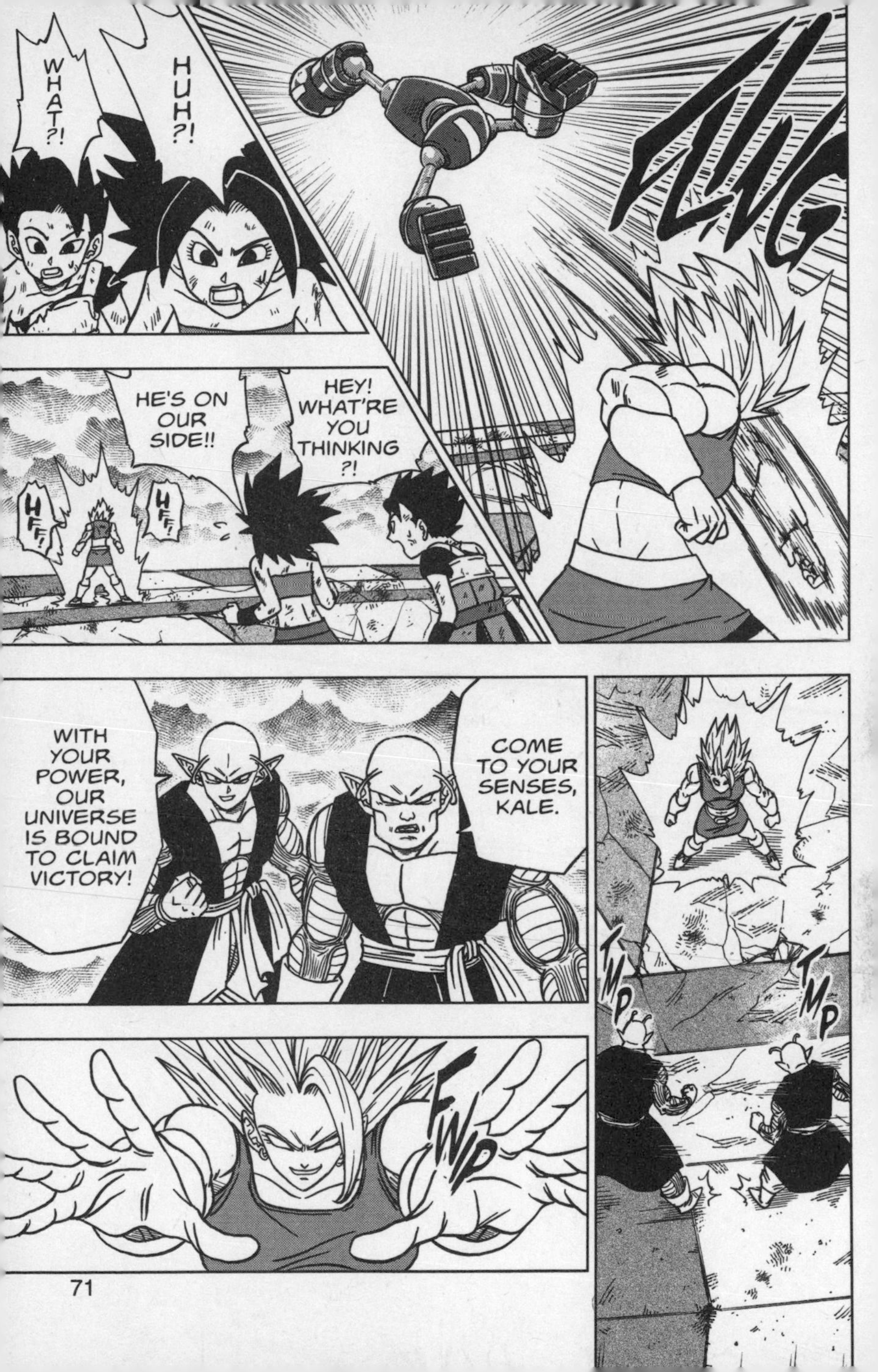
HUH?!
WHAT?!
HEY! WHAT'RE YOU THINKING?!
HE'S ON OUR SIDE!!
HFF
HFF
TMP
TMP
COME TO YOUR SENSES, KALE.
WITH YOUR POWER, OUR UNIVERSE IS BOUND TO CLAIM VICTORY!
FWP

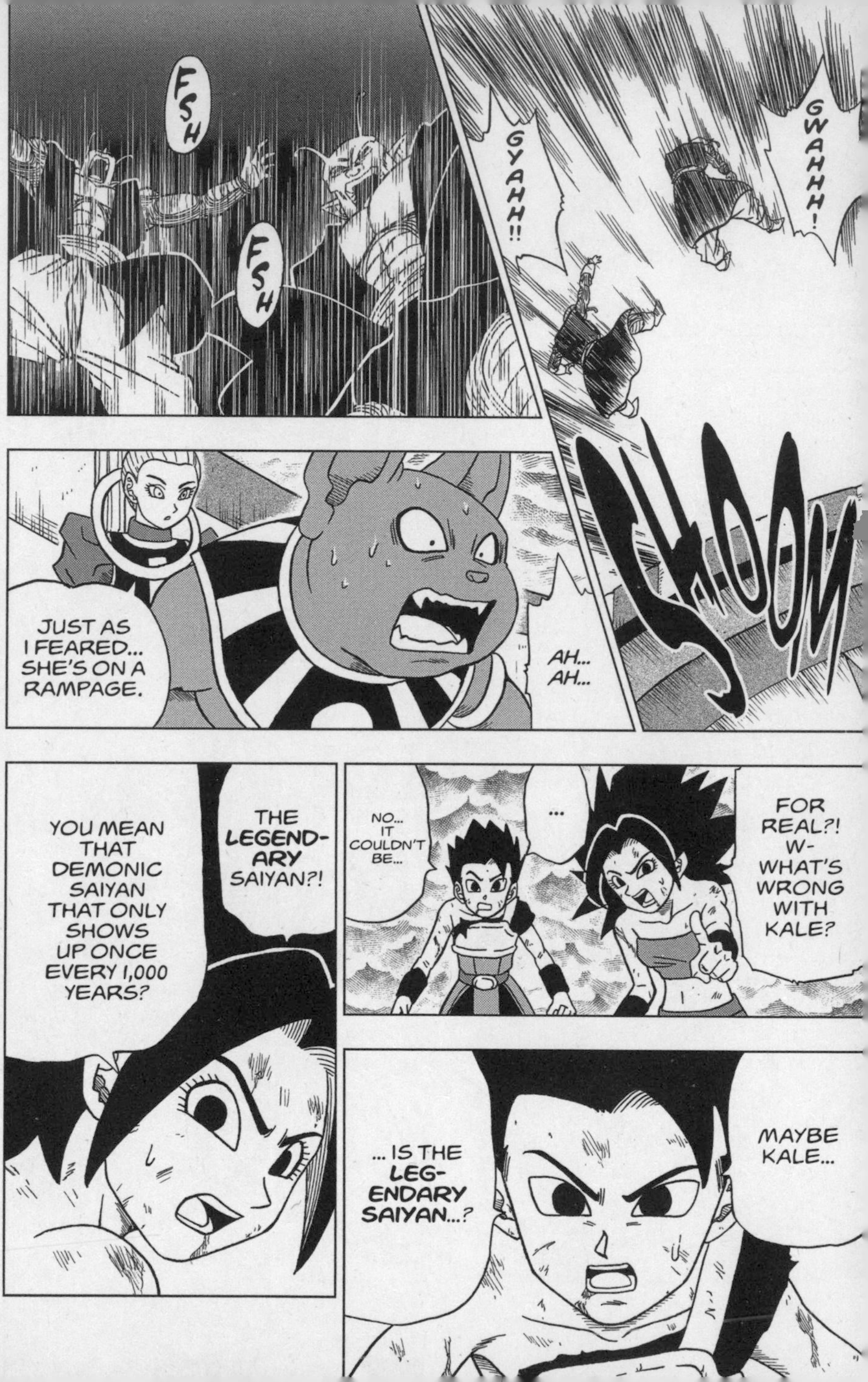
GWAHHH!
GYAHH!!
SHOOM
FSH
FSH
AH... AH...
JUST AS I FEARED... SHE'S ON A RAMPAGE.
FOR REAL?! W-WHAT'S WRONG WITH KALE?
...
NO... IT COULDN'T BE...
THE **LEGENDARY** SAIYAN?!
YOU MEAN THAT DEMONIC SAIYAN THAT ONLY SHOWS UP ONCE EVERY 1,000 YEARS?
MAYBE KALE...
... IS THE **LEGENDARY SAIYAN**...?

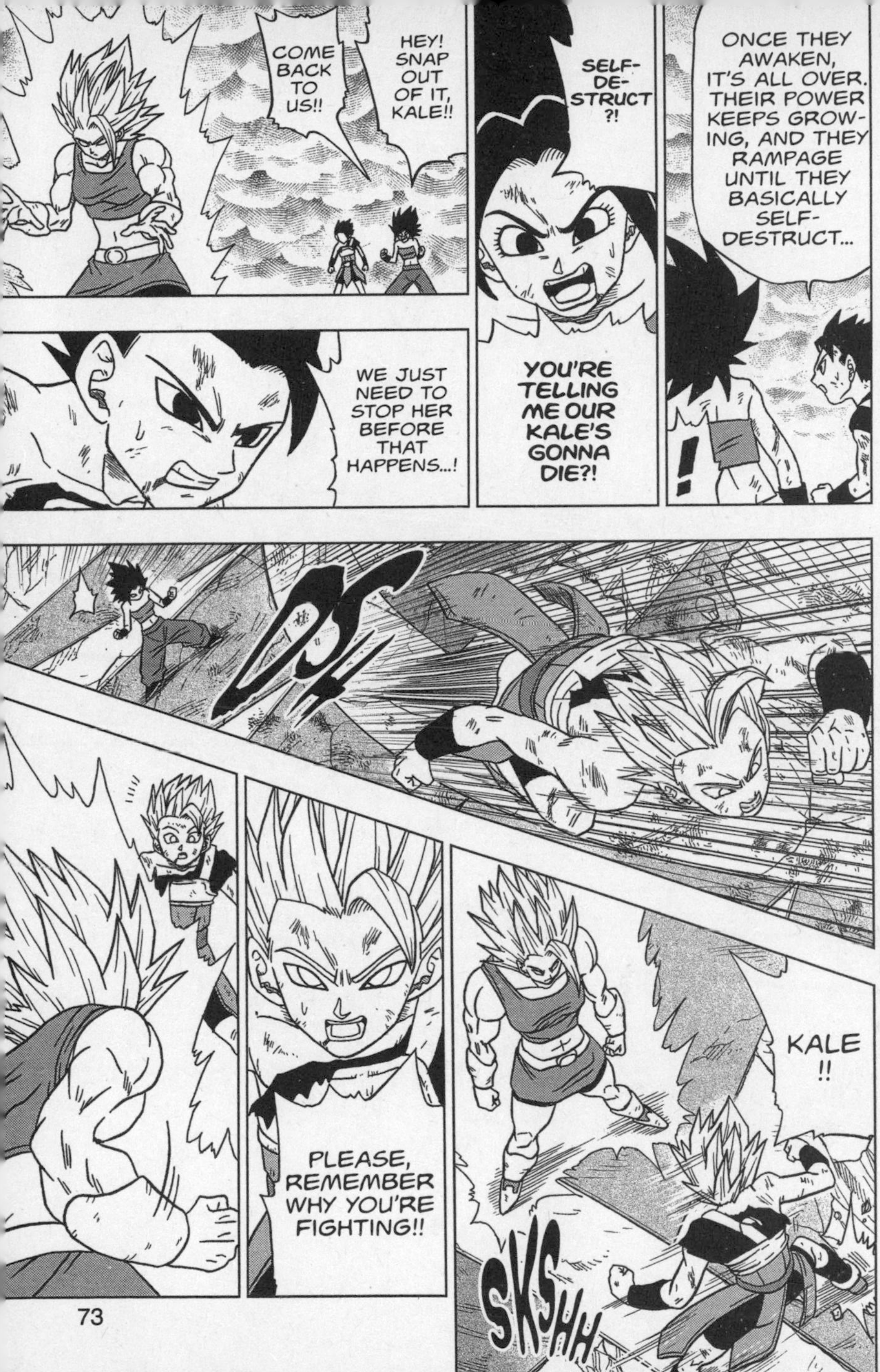
ONCE THEY AWAKEN, IT'S ALL OVER. THEIR POWER KEEPS GROW-ING, AND THEY RAMPAGE UNTIL THEY BASICALLY SELF-DESTRUCT...
!
SELF-DE-STRUCT?!
YOU'RE TELLING ME OUR KALE'S GONNA DIE?!
HEY! SNAP OUT OF IT, KALE!!
COME BACK TO US!!
WE JUST NEED TO STOP HER BEFORE THAT HAPPENS...!
KALE !!
SKSHH
PLEASE, REMEMBER WHY YOU'RE FIGHTING!!

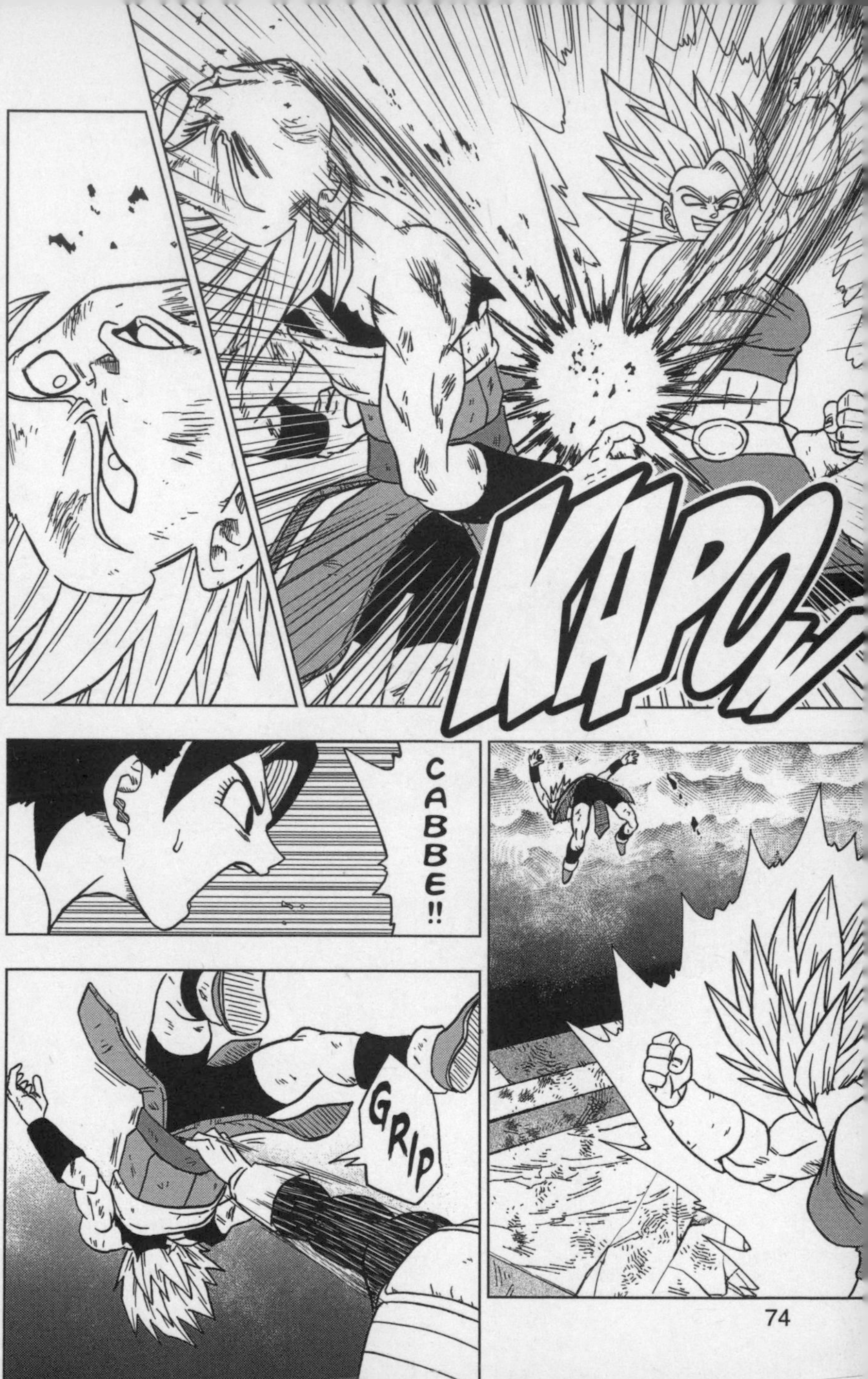
KAPOW
CABBE!!
GRIP

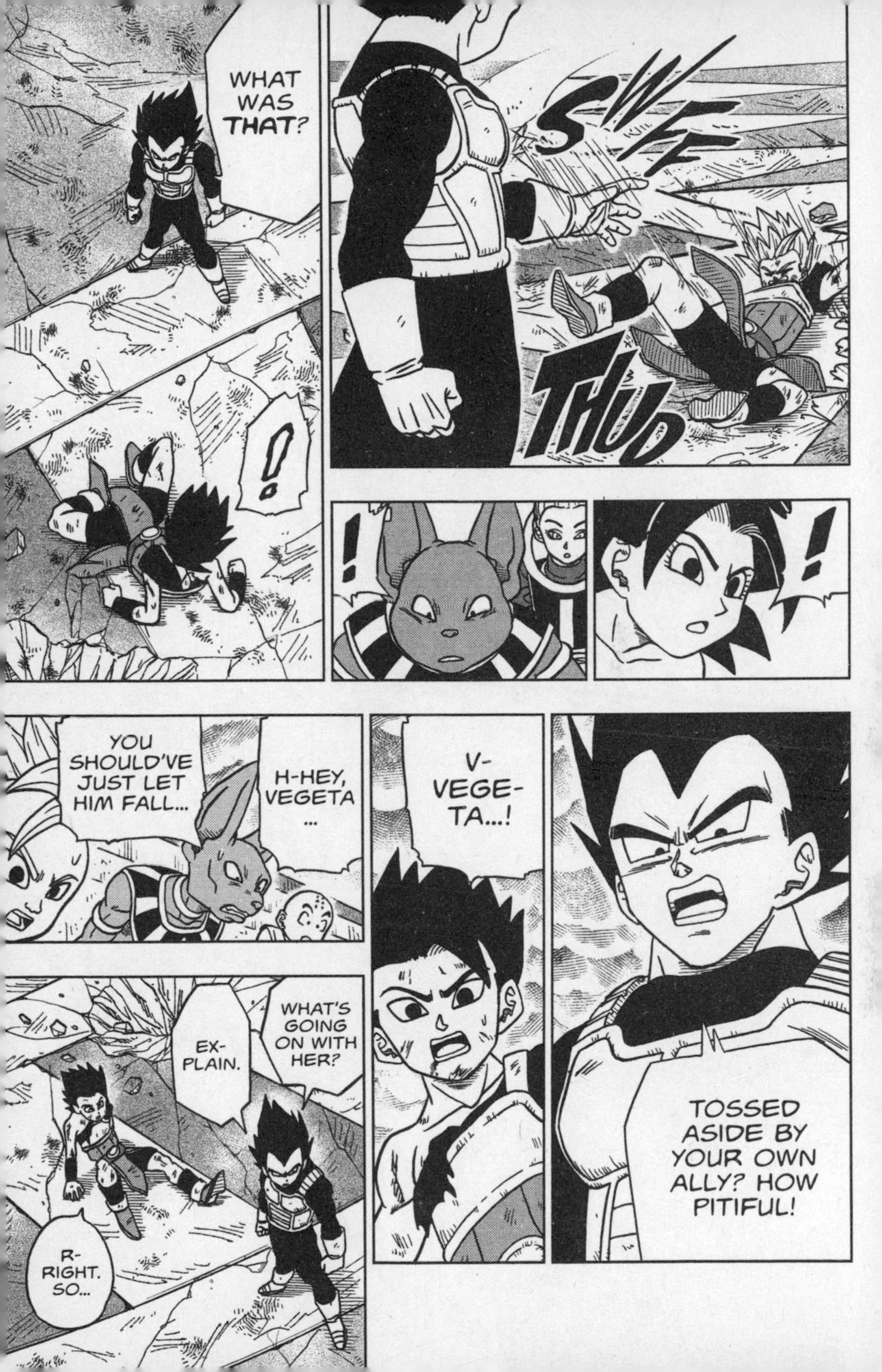
SWFF
THUD
!
!
WHAT WAS THAT?
!
TOSSED ASIDE BY YOUR OWN ALLY? HOW PITIFUL!
V-VEGETA...!
H-HEY, VEGETA...
YOU SHOULD'VE JUST LET HIM FALL...
WHAT'S GOING ON WITH HER?
EX-PLAIN.
R-RIGHT. SO...

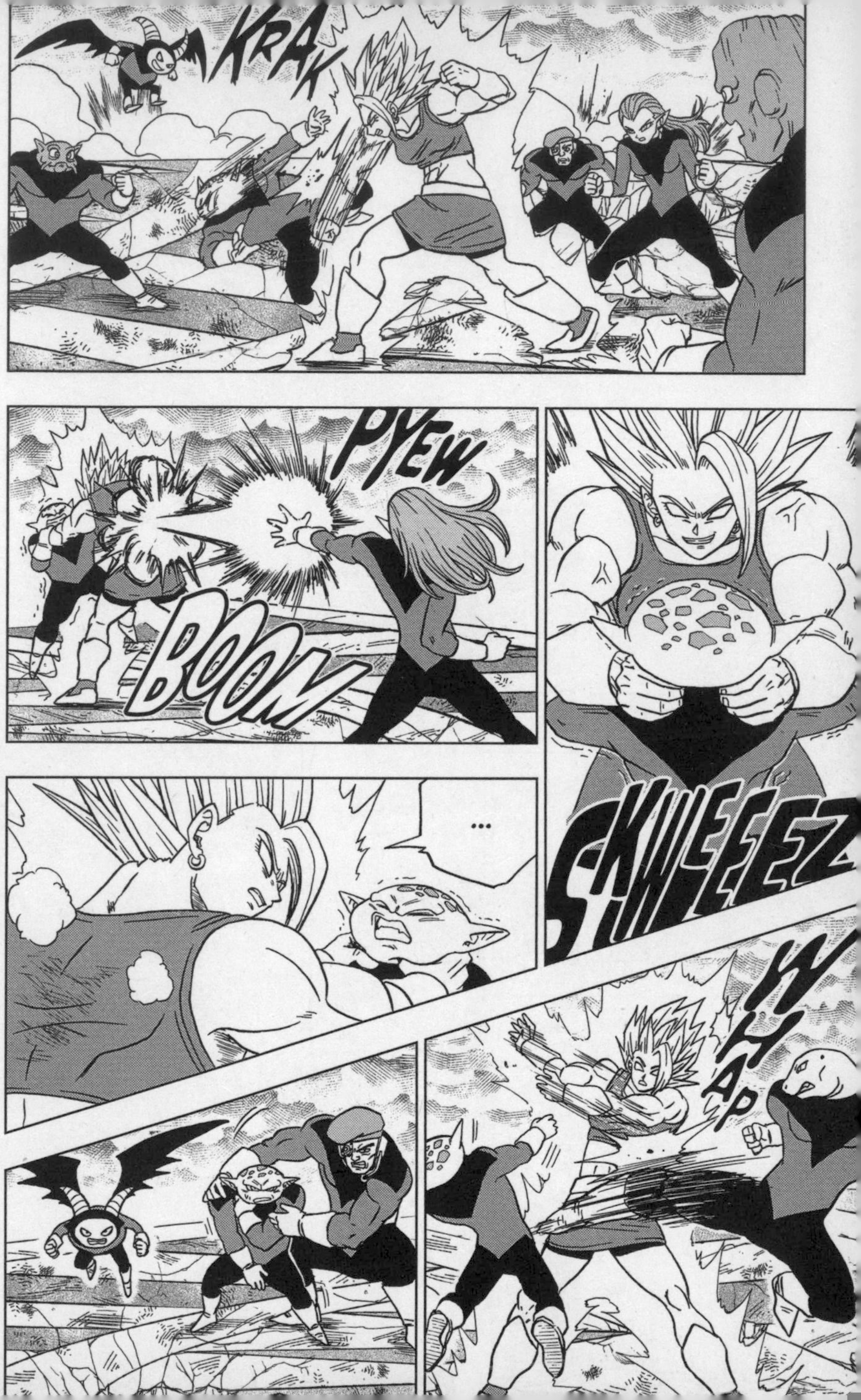
KRAK
SKWEEEZ
PYEW
BOOM
...
WHAP

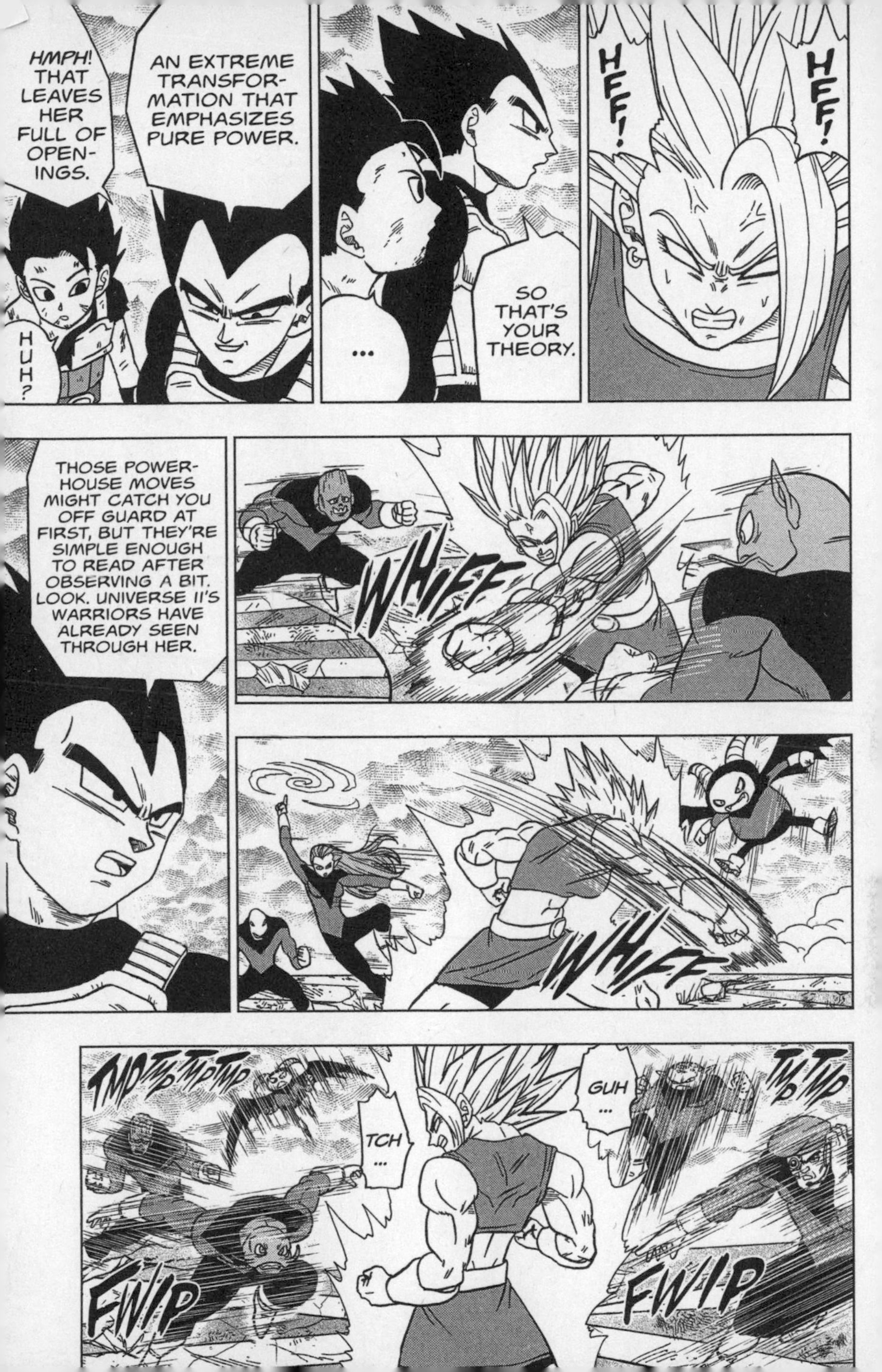
HEFF! HEFF!
SO THAT'S YOUR THEORY.
...
AN EXTREME TRANSFORMATION THAT EMPHASIZES PURE POWER.
HMPH! THAT LEAVES HER FULL OF OPENINGS.
HUH?
WHIFF
WHIFF
THOSE POWERHOUSE MOVES MIGHT CATCH YOU OFF GUARD AT FIRST, BUT THEY'RE SIMPLE ENOUGH TO READ AFTER OBSERVING A BIT. LOOK. UNIVERSE 11'S WARRIORS HAVE ALREADY SEEN THROUGH HER.
TMPTMP
GUH ...
TCH ...
TMPTMPTMPTMP
FWIP
FWIP

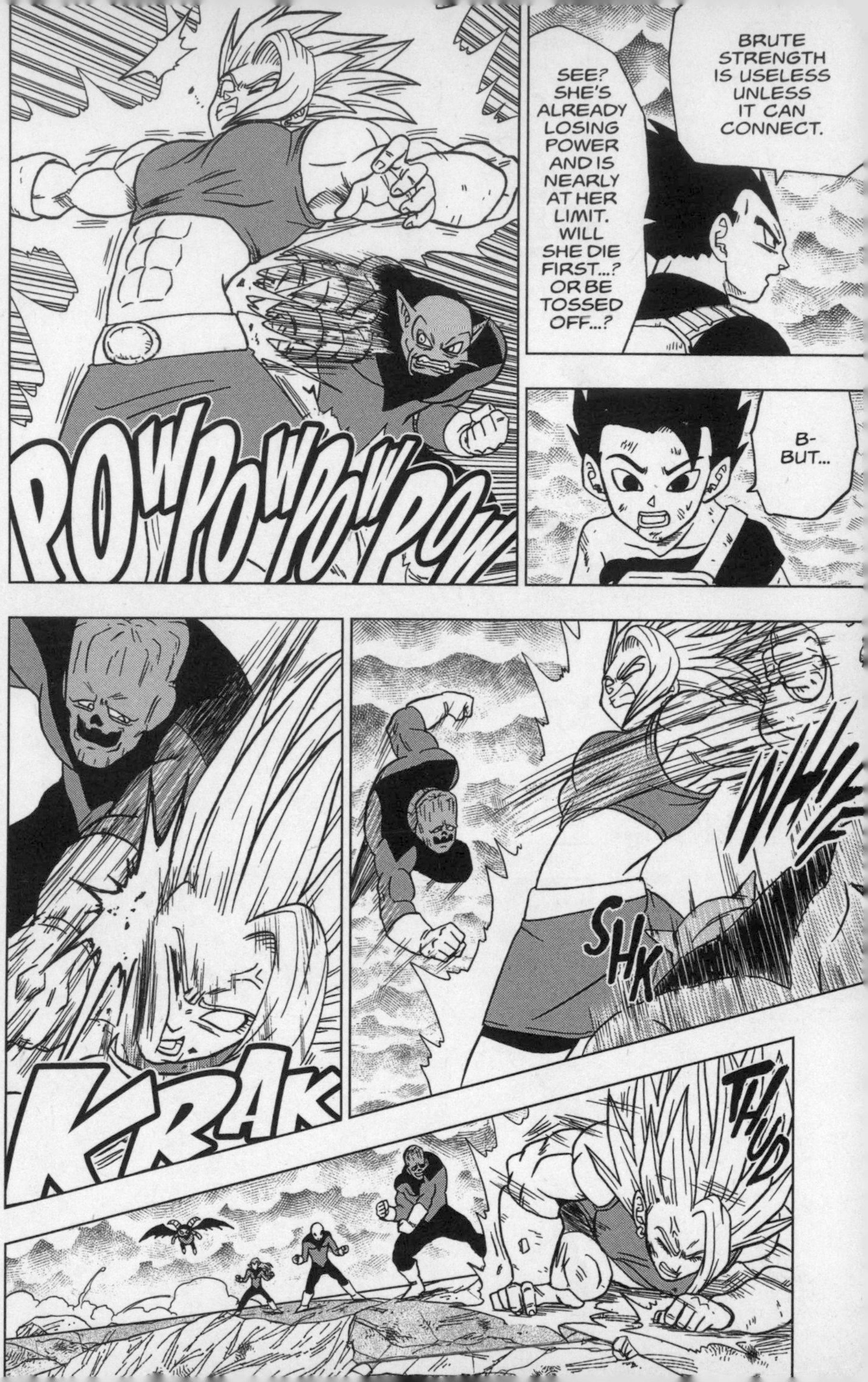
BRUTE STRENGTH IS USELESS UNLESS IT CAN CONNECT.
SEE? SHE'S ALREADY LOSING POWER AND IS NEARLY AT HER LIMIT. WILL SHE DIE FIRST...? OR BE TOSSED OFF...?
B- BUT...
POW POW POW POW POW
SHK
KRAK
THUD

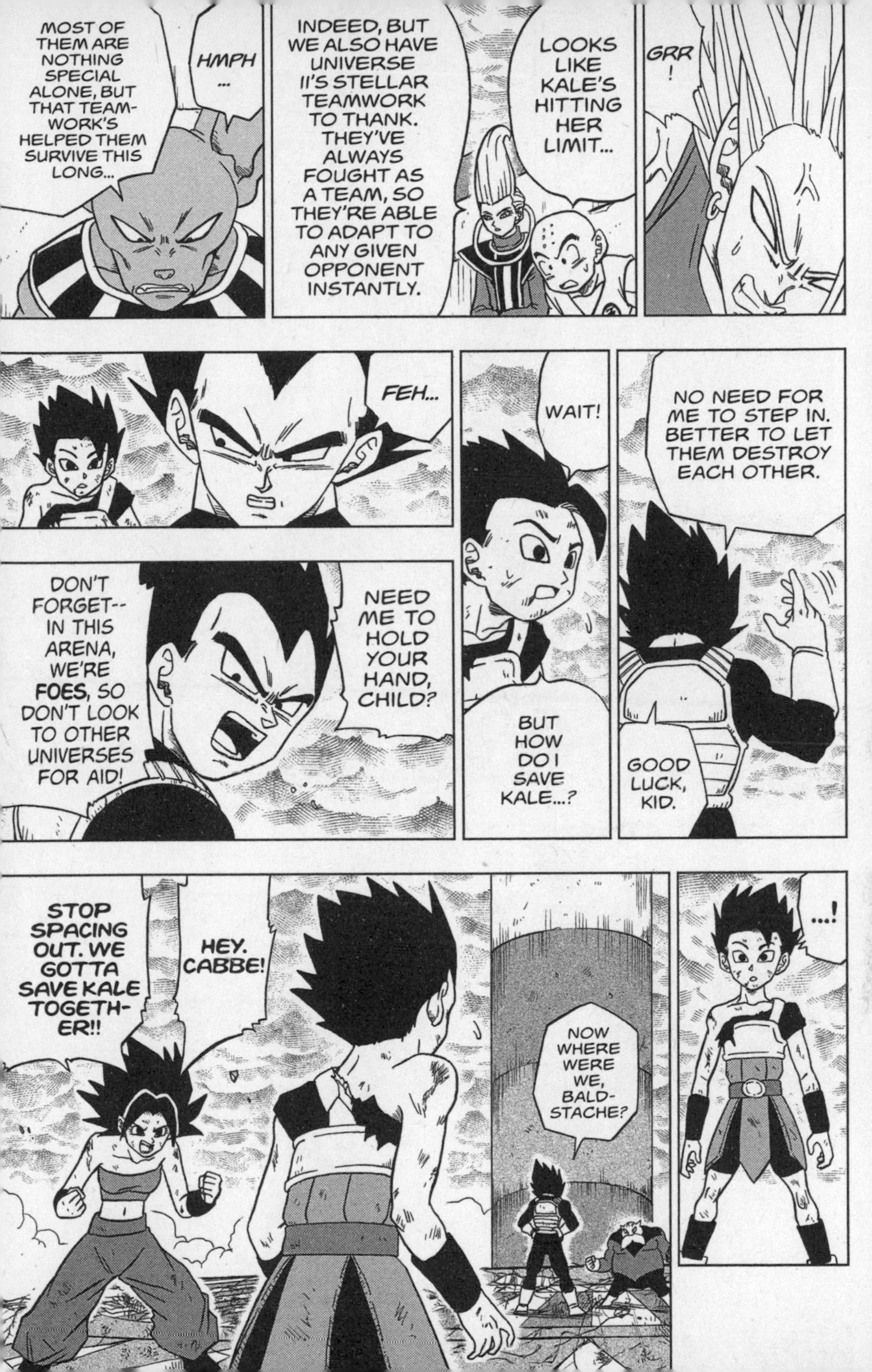
GRR!
LOOKS LIKE KALE'S HITTING HER LIMIT...
INDEED, BUT WE ALSO HAVE UNIVERSE 11'S STELLAR TEAMWORK TO THANK. THEY'VE ALWAYS FOUGHT AS A TEAM, SO THEY'RE ABLE TO ADAPT TO ANY GIVEN OPPONENT INSTANTLY.
HMPH...
MOST OF THEM ARE NOTHING SPECIAL ALONE, BUT THAT TEAMWORK'S HELPED THEM SURVIVE THIS LONG...
NO NEED FOR ME TO STEP IN. BETTER TO LET THEM DESTROY EACH OTHER.
GOOD LUCK, KID.
WAIT!
BUT HOW DO I SAVE KALE...?
FEH...
NEED ME TO HOLD YOUR HAND, CHILD?
DON'T FORGET-- IN THIS ARENA, WE'RE **FOES**, SO DON'T LOOK TO OTHER UNIVERSES FOR AID!
...!
NOW WHERE WERE WE, BALD-STACHE?
HEY. CABBE!
STOP SPACING OUT. WE GOTTA SAVE KALE TOGETHER!!

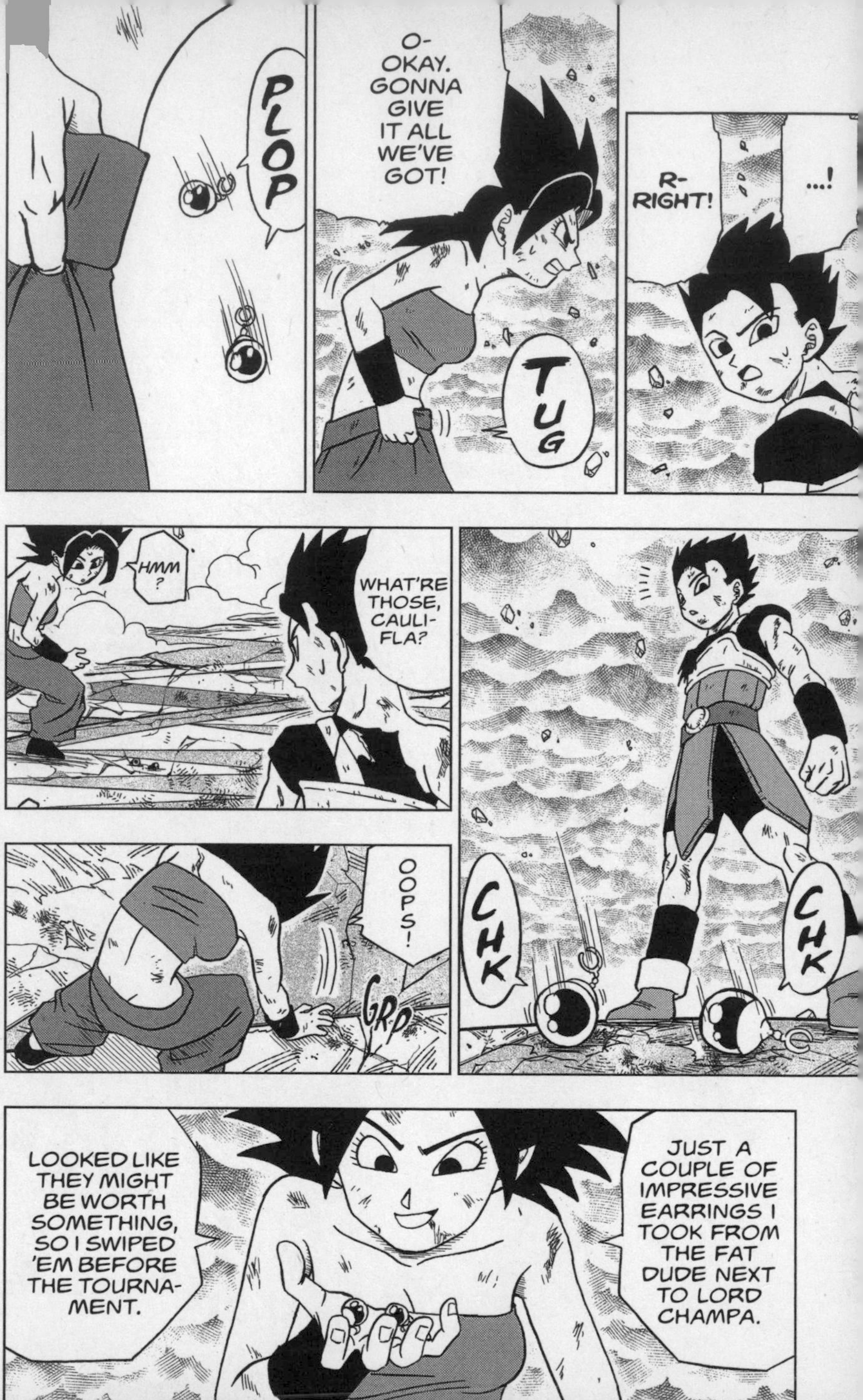
...!
R-RIGHT!
O-OKAY. GONNA GIVE IT ALL WE'VE GOT!
TUG
PLOP
CHK
CHK
WHAT'RE THOSE, CAULI-FLA?
HMM?
OOPS!
GRP
JUST A COUPLE OF IMPRESSIVE EARRINGS I TOOK FROM THE FAT DUDE NEXT TO LORD CHAMPA.
LOOKED LIKE THEY MIGHT BE WORTH SOMETHING, SO I SWIPED 'EM BEFORE THE TOURNA-MENT.

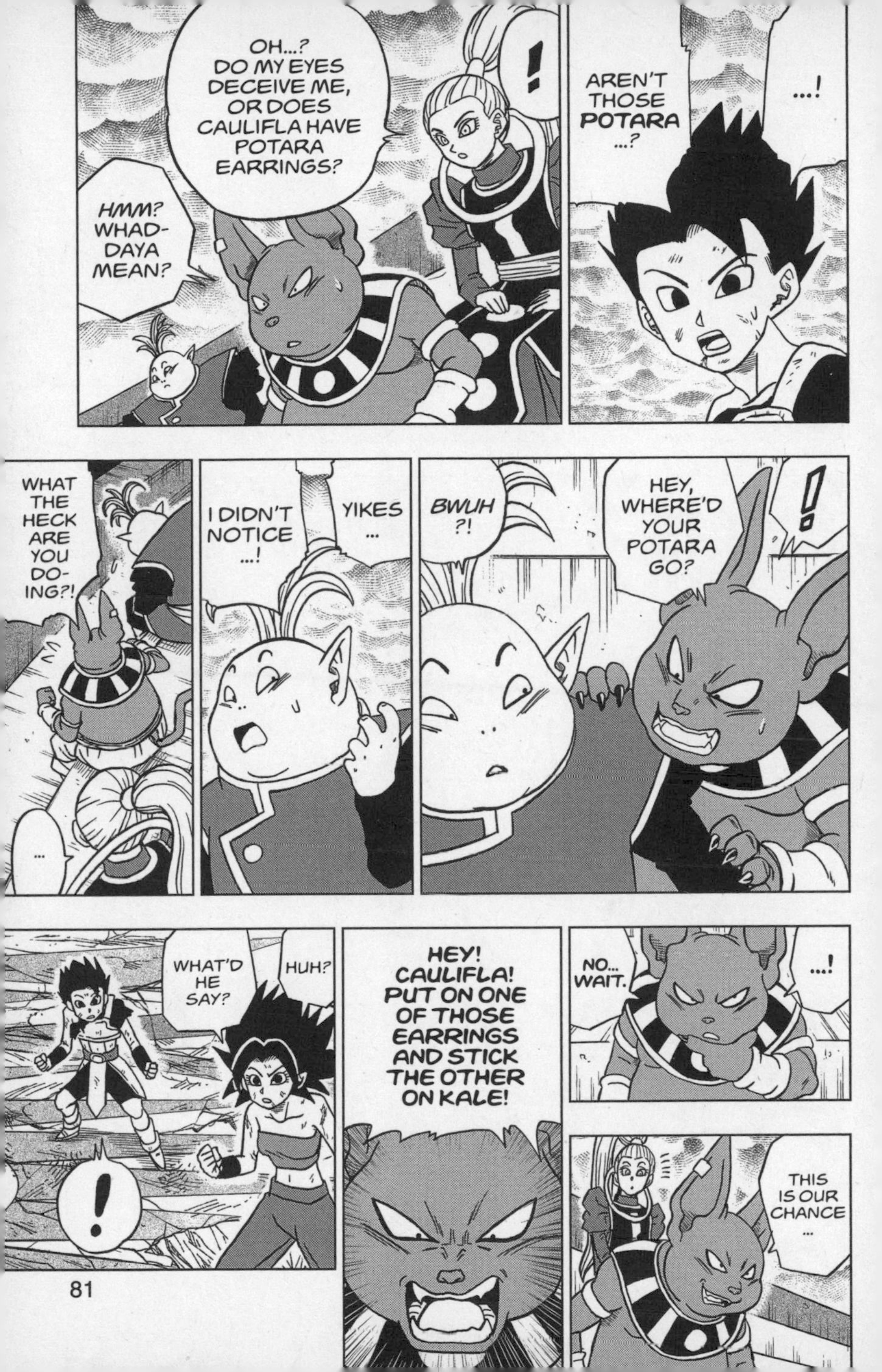
AREN'T THOSE POTARA ...?
...!
!
OH...? DO MY EYES DECEIVE ME, OR DOES CAULIFLA HAVE POTARA EARRINGS?
HMM? WHAD-DAYA MEAN?
!
HEY, WHERE'D YOUR POTARA GO?
BWUH ?!
YIKES ...
I DIDN'T NOTICE ...!
WHAT THE HECK ARE YOU DO-ING?!
...
...!
NO... WAIT.
THIS IS OUR CHANCE ...
HEY! CAULIFLA! PUT ON ONE OF THOSE EARRINGS AND STICK THE OTHER ON KALE!
HUH?
WHAT'D HE SAY?
!

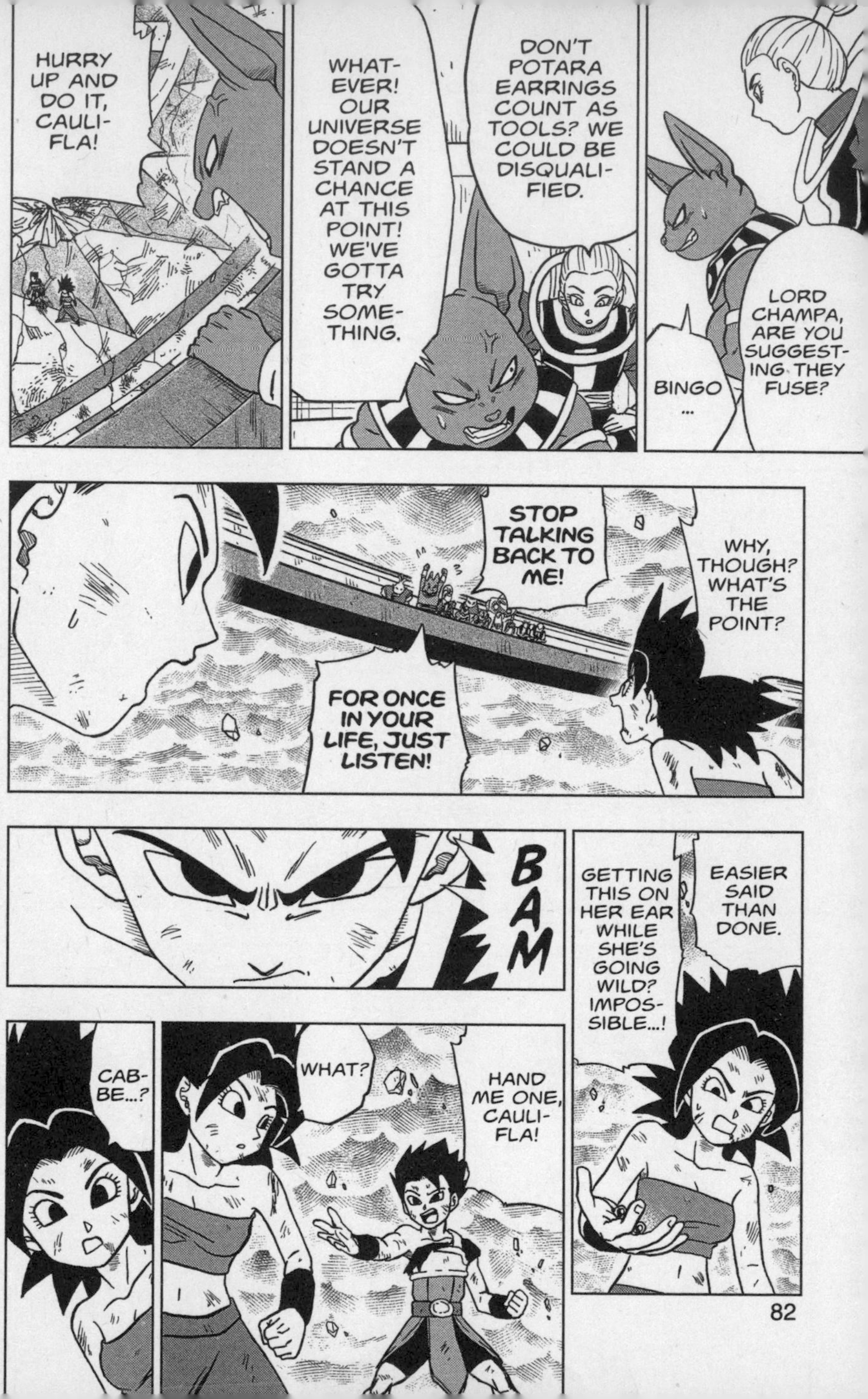

LORD CHAMPA, ARE YOU SUGGESTING THEY FUSE?
BINGO...
DON'T POTARA EARRINGS COUNT AS TOOLS? WE COULD BE DISQUALIFIED.
WHATEVER! OUR UNIVERSE DOESN'T STAND A CHANCE AT THIS POINT! WE'VE GOTTA TRY SOMETHING.
HURRY UP AND DO IT, CAULIFLA!
WHY, THOUGH? WHAT'S THE POINT?
STOP TALKING BACK TO ME!
FOR ONCE IN YOUR LIFE, JUST LISTEN!
EASIER SAID THAN DONE.
GETTING THIS ON HER EAR WHILE SHE'S GOING WILD? IMPOSSIBLE...!
BAM
HAND ME ONE, CAULIFLA!
WHAT?
CABBE...?

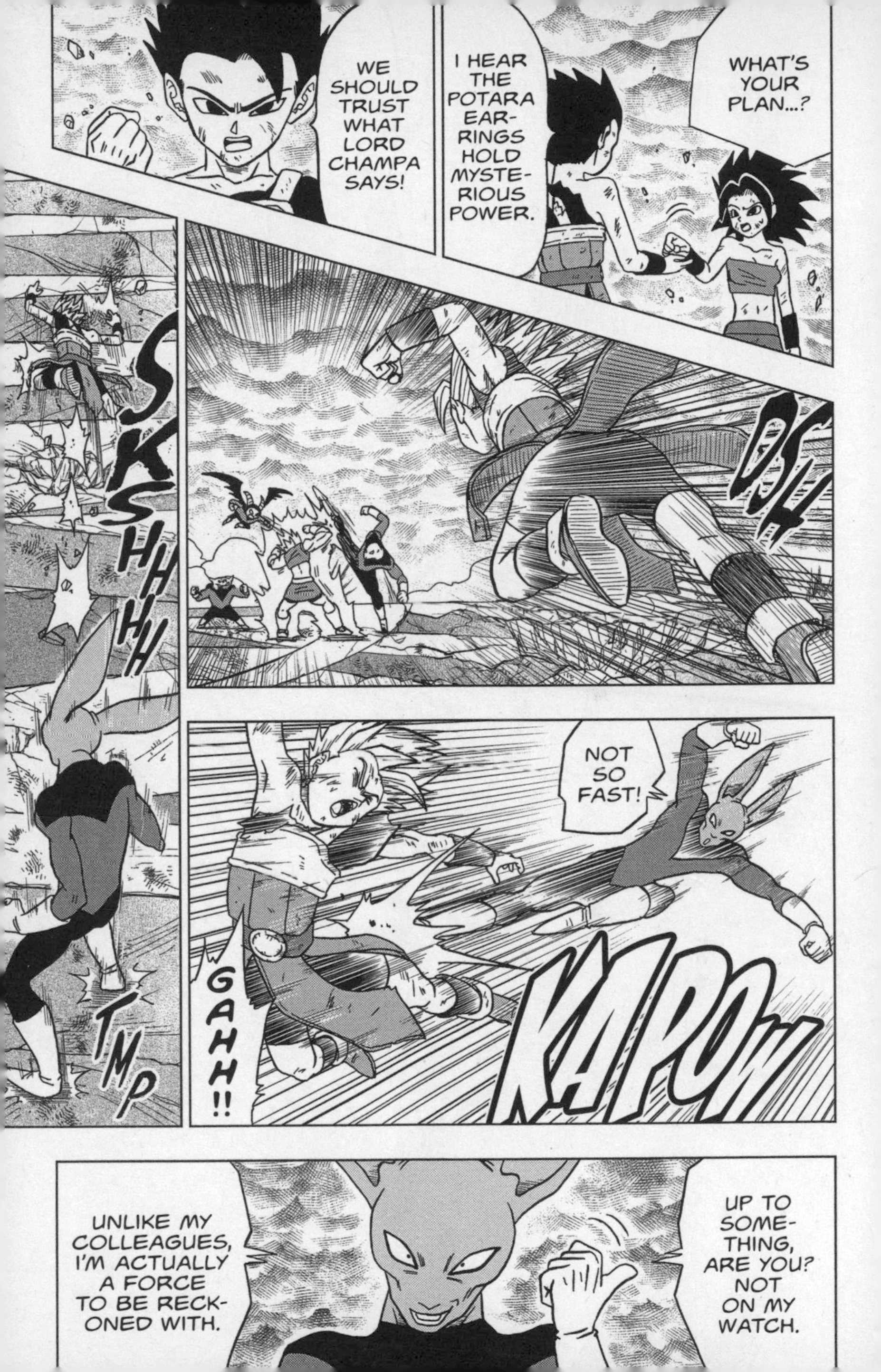
WHAT'S YOUR PLAN...?
I HEAR THE POTARA EAR-RINGS HOLD MYSTERIOUS POWER.
WE SHOULD TRUST WHAT LORD CHAMPA SAYS!
DSH
NOT SO FAST!
GAHH!!
KAPOW
SKSHHHHH
TMP
UP TO SOMETHING, ARE YOU? NOT ON MY WATCH.
UNLIKE MY COLLEAGUES, I'M ACTUALLY A FORCE TO BE RECKONED WITH.

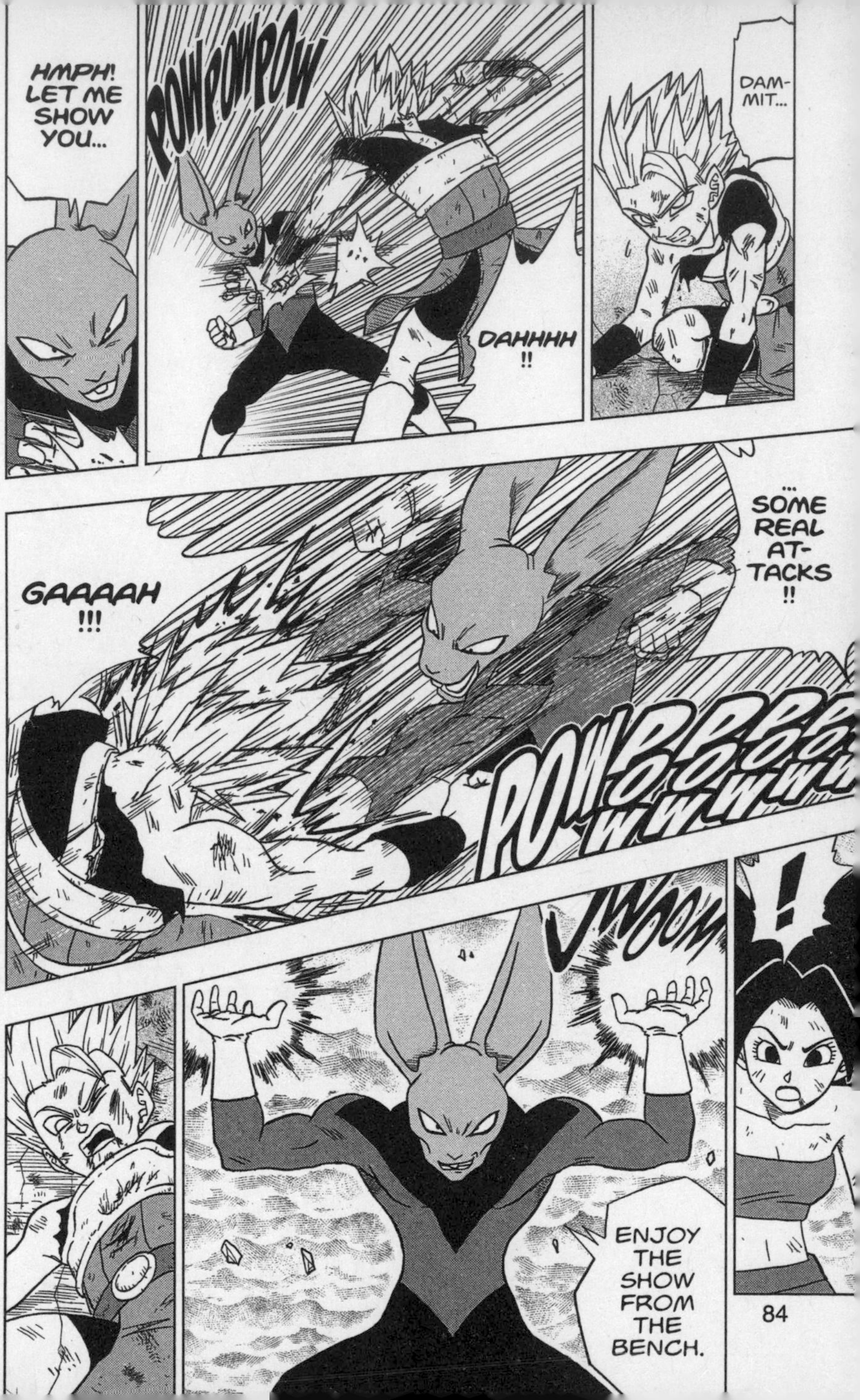
DAM- MIT...
POWPOWPOW
DAHHHH !!
HMPH! LET ME SHOW YOU...
... SOME REAL AT- TACKS !!
GAAAAH !!!
!
JWOOM
ENJOY THE SHOW FROM THE BENCH.

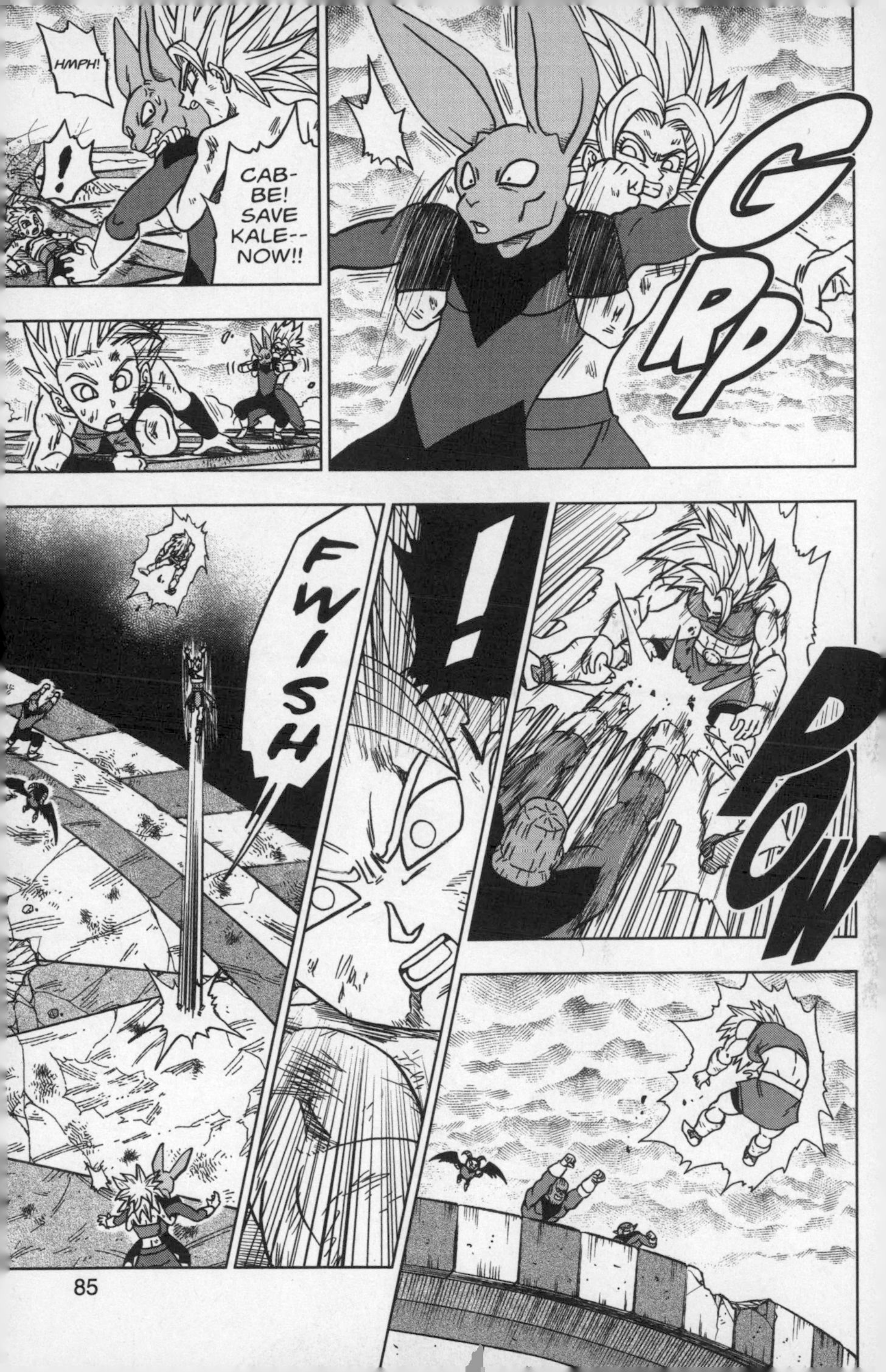
GRP
HMPH!
!
CAB-BE! SAVE KALE--NOW!!
POW
!
FWISH

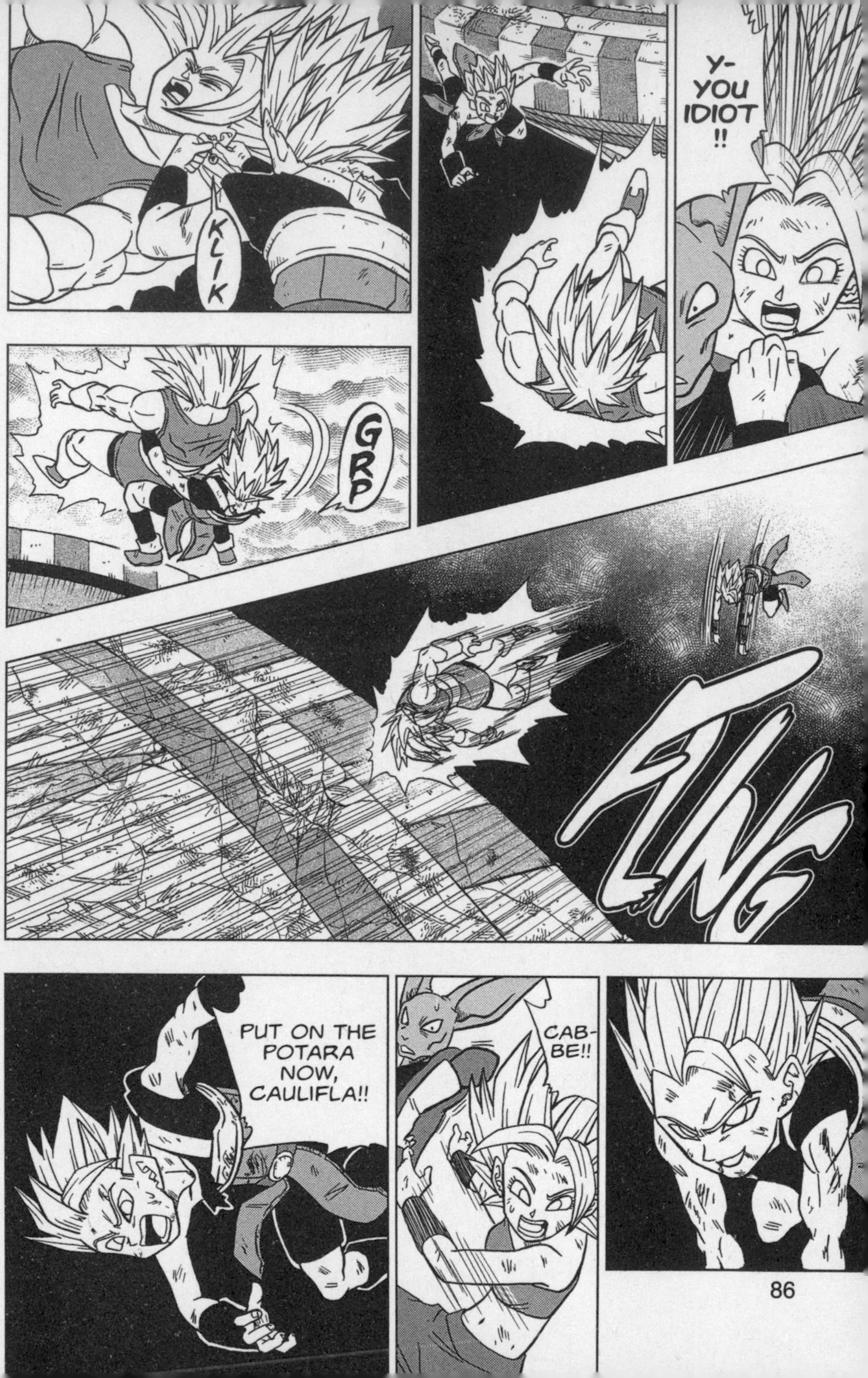
Y-YOU IDIOT!!
KLIK
GRP
FWING
CAB-BE!!
PUT ON THE POTARA NOW, CAULIFLA!!

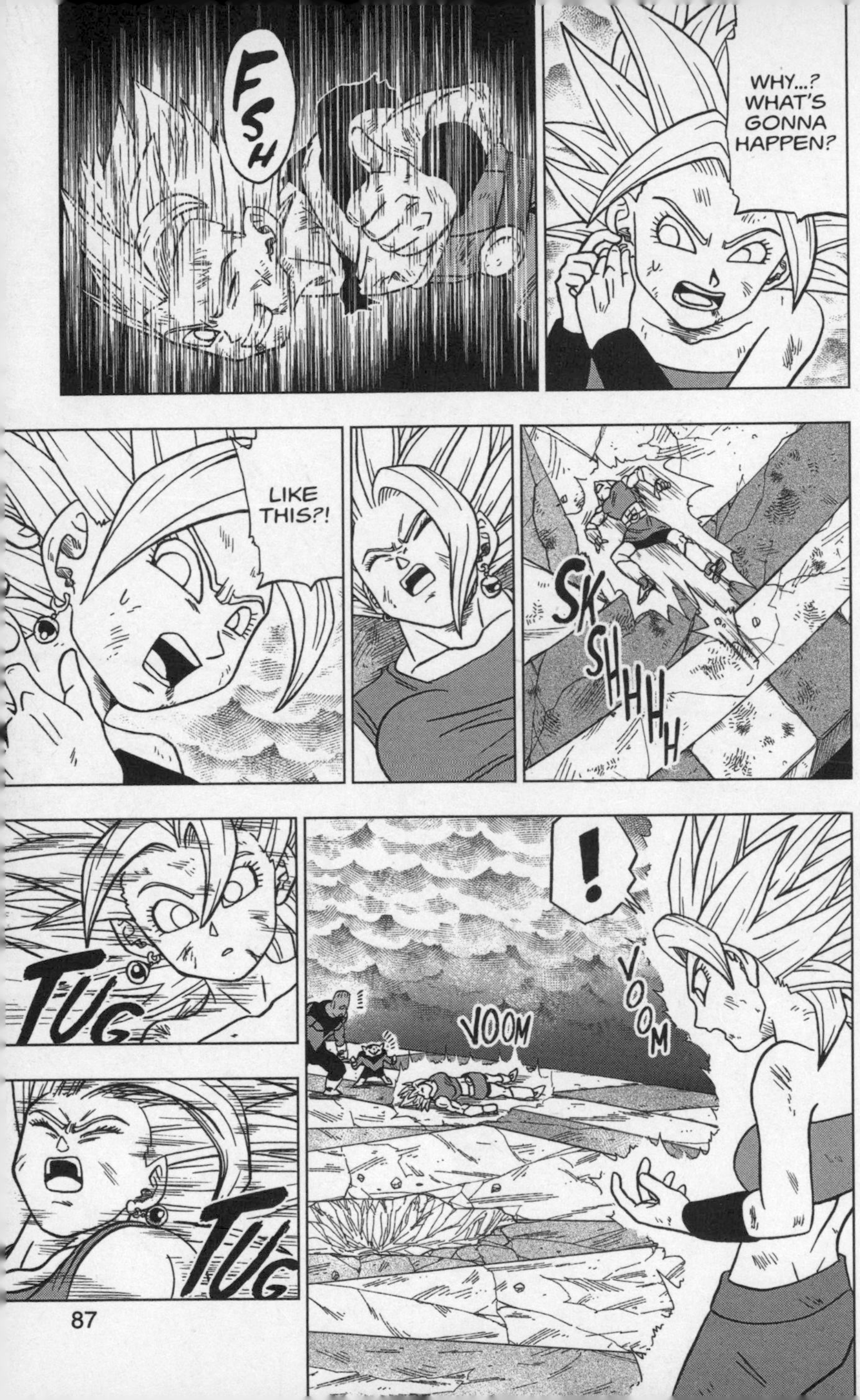
WHY...? WHAT'S GONNA HAPPEN?
FSH
SKSHHHHH
LIKE THIS?!
!
VOOM VOOM
VOOM
TUG
TUG TUG

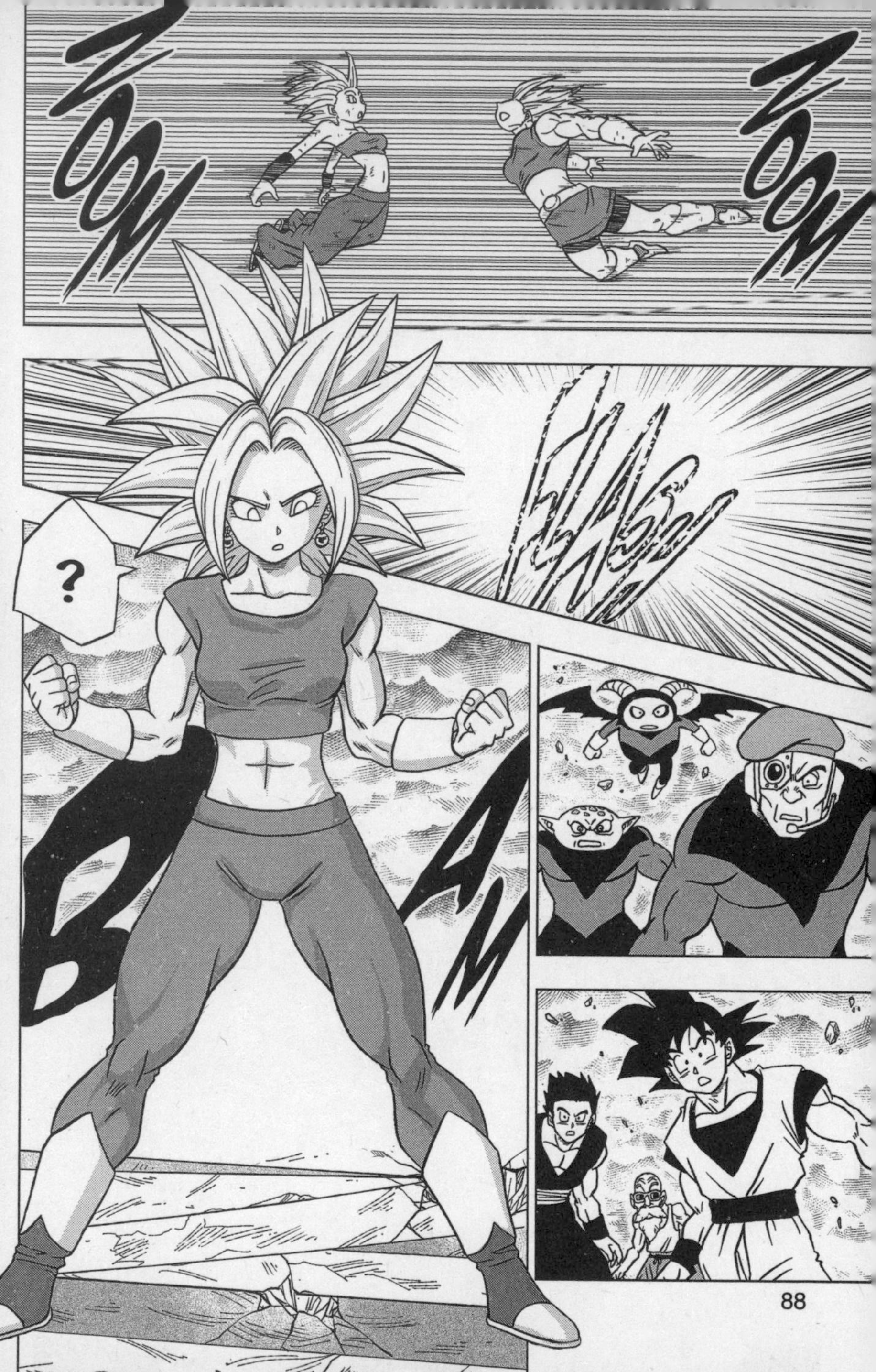
VOOM
VOOM
?
BAM

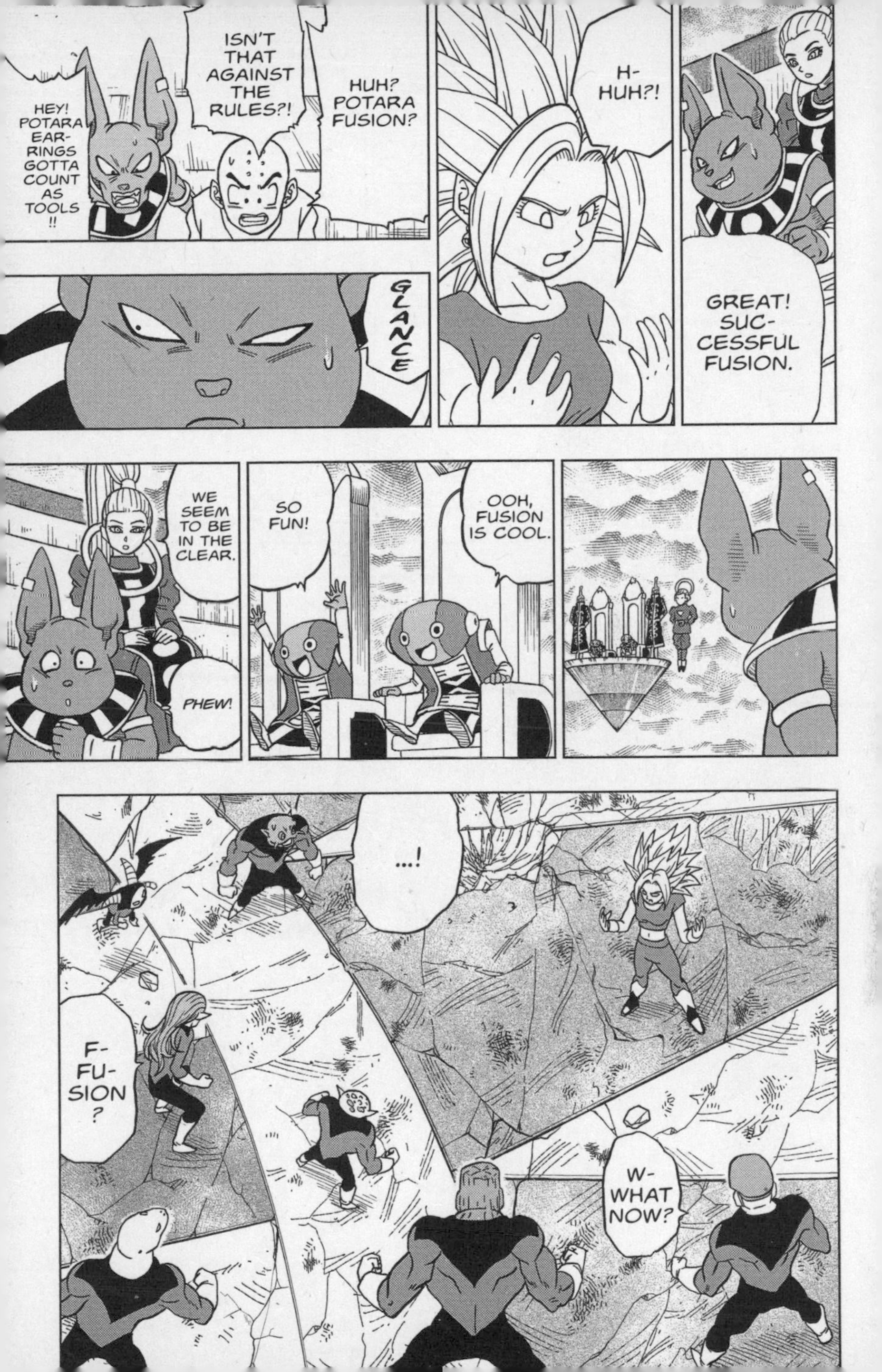
GREAT! SUCCESSFUL FUSION.
H- HUH?!
HUH? POTARA FUSION?
ISN'T THAT AGAINST THE RULES?!
HEY! POTARA EARRINGS GOTTA COUNT AS TOOLS!!
GLANCE
OOH, FUSION IS COOL.
SO FUN!
WE SEEM TO BE IN THE CLEAR.
PHEW!
...!
W- WHAT NOW?
F- FUSION?

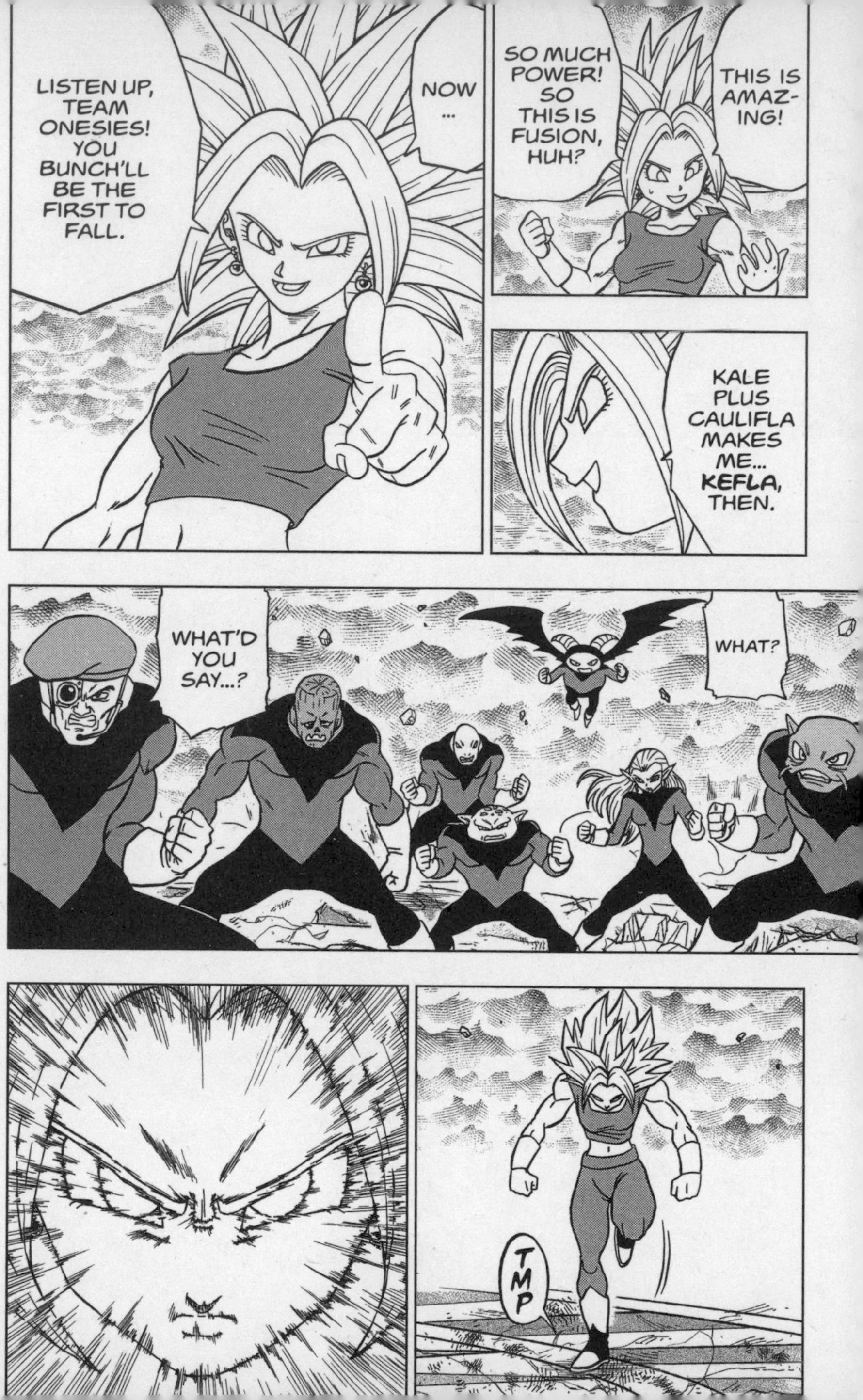
THIS IS AMAZ-ING!
SO MUCH POWER! SO THIS IS FUSION, HUH?
KALE PLUS CAULIFLA MAKES ME... **KEFLA**, THEN.
NOW ...
LISTEN UP, TEAM ONESIES! YOU BUNCH'LL BE THE FIRST TO FALL.
WHAT?
WHAT'D YOU SAY...?
TMP

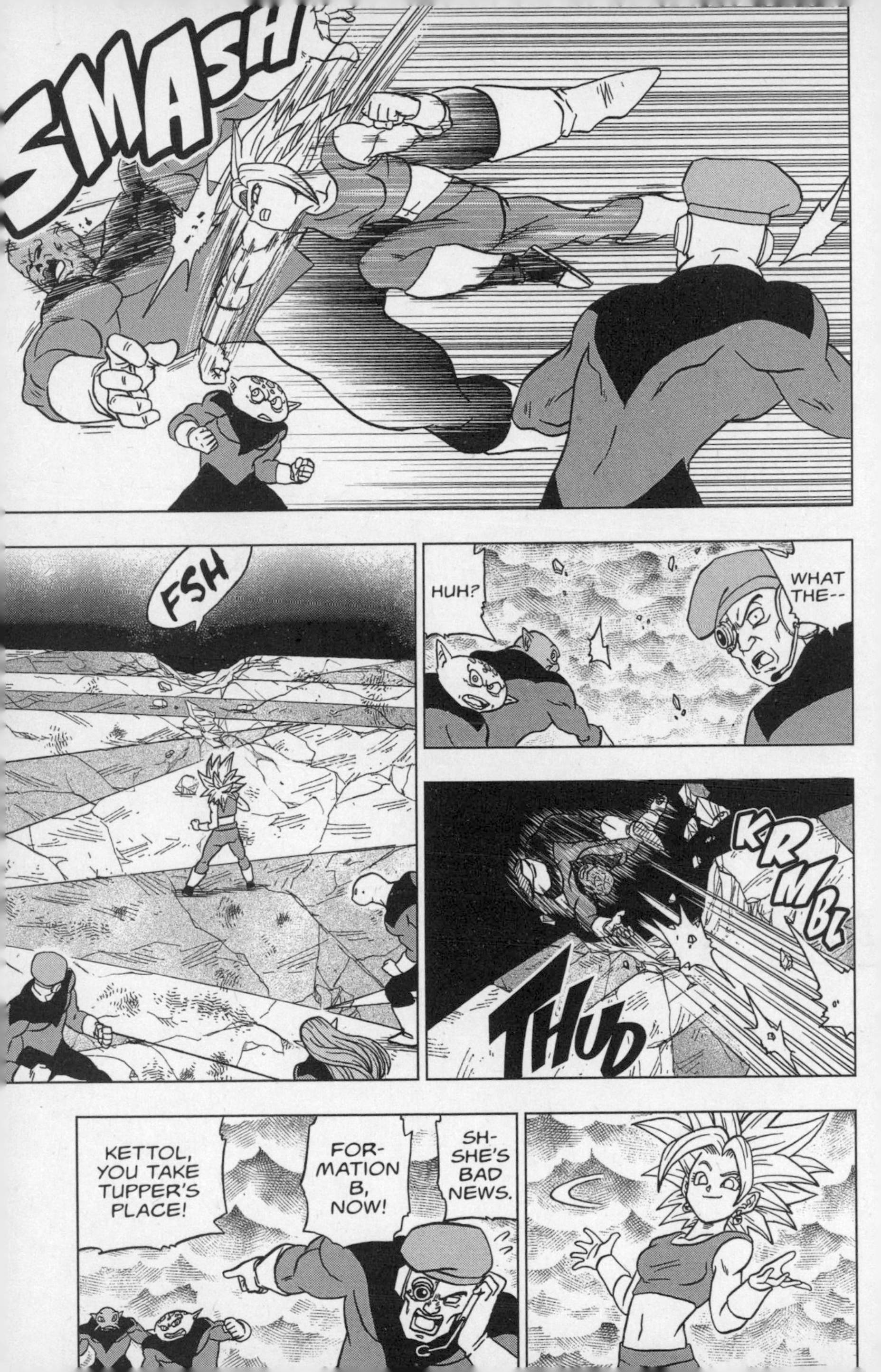
SMASH
WHAT THE--
HUH?
KRMBL
THUD
FSH
SH-SHE'S BAD NEWS.
FOR-MATION B, NOW!
KETTOL, YOU TAKE TUPPER'S PLACE!

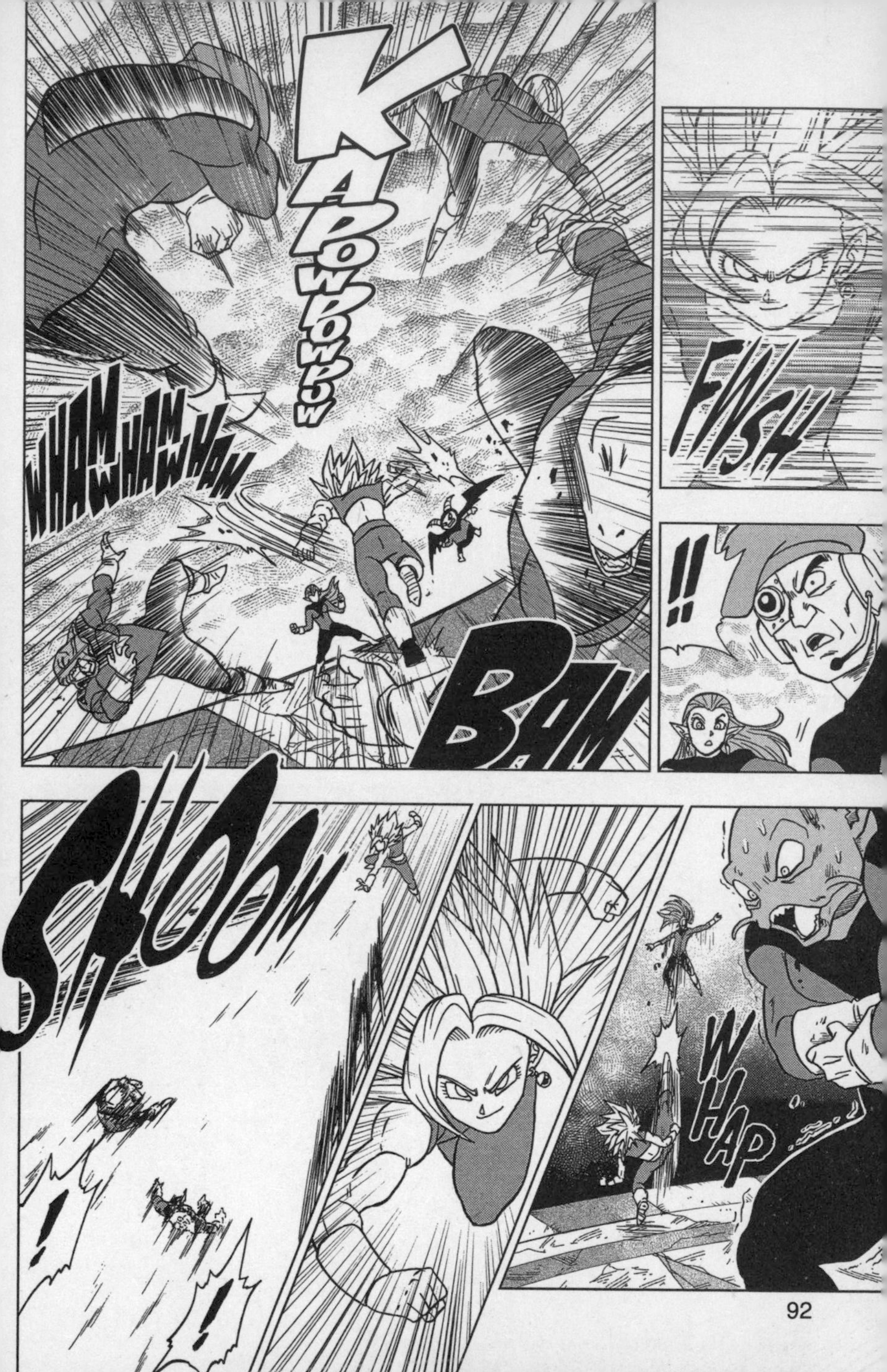
FWSH
!!
KAPOWPOWPOW
WHAMWHAMWHAM
BAM
WHAP
SHOOOM
!
!

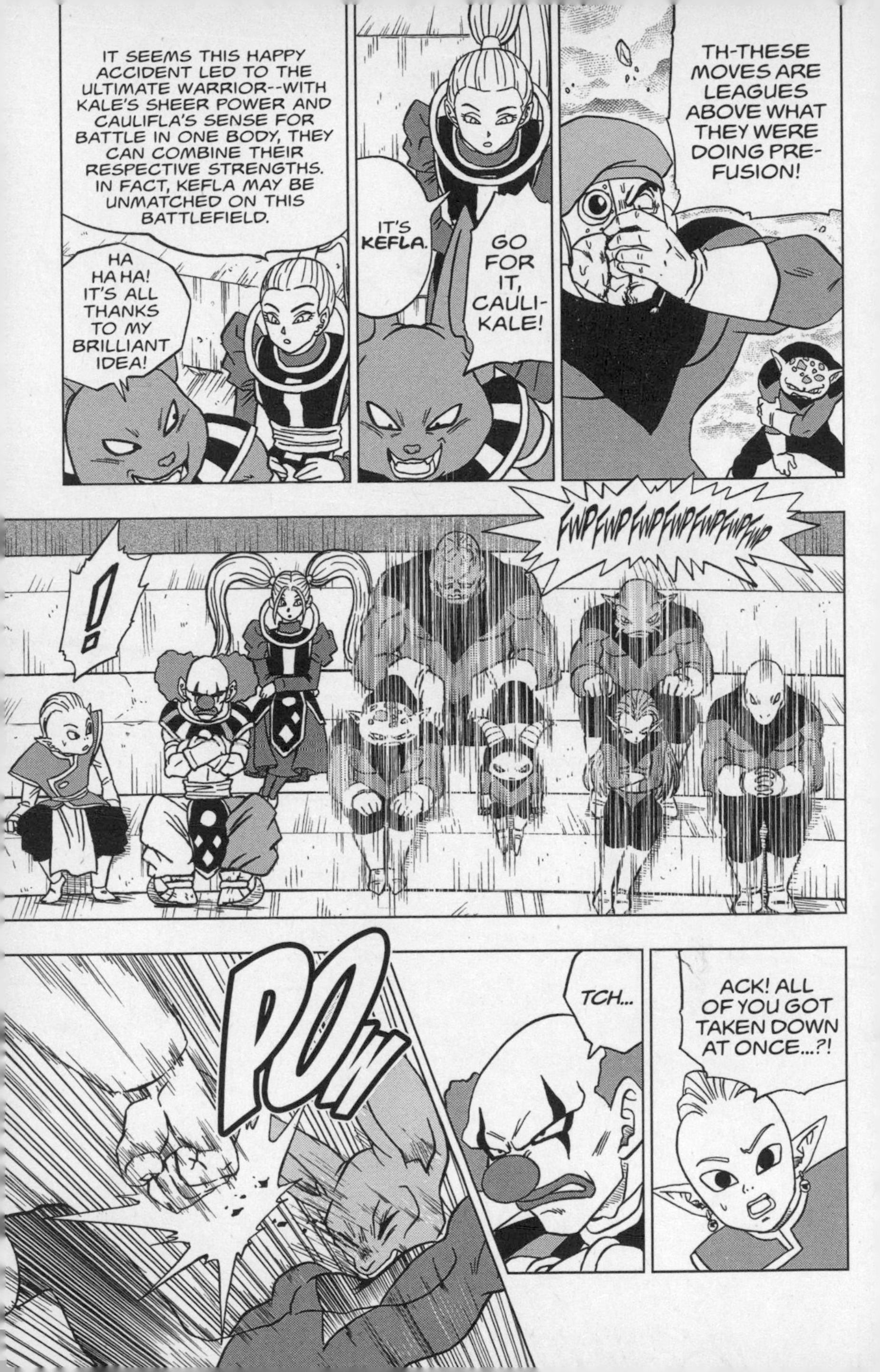

TH-THESE MOVES ARE LEAGUES ABOVE WHAT THEY WERE DOING PRE-FUSION!
GO FOR IT, CAULI-KALE!
IT'S KEFLA.
IT SEEMS THIS HAPPY ACCIDENT LED TO THE ULTIMATE WARRIOR--WITH KALE'S SHEER POWER AND CAULIFLA'S SENSE FOR BATTLE IN ONE BODY, THEY CAN COMBINE THEIR RESPECTIVE STRENGTHS. IN FACT, KEFLA MAY BE UNMATCHED ON THIS BATTLEFIELD.
HA HA HA! IT'S ALL THANKS TO MY BRILLIANT IDEA!
FWP FWP FWP FWP FWP FWP FWP
!
ACK! ALL OF YOU GOT TAKEN DOWN AT ONCE...?!
TCH...
POW

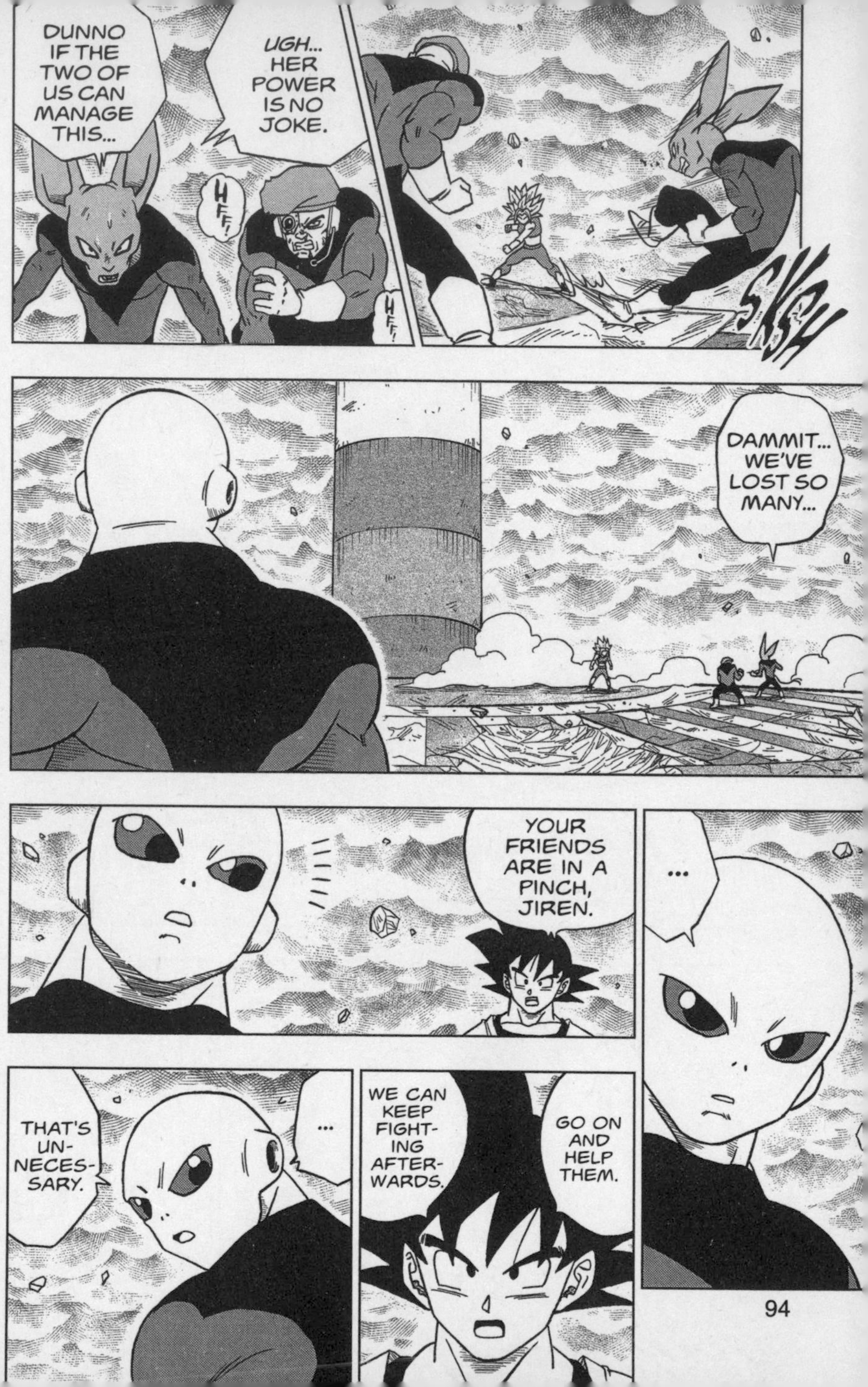
SKSH
UGH... HER POWER IS NO JOKE.
DUNNO IF THE TWO OF US CAN MANAGE THIS...
HFF!
HFF!
DAMMIT... WE'VE LOST SO MANY...
...
YOUR FRIENDS ARE IN A PINCH, JIREN.
GO ON AND HELP THEM.
WE CAN KEEP FIGHT-ING AFTER-WARDS.
...
THAT'S UN-NECES-SARY.

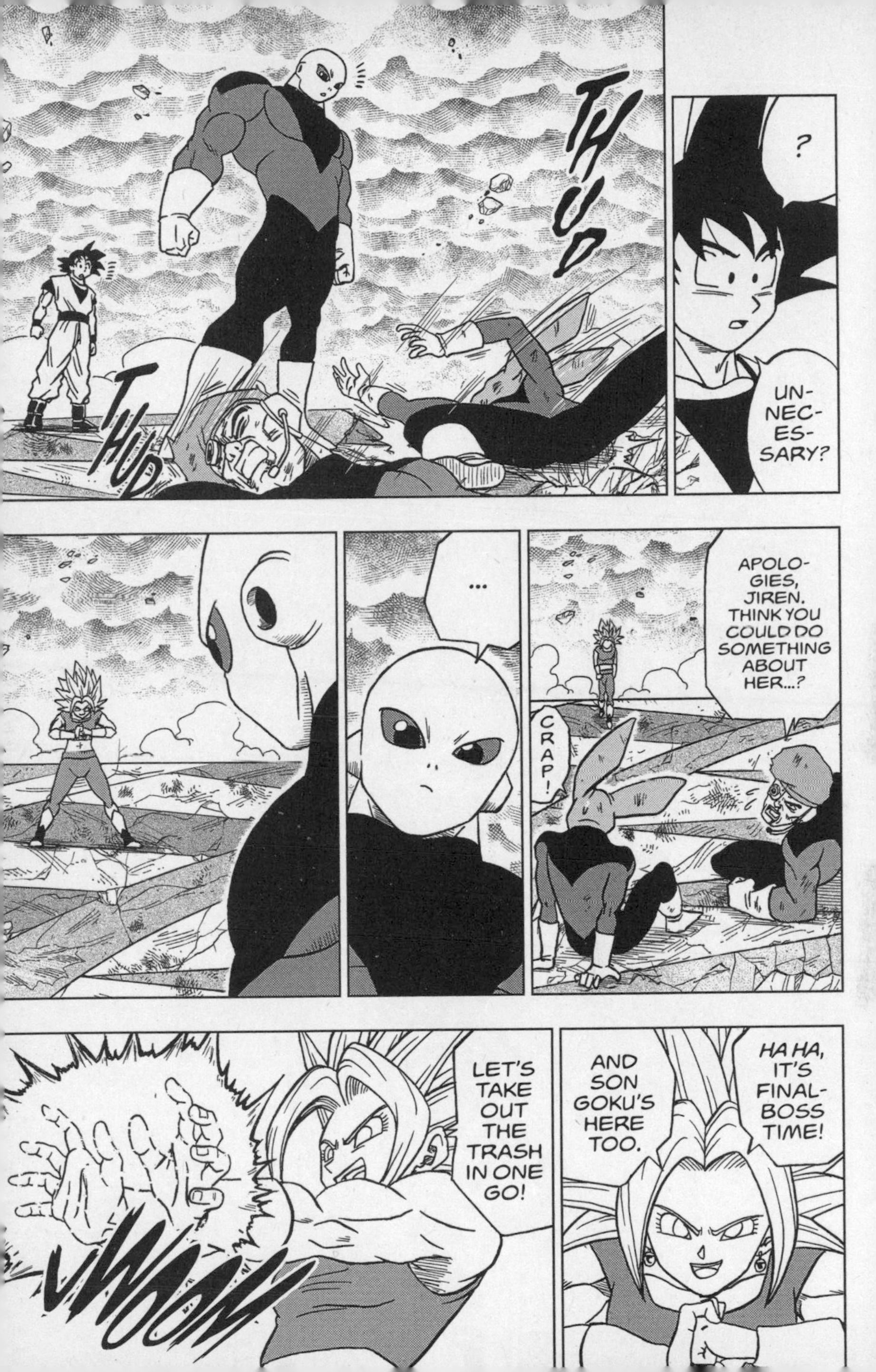
?
UN-NEC-ES-SARY?
THUD
THUD
APOLO-GIES, JIREN. THINK YOU COULD DO SOMETHING ABOUT HER...?
CRAP!
...
HA HA, IT'S FINAL-BOSS TIME!
AND SON GOKU'S HERE TOO.
LET'S TAKE OUT THE TRASH IN ONE GO!
VWOOM

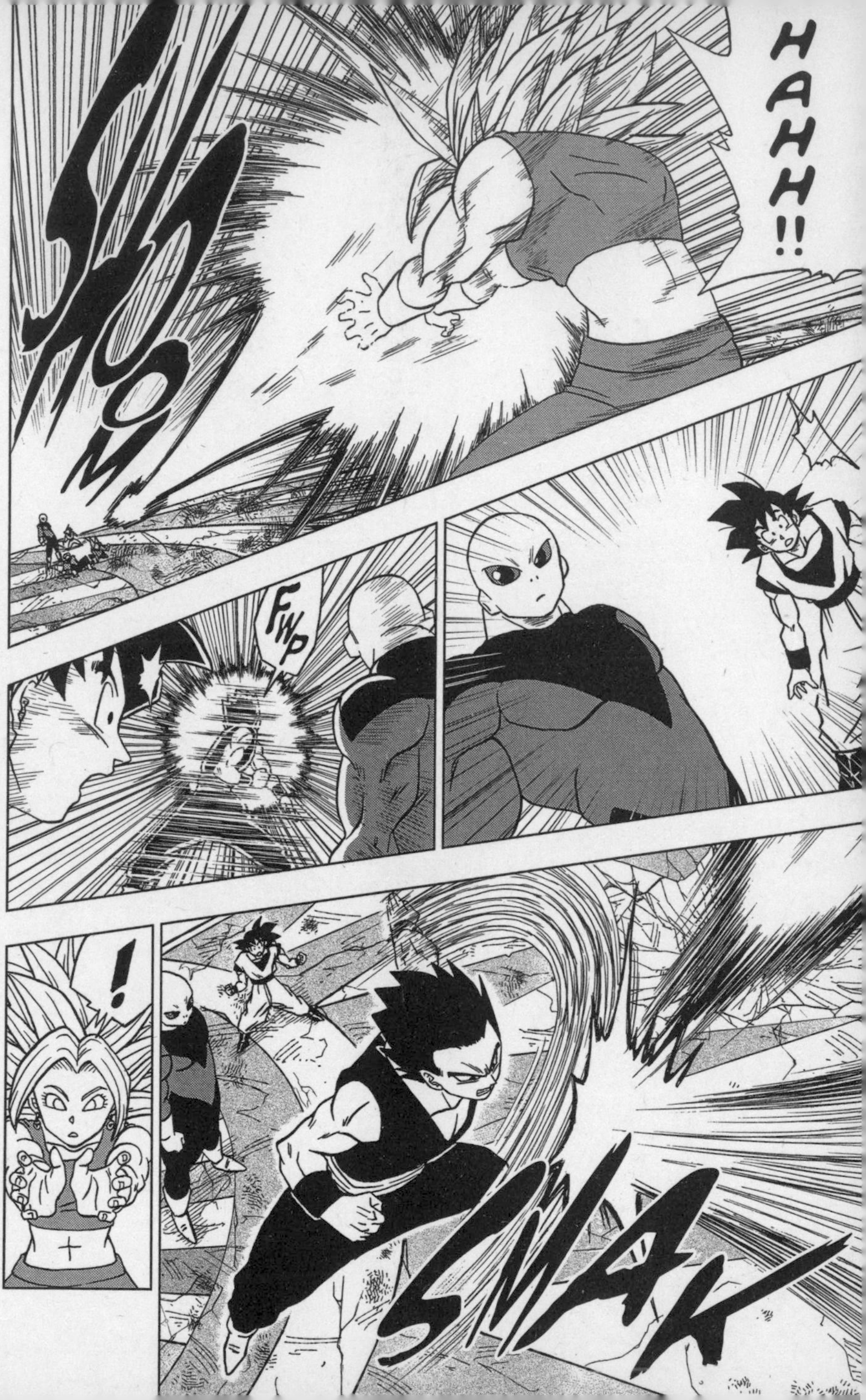
HAHHH!!
SHOOM
FWP
SMAK
!

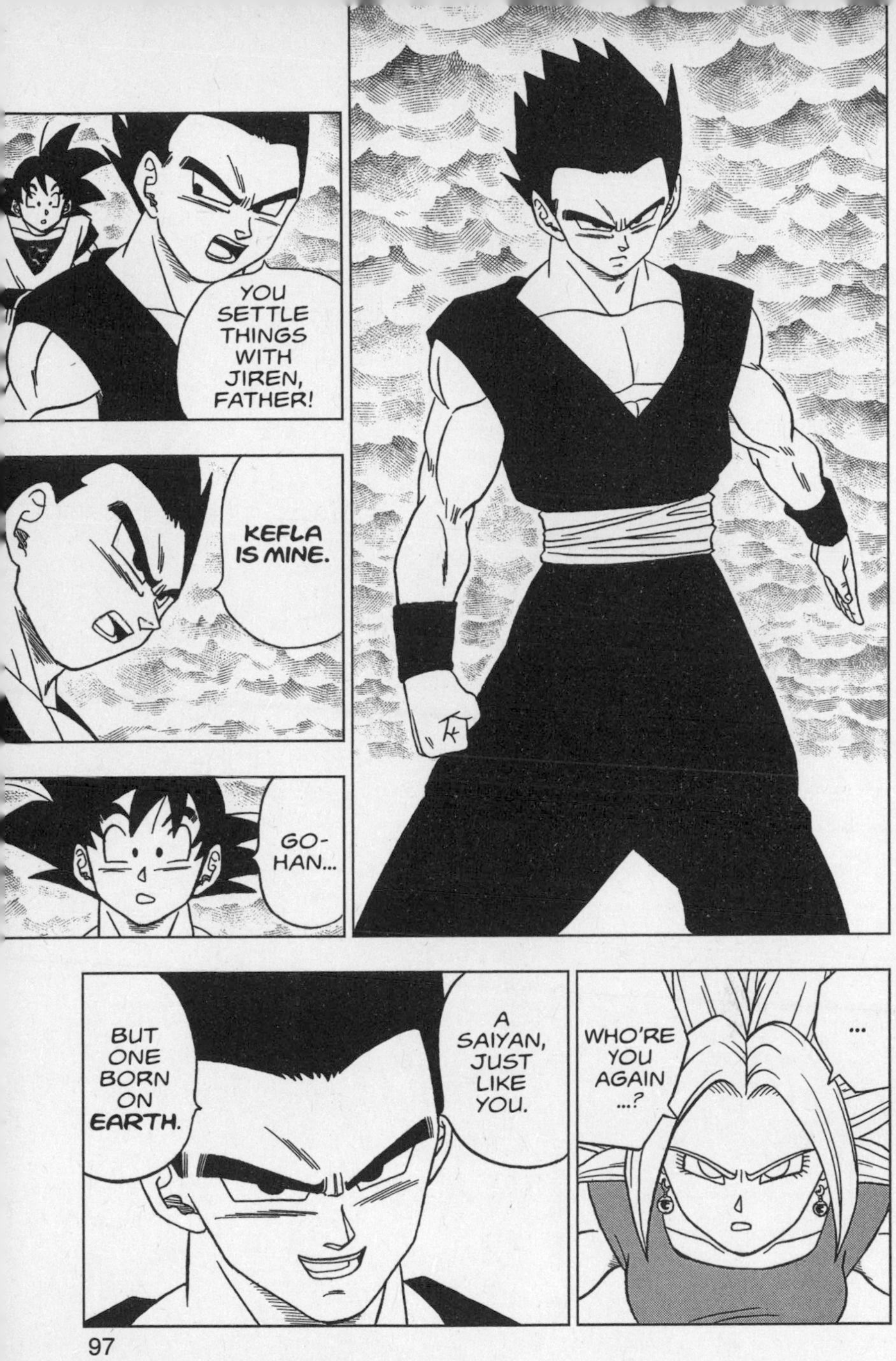
YOU SETTLE THINGS WITH JIREN, FATHER!
KEFLA IS MINE.
GO-HAN...
...
WHO'RE YOU AGAIN ...?
A SAIYAN, JUST LIKE YOU.
BUT ONE BORN ON EARTH.

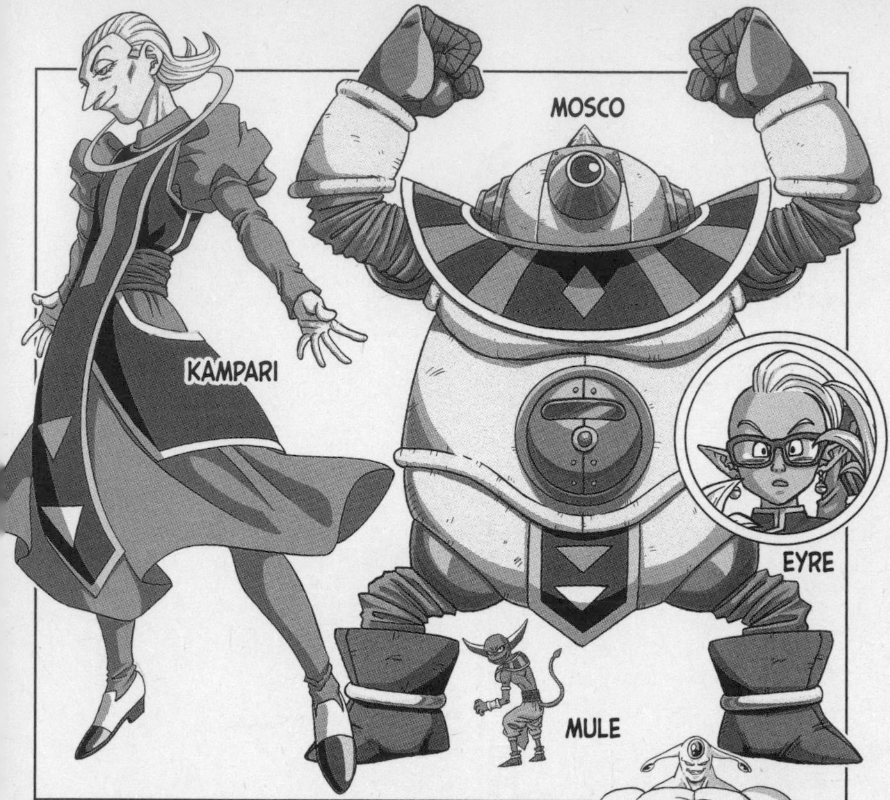
MOSCO
KAMPARI
EYRE
MULE

UNIVERSE 3

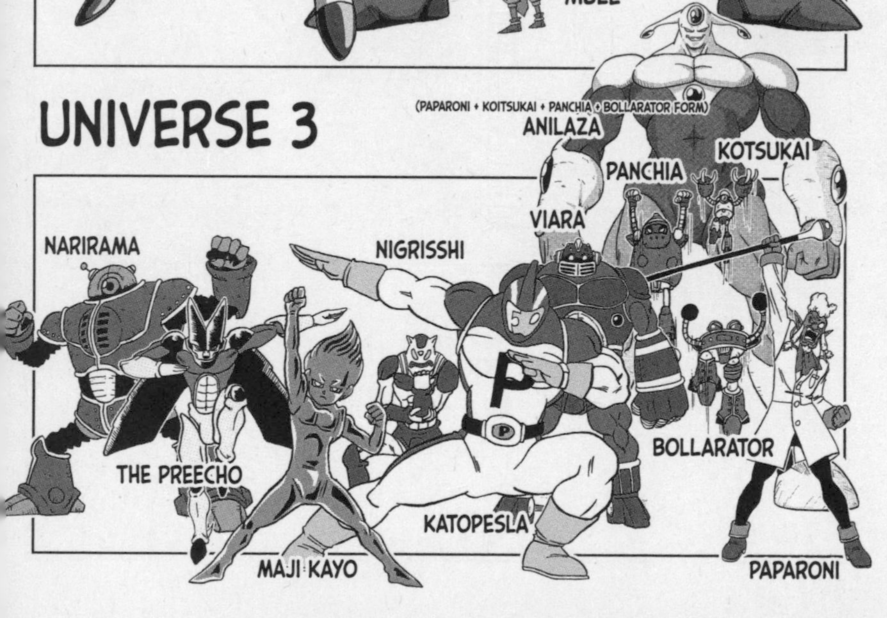
(PAPARONI + KOITSUKAI + PANCHIA + BOLLARATOR FORM)
ANILAZA
KOTSUKAI
PANCHIA
VIARA
NIGRISSHI
NARIRAMA
BOLLARATOR
THE PREECHO
KATOPESLA
MAJI KAYO
PAPARONI

DRAGON BALL SUPER

CHAPTER 39: SIGN OF SON GOKU'S AWAKENING

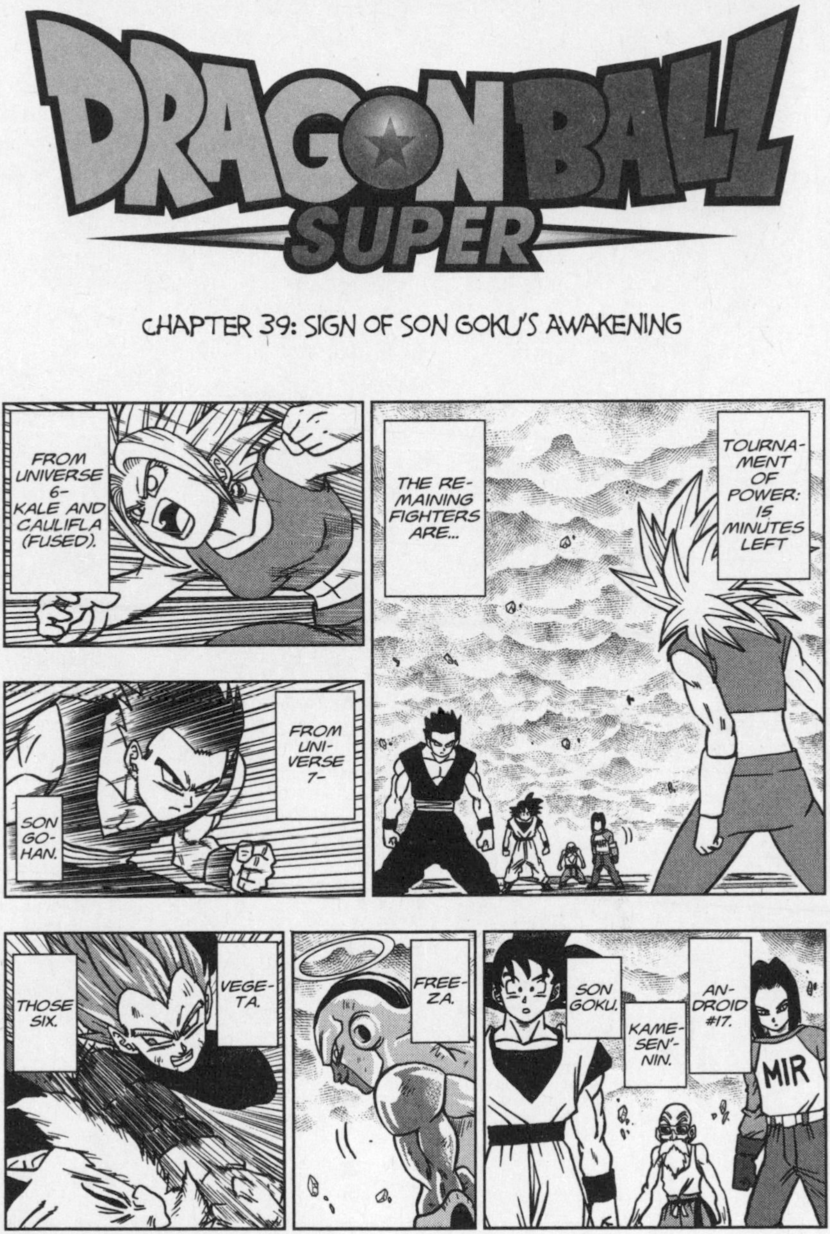
TOURNAMENT OF POWER: 15 MINUTES LEFT
THE REMAINING FIGHTERS ARE...
FROM UNIVERSE 6- KALE AND CAULIFLA (FUSED).
FROM UNIVERSE 7-
SON GOHAN.
ANDROID #17.
KAMESEN'NIN.
SON GOKU.
FREEZA.
VEGETA.
THOSE SIX.
MIR

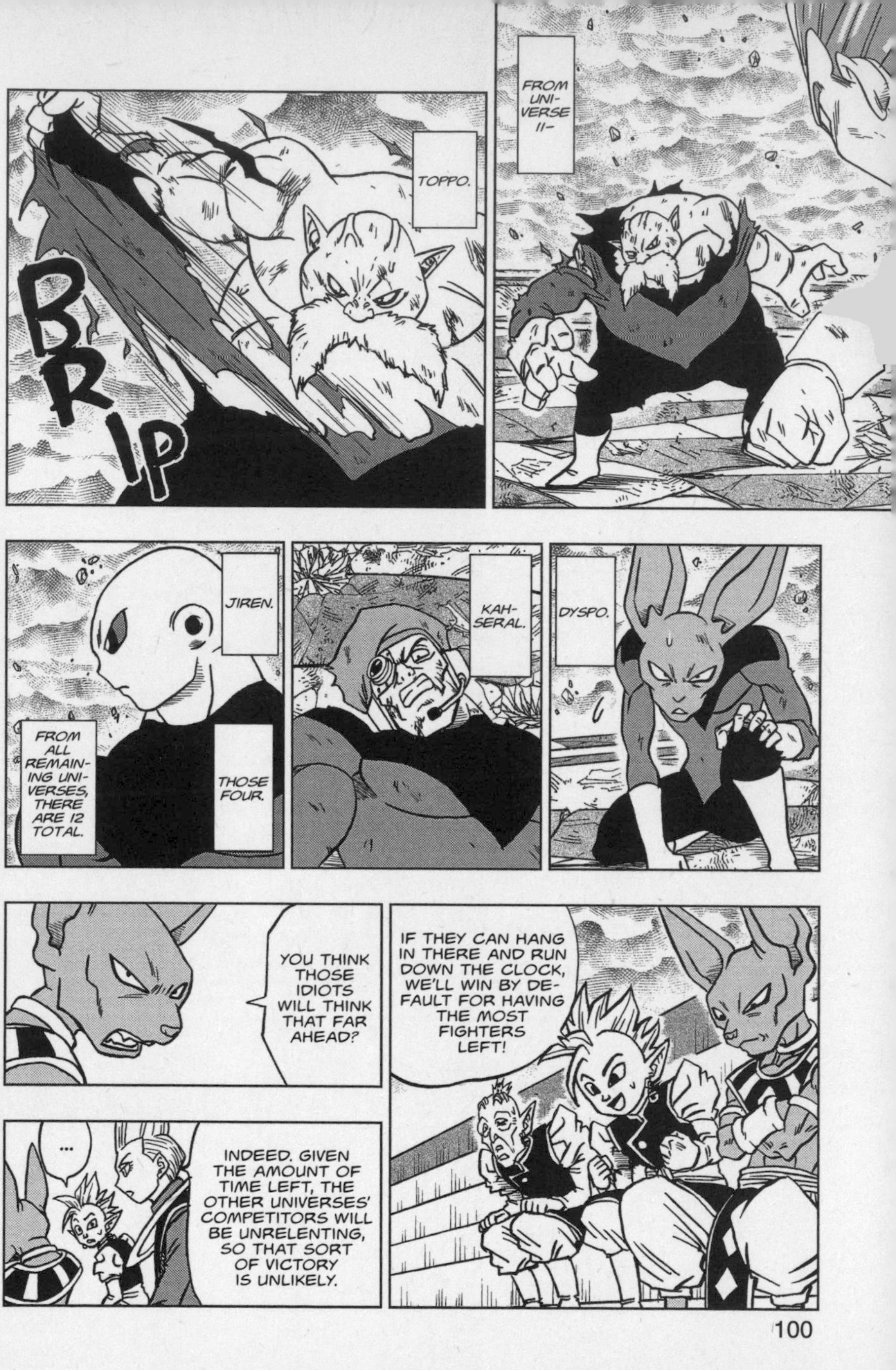
FROM UNI-VERSE 11—
TOPPO.
BRIP
DYSPO.
KAH-SERAL.
JIREN.
THOSE FOUR.
FROM ALL REMAINING UNI-VERSES, THERE ARE 12 TOTAL.
IF THEY CAN HANG IN THERE AND RUN DOWN THE CLOCK, WE'LL WIN BY DE-FAULT FOR HAVING THE MOST FIGHTERS LEFT!
YOU THINK THOSE IDIOTS WILL THINK THAT FAR AHEAD?
INDEED. GIVEN THE AMOUNT OF TIME LEFT, THE OTHER UNIVERSES' COMPETITORS WILL BE UNRELENTING, SO THAT SORT OF VICTORY IS UNLIKELY.
...

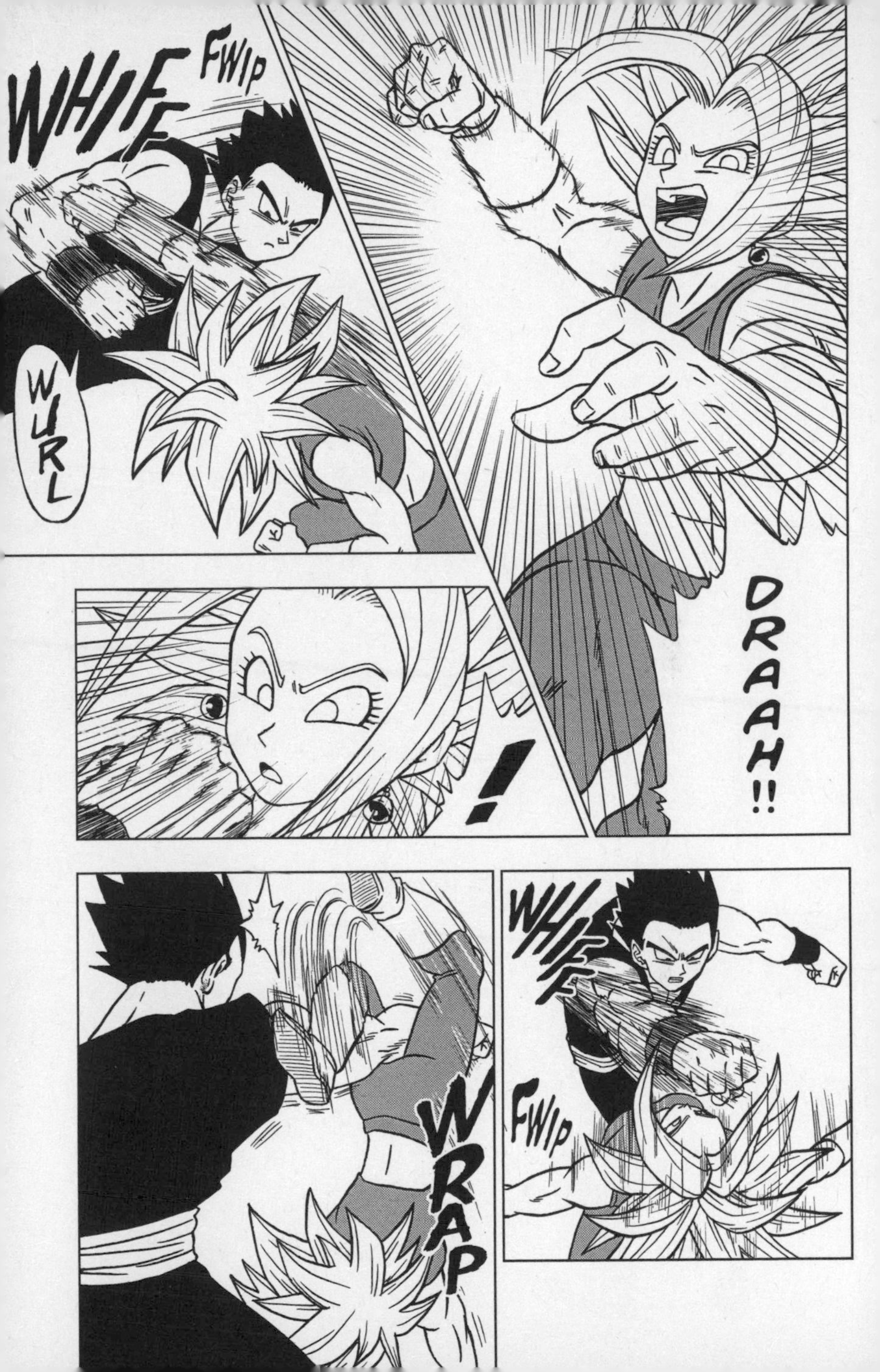
DRAAAH!!
WHIFF
FWIP
WURL
!
WHIFF
FWIP
WRAP

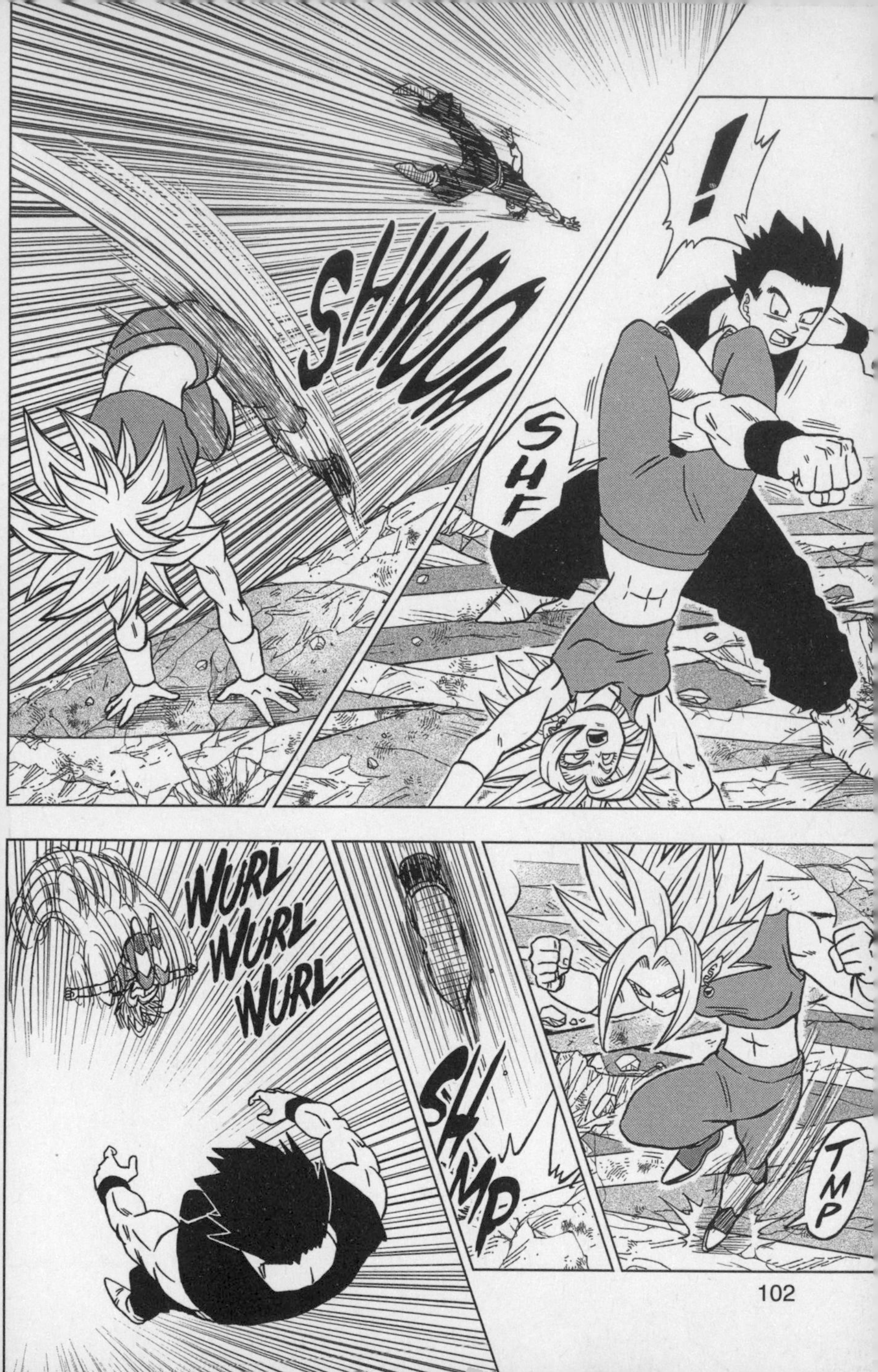
!
SHF
SHWOOM
TMP
SHMP
WURL WURL WURL

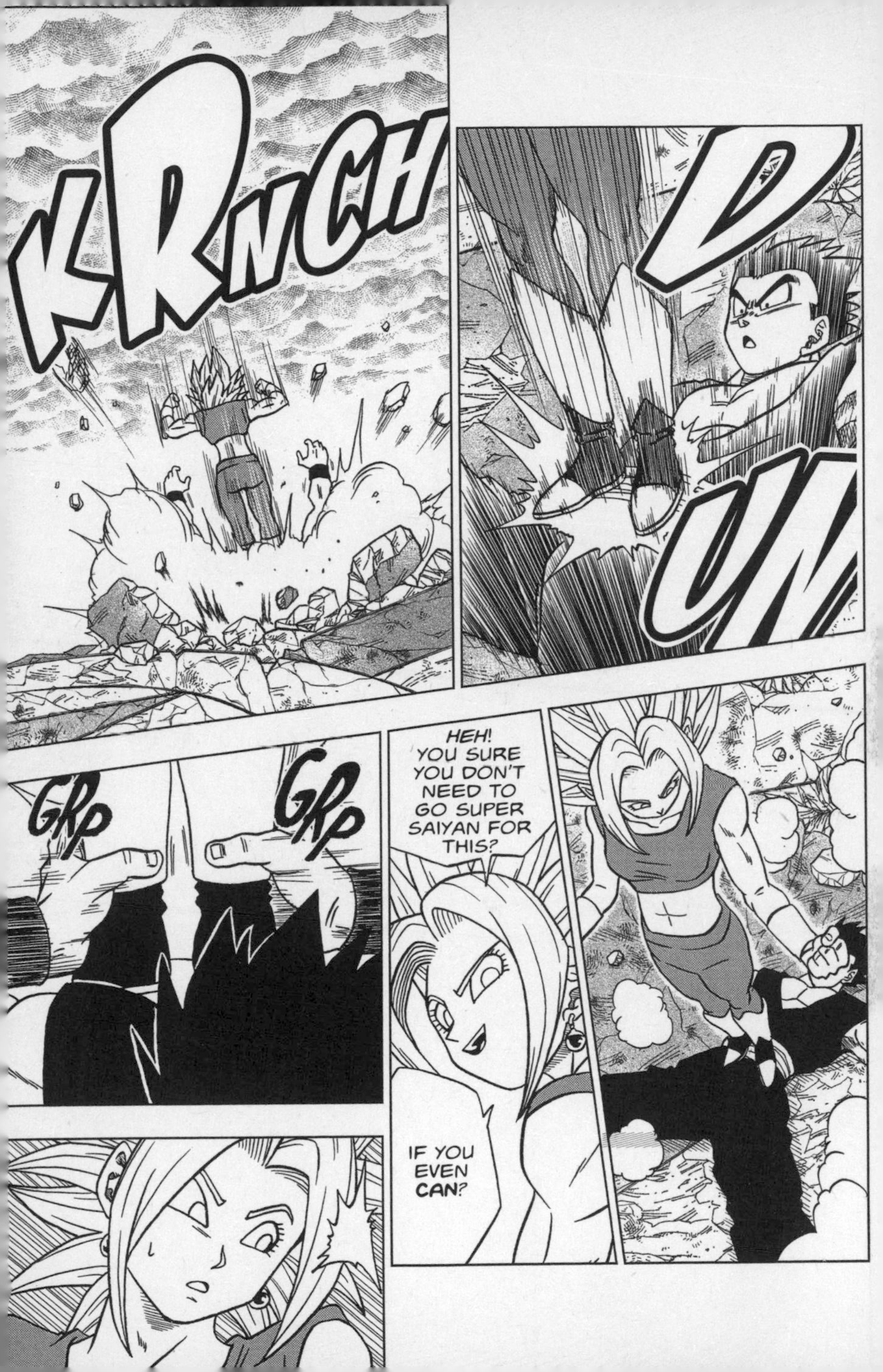
DUN
KRNCH
HEH! YOU SURE YOU DON'T NEED TO GO SUPER SAIYAN FOR THIS?
IF YOU EVEN CAN?
GRP
GRP

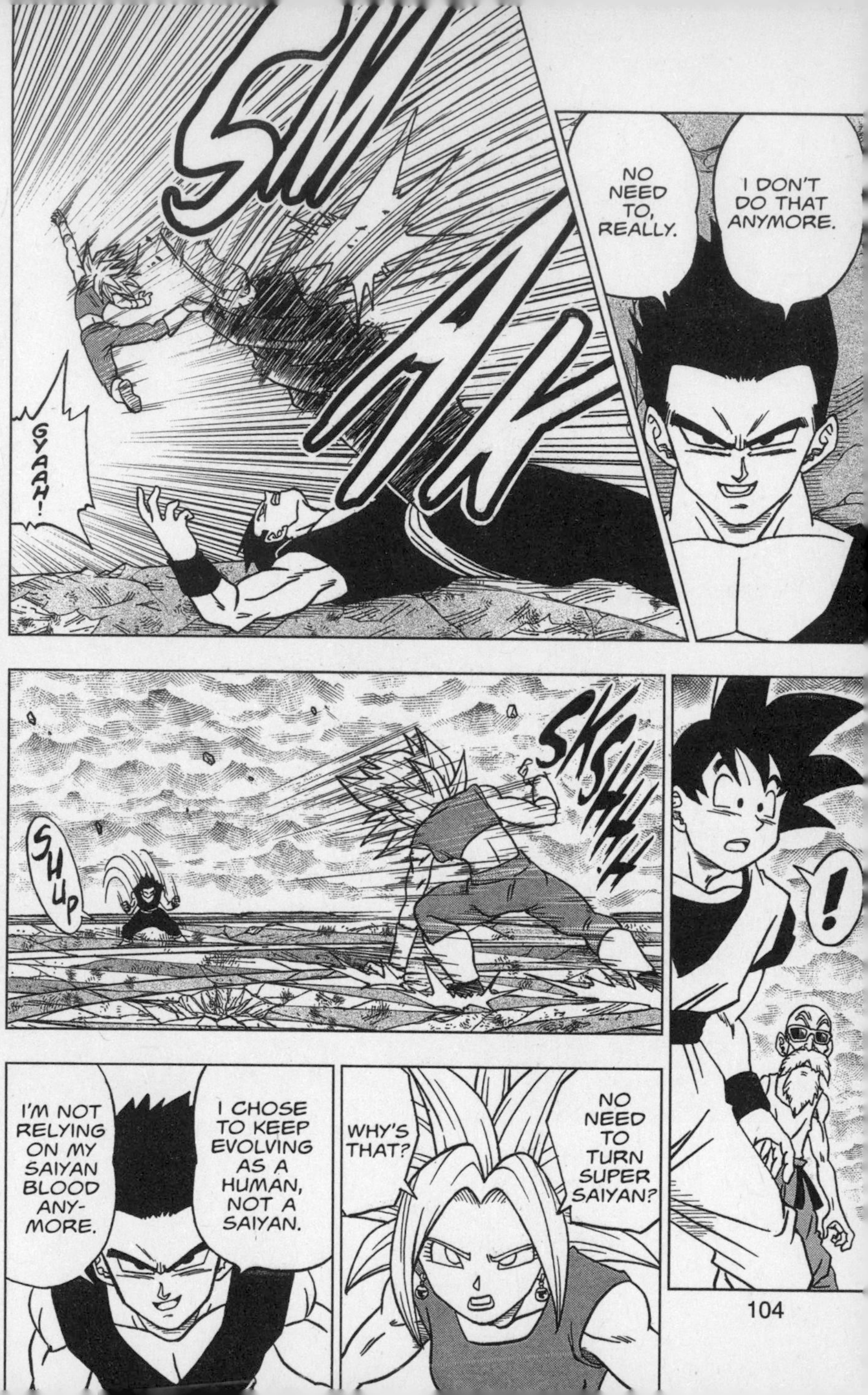
NO NEED TO, REALLY.
I DON'T DO THAT ANYMORE.
SWAM
GYAAH!
!
SKSHHH
SHUP
NO NEED TO TURN SUPER SAIYAN?
WHY'S THAT?
I CHOSE TO KEEP EVOLVING AS A HUMAN, NOT A SAIYAN.
I'M NOT RELYING ON MY SAIYAN BLOOD ANYMORE.

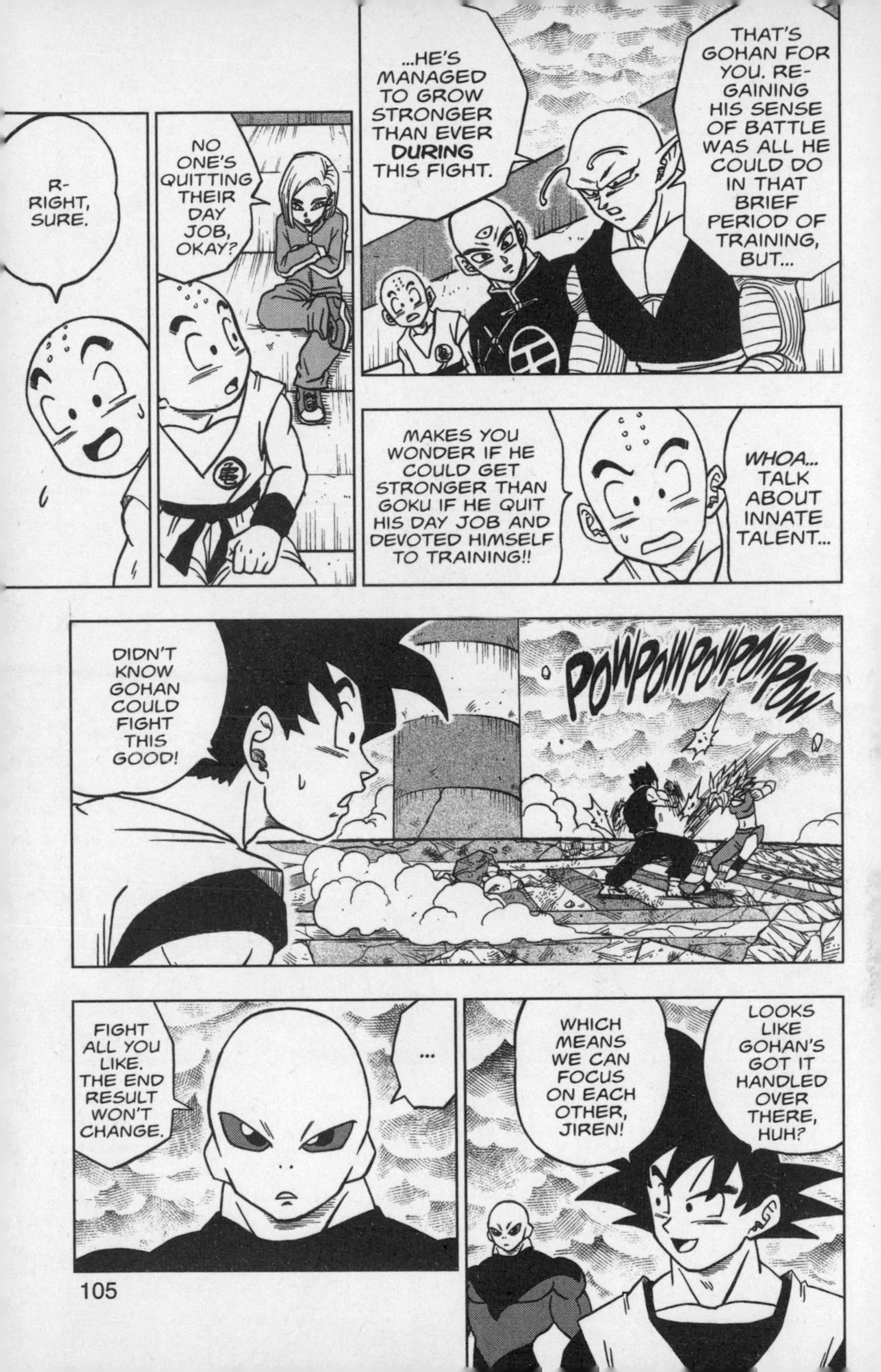
THAT'S GOHAN FOR YOU. RE-GAINING HIS SENSE OF BATTLE WAS ALL HE COULD DO IN THAT BRIEF PERIOD OF TRAINING, BUT...
...HE'S MANAGED TO GROW STRONGER THAN EVER **DURING** THIS FIGHT.
WHOA... TALK ABOUT INNATE TALENT...
MAKES YOU WONDER IF HE COULD GET STRONGER THAN GOKU IF HE QUIT HIS DAY JOB AND DEVOTED HIMSELF TO TRAINING!!
NO ONE'S QUITTING THEIR DAY JOB, OKAY?
R-RIGHT, SURE.
POWPOWPOWPOWPOW
DIDN'T KNOW GOHAN COULD FIGHT THIS GOOD!
LOOKS LIKE GOHAN'S GOT IT HANDLED OVER THERE, HUH?
WHICH MEANS WE CAN FOCUS ON EACH OTHER, JIREN!
...
FIGHT ALL YOU LIKE. THE END RESULT WON'T CHANGE.

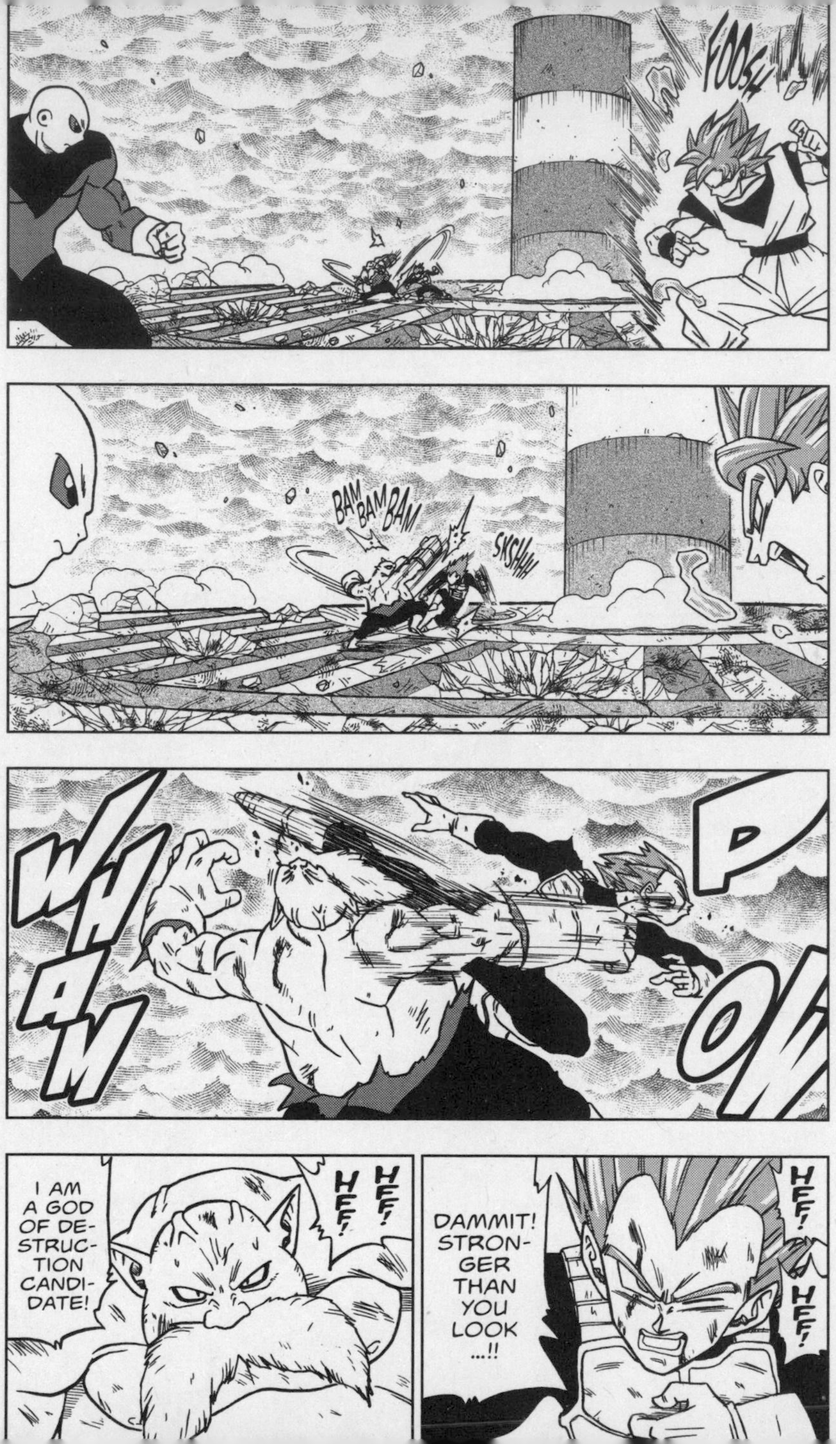
FOOSH
BAM BAM BAM
SKSHH
POW
WHAM
HEF! HEF!
DAMMIT! STRONGER THAN YOU LOOK ...!!
HEF! HEF!
I AM A GOD OF DESTRUCTION CANDIDATE!

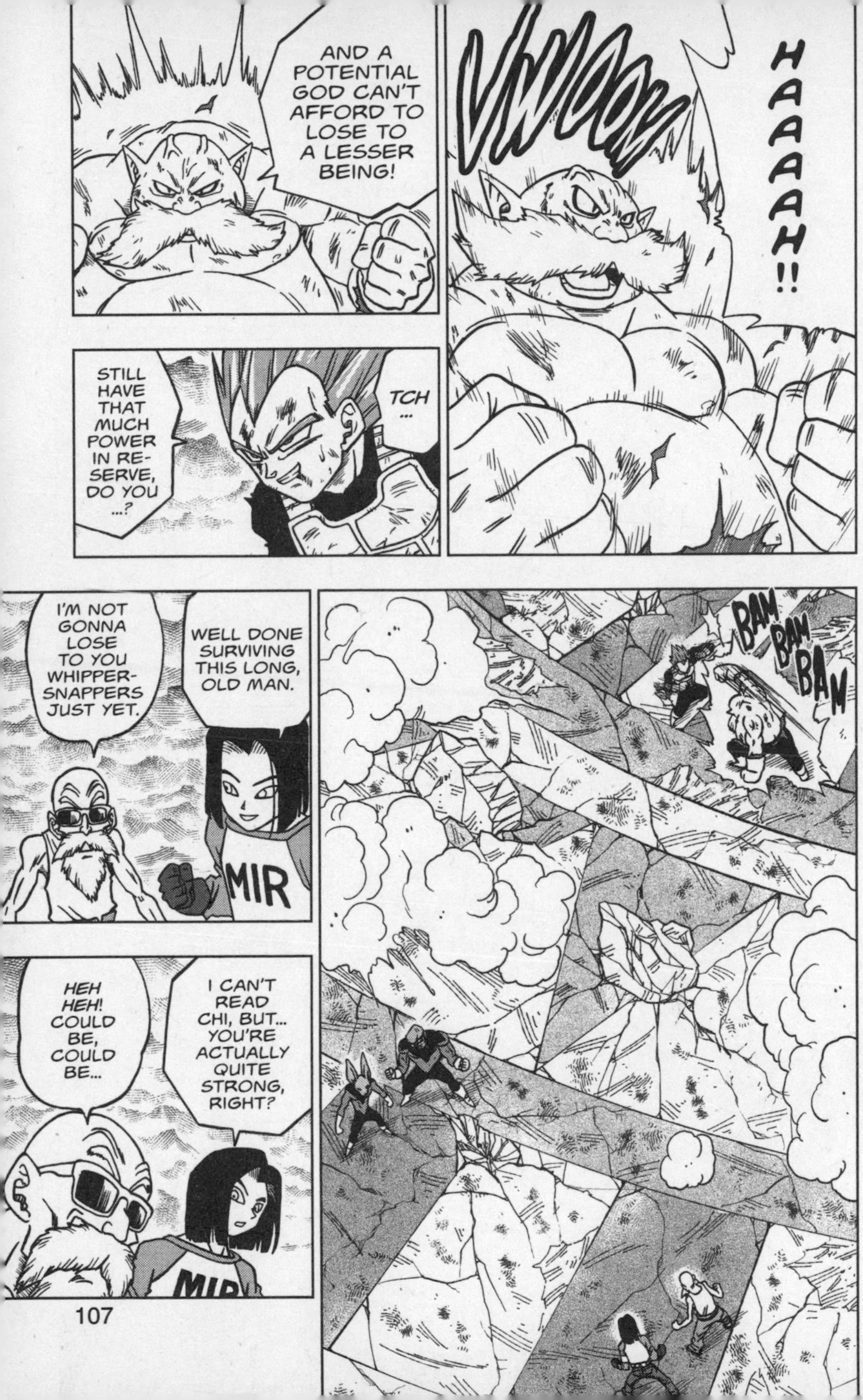
VWOOM
HAAAAAH!!
AND A POTENTIAL GOD CAN'T AFFORD TO LOSE TO A LESSER BEING!
TCH...
STILL HAVE THAT MUCH POWER IN RE-SERVE, DO YOU ...?
BAM BAM BAM
WELL DONE SURVIVING THIS LONG, OLD MAN.
I'M NOT GONNA LOSE TO YOU WHIPPER-SNAPPERS JUST YET.
MIR
I CAN'T READ CHI, BUT... YOU'RE ACTUALLY QUITE STRONG, RIGHT?
HEH HEH! COULD BE, COULD BE...
MIR

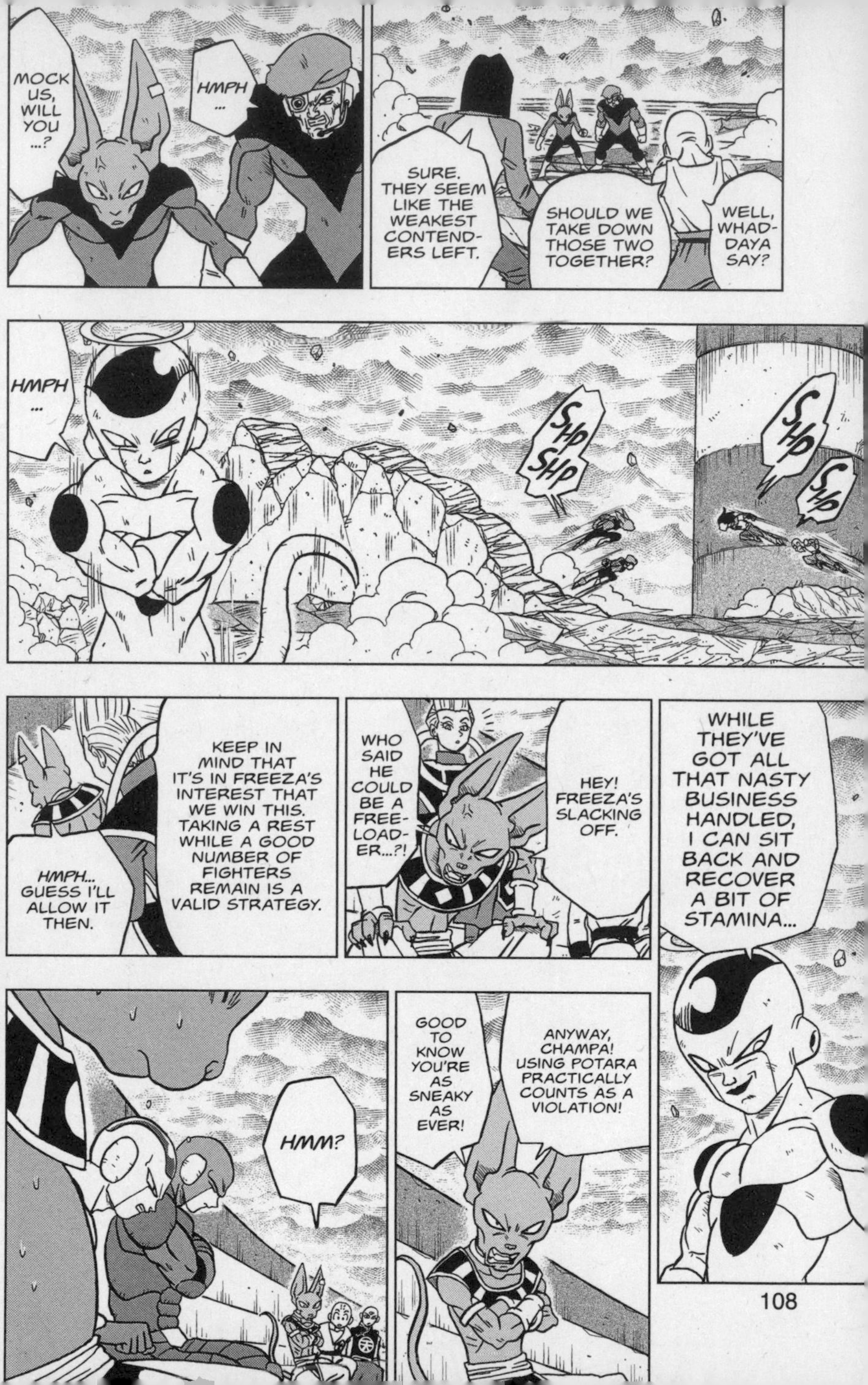

WELL, WHAD-DAYA SAY?
SHOULD WE TAKE DOWN THOSE TWO TOGETHER?
SURE. THEY SEEM LIKE THE WEAKEST CONTEND-ERS LEFT.
HMPH ...
MOCK US, WILL YOU ...?
SHP SHP
SHP SHP
HMPH ...
WHILE THEY'VE GOT ALL THAT NASTY BUSINESS HANDLED, I CAN SIT BACK AND RECOVER A BIT OF STAMINA...
HEY! FREEZA'S SLACKING OFF.
WHO SAID HE COULD BE A FREE-LOAD-ER...?!
KEEP IN MIND THAT IT'S IN FREEZA'S INTEREST THAT WE WIN THIS. TAKING A REST WHILE A GOOD NUMBER OF FIGHTERS REMAIN IS A VALID STRATEGY.
HMPH... GUESS I'LL ALLOW IT THEN.
ANYWAY, CHAMPA! USING POTARA PRACTICALLY COUNTS AS A VIOLATION!
GOOD TO KNOW YOU'RE AS SNEAKY AS EVER!
HMM?

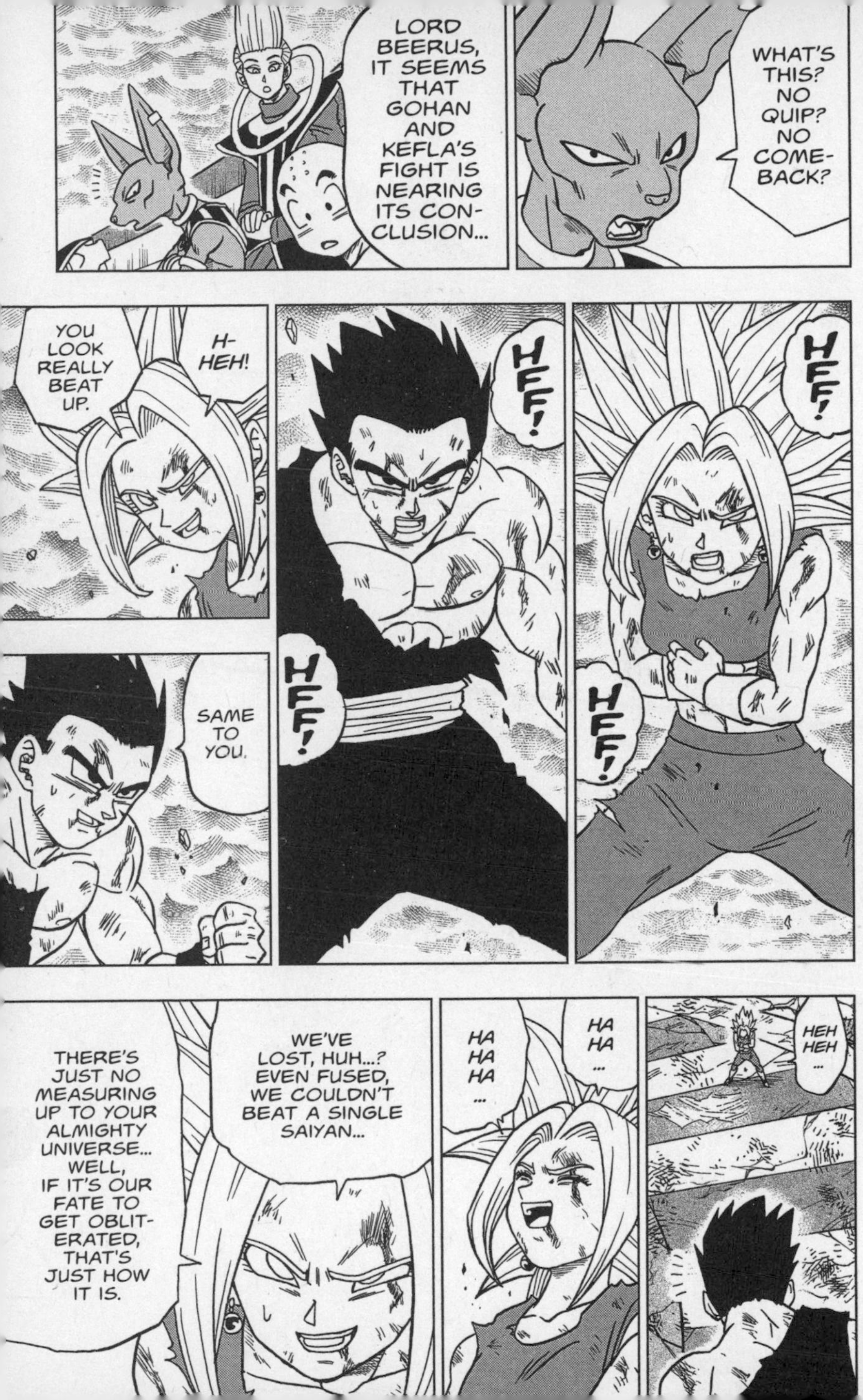
WHAT'S THIS? NO QUIP? NO COME-BACK?
LORD BEERUS, IT SEEMS THAT GOHAN AND KEFLA'S FIGHT IS NEARING ITS CON-CLUSION...
HEFF!
HEFF!
HEFF!
HEFF!
H-HEH!
YOU LOOK REALLY BEAT UP.
SAME TO YOU.
HEH HEH ...
HA HA ...
HA HA HA ...
WE'VE LOST, HUH...? EVEN FUSED, WE COULDN'T BEAT A SINGLE SAIYAN...
THERE'S JUST NO MEASURING UP TO YOUR ALMIGHTY UNIVERSE... WELL, IF IT'S OUR FATE TO GET OBLIT-ERATED, THAT'S JUST HOW IT IS.

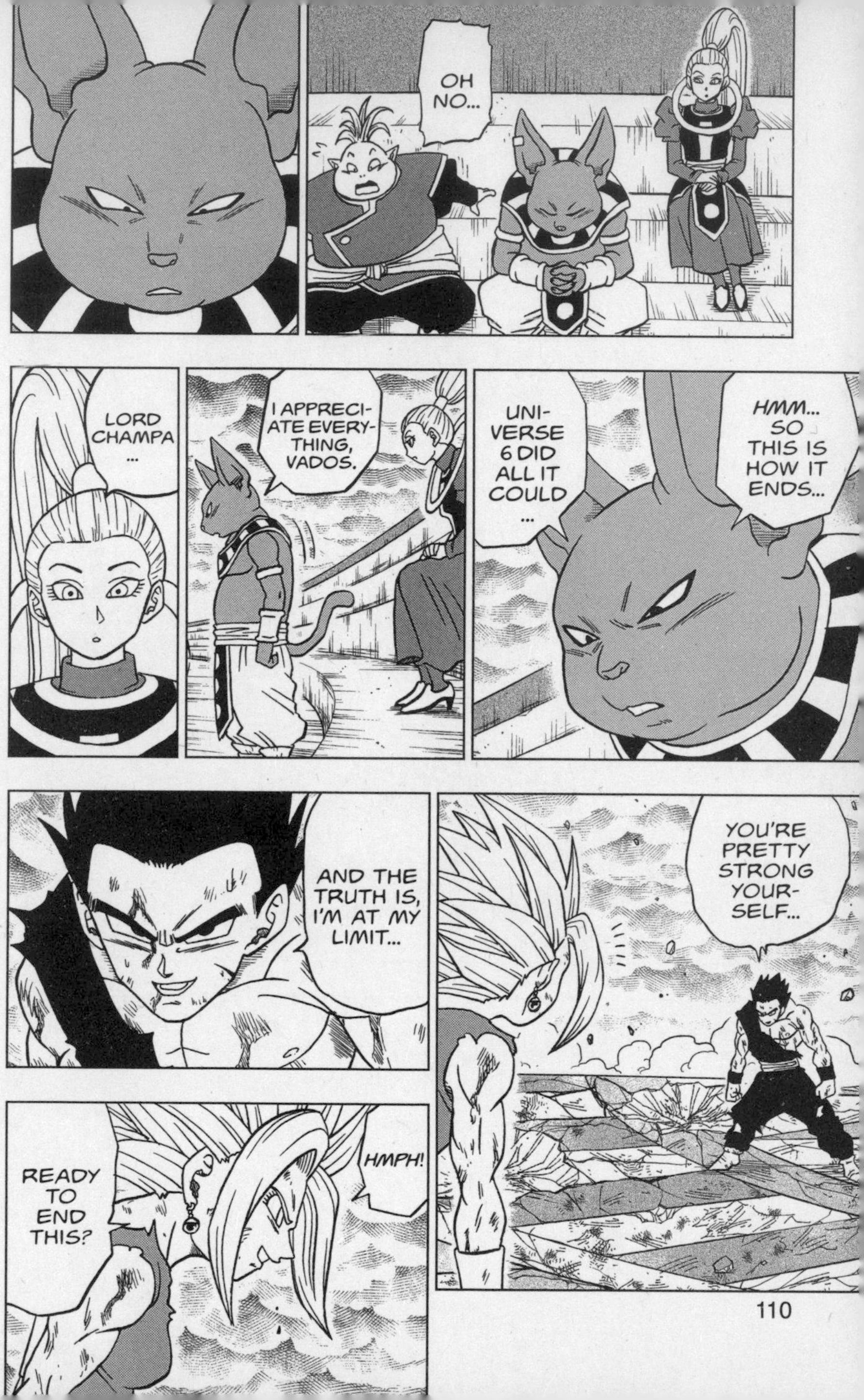
OH NO...
HMM... SO THIS IS HOW IT ENDS...
UNIVERSE 6 DID ALL IT COULD...
I APPRECIATE EVERYTHING, VADOS.
LORD CHAMPA...
YOU'RE PRETTY STRONG YOURSELF...
AND THE TRUTH IS, I'M AT MY LIMIT...
HMPH!
READY TO END THIS?

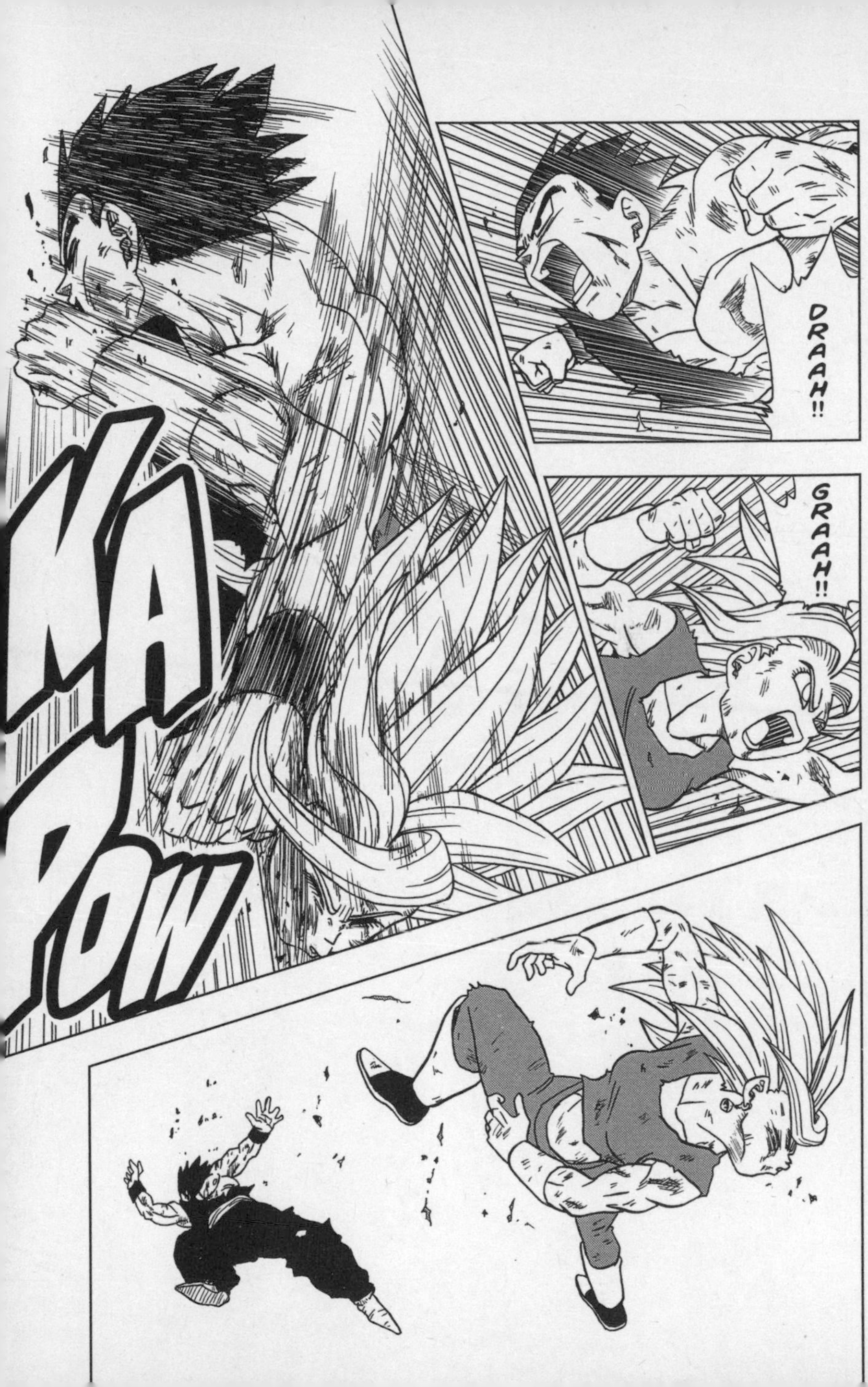
DRAAH!!
GRAAAH!!

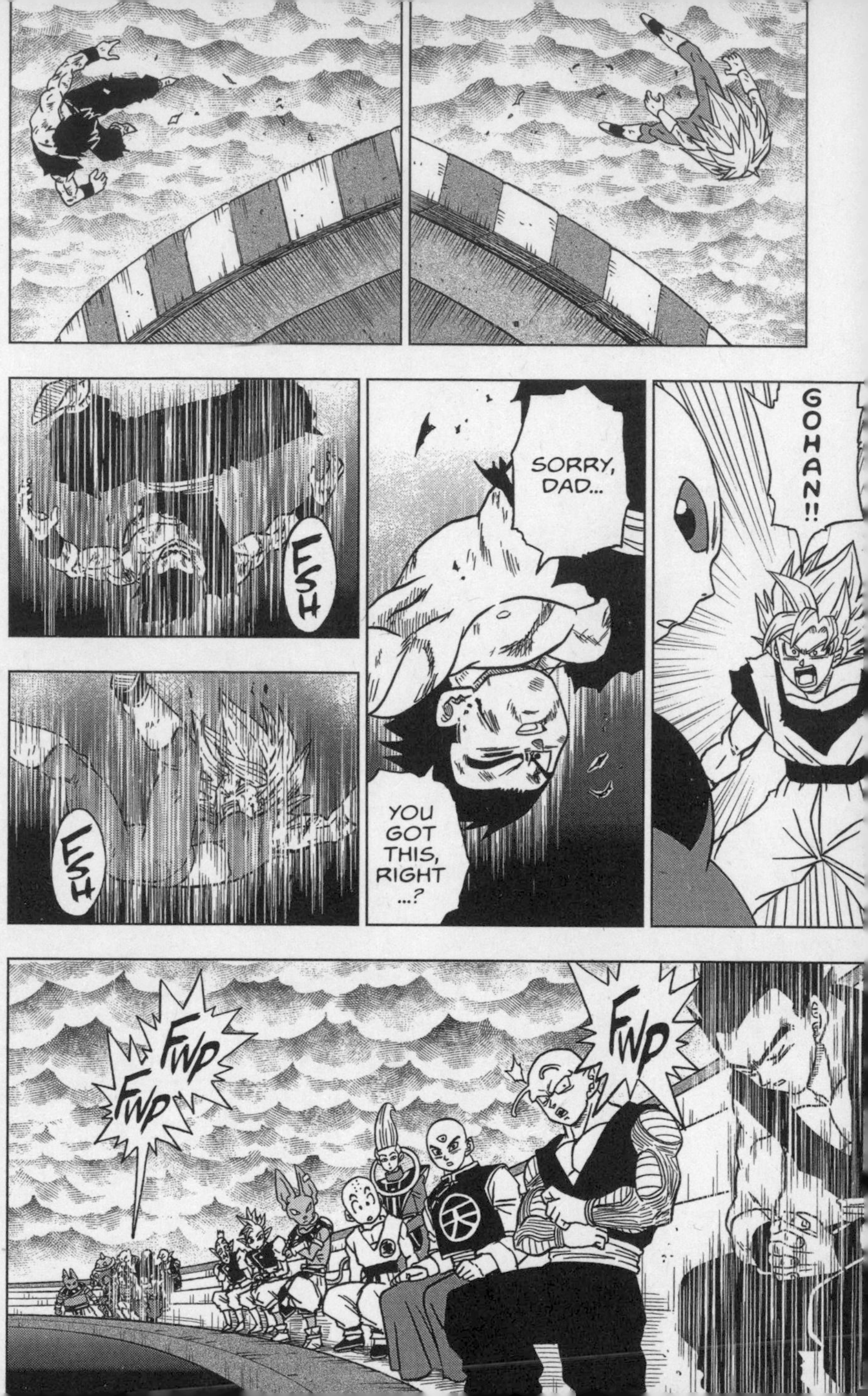
GOHAN!!
SORRY, DAD...
YOU GOT THIS, RIGHT ...?
FSH
FSH
FWP
FWP
FWP

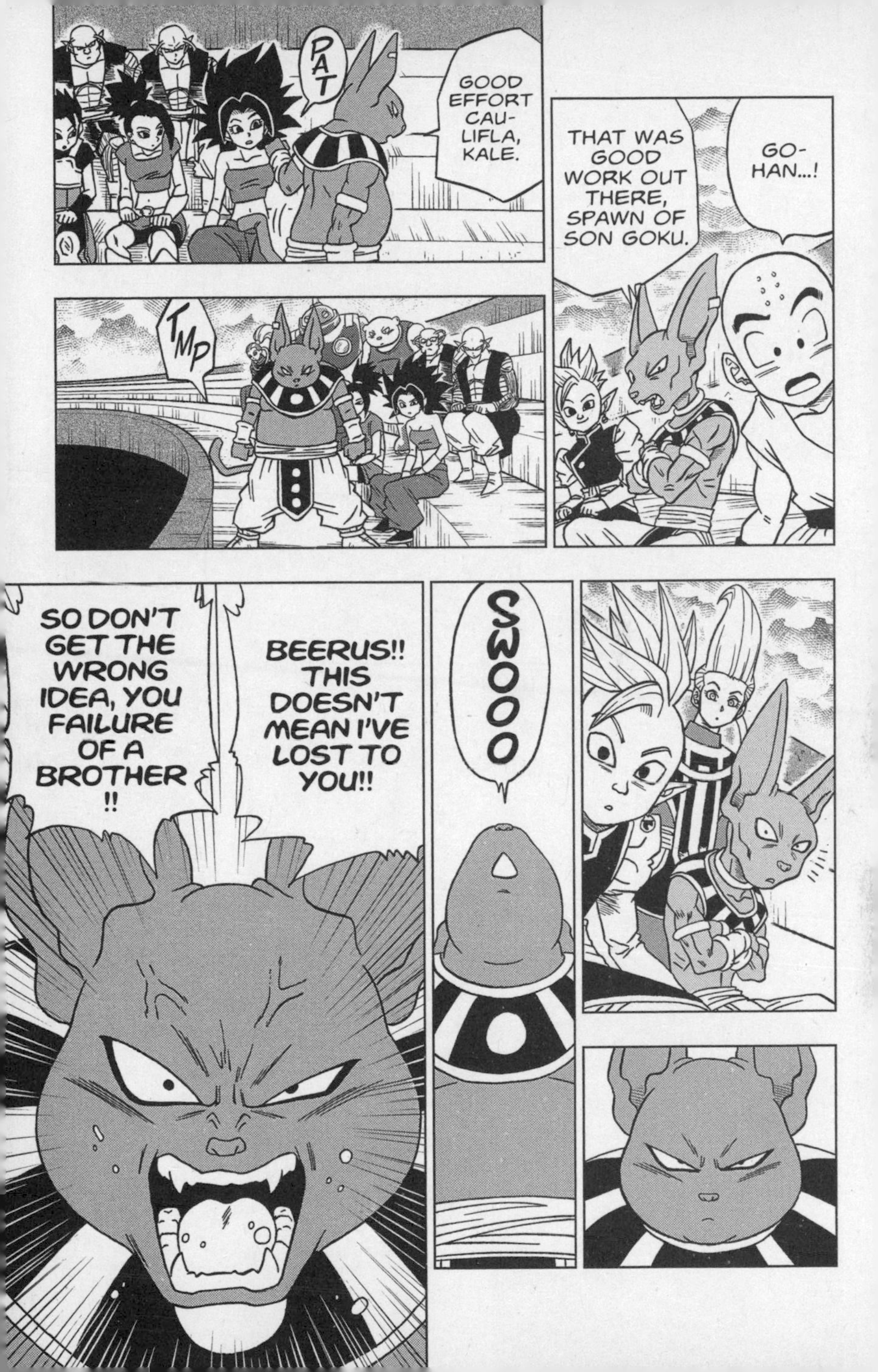
GO-HAN...!
THAT WAS GOOD WORK OUT THERE, SPAWN OF SON GOKU.
GOOD EFFORT CAU-LIFLA, KALE.
PAT
TMP
SWOOO
BEERUS!! THIS DOESN'T MEAN I'VE LOST TO YOU!!
SO DON'T GET THE WRONG IDEA, YOU FAILURE OF A BROTHER!!

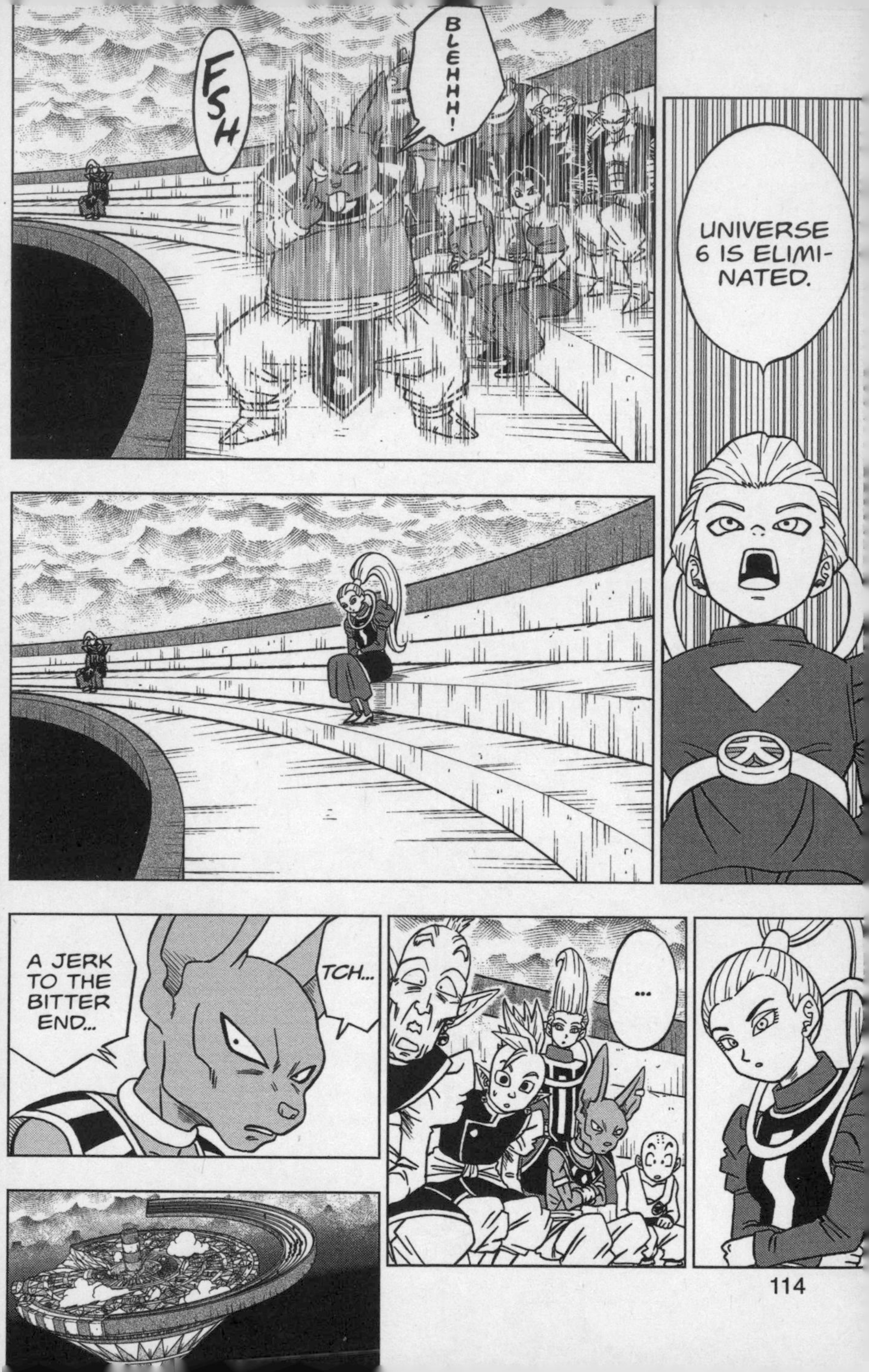
UNIVERSE 6 IS ELIMINATED.
BLEHHH!
FSH
...
TCH...
A JERK TO THE BITTER END...

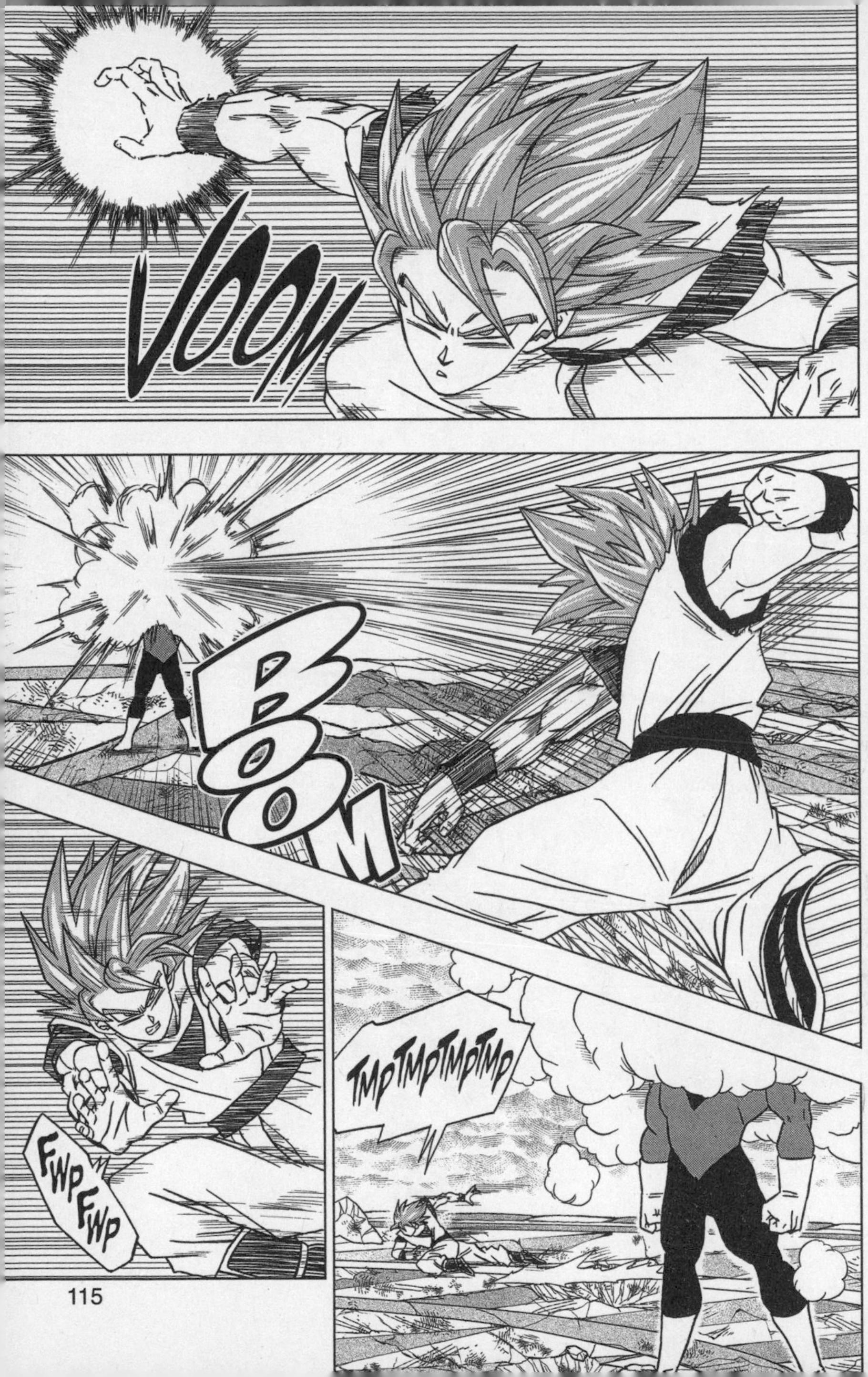
VOOM
BOOOM
TMPTMPTMPTMP
FWP FWP

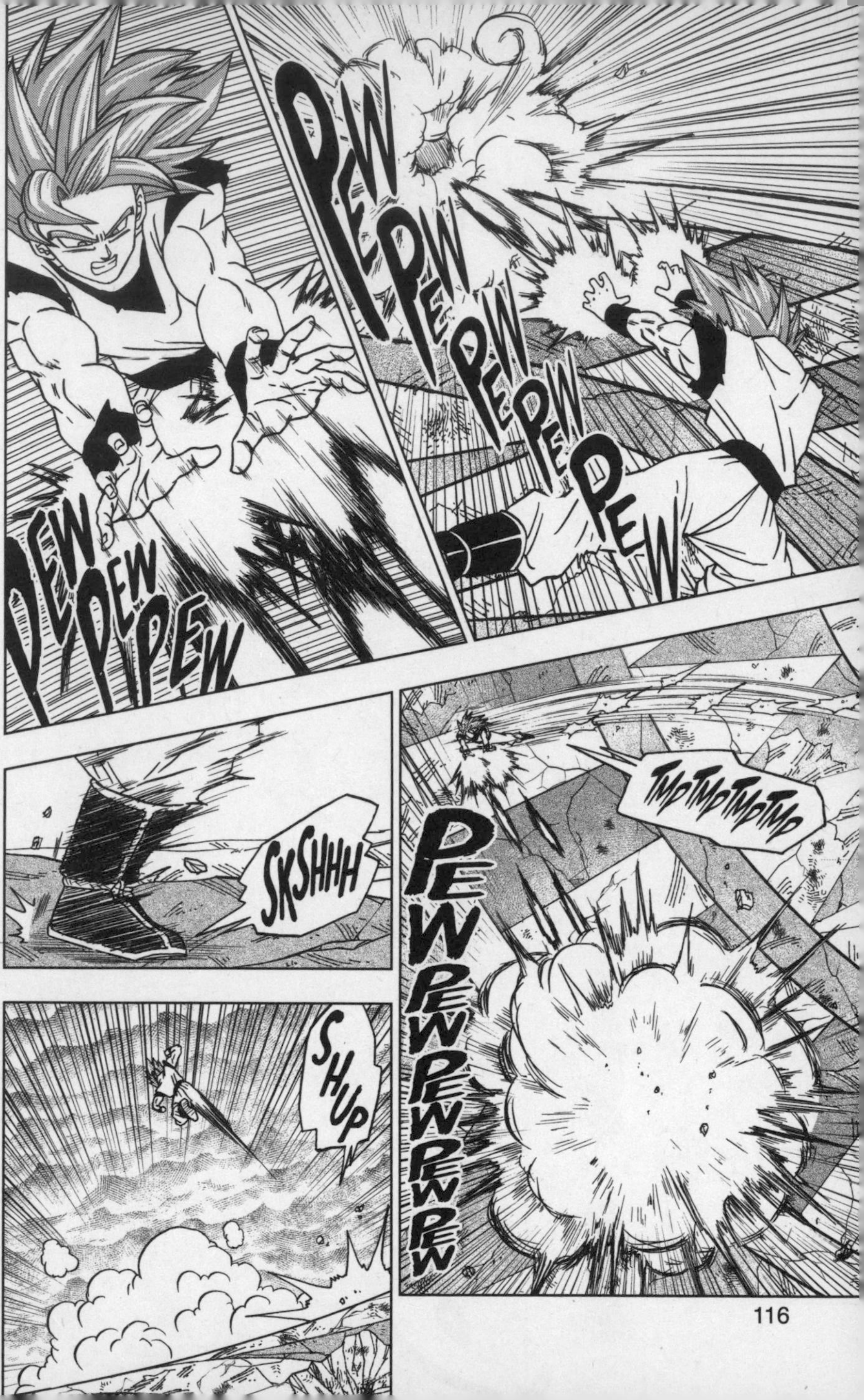
PEW PEW PEW PEW PEW PEW PEW
PEW PEW PEW
TMPTMPTMPTMP
PEWPEWPEWPEWPEWPEWPEW
SKSHHH
SHUP

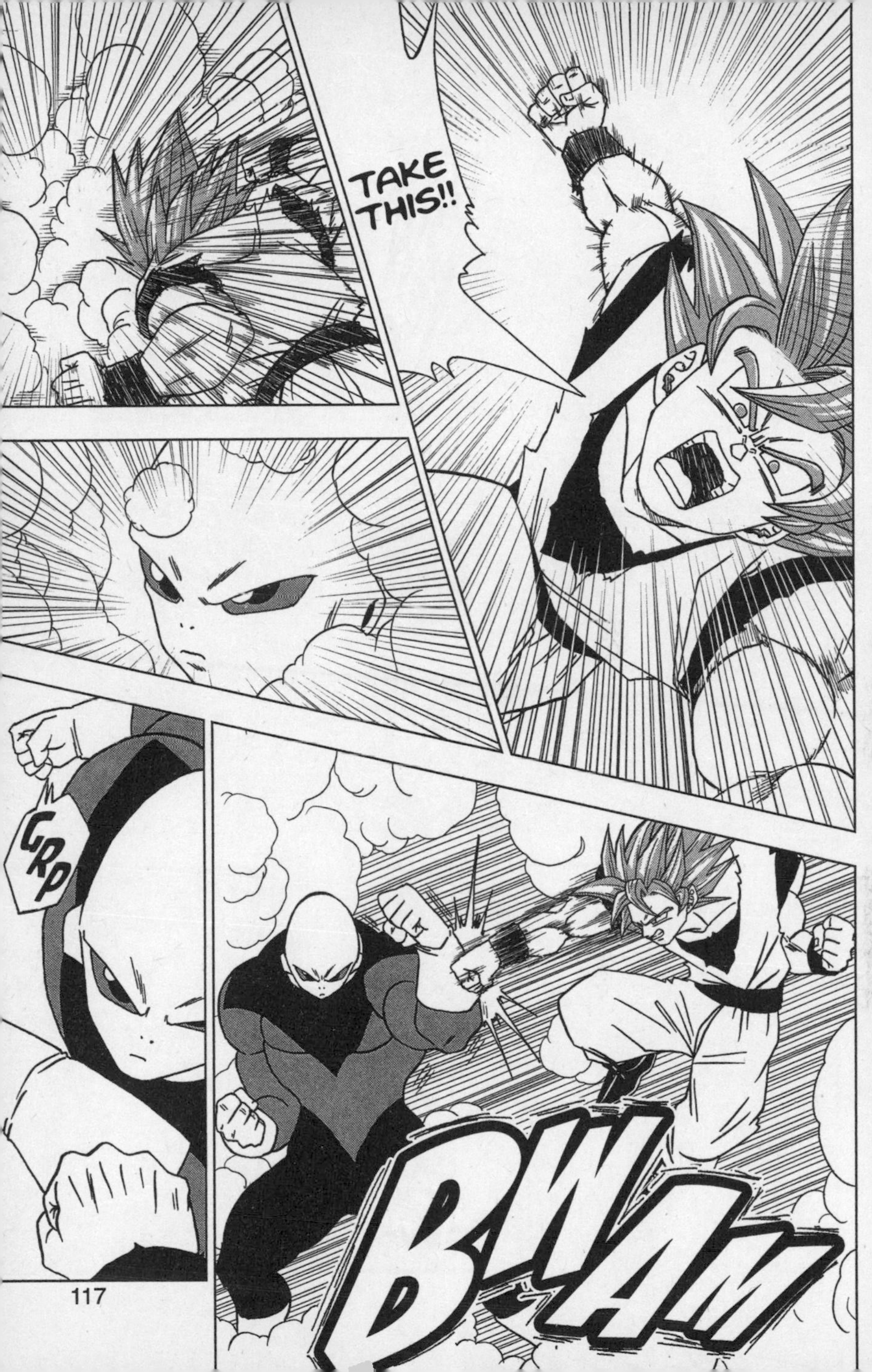
TAKE THIS!!
GRP
BWAM

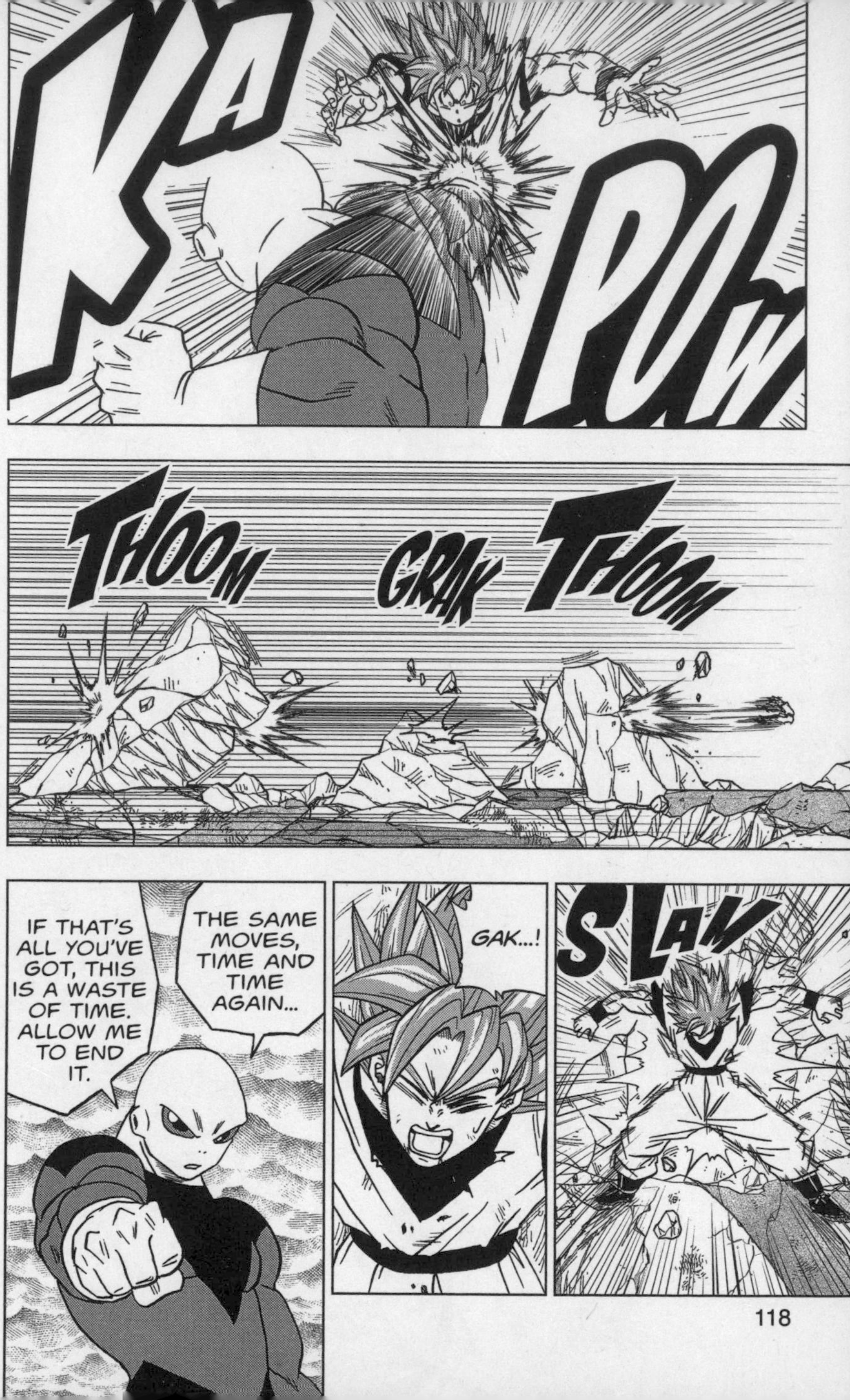
KA POW
THOOM
GRAK
THOOM
SLAM
GAK...!
THE SAME MOVES, TIME AND TIME AGAIN...
IF THAT'S ALL YOU'VE GOT, THIS IS A WASTE OF TIME. ALLOW ME TO END IT.

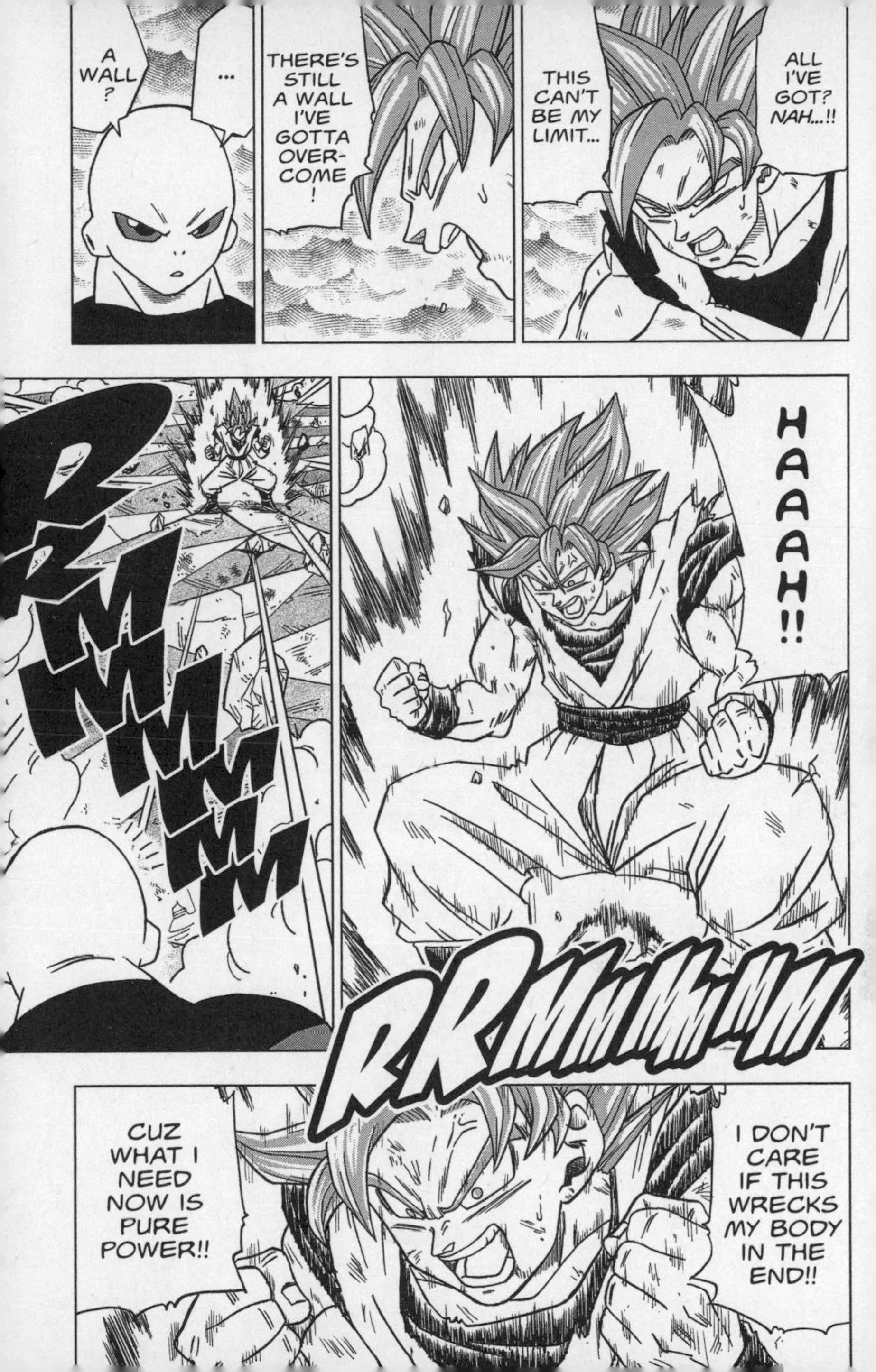
ALL I'VE GOT? NAH...!!
THIS CAN'T BE MY LIMIT...
THERE'S STILL A WALL I'VE GOTTA OVERCOME!
...
A WALL?
HAAAAH!!
I DON'T CARE IF THIS WRECKS MY BODY IN THE END!!
CUZ WHAT I NEED NOW IS PURE POWER!!

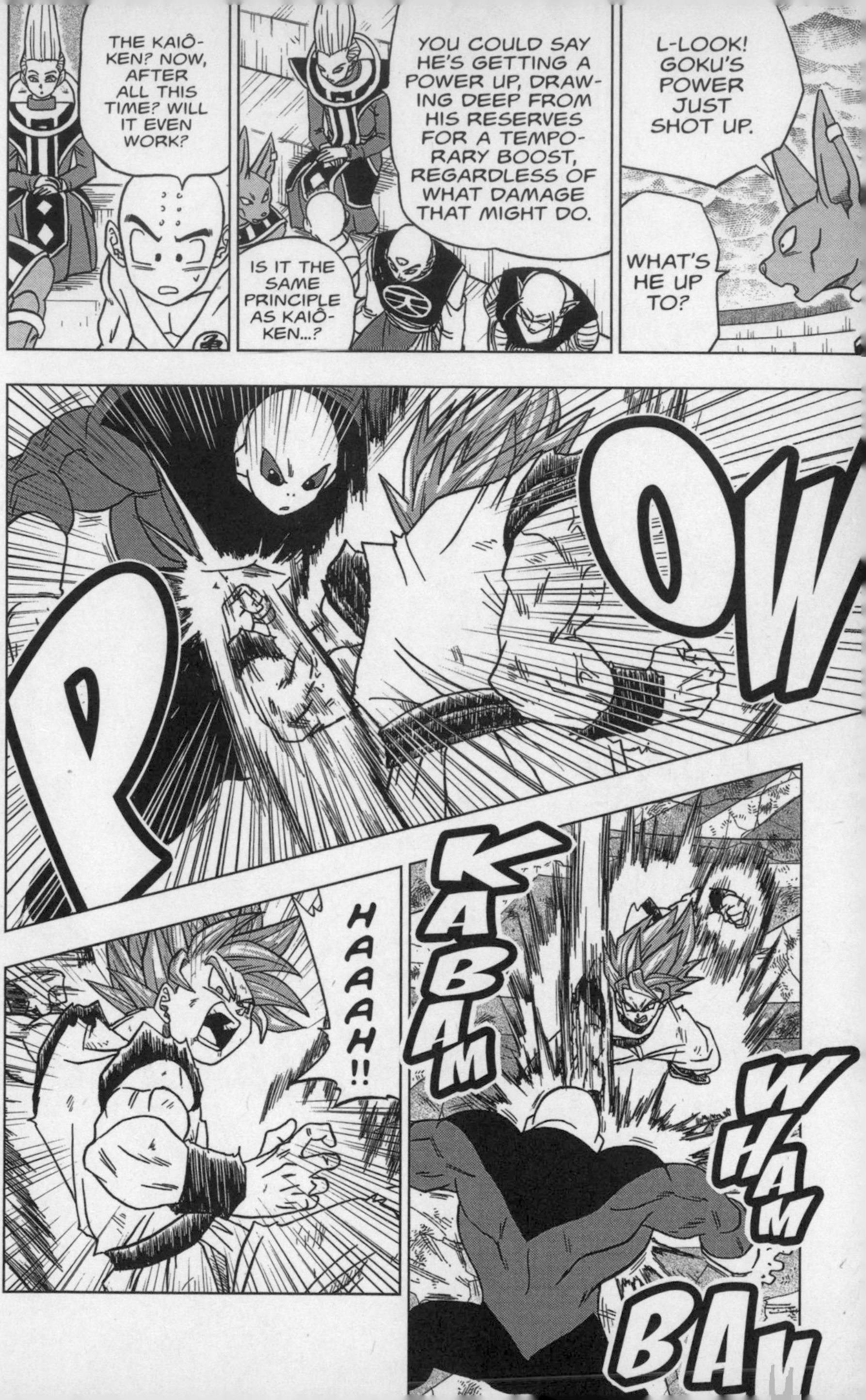
L-LOOK! GOKU'S POWER JUST SHOT UP.
WHAT'S HE UP TO?
IS IT THE SAME PRINCIPLE AS KAIÔ-KEN...?
YOU COULD SAY HE'S GETTING A POWER UP, DRAWING DEEP FROM HIS RESERVES FOR A TEMPORARY BOOST, REGARDLESS OF WHAT DAMAGE THAT MIGHT DO.
THE KAIÔ-KEN? NOW, AFTER ALL THIS TIME? WILL IT EVEN WORK?
POW
KABAM
WHAM
BAM
HAAAAH!!

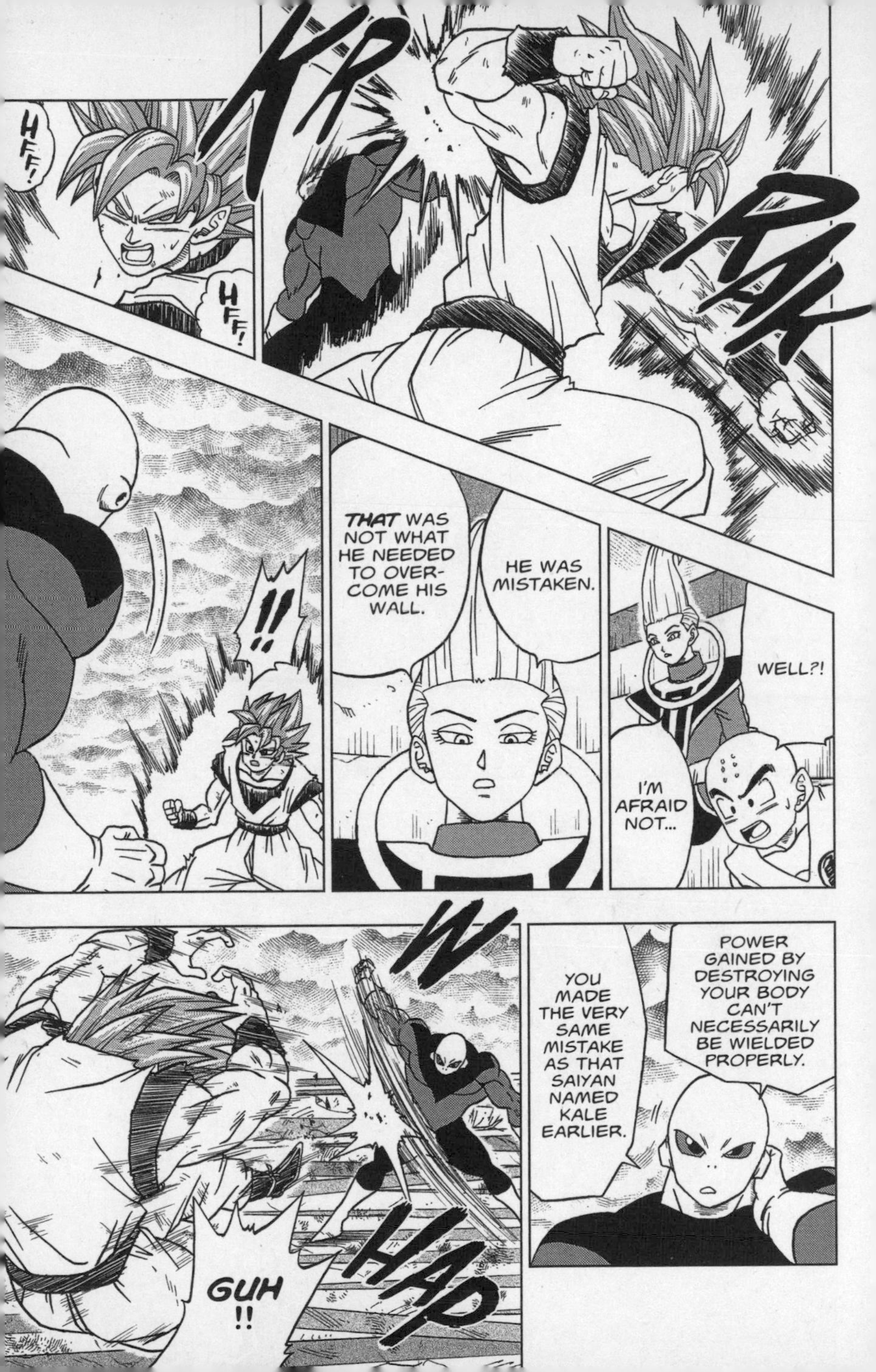

KR
RAK
HFF!
HFF!
WELL?!
I'M AFRAID NOT...
HE WAS MISTAKEN.
THAT WAS NOT WHAT HE NEEDED TO OVER-COME HIS WALL.
!!
POWER GAINED BY DESTROYING YOUR BODY CAN'T NECESSARILY BE WIELDED PROPERLY.
YOU MADE THE VERY SAME MISTAKE AS THAT SAIYAN NAMED KALE EARLIER.
W
HAP
GUH !!

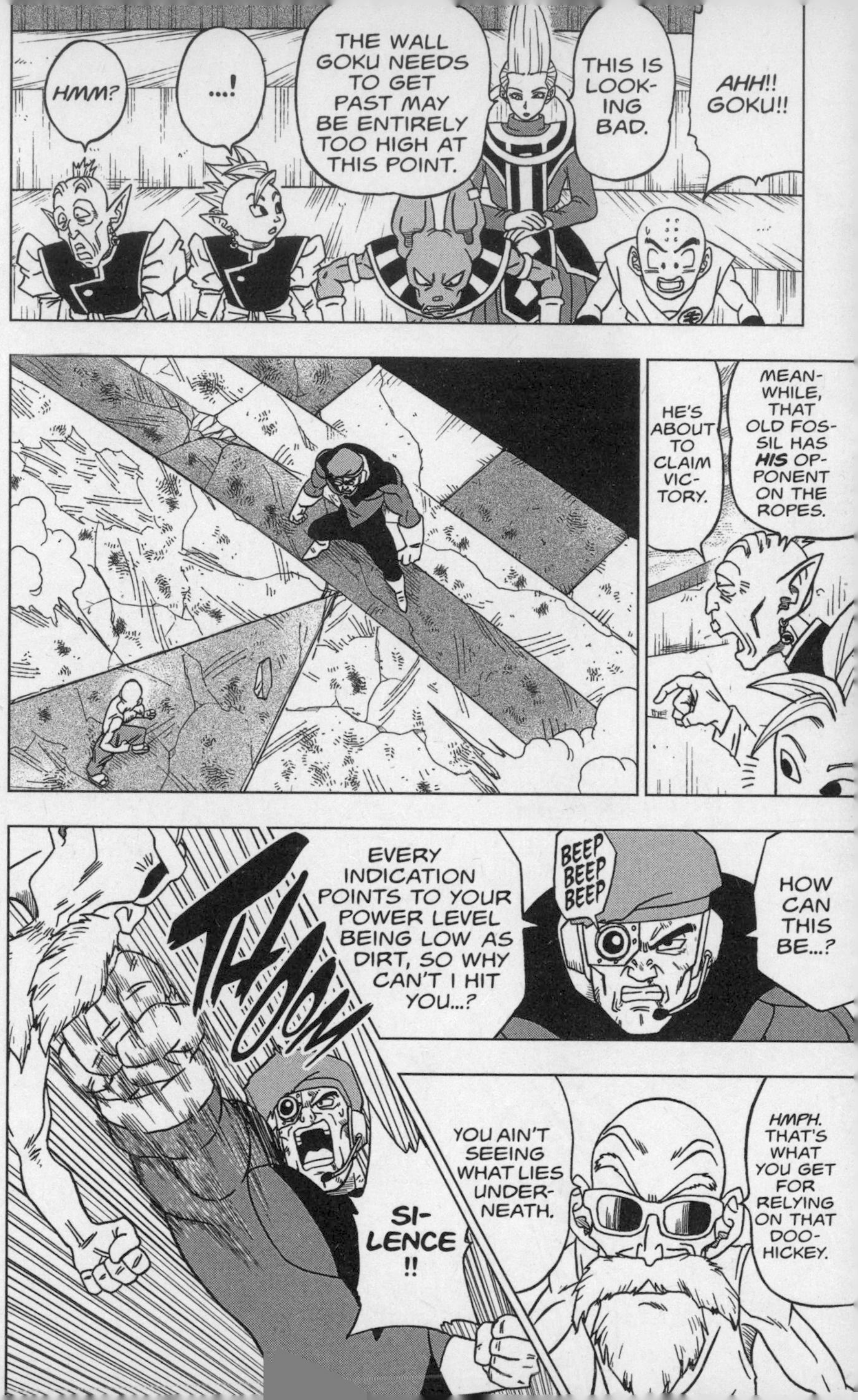
AHH!! GOKU!!
THIS IS LOOKING BAD.
THE WALL GOKU NEEDS TO GET PAST MAY BE ENTIRELY TOO HIGH AT THIS POINT.
...!
HMM?
MEANWHILE, THAT OLD FOSSIL HAS **HIS** OPPONENT ON THE ROPES.
HE'S ABOUT TO CLAIM VICTORY.
HOW CAN THIS BE...?
BEEP BEEP BEEP
EVERY INDICATION POINTS TO YOUR POWER LEVEL BEING LOW AS DIRT, SO WHY CAN'T I HIT YOU...?
HMPH. THAT'S WHAT YOU GET FOR RELYING ON THAT DOOHICKEY.
YOU AIN'T SEEING WHAT LIES UNDERNEATH.
SILENCE!!
THOOM

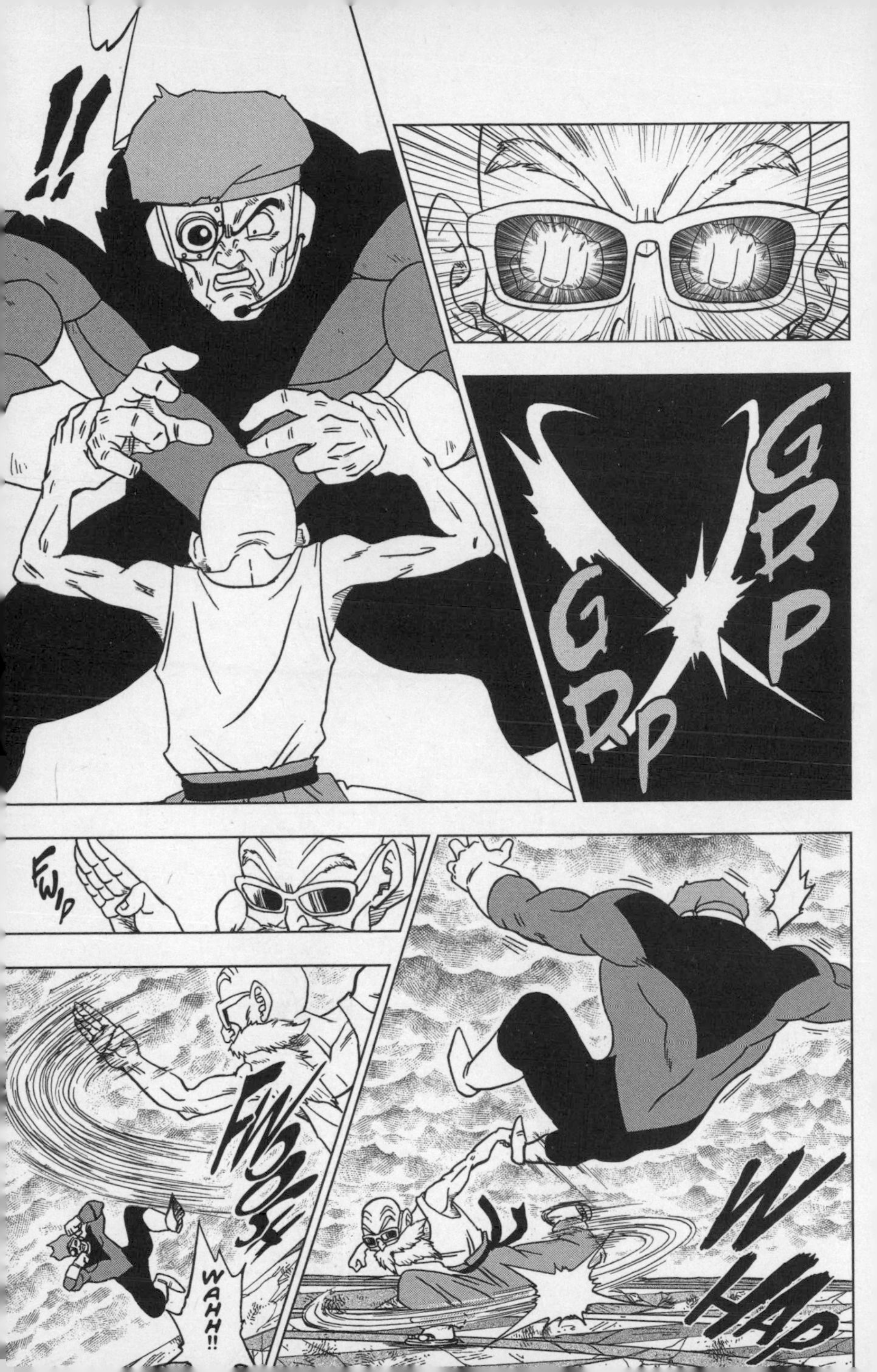
GRIP GRIP
!!
WHAP
FWIP
FWOOSH
WAHH!!

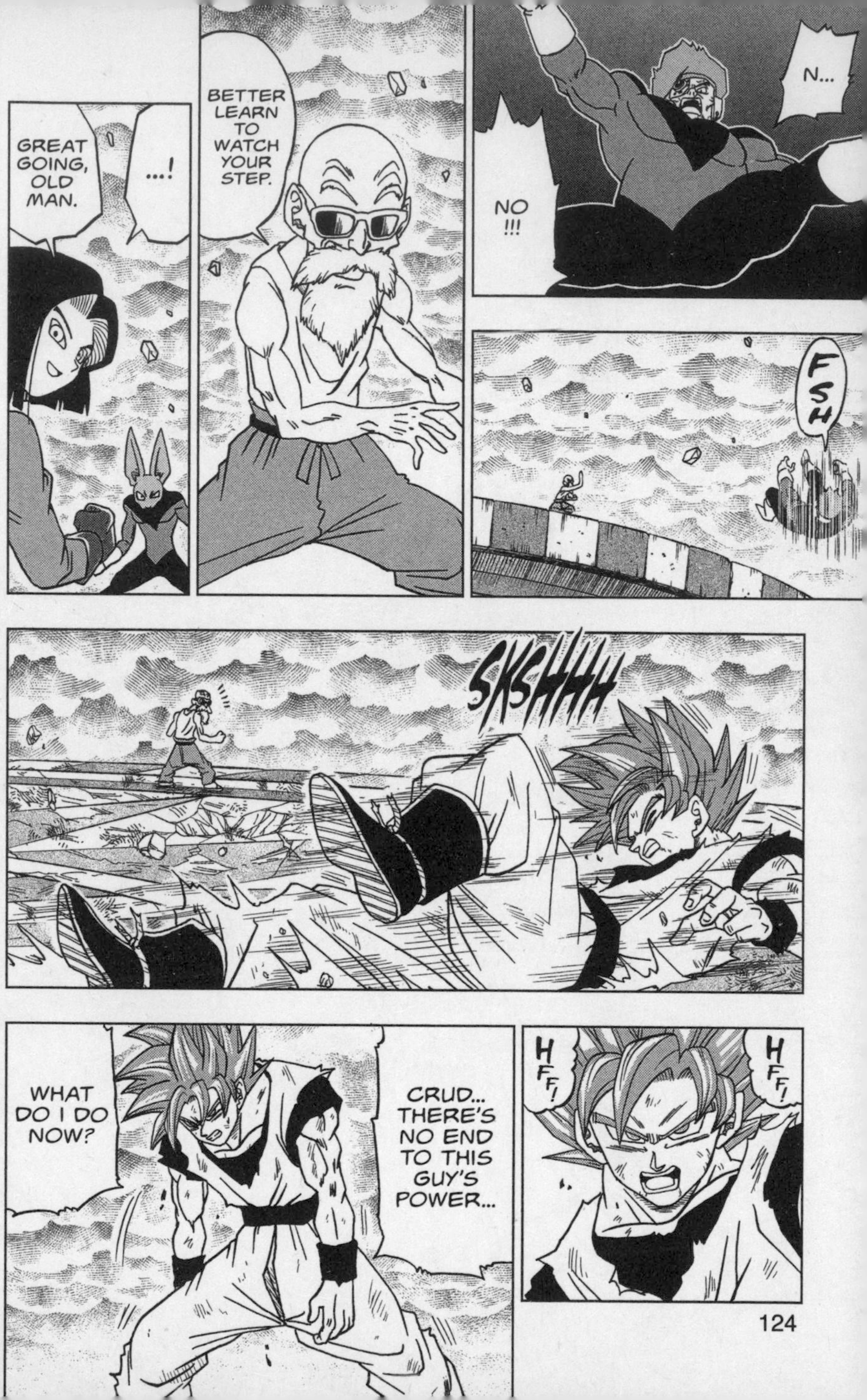
N...
NO !!!
FSH
BETTER LEARN TO WATCH YOUR STEP.
...!
GREAT GOING, OLD MAN.
SKSHHH
HFF!
HFF!
CRUD... THERE'S NO END TO THIS GUY'S POWER...
WHAT DO I DO NOW?

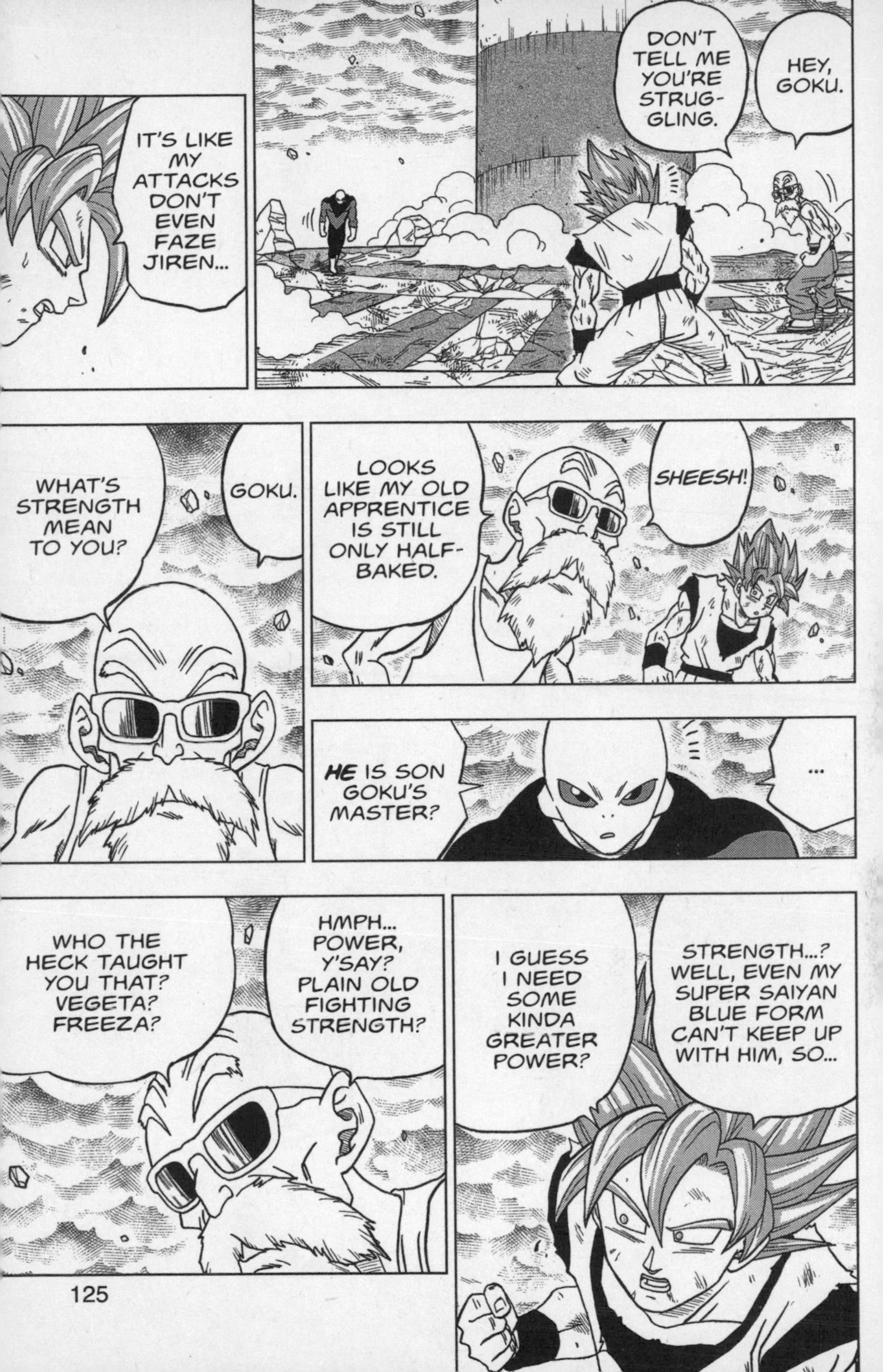
HEY, GOKU.
DON'T TELL ME YOU'RE STRUG-GLING.
IT'S LIKE MY ATTACKS DON'T EVEN FAZE JIREN...
SHEESH!
LOOKS LIKE MY OLD APPRENTICE IS STILL ONLY HALF-BAKED.
...
HE IS SON GOKU'S MASTER?
GOKU.
WHAT'S STRENGTH MEAN TO YOU?
STRENGTH...? WELL, EVEN MY SUPER SAIYAN BLUE FORM CAN'T KEEP UP WITH HIM, SO...
I GUESS I NEED SOME KINDA GREATER POWER?
HMPH... POWER, Y'SAY? PLAIN OLD FIGHTING STRENGTH?
WHO THE HECK TAUGHT YOU THAT? VEGETA? FREEZA?

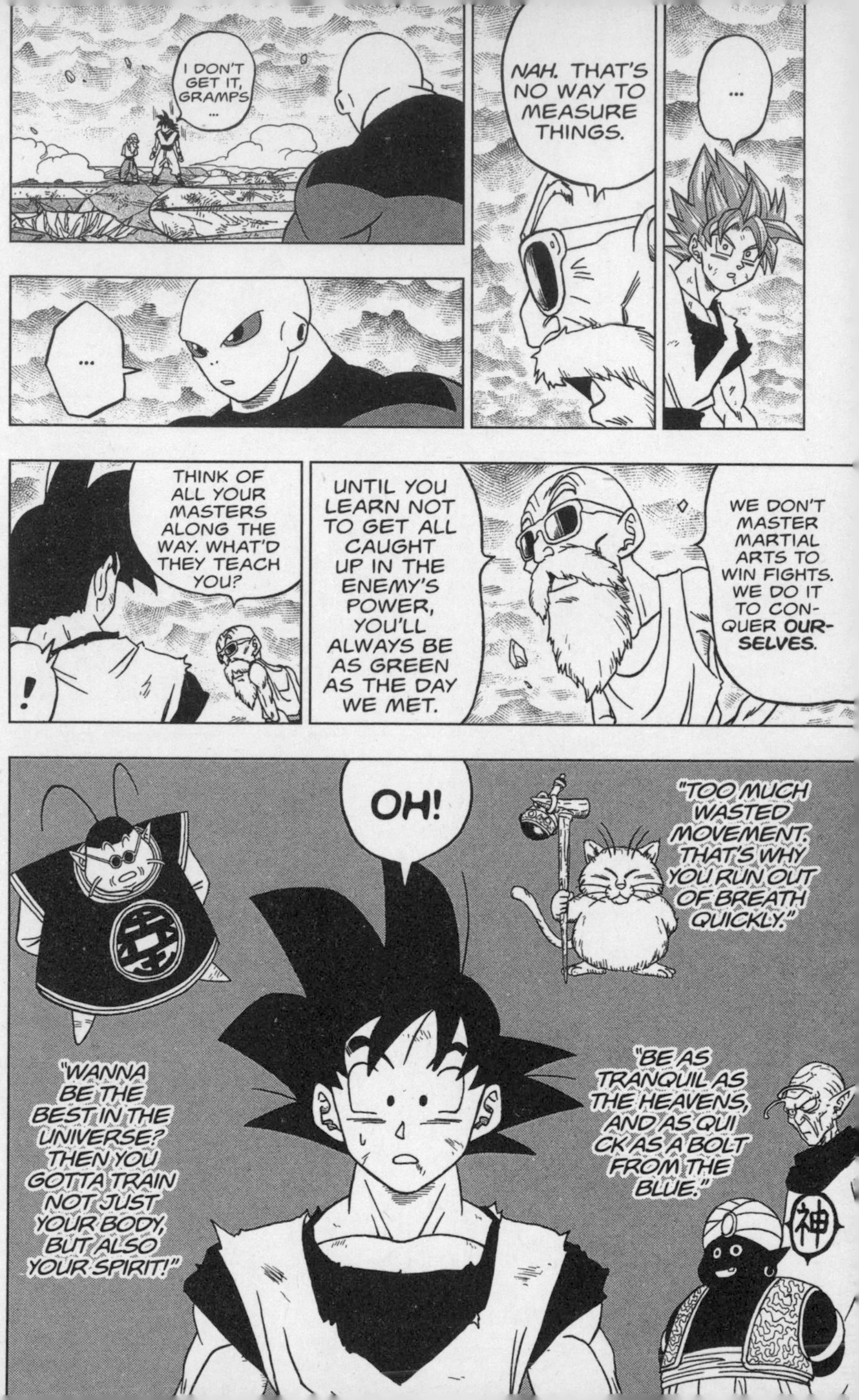
...
NAH. THAT'S NO WAY TO MEASURE THINGS.
I DON'T GET IT, GRAMPS...
...
WE DON'T MASTER MARTIAL ARTS TO WIN FIGHTS. WE DO IT TO CONQUER **OURSELVES**.
UNTIL YOU LEARN NOT TO GET ALL CAUGHT UP IN THE ENEMY'S POWER, YOU'LL ALWAYS BE AS GREEN AS THE DAY WE MET.
THINK OF ALL YOUR MASTERS ALONG THE WAY. WHAT'D THEY TEACH YOU?
!
"TOO MUCH WASTED MOVEMENT. THAT'S WHY YOU RUN OUT OF BREATH QUICKLY."
OH!
"BE AS TRANQUIL AS THE HEAVENS, AND AS QUICK AS A BOLT FROM THE BLUE."
"WANNA BE THE BEST IN THE UNIVERSE? THEN YOU GOTTA TRAIN NOT JUST YOUR BODY, BUT ALSO YOUR SPIRIT!"
神

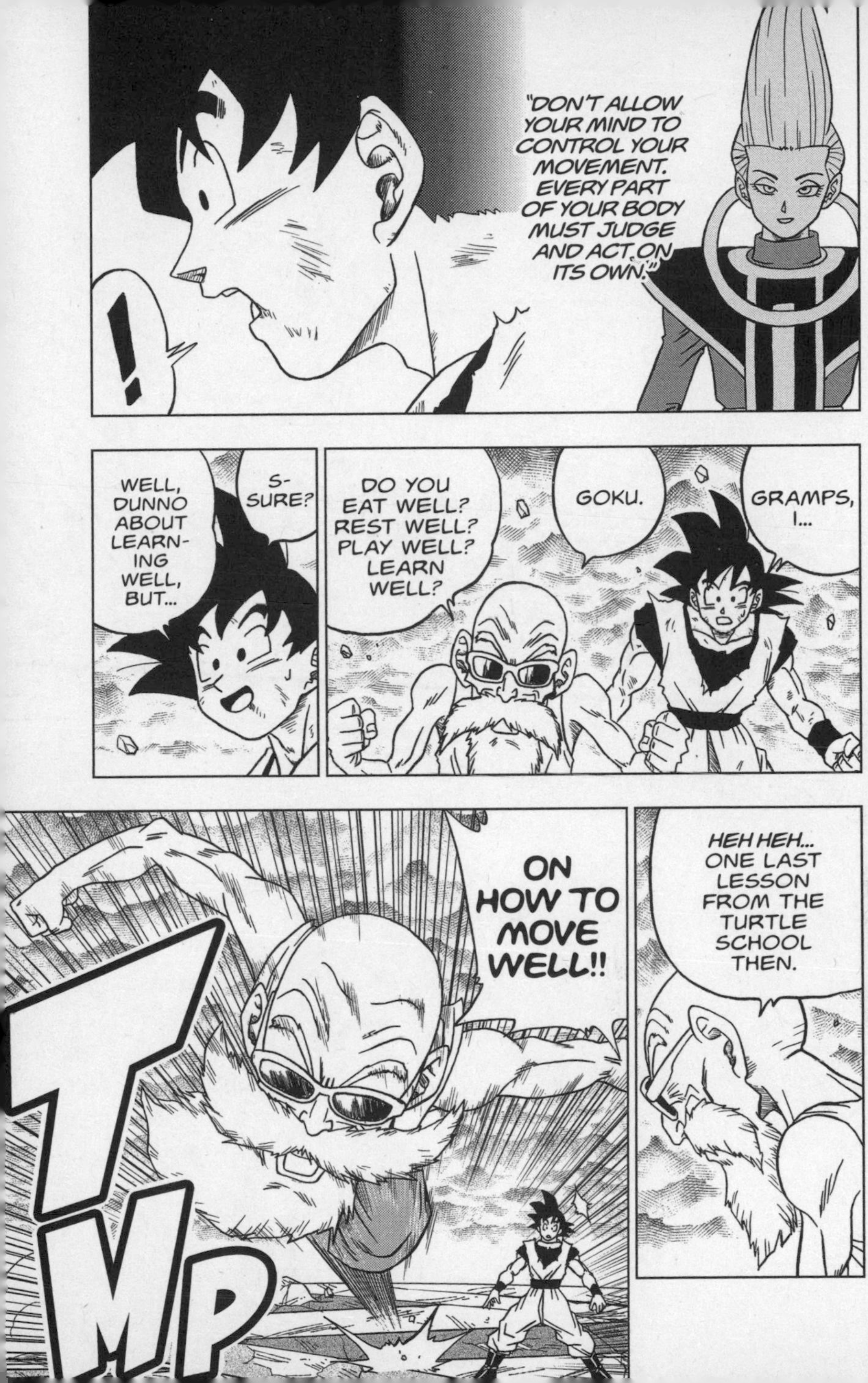
"DON'T ALLOW YOUR MIND TO CONTROL YOUR MOVEMENT. EVERY PART OF YOUR BODY MUST JUDGE AND ACT ON ITS OWN."
!
GRAMPS, I...
GOKU.
DO YOU EAT WELL? REST WELL? PLAY WELL? LEARN WELL?
S-SURE?
WELL, DUNNO ABOUT LEARN-ING WELL, BUT...
HEH HEH... ONE LAST LESSON FROM THE TURTLE SCHOOL THEN.
ON HOW TO MOVE WELL!!
TMP

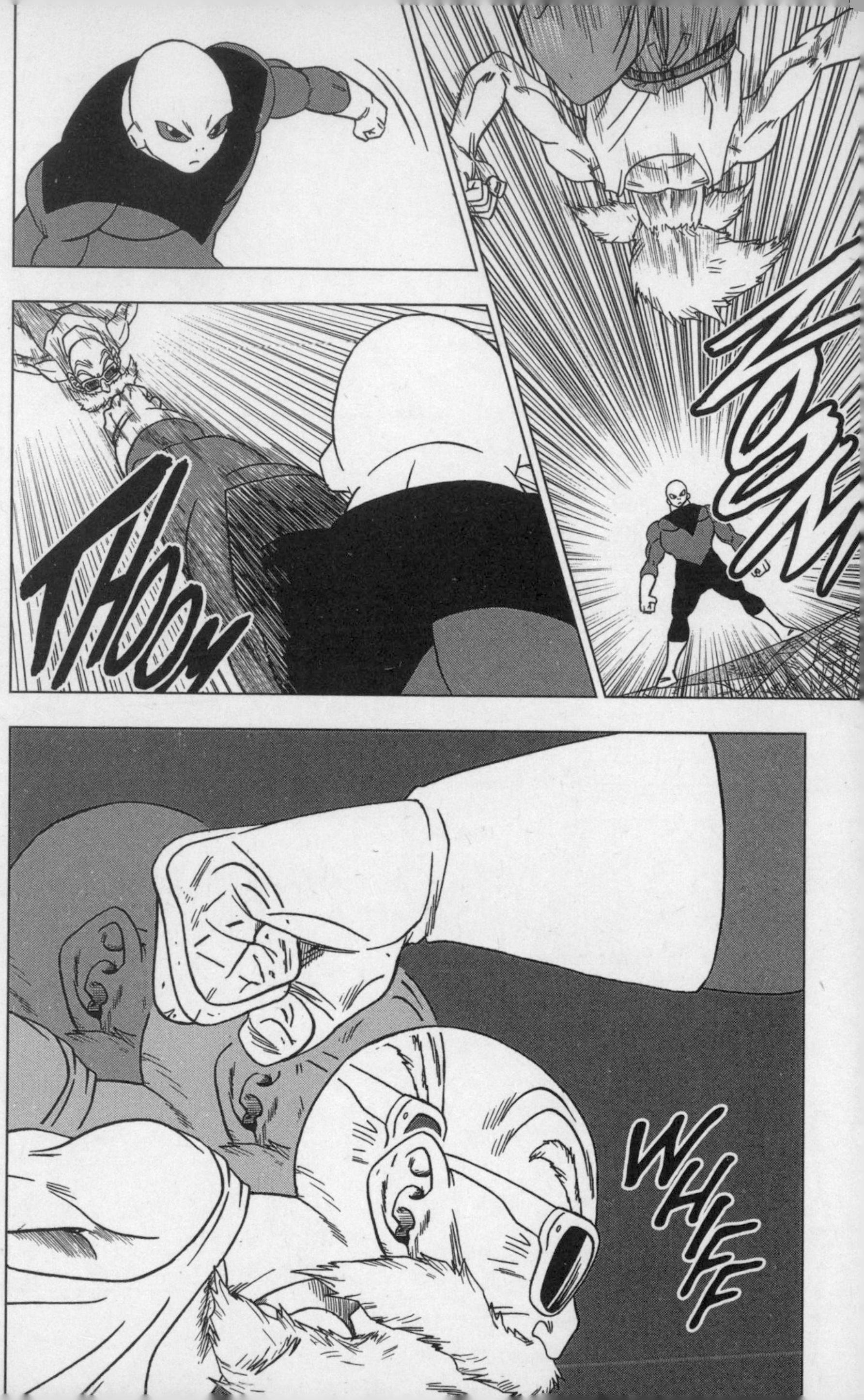
THOOM
WHIFF

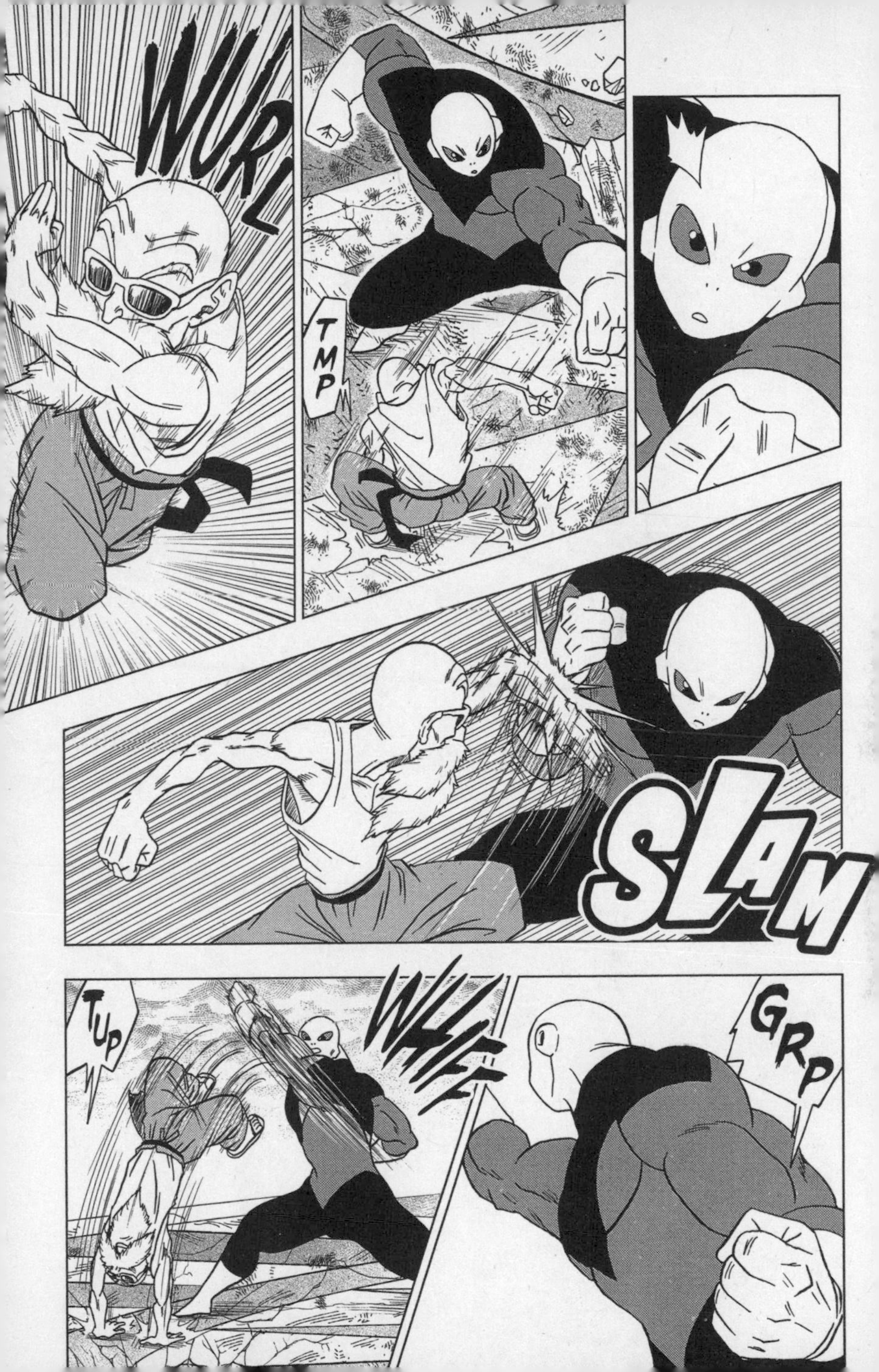
TMP
WURL
SLAM
GRP
WHF
TUP

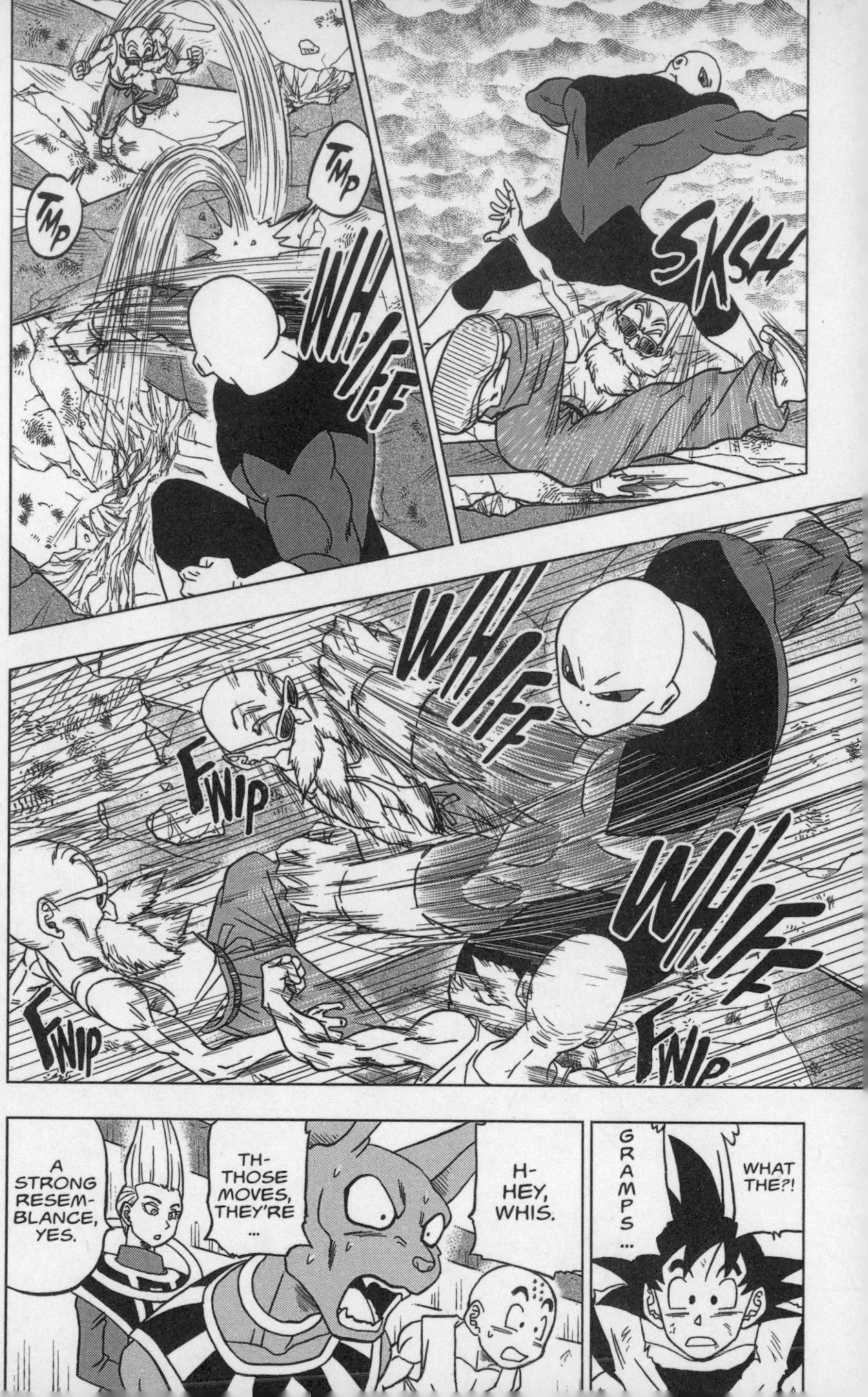
SKSH
TMP
TMP
WHIFF
WHIFF
FWIP
WHIFF
FWIP
FWIP
WHAT THE?!
GRAMPS...
H- HEY, WHIS.
TH- THOSE MOVES, THEY'RE ...
A STRONG RESEMBLANCE, YES.

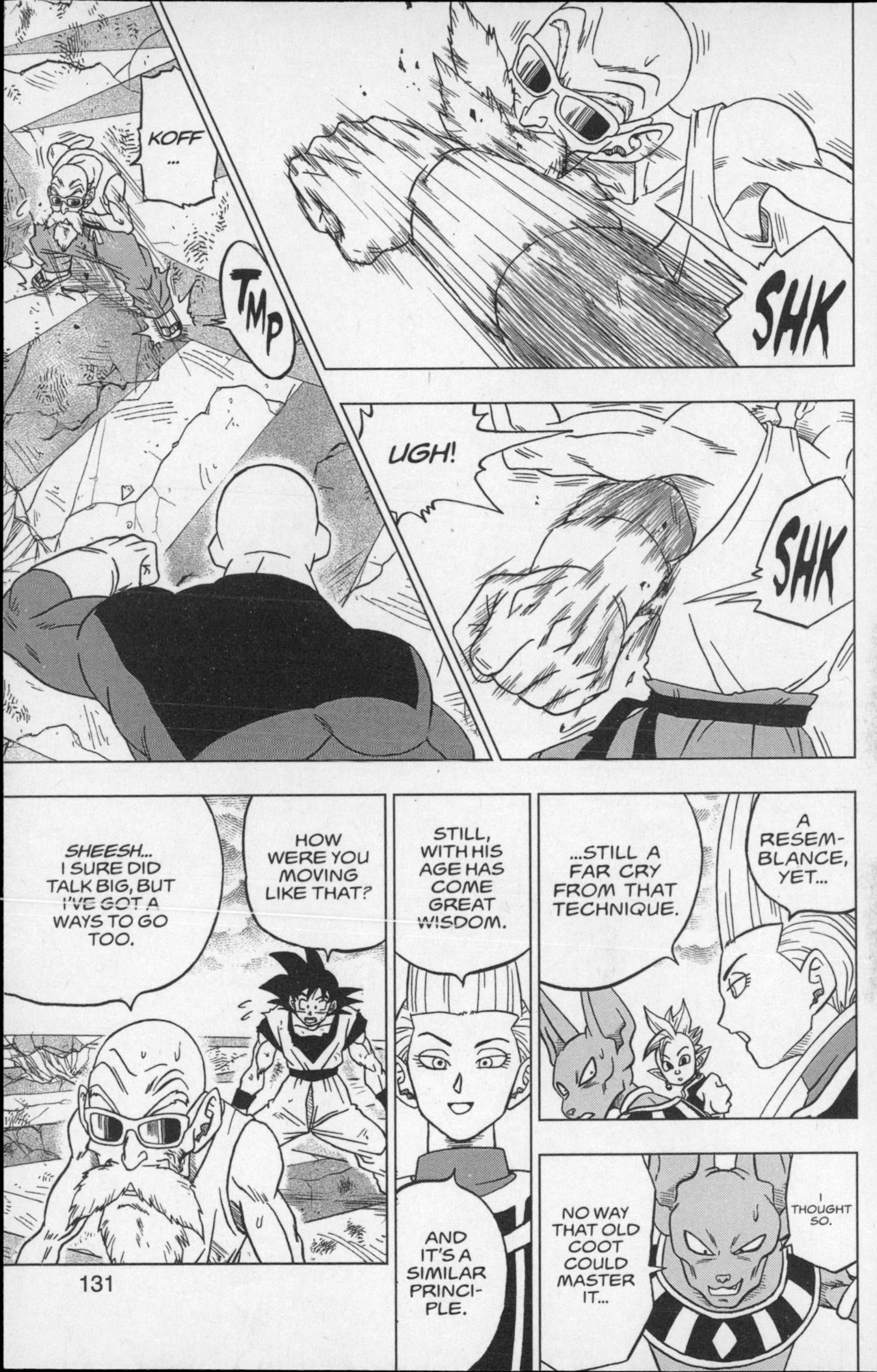
SHK
UGH!
SHK
KOFF ...
TMP
A RESEMBLANCE, YET...
...STILL A FAR CRY FROM THAT TECHNIQUE.
I THOUGHT SO.
NO WAY THAT OLD COOT COULD MASTER IT...
STILL, WITH HIS AGE HAS COME GREAT WISDOM.
AND IT'S A SIMILAR PRINCIPLE.
HOW WERE YOU MOVING LIKE THAT?
SHEESH... I SURE DID TALK BIG, BUT I'VE GOT A WAYS TO GO TOO.

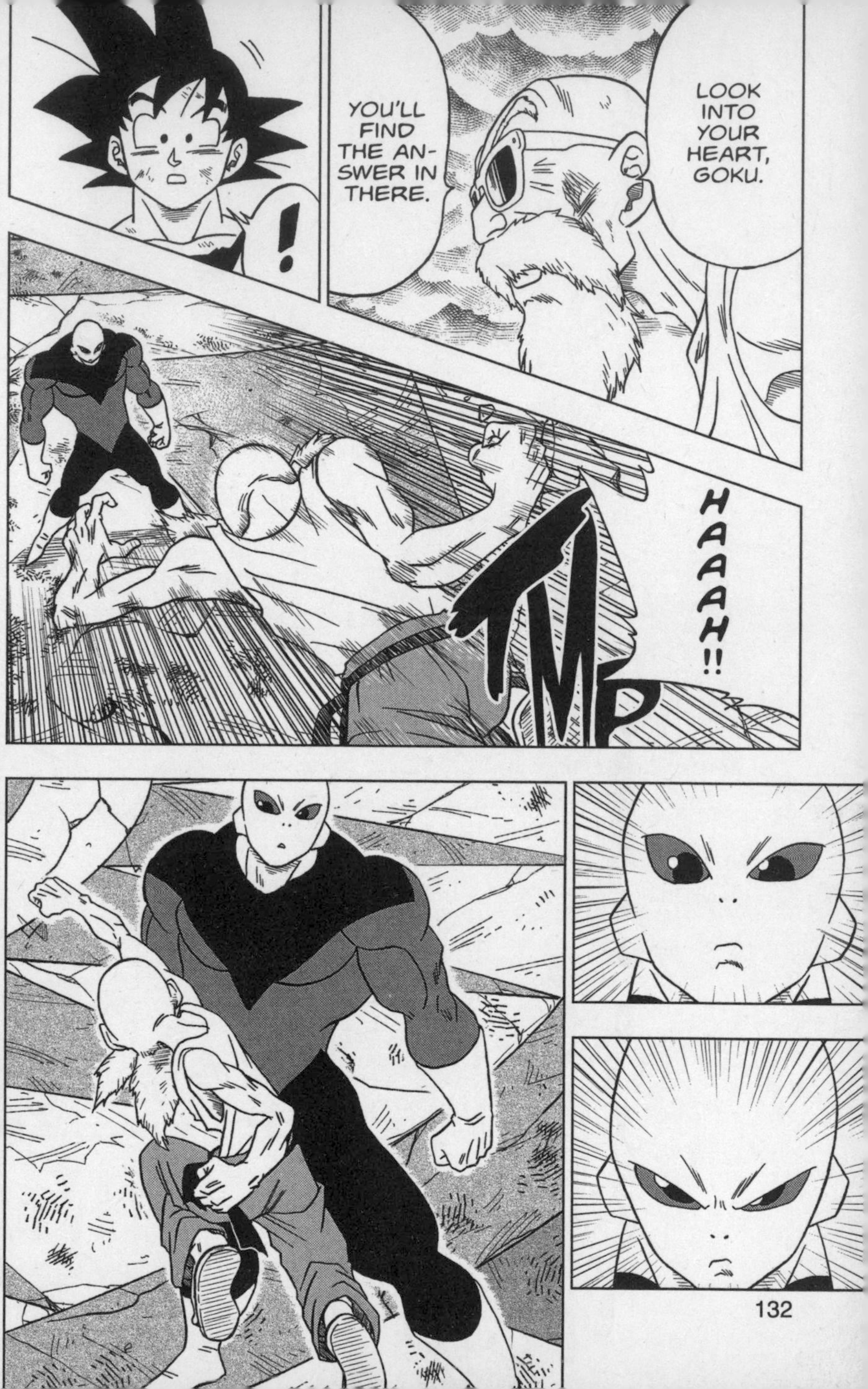
LOOK INTO YOUR HEART, GOKU.
YOU'LL FIND THE AN- SWER IN THERE.
!
HAAAAH!!
TMP

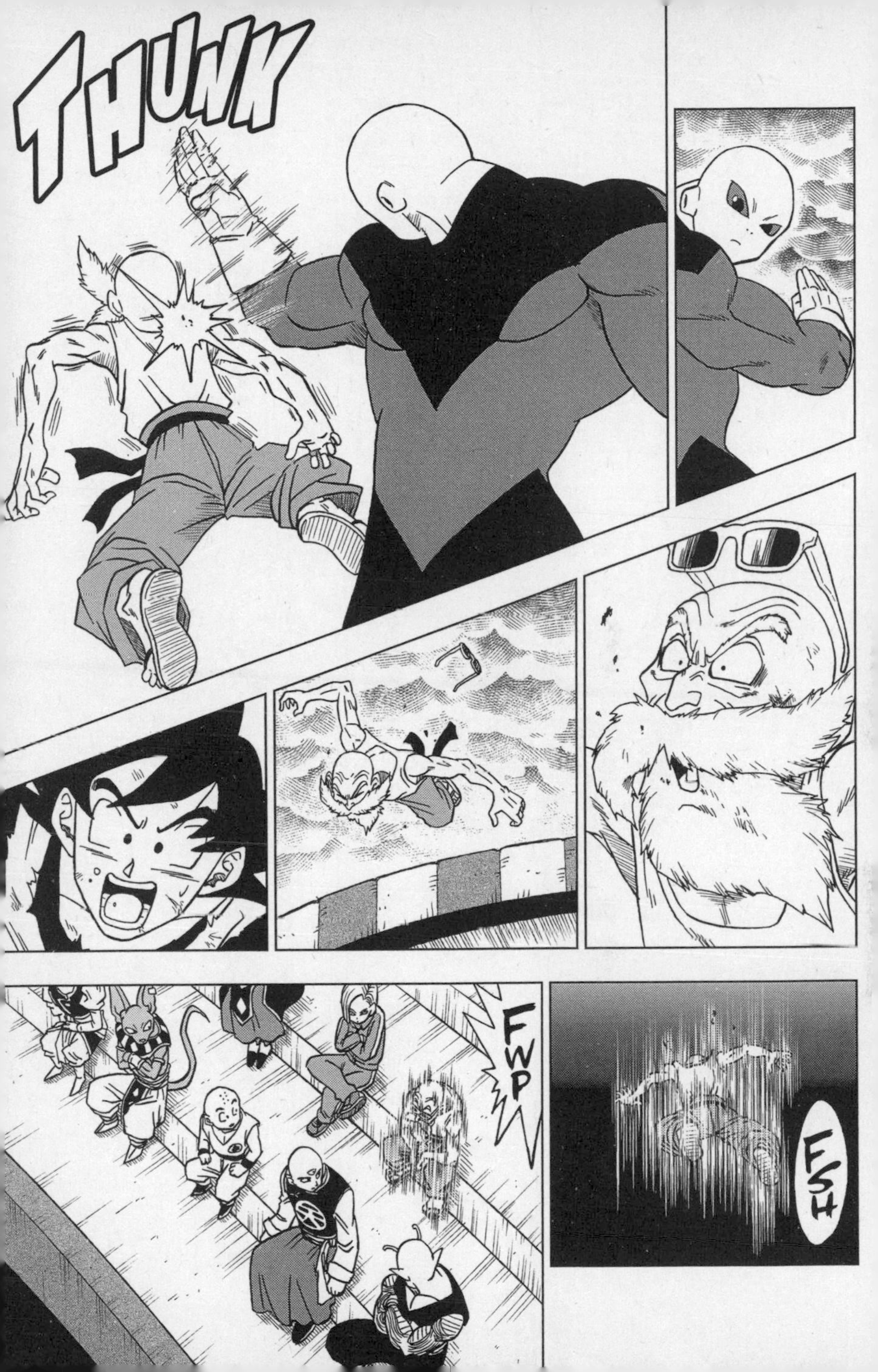
THUNK
FWP
FSH

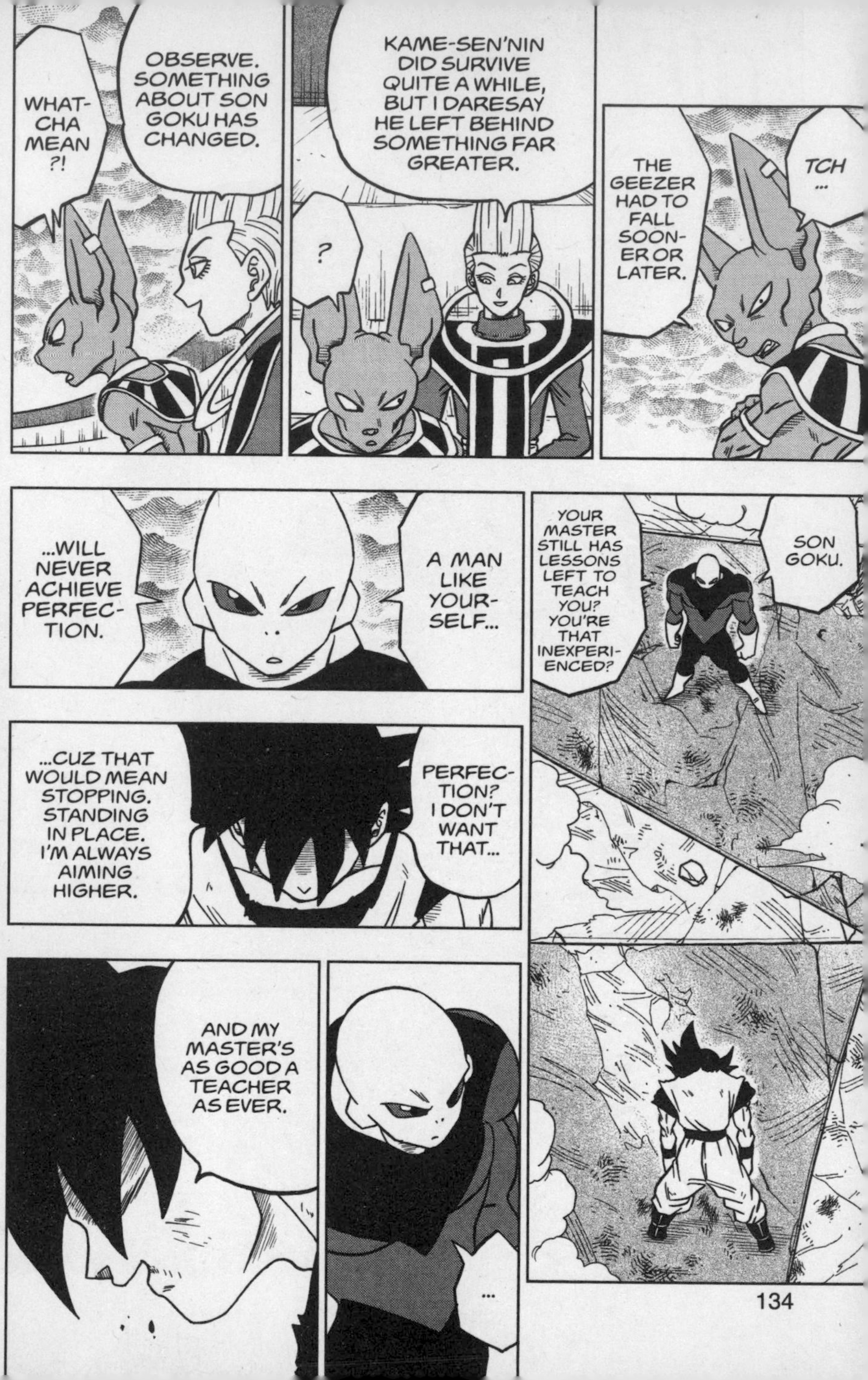
TCH...
THE GEEZER HAD TO FALL SOONER OR LATER.
KAME-SEN'NIN DID SURVIVE QUITE A WHILE, BUT I DARESAY HE LEFT BEHIND SOMETHING FAR GREATER.
?
OBSERVE. SOMETHING ABOUT SON GOKU HAS CHANGED.
WHAT-CHA MEAN?!
SON GOKU.
YOUR MASTER STILL HAS LESSONS LEFT TO TEACH YOU? YOU'RE THAT INEXPERIENCED?
A MAN LIKE YOURSELF...
...WILL NEVER ACHIEVE PERFECTION.
PERFECTION? I DON'T WANT THAT...
...CUZ THAT WOULD MEAN STOPPING. STANDING IN PLACE. I'M ALWAYS AIMING HIGHER.
AND MY MASTER'S AS GOOD A TEACHER AS EVER.
...

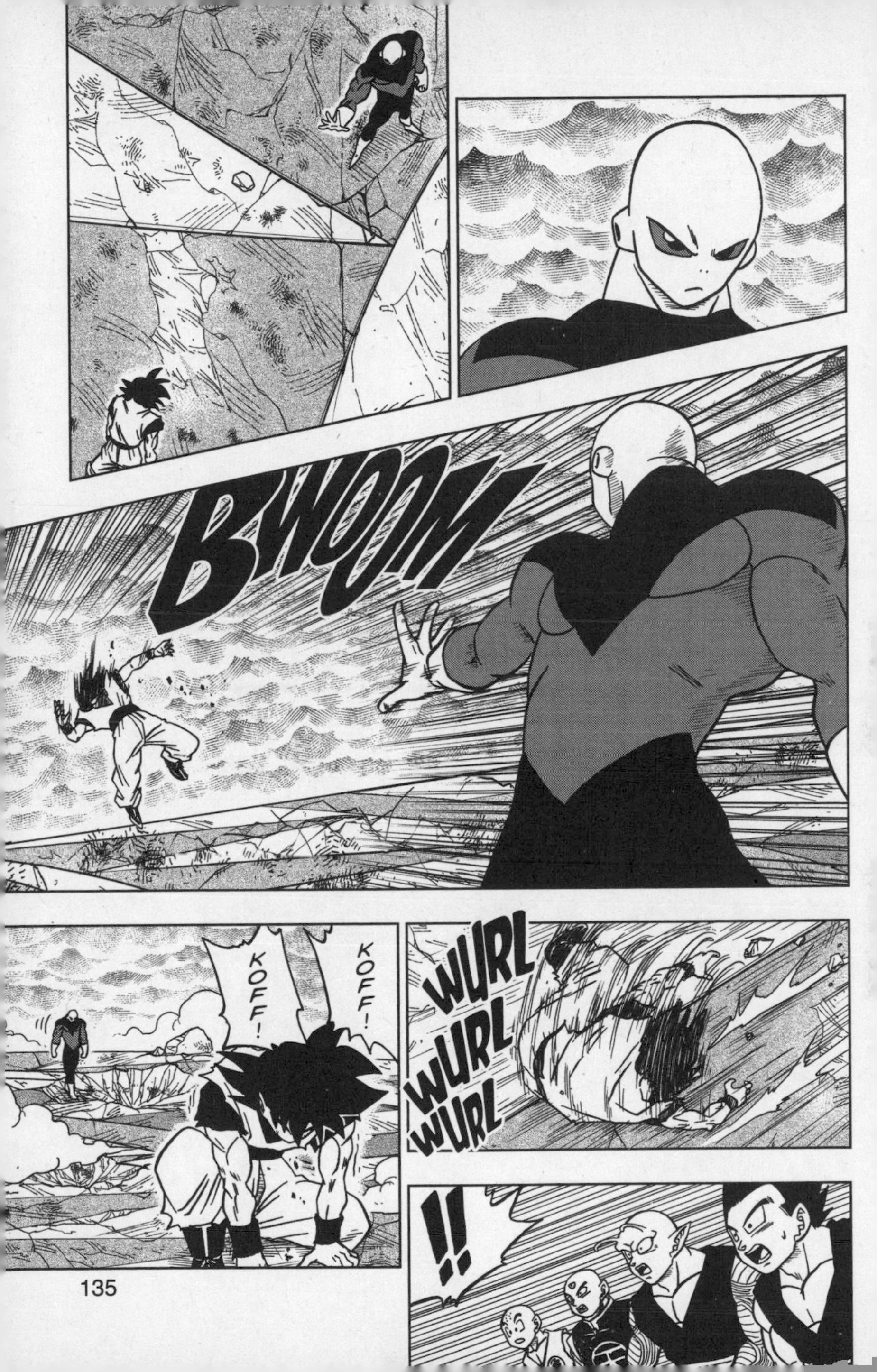

BWOOM
WURL WURL WURL
!!
KOFF!
KOFF!

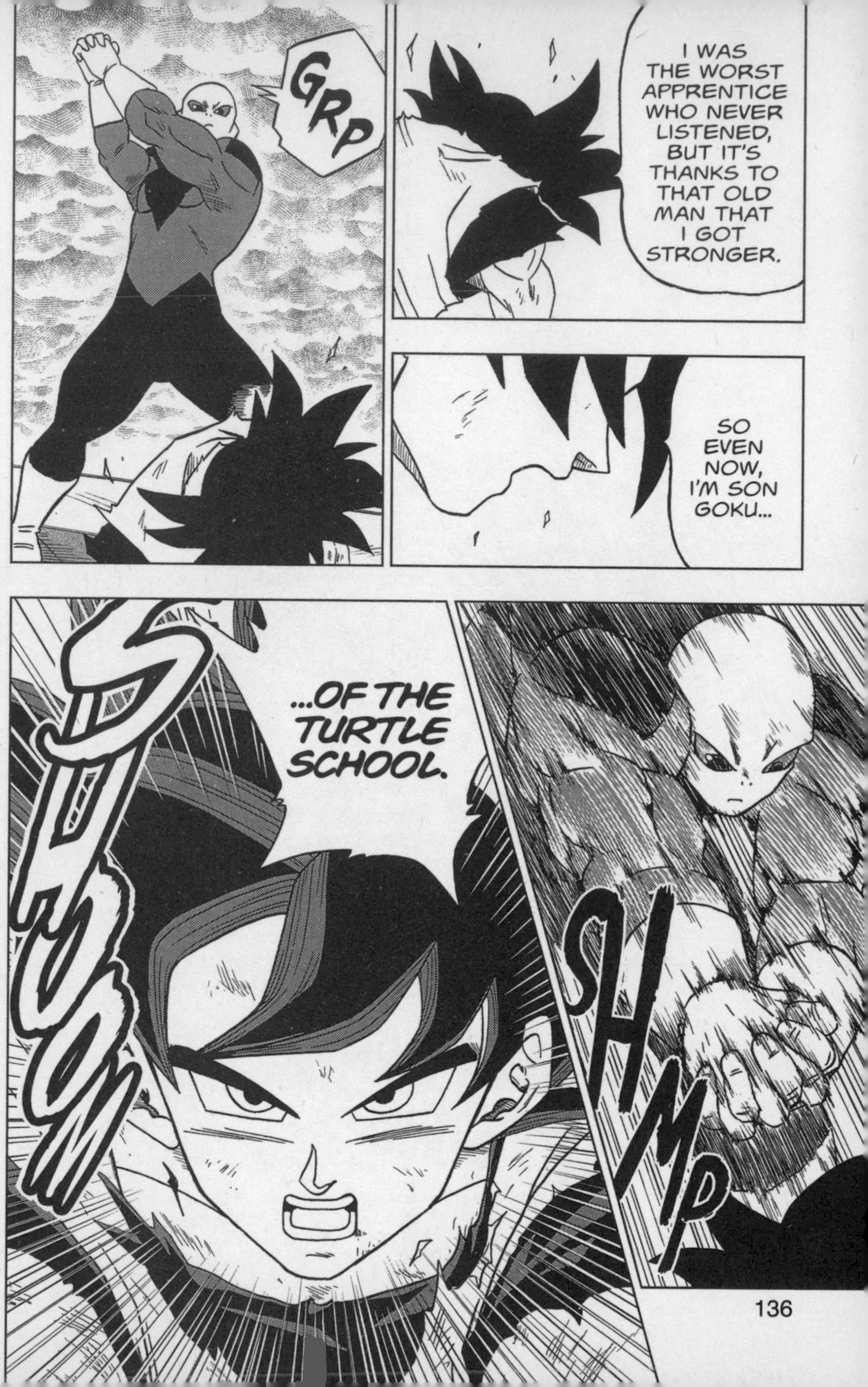
I WAS THE WORST APPRENTICE WHO NEVER LISTENED, BUT IT'S THANKS TO THAT OLD MAN THAT I GOT STRONGER.
SO EVEN NOW, I'M SON GOKU...
GRP
SHMP
...OF THE TURTLE SCHOOL.

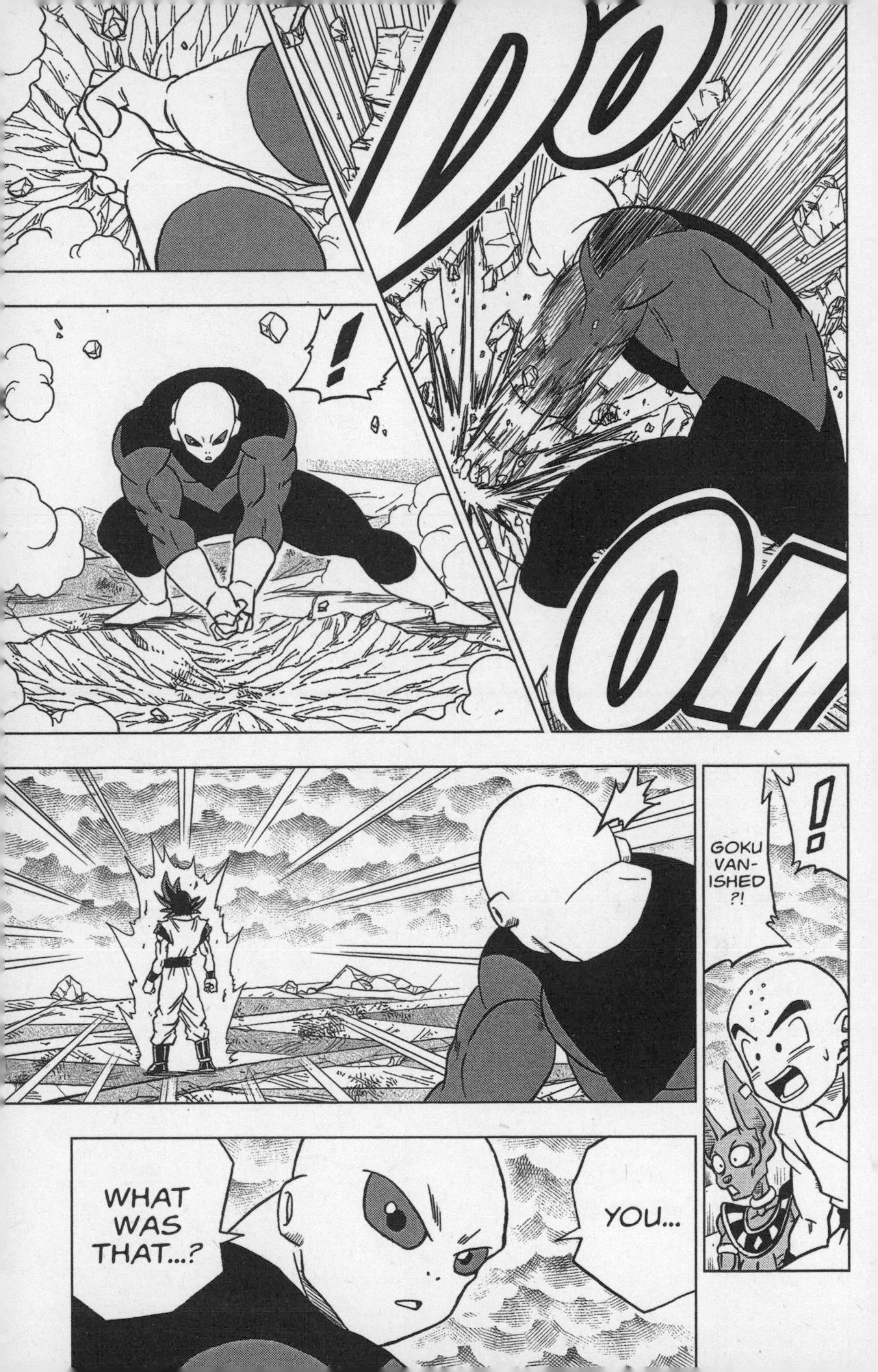
DOOM
!
!
GOKU VANISHED ?!
YOU...
WHAT WAS THAT...?

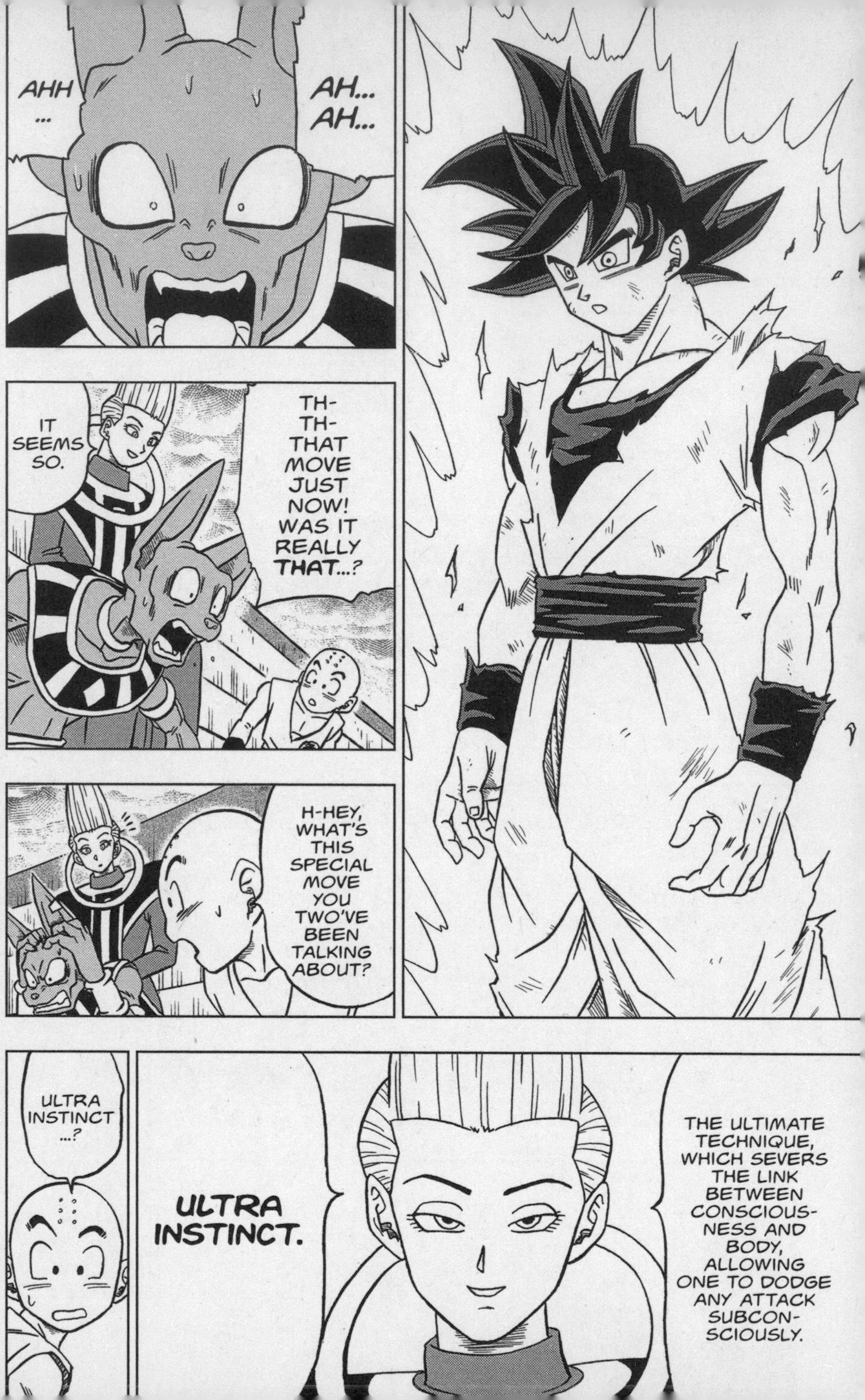
AH... AH...
AHH ...
TH-TH-THAT MOVE JUST NOW! WAS IT REALLY THAT...?
IT SEEMS SO.
H-HEY, WHAT'S THIS SPECIAL MOVE YOU TWO'VE BEEN TALKING ABOUT?
THE ULTIMATE TECHNIQUE, WHICH SEVERS THE LINK BETWEEN CONSCIOUSNESS AND BODY, ALLOWING ONE TO DODGE ANY ATTACK SUBCONSCIOUSLY.
ULTRA INSTINCT.
ULTRA INSTINCT ...?

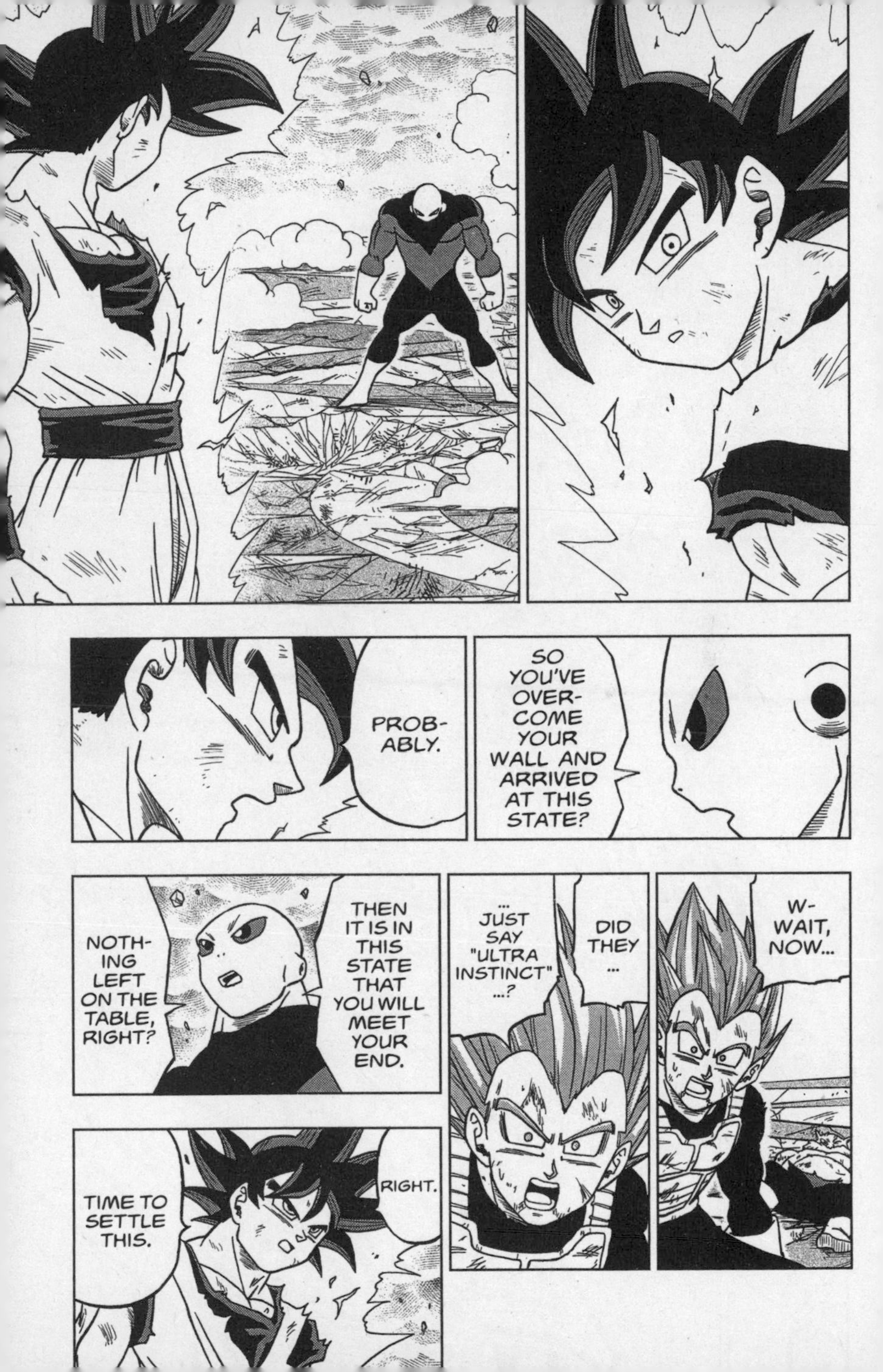
SO YOU'VE OVERCOME YOUR WALL AND ARRIVED AT THIS STATE?
PROBABLY.
W-WAIT, NOW...
DID THEY ...
... JUST SAY "ULTRA INSTINCT" ...?
THEN IT IS IN THIS STATE THAT YOU WILL MEET YOUR END.
NOTHING LEFT ON THE TABLE, RIGHT?
RIGHT.
TIME TO SETTLE THIS.

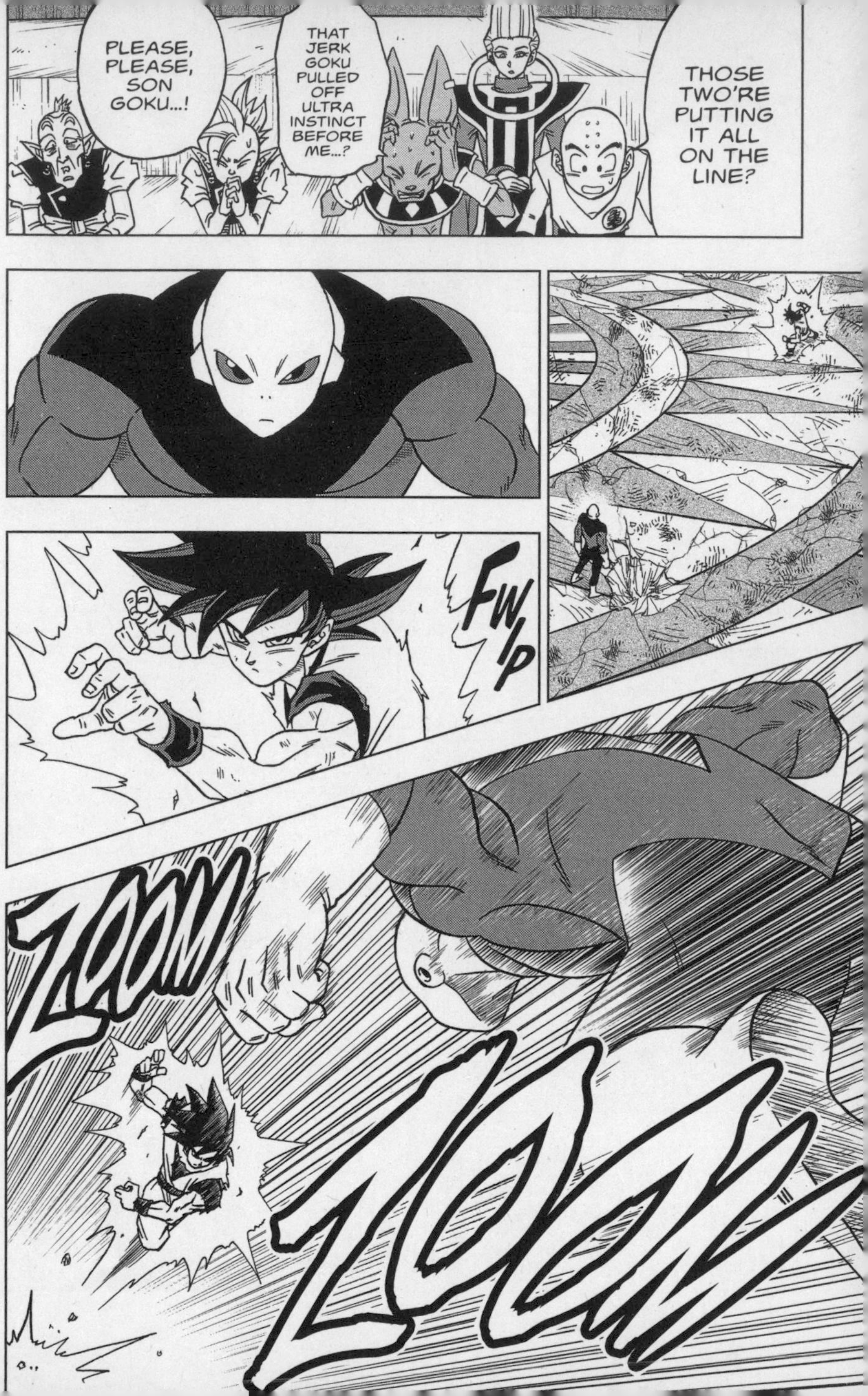
THOSE TWO'RE PUTTING IT ALL ON THE LINE?
THAT JERK GOKU PULLED OFF ULTRA INSTINCT BEFORE ME...?
PLEASE, PLEASE, SON GOKU...!
FWIP
ZOOM
ZOOM

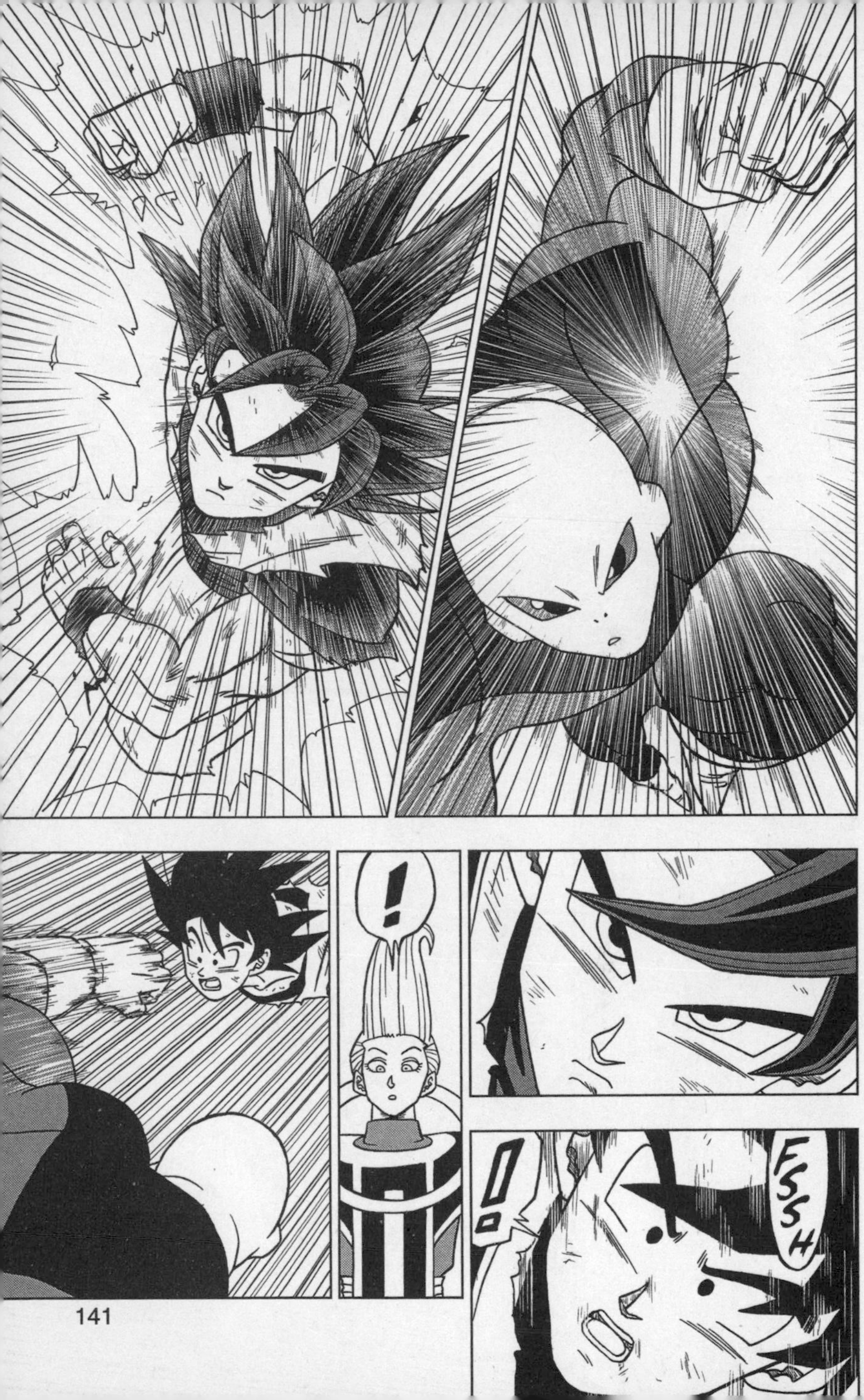
!
FSSH
!

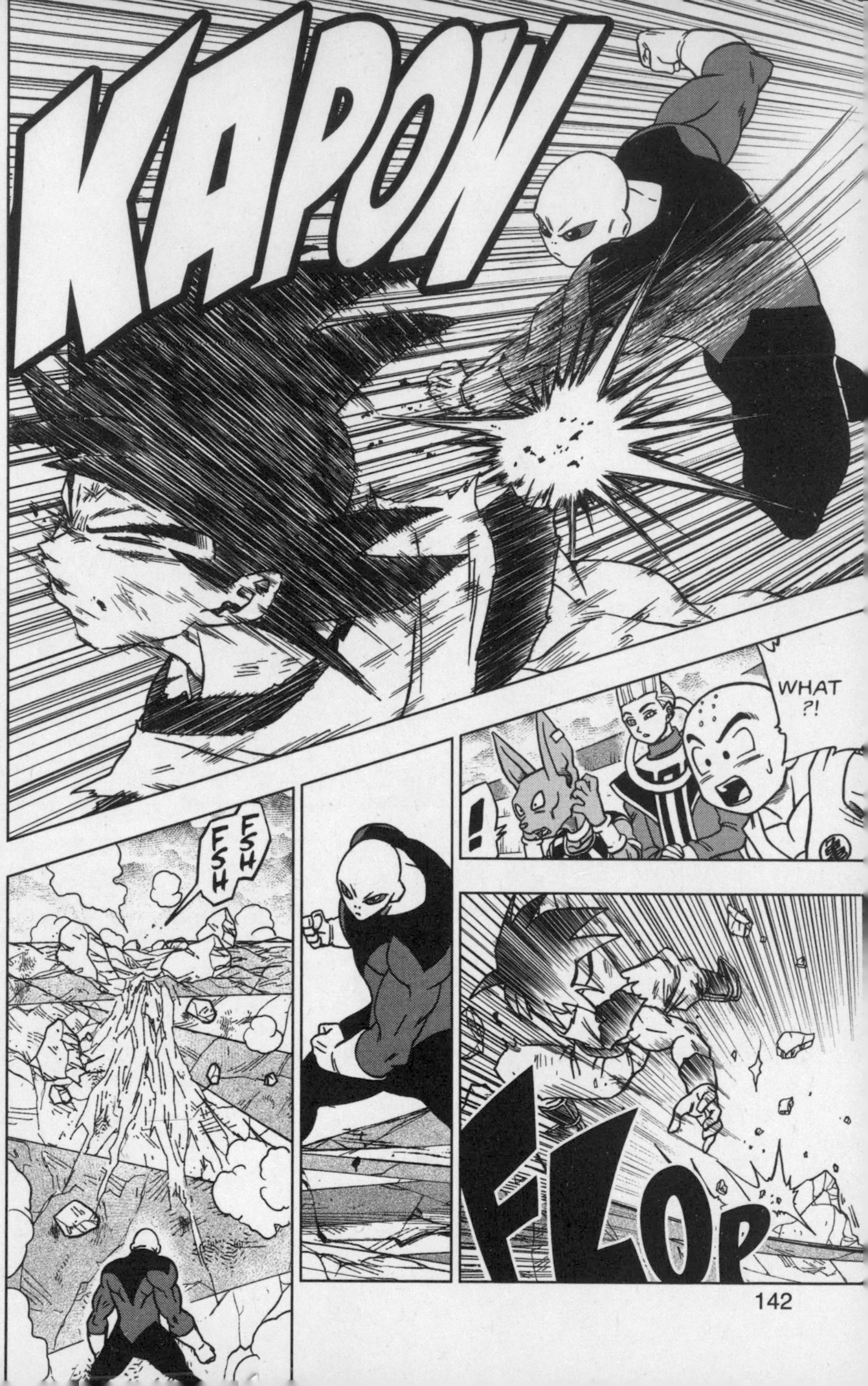
KAPOW
WHAT ?!
!
FLOP
FSH FSH

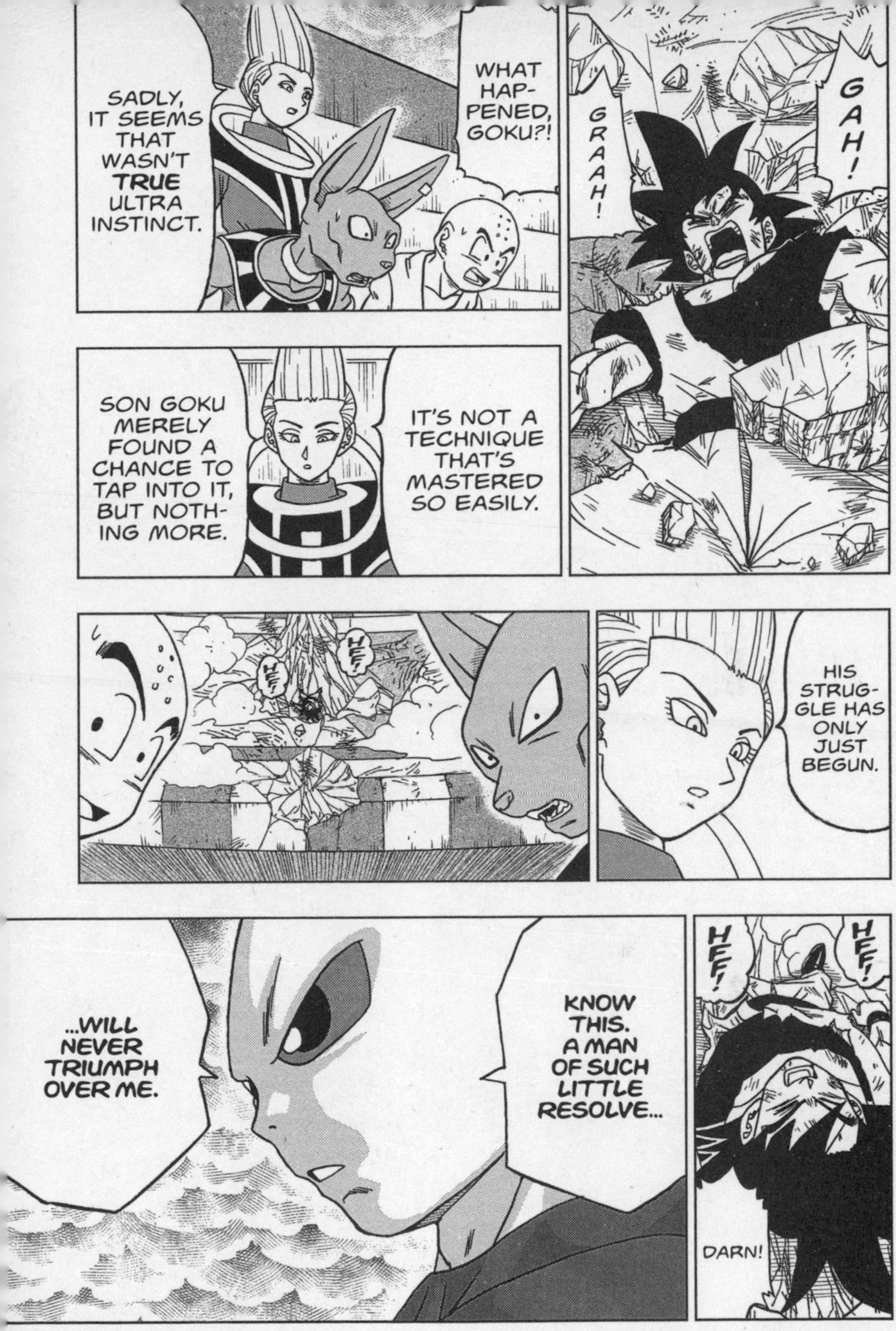
GAH!
GRAAAH!
WHAT HAP-PENED, GOKU?!
SADLY, IT SEEMS THAT WASN'T **TRUE** ULTRA INSTINCT.
IT'S NOT A TECHNIQUE THAT'S MASTERED SO EASILY.
SON GOKU MERELY FOUND A CHANCE TO TAP INTO IT, BUT NOTH-ING MORE.
HIS STRUG-GLE HAS ONLY JUST BEGUN.
HEF!
HEF!
HEF!
HEF!
DARN!
KNOW THIS. A MAN OF SUCH LITTLE RESOLVE...
...WILL NEVER TRIUMPH OVER ME.

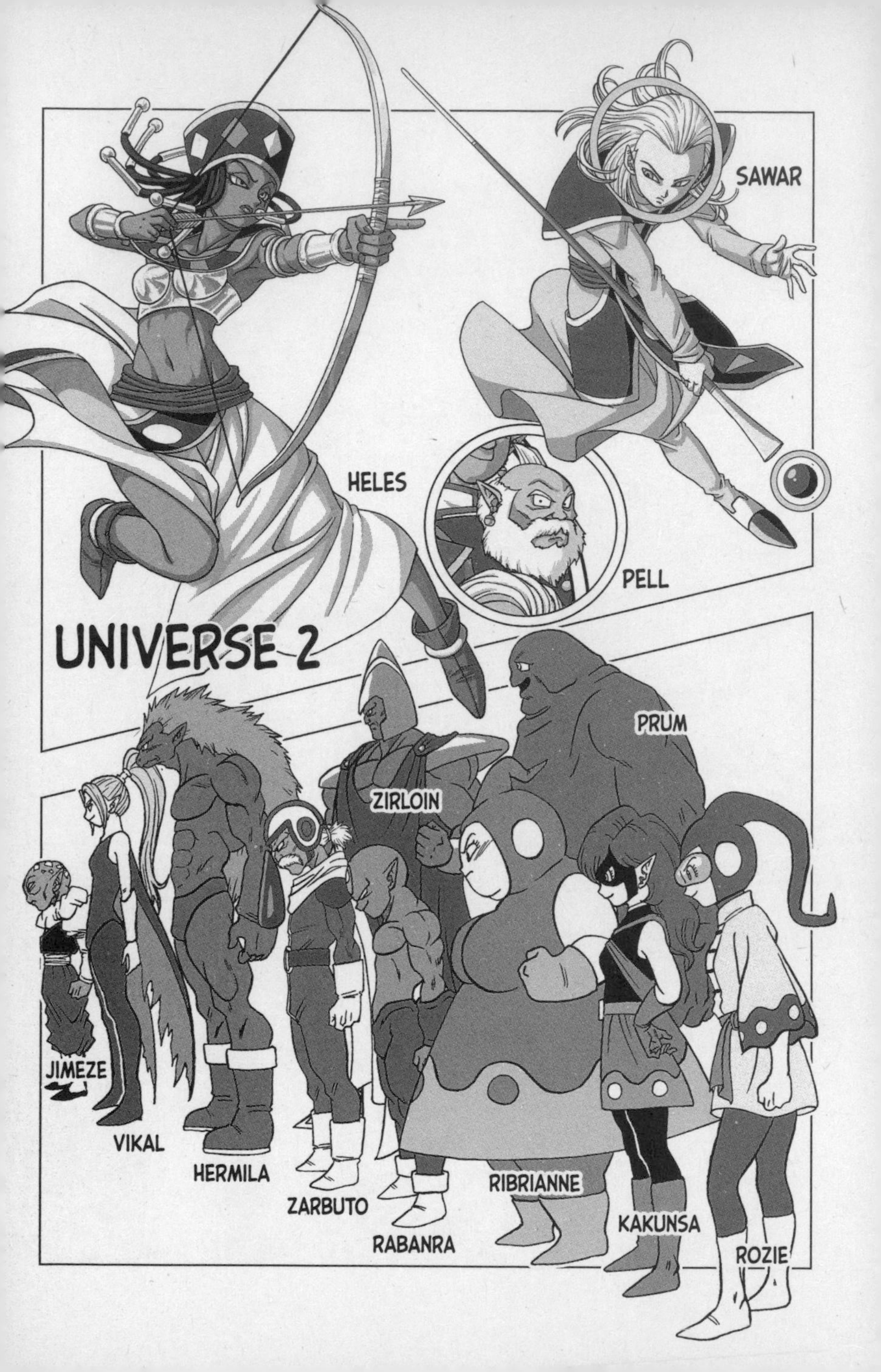
SAWAR
PELL
HELES
UNIVERSE 2
PRUM
ZIRLOIN
ROZIE
KAKUNSA
RIBRIANNE
RABANRA
ZARBUTO
HERMILA
VIKAL
JIMEZE

DRAGON BALL SUPER

CHAPTER 40: JIREN VS. UNIVERSE 7

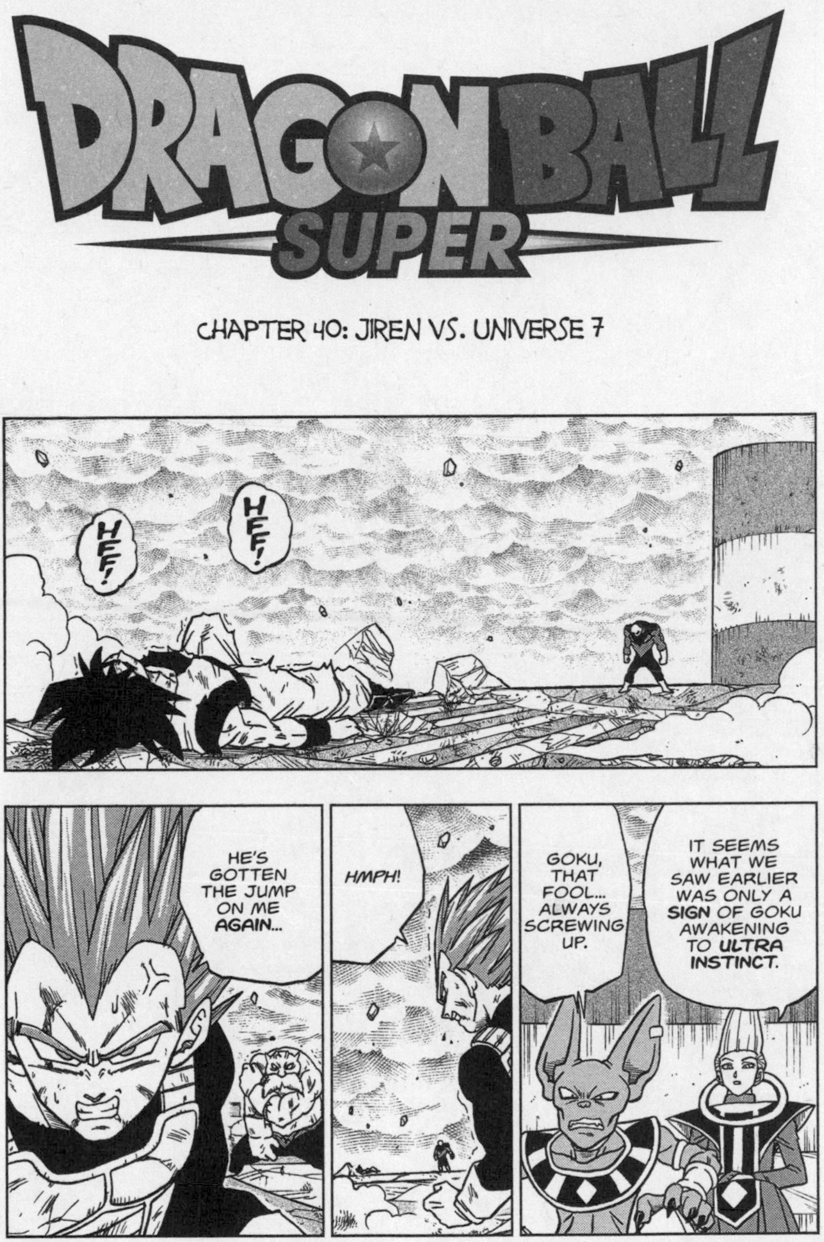
HEF!
HEF!
IT SEEMS WHAT WE SAW EARLIER WAS ONLY A **SIGN** OF GOKU AWAKENING TO **ULTRA INSTINCT**.
GOKU, THAT FOOL... ALWAYS SCREWING UP.
HMPH!
HE'S GOTTEN THE JUMP ON ME **AGAIN**...

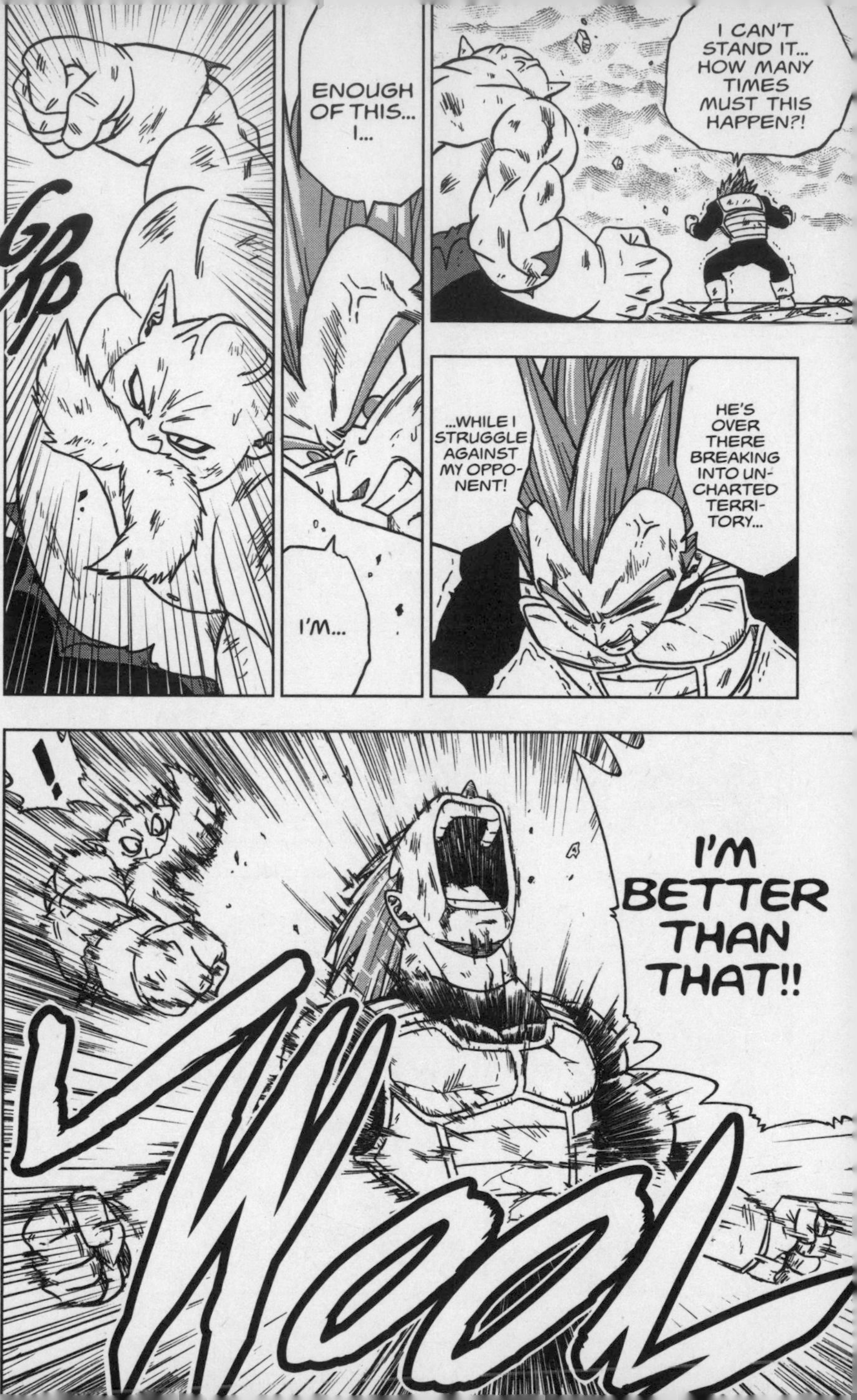
I CAN'T STAND IT... HOW MANY TIMES MUST THIS HAPPEN?!
HE'S OVER THERE BREAKING INTO UNCHARTED TERRITORY...
...WHILE I STRUGGLE AGAINST MY OPPONENT!
ENOUGH OF THIS... I...
I'M...
GRP
I'M BETTER THAN THAT!!
!

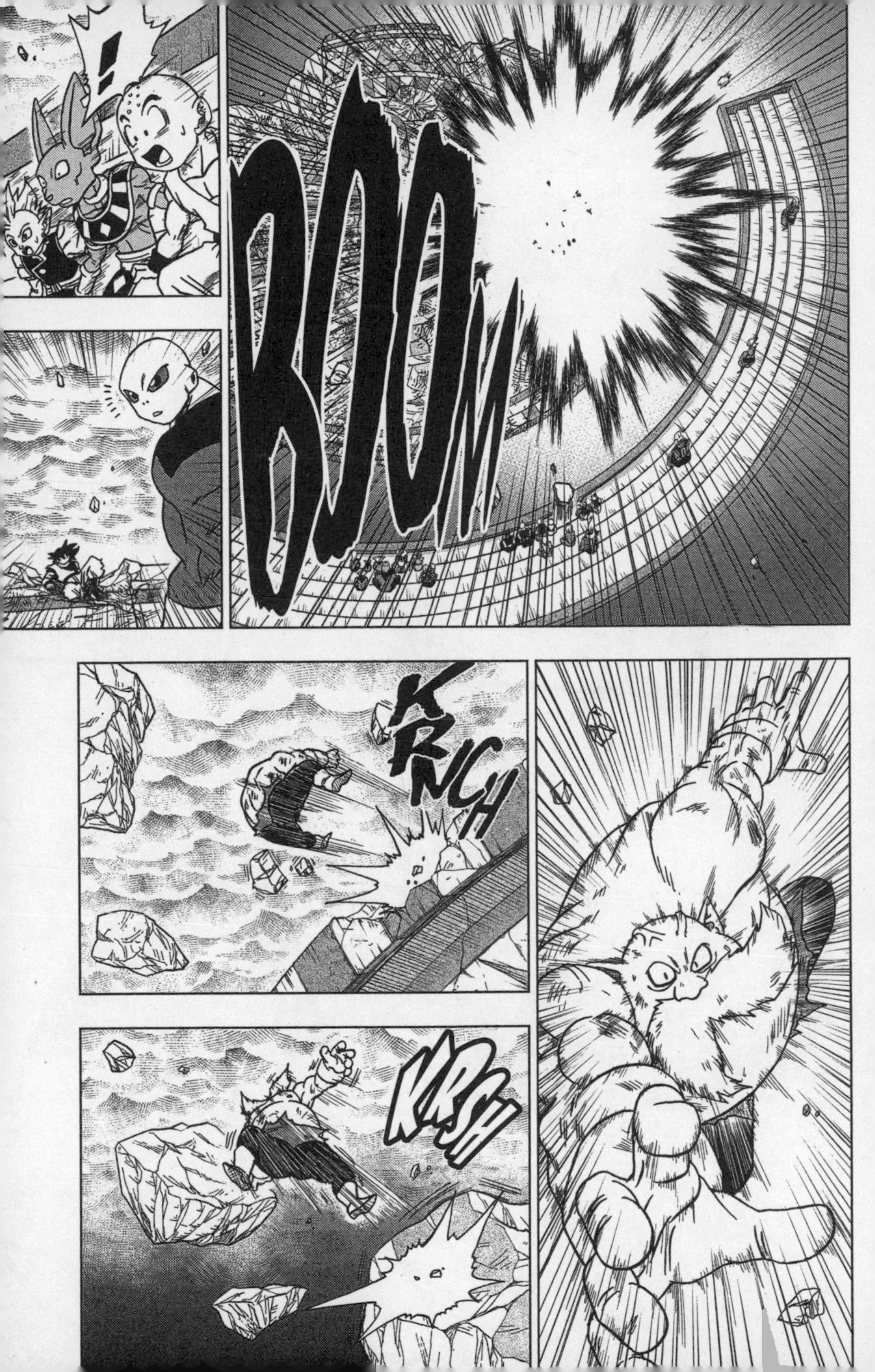

!
BOOM
KRNCH
KRSH

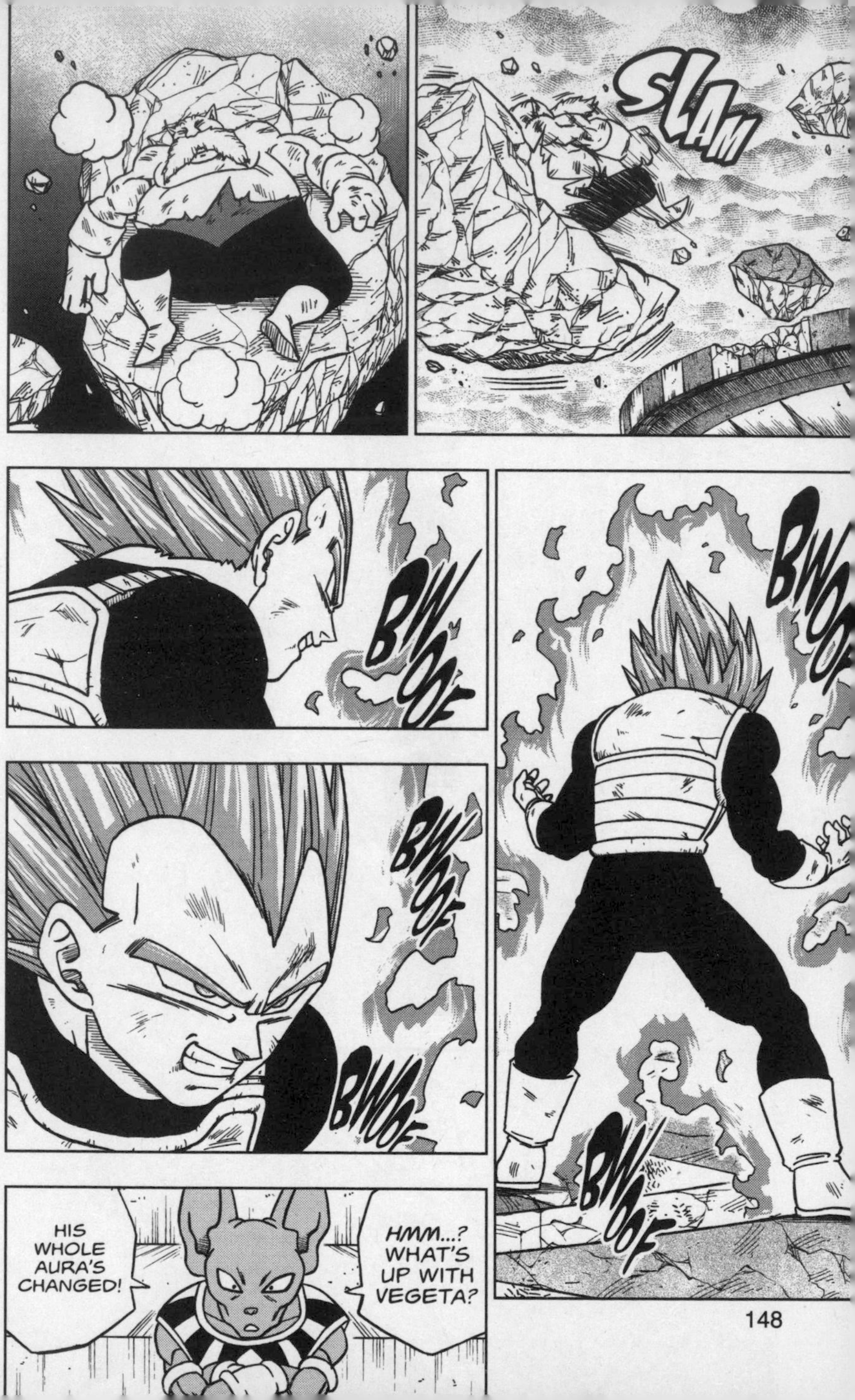

SLAM
BWOOF
BWOOF
BWOOF
BWOOF
BWOOF
HMM...? WHAT'S UP WITH VEGETA?
HIS WHOLE AURA'S CHANGED!

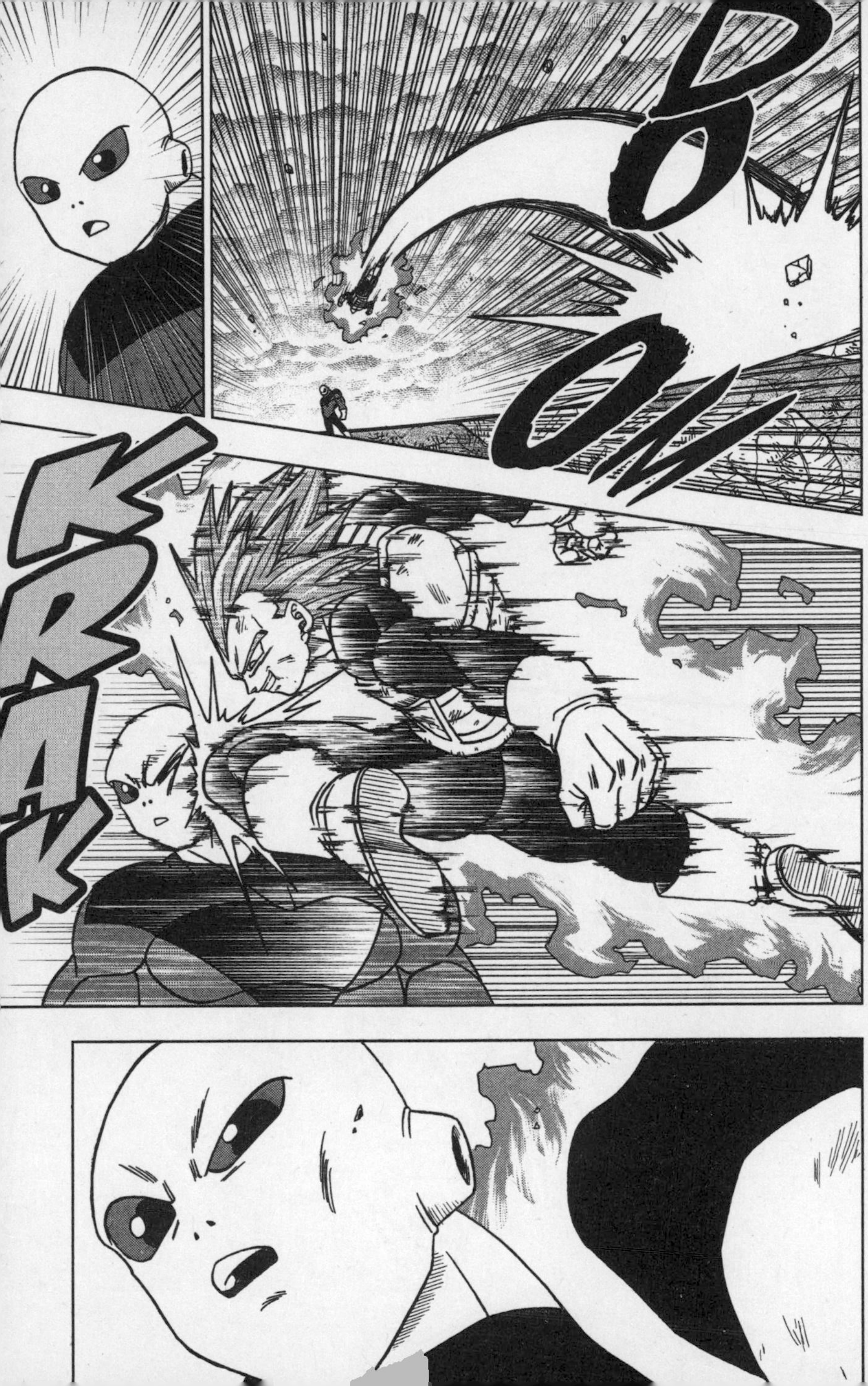
BOOM
KRAK

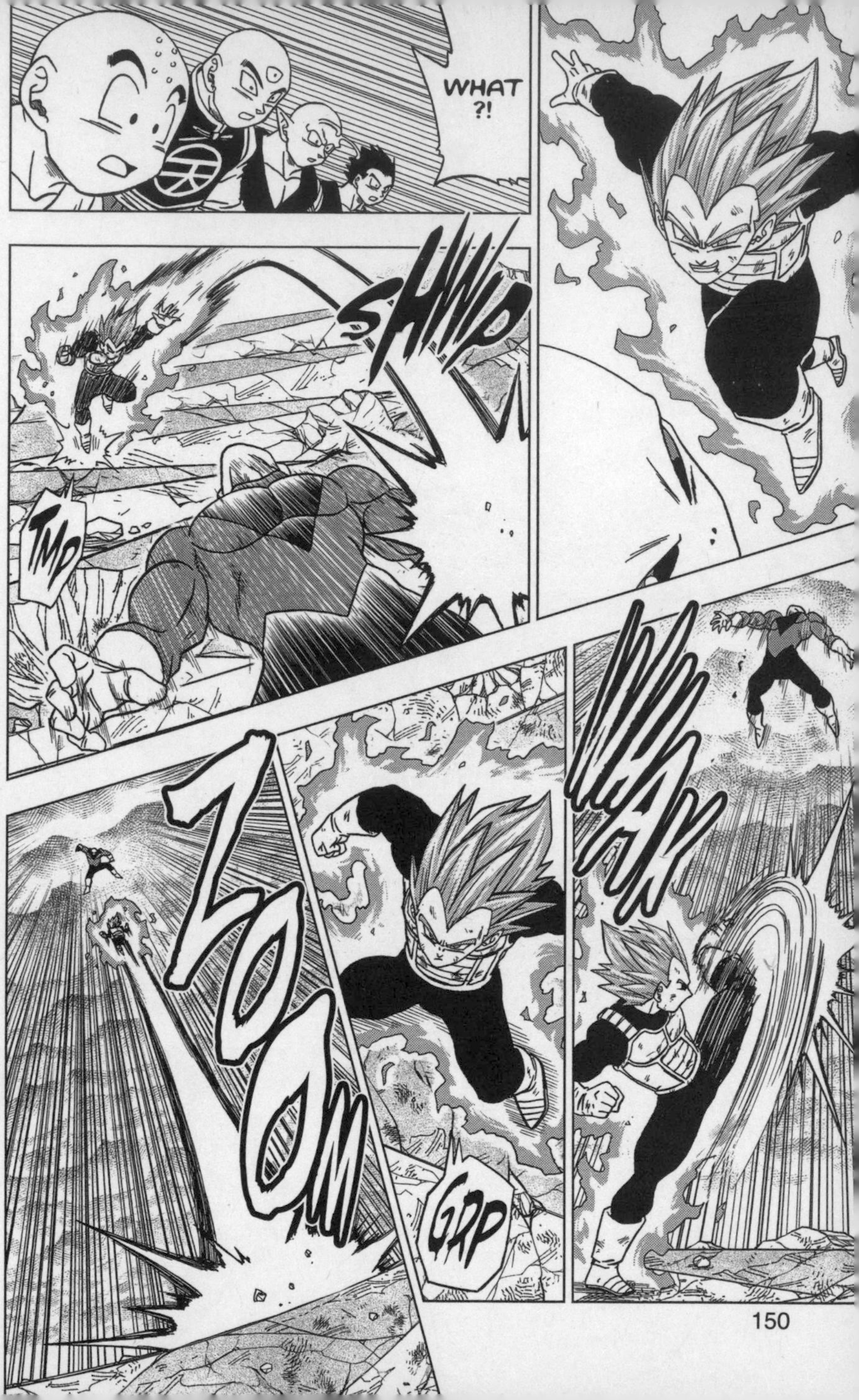
WHAT ?!
SHWP
TMP
WHAK
GRP
ZOOM

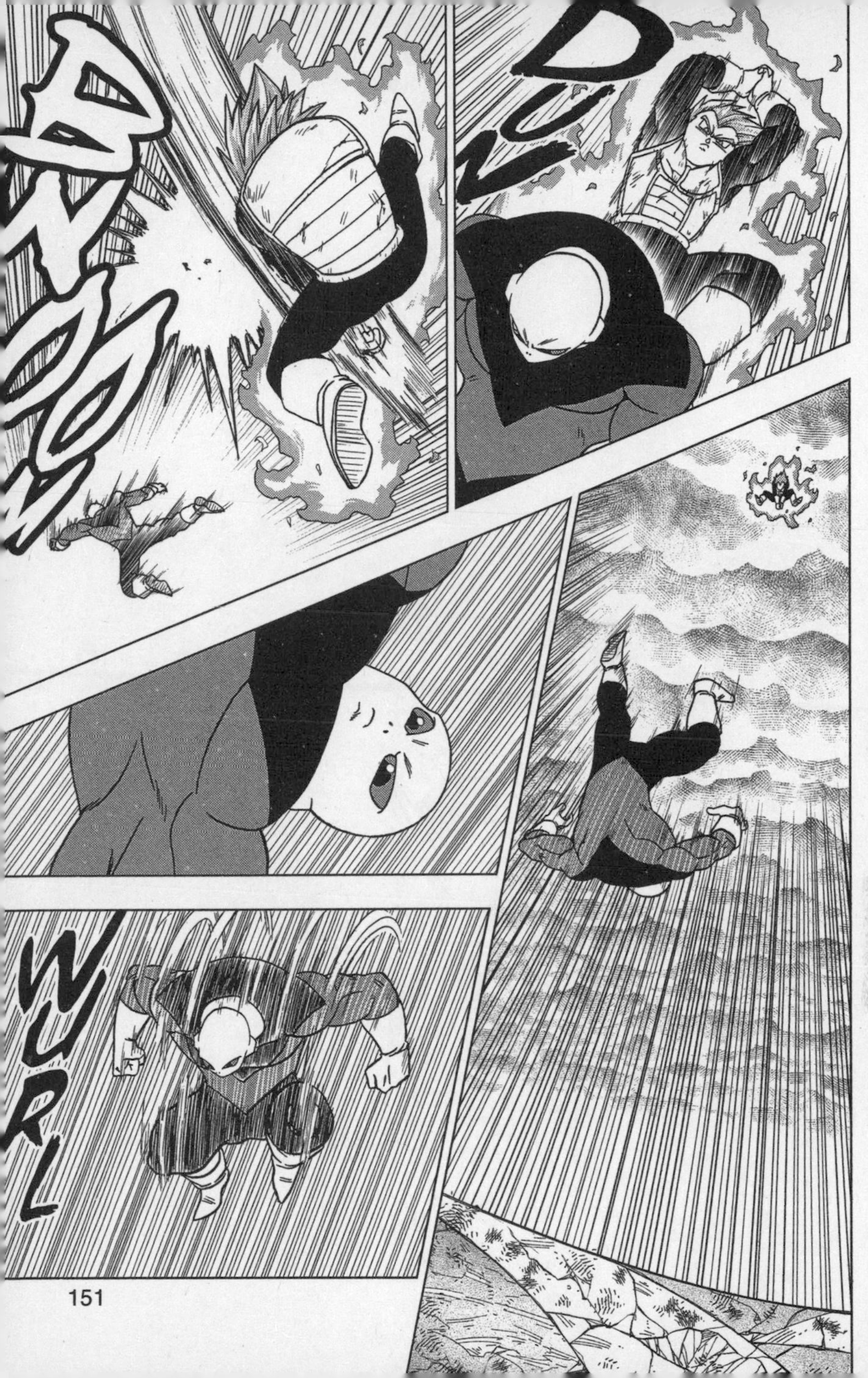
DUN
WURL

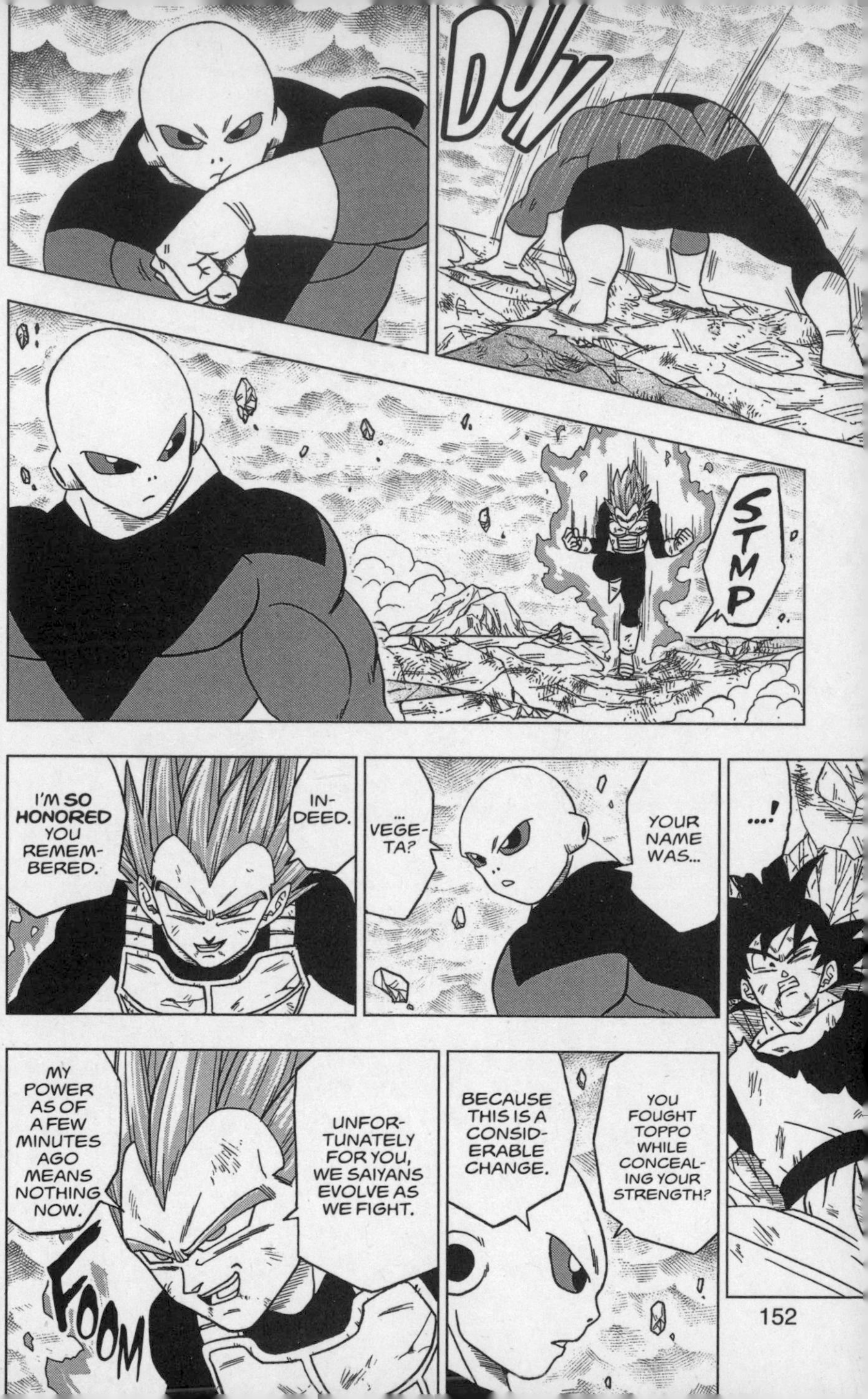
DUN
STMP
...!
YOUR NAME WAS...
...VEGETA?
INDEED.
I'M SO **HONORED** YOU REMEMBERED.
YOU FOUGHT TOPPO WHILE CONCEALING YOUR STRENGTH?
BECAUSE THIS IS A CONSIDERABLE CHANGE.
UNFORTUNATELY FOR YOU, WE SAIYANS EVOLVE AS WE FIGHT.
MY POWER AS OF A FEW MINUTES AGO MEANS NOTHING NOW.
FOOM

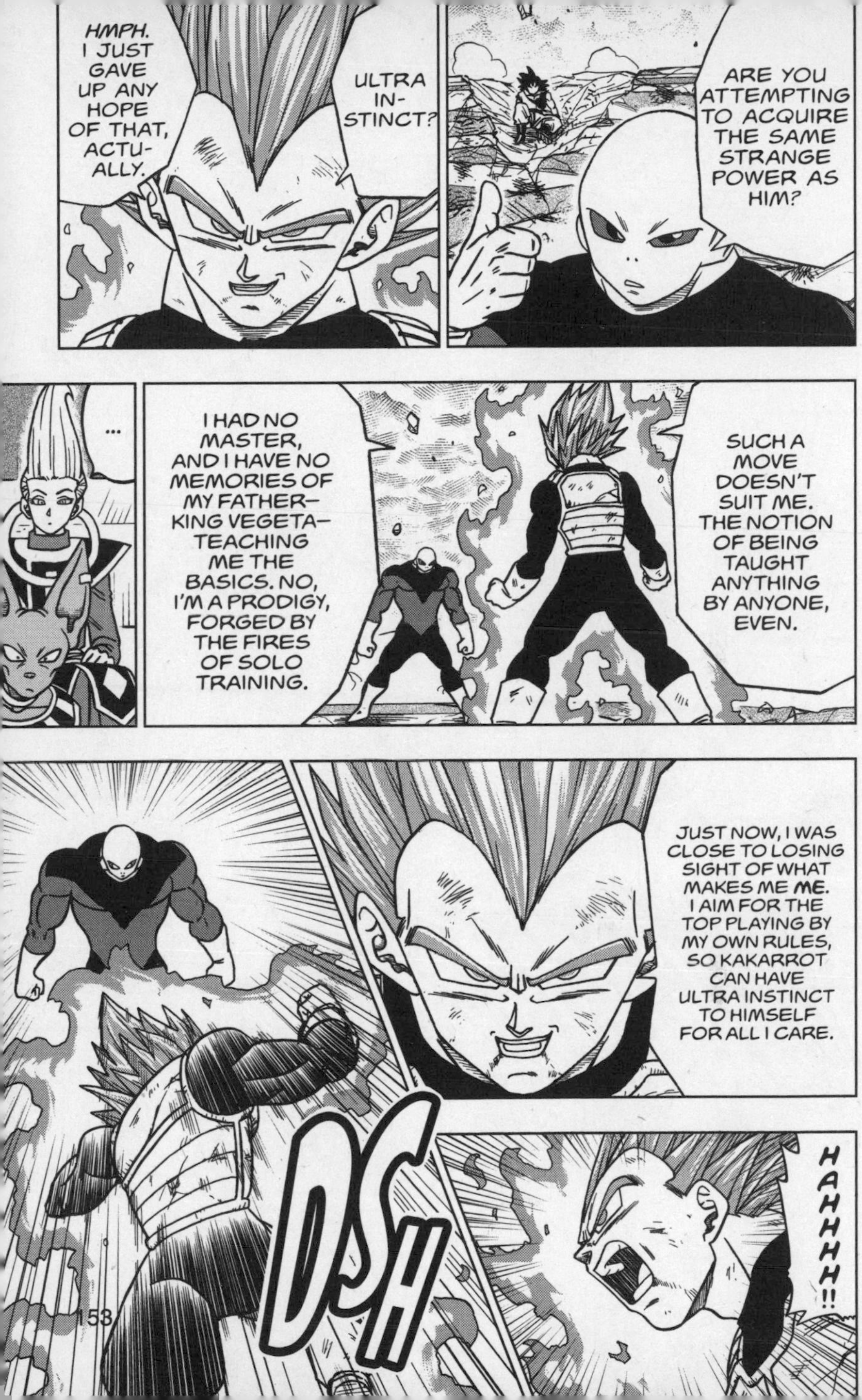
ARE YOU ATTEMPTING TO ACQUIRE THE SAME STRANGE POWER AS HIM?
ULTRA IN-STINCT?
HMPH. I JUST GAVE UP ANY HOPE OF THAT, ACTU-ALLY.
SUCH A MOVE DOESN'T SUIT ME. THE NOTION OF BEING TAUGHT ANYTHING BY ANYONE, EVEN.
I HAD NO MASTER, AND I HAVE NO MEMORIES OF MY FATHER—KING VEGETA—TEACHING ME THE BASICS. NO, I'M A PRODIGY, FORGED BY THE FIRES OF SOLO TRAINING.
...
JUST NOW, I WAS CLOSE TO LOSING SIGHT OF WHAT MAKES ME ME. I AIM FOR THE TOP PLAYING BY MY OWN RULES, SO KAKARROT CAN HAVE ULTRA INSTINCT TO HIMSELF FOR ALL I CARE.
HAHHHHH!!
DSH

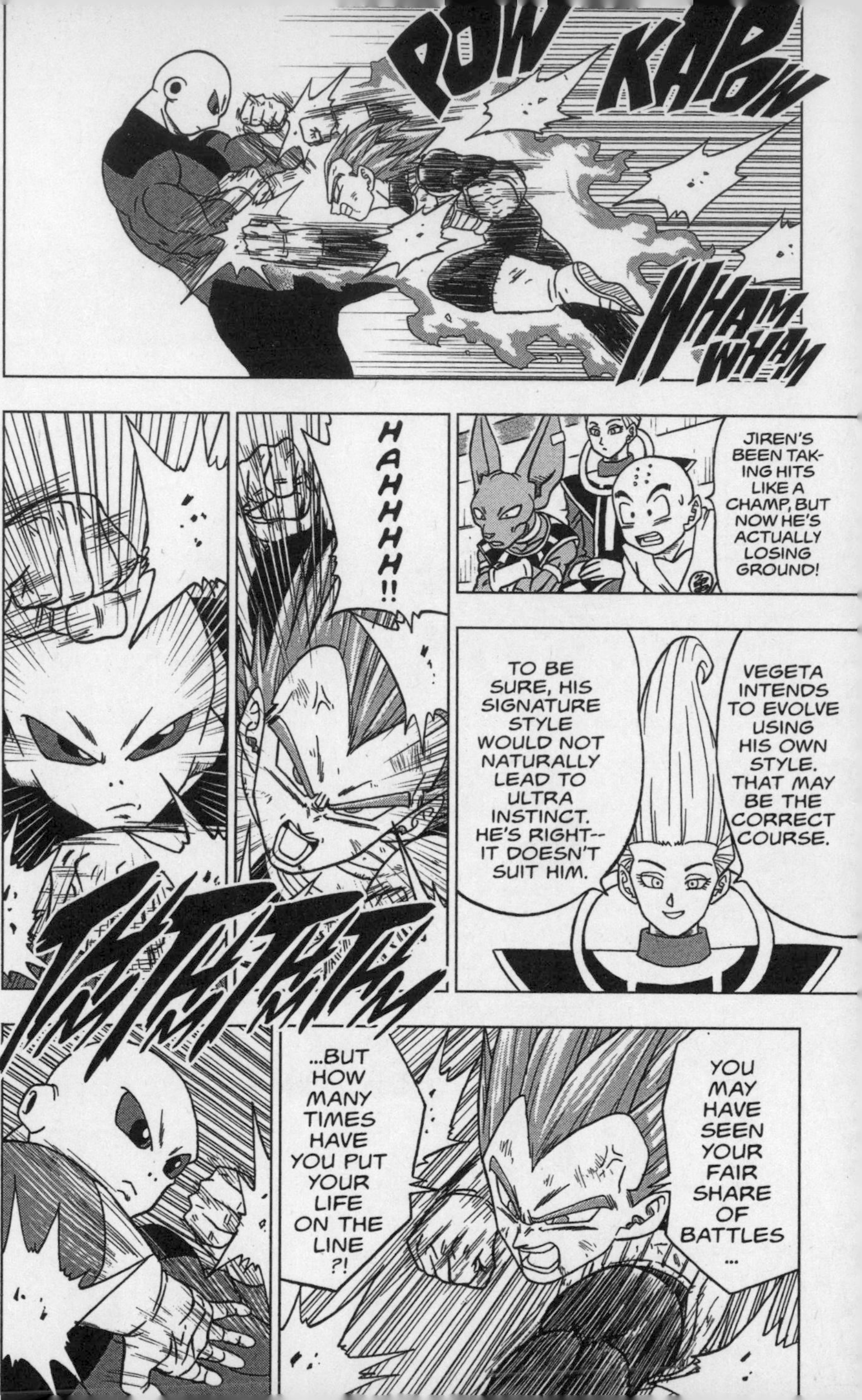
KAPOW
POW
WHAM WHAM
JIREN'S BEEN TAKING HITS LIKE A CHAMP, BUT NOW HE'S ACTUALLY LOSING GROUND!
VEGETA INTENDS TO EVOLVE USING HIS OWN STYLE. THAT MAY BE THE CORRECT COURSE.
TO BE SURE, HIS SIGNATURE STYLE WOULD NOT NATURALLY LEAD TO ULTRA INSTINCT. HE'S RIGHT-- IT DOESN'T SUIT HIM.
HAHHHHH!!
YOU MAY HAVE SEEN YOUR FAIR SHARE OF BATTLES...
...BUT HOW MANY TIMES HAVE YOU PUT YOUR LIFE ON THE LINE?!

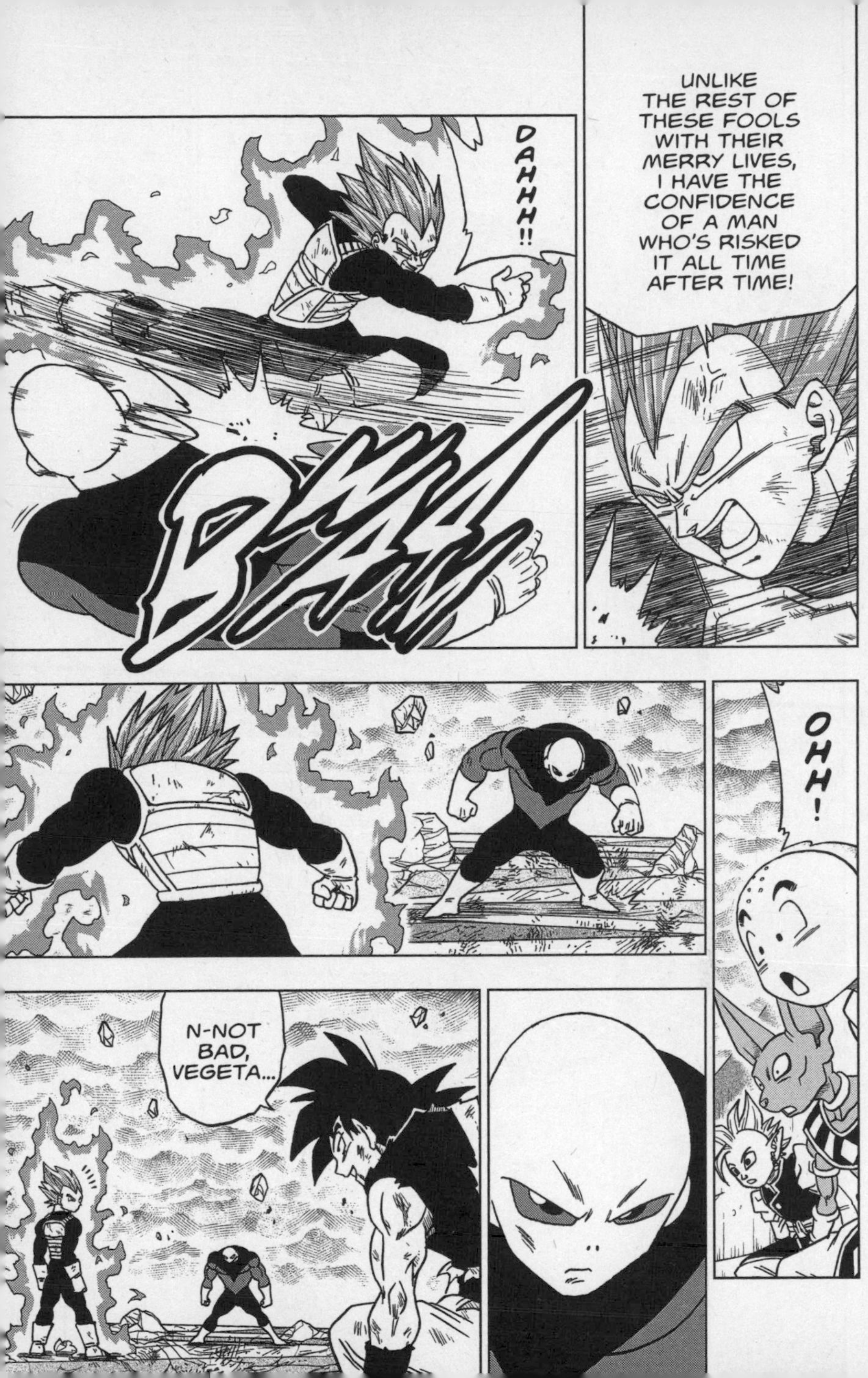
UNLIKE THE REST OF THESE FOOLS WITH THEIR MERRY LIVES, I HAVE THE CONFIDENCE OF A MAN WHO'S RISKED IT ALL TIME AFTER TIME!
DAHHHH!!
BAM
OHH!
N-NOT BAD, VEGETA...

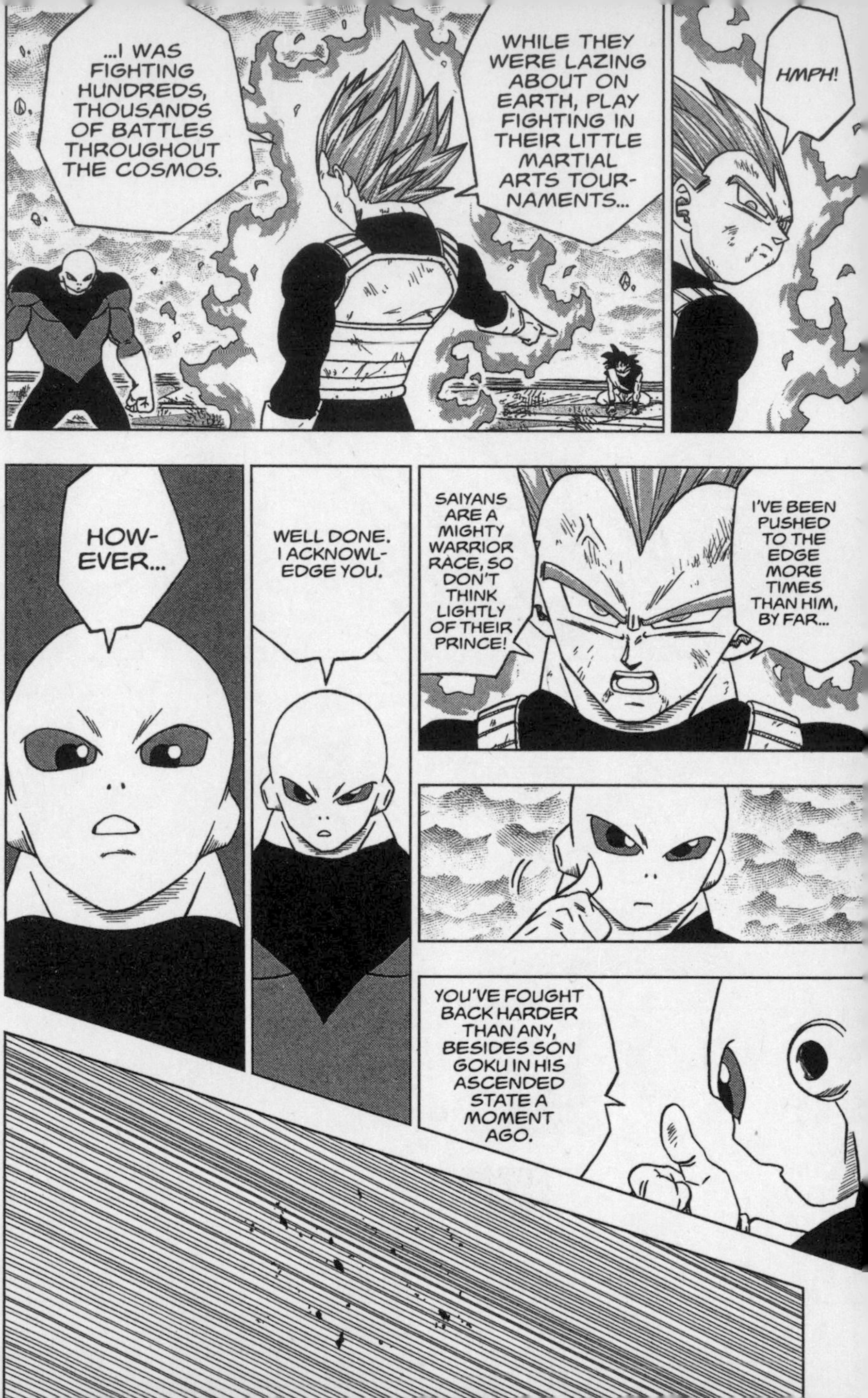
HMPH!
WHILE THEY WERE LAZING ABOUT ON EARTH, PLAY FIGHTING IN THEIR LITTLE MARTIAL ARTS TOURNAMENTS...
...I WAS FIGHTING HUNDREDS, THOUSANDS OF BATTLES THROUGHOUT THE COSMOS.
I'VE BEEN PUSHED TO THE EDGE MORE TIMES THAN HIM, BY FAR...
SAIYANS ARE A MIGHTY WARRIOR RACE, SO DON'T THINK LIGHTLY OF THEIR PRINCE!
YOU'VE FOUGHT BACK HARDER THAN ANY, BESIDES SON GOKU IN HIS ASCENDED STATE A MOMENT AGO.
WELL DONE. I ACKNOWL-EDGE YOU.
HOW-EVER...

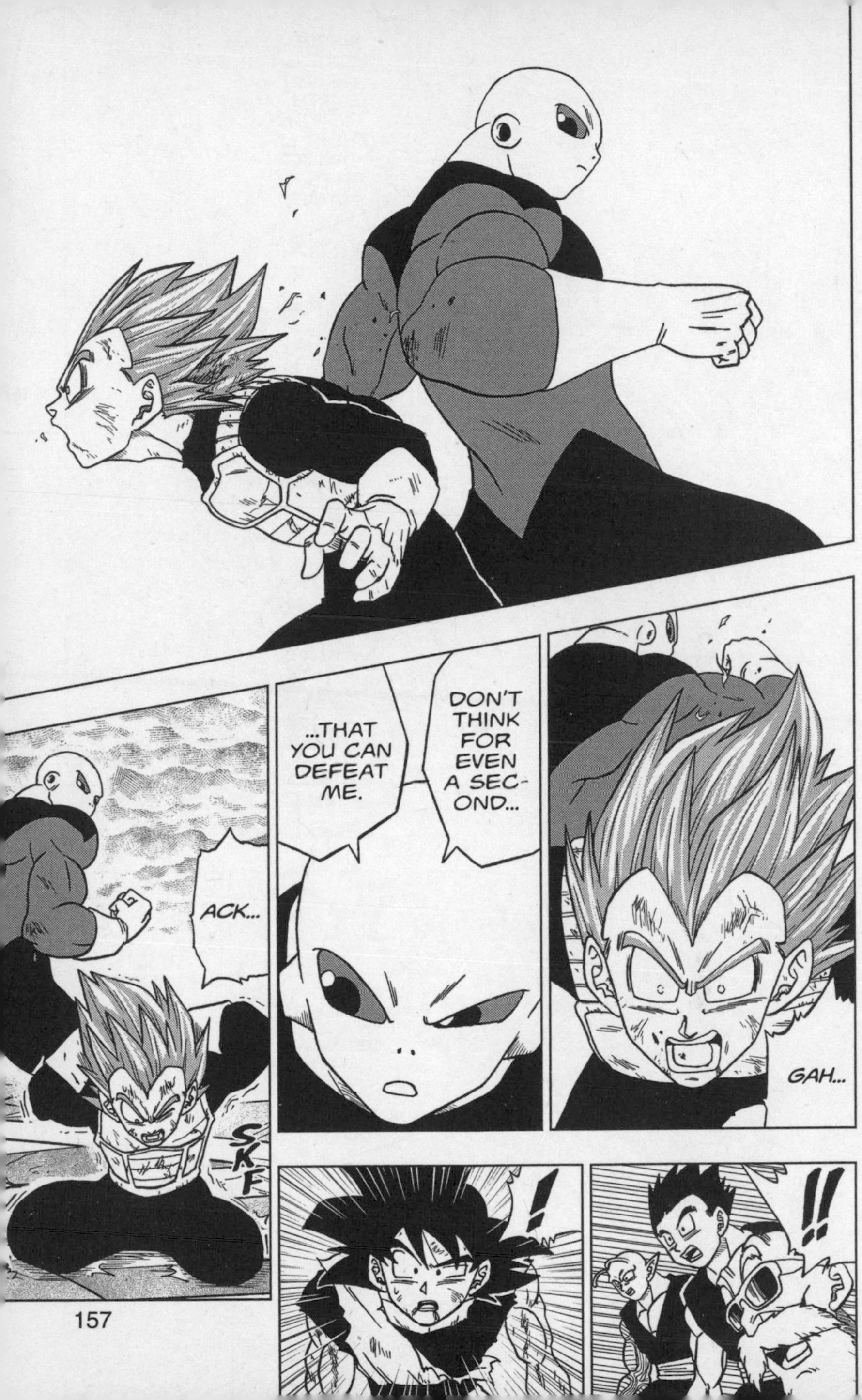
GAH...
DON'T THINK FOR EVEN A SECOND...
...THAT YOU CAN DEFEAT ME.
ACK...
SKF
!!
!

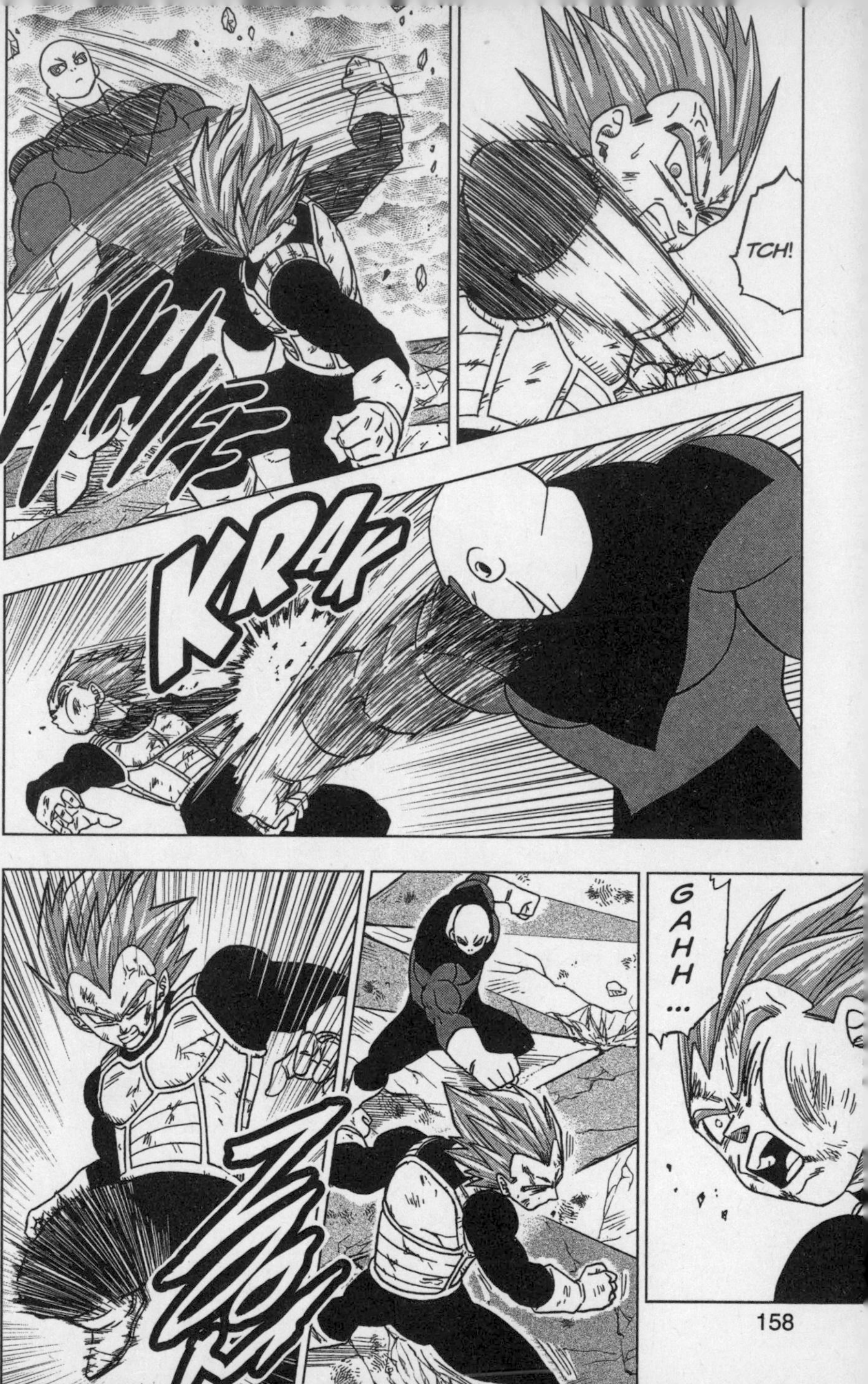
TCH!
WHIFF
KRAK
GAHH ...

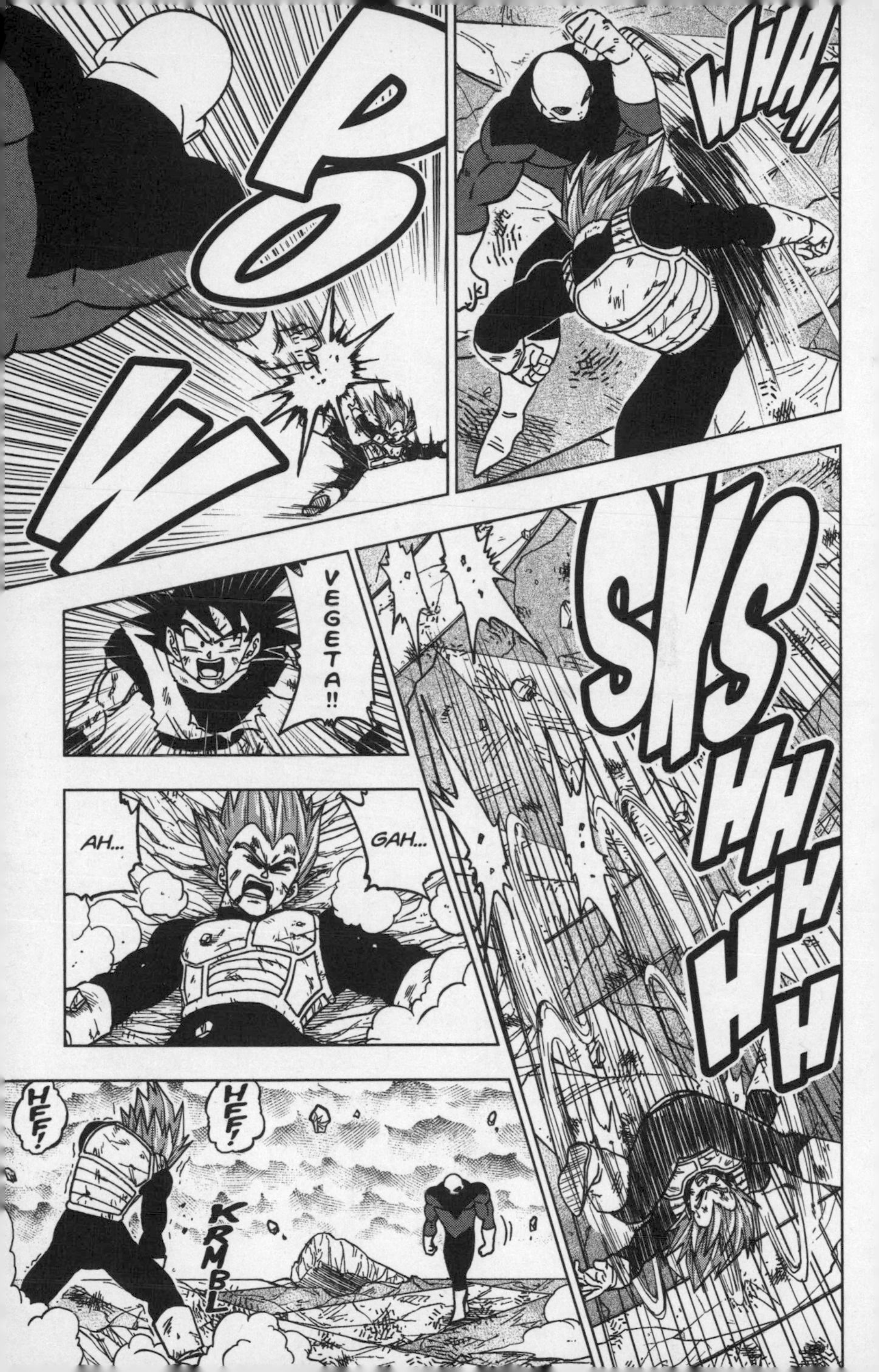
WHAM
POW
SHSHHHHHH
VEGETA!!
GAH...
AH...
HEF!
HEF!
KRMBL

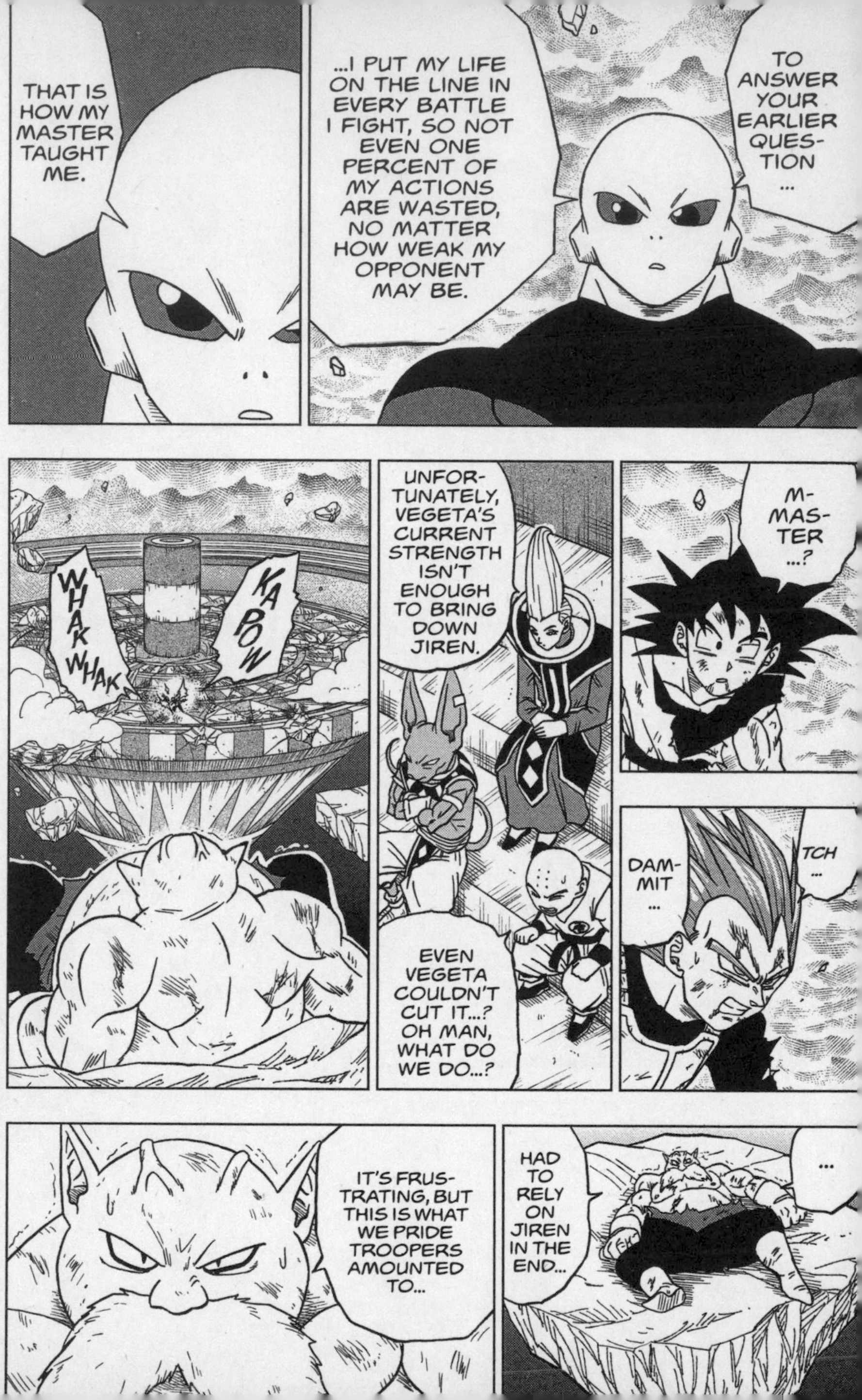

TO ANSWER YOUR EARLIER QUESTION...
...I PUT MY LIFE ON THE LINE IN EVERY BATTLE I FIGHT, SO NOT EVEN ONE PERCENT OF MY ACTIONS ARE WASTED, NO MATTER HOW WEAK MY OPPONENT MAY BE.
THAT IS HOW MY MASTER TAUGHT ME.
M-MASTER...?
TCH...
DAMMIT...
UNFORTUNATELY, VEGETA'S CURRENT STRENGTH ISN'T ENOUGH TO BRING DOWN JIREN.
EVEN VEGETA COULDN'T CUT IT...? OH MAN, WHAT DO WE DO...?
KA POW
WHAK WHAK
...
HAD TO RELY ON JIREN IN THE END...
IT'S FRUSTRATING, BUT THIS IS WHAT WE PRIDE TROOPERS AMOUNTED TO...

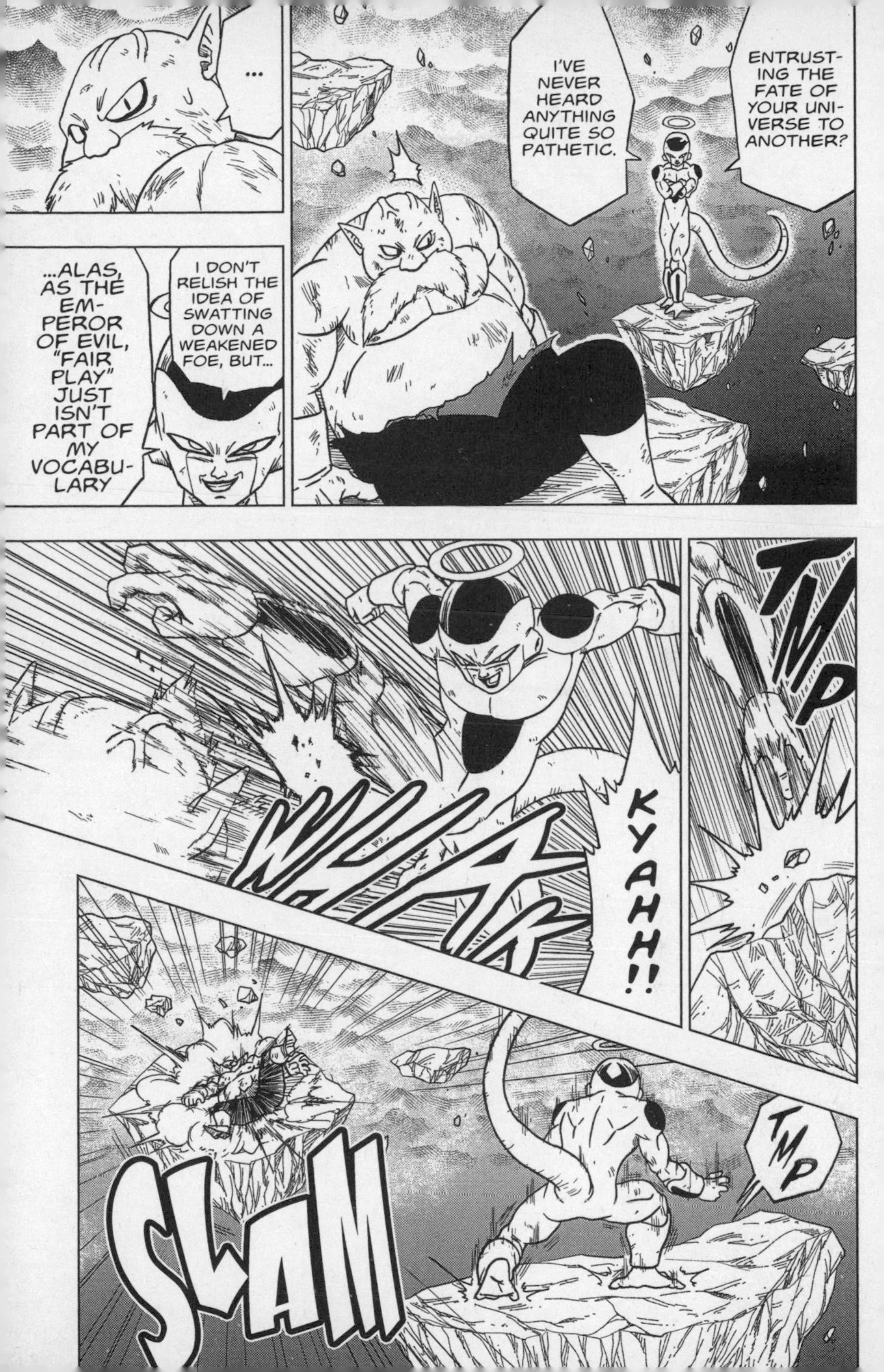
ENTRUSTING THE FATE OF YOUR UNIVERSE TO ANOTHER?
I'VE NEVER HEARD ANYTHING QUITE SO PATHETIC.
...
I DON'T RELISH THE IDEA OF SWATTING DOWN A WEAKENED FOE, BUT...
...ALAS, AS THE EMPEROR OF EVIL, "FAIR PLAY" JUST ISN'T PART OF MY VOCABULARY
TMP
WHAK
KYAHH!!
TMP
SLAM

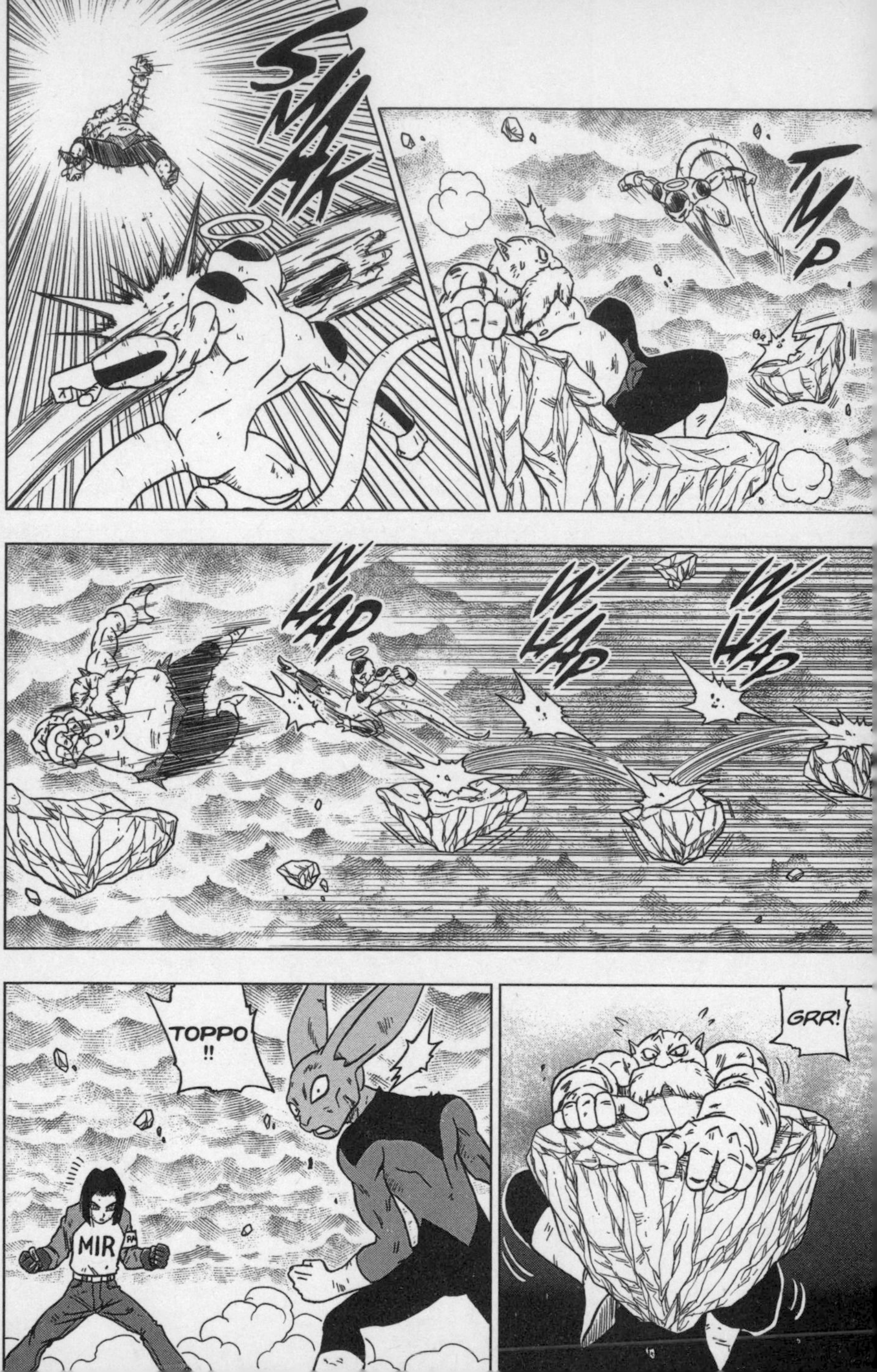
TMP
SMAAK
WHAP
WHAP
WHAP
GRR!
TOPPO !!

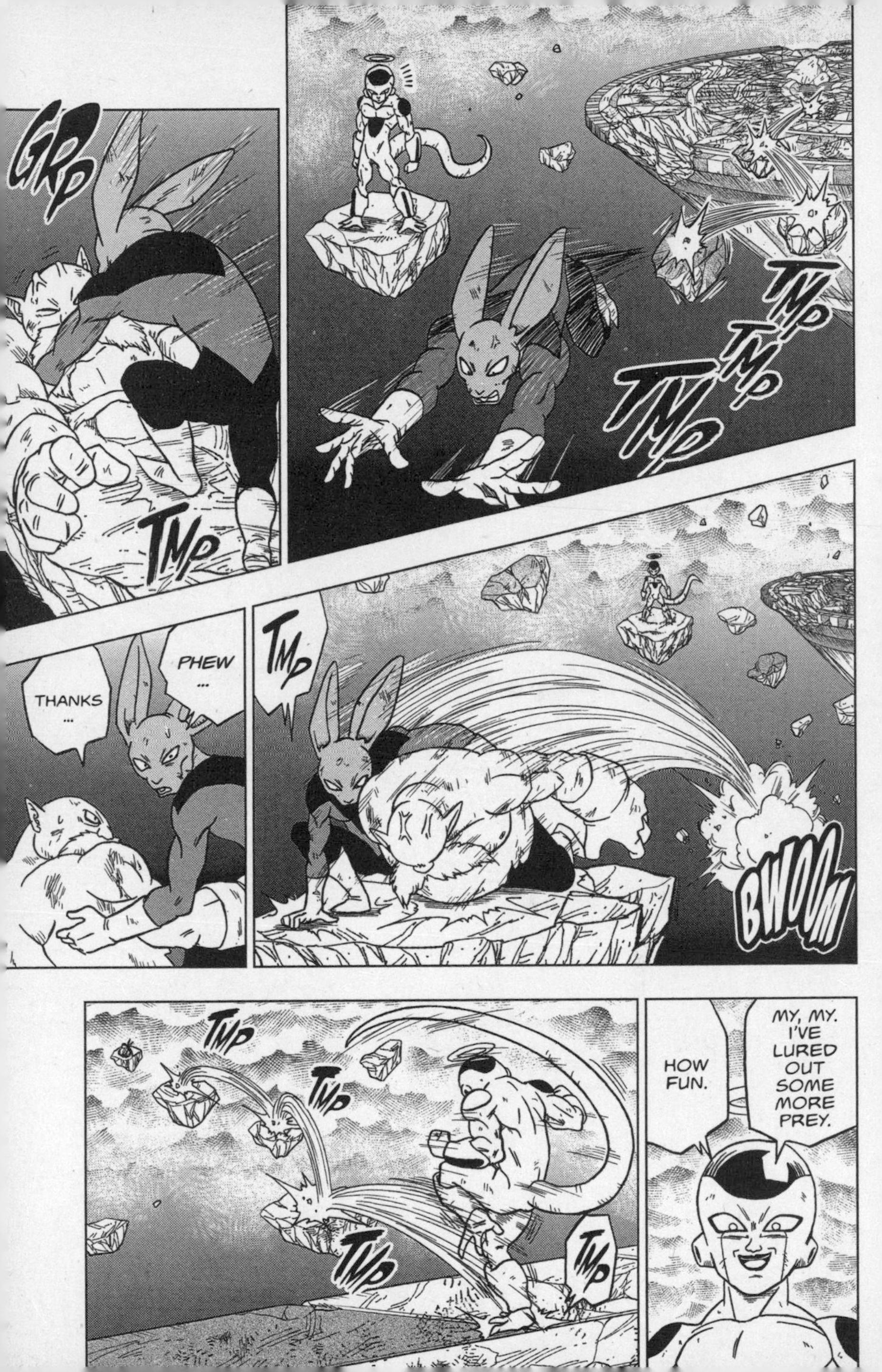
TMP
TMP
TMP
GRP
TMP
TMP
BWOOM
PHEW ...
THANKS ...
MY, MY. I'VE LURED OUT SOME MORE PREY.
HOW FUN.
TMP
TMP
TMP
TMP

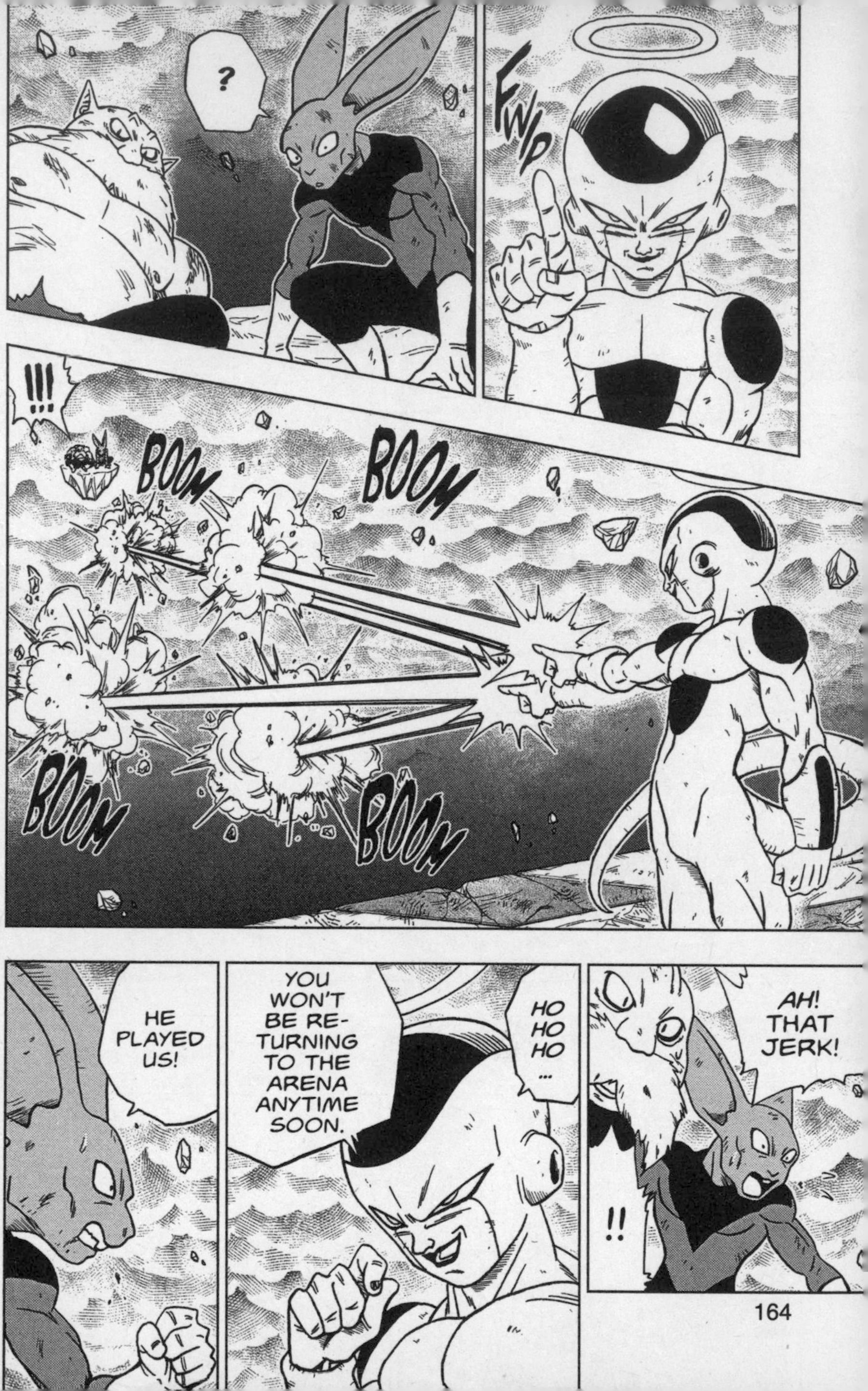
FWIP
?
!!!
BOOM
BOOM
BOOM
BOOM
AH! THAT JERK!
!!
HO HO HO ...
YOU WON'T BE RE-TURNING TO THE ARENA ANYTIME SOON.
HE PLAYED US!

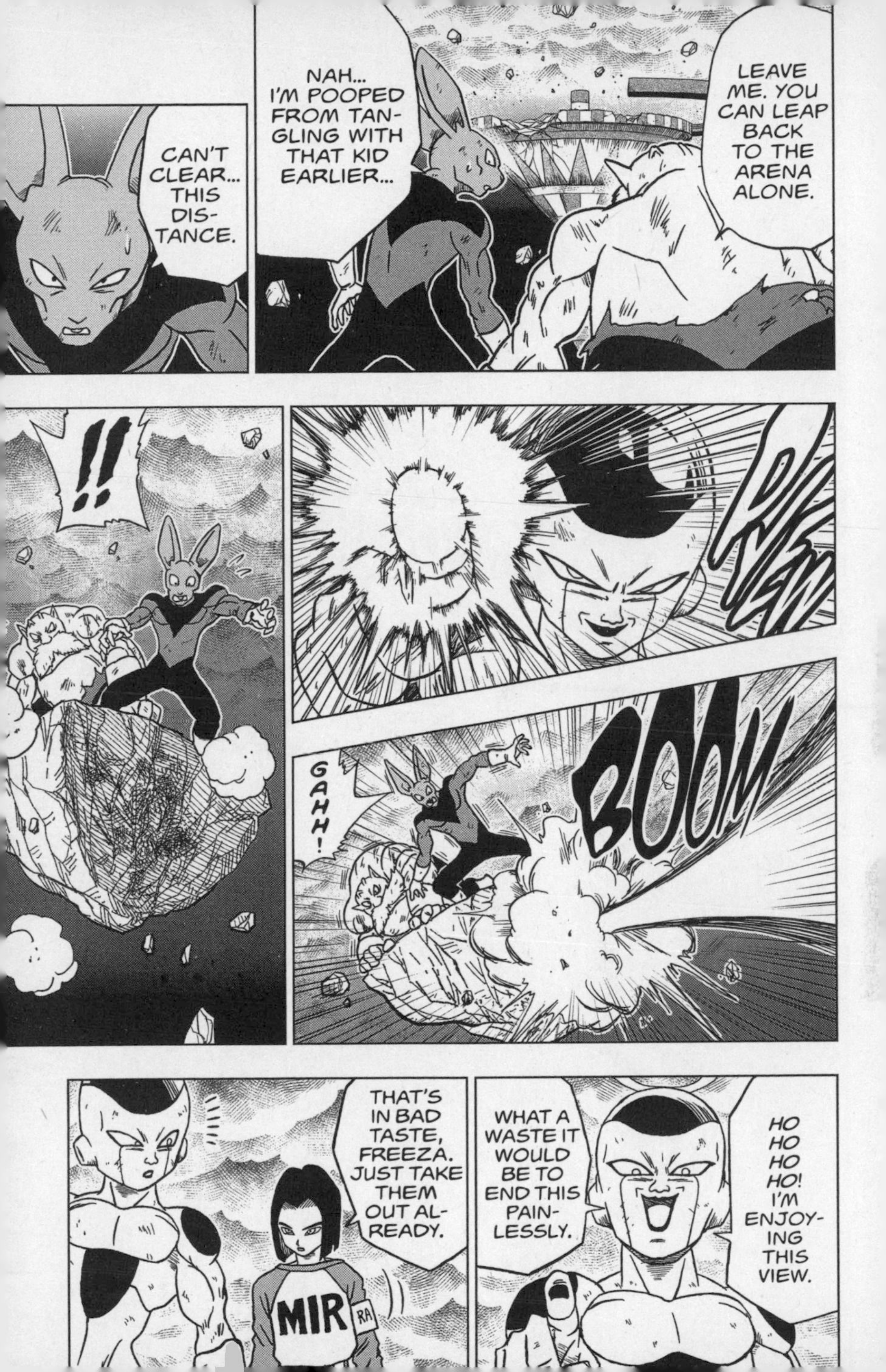
LEAVE ME. YOU CAN LEAP BACK TO THE ARENA ALONE.
NAH... I'M POOPED FROM TANGLING WITH THAT KID EARLIER...
CAN'T CLEAR... THIS DISTANCE.
BOOM
GAHH!
!!
HO HO HO HO! I'M ENJOYING THIS VIEW.
WHAT A WASTE IT WOULD BE TO END THIS PAINLESSLY.
THAT'S IN BAD TASTE, FREEZA. JUST TAKE THEM OUT ALREADY.
MIR
RA

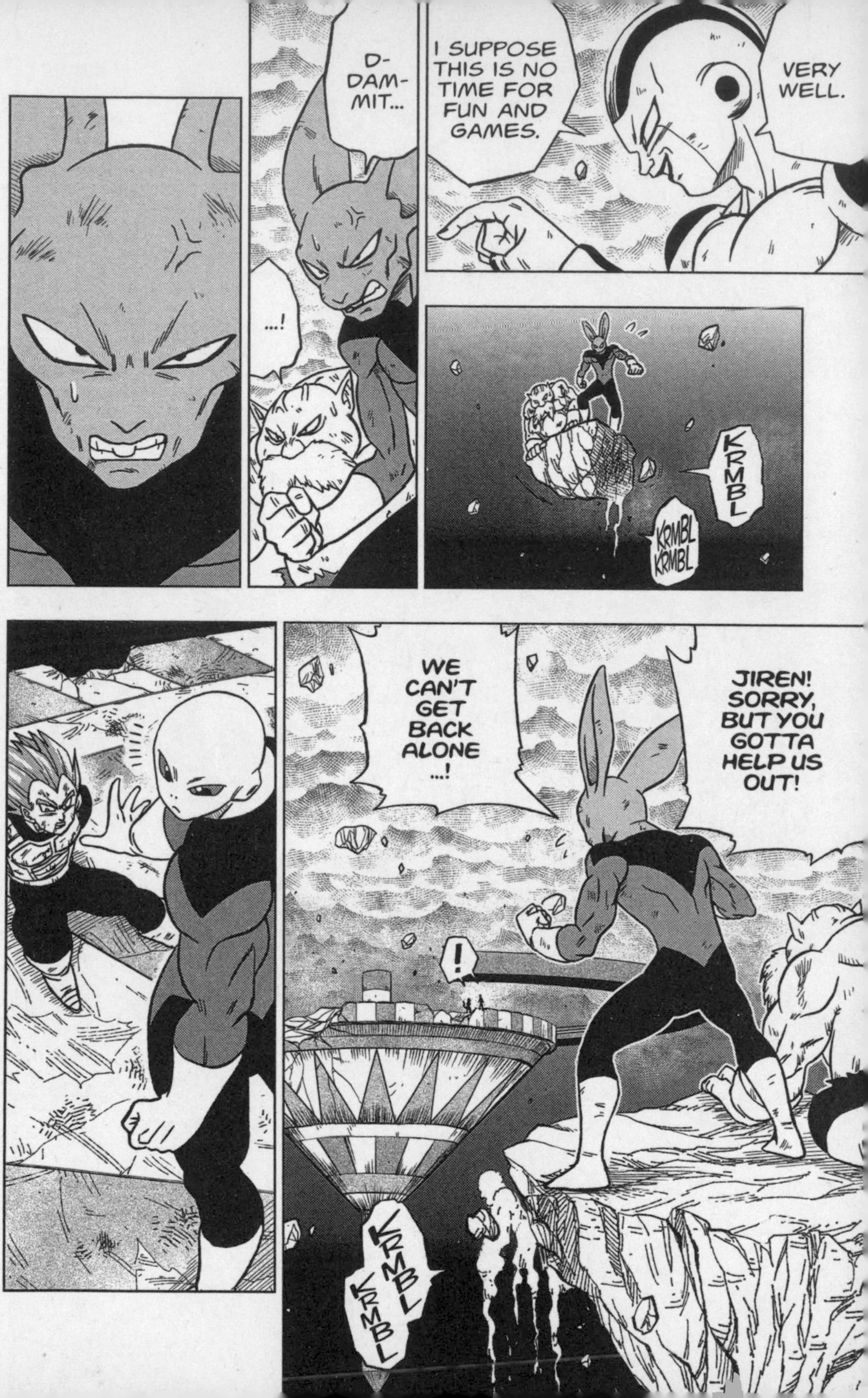
VERY WELL.
I SUPPOSE THIS IS NO TIME FOR FUN AND GAMES.
KRMBL
KRMBL KRMBL
D-DAM-MIT...
...!
JIREN! SORRY, BUT YOU GOTTA HELP US OUT!
WE CAN'T GET BACK ALONE ...!
!
KRMBL
KRMBL

FWP

FSH

SHHH

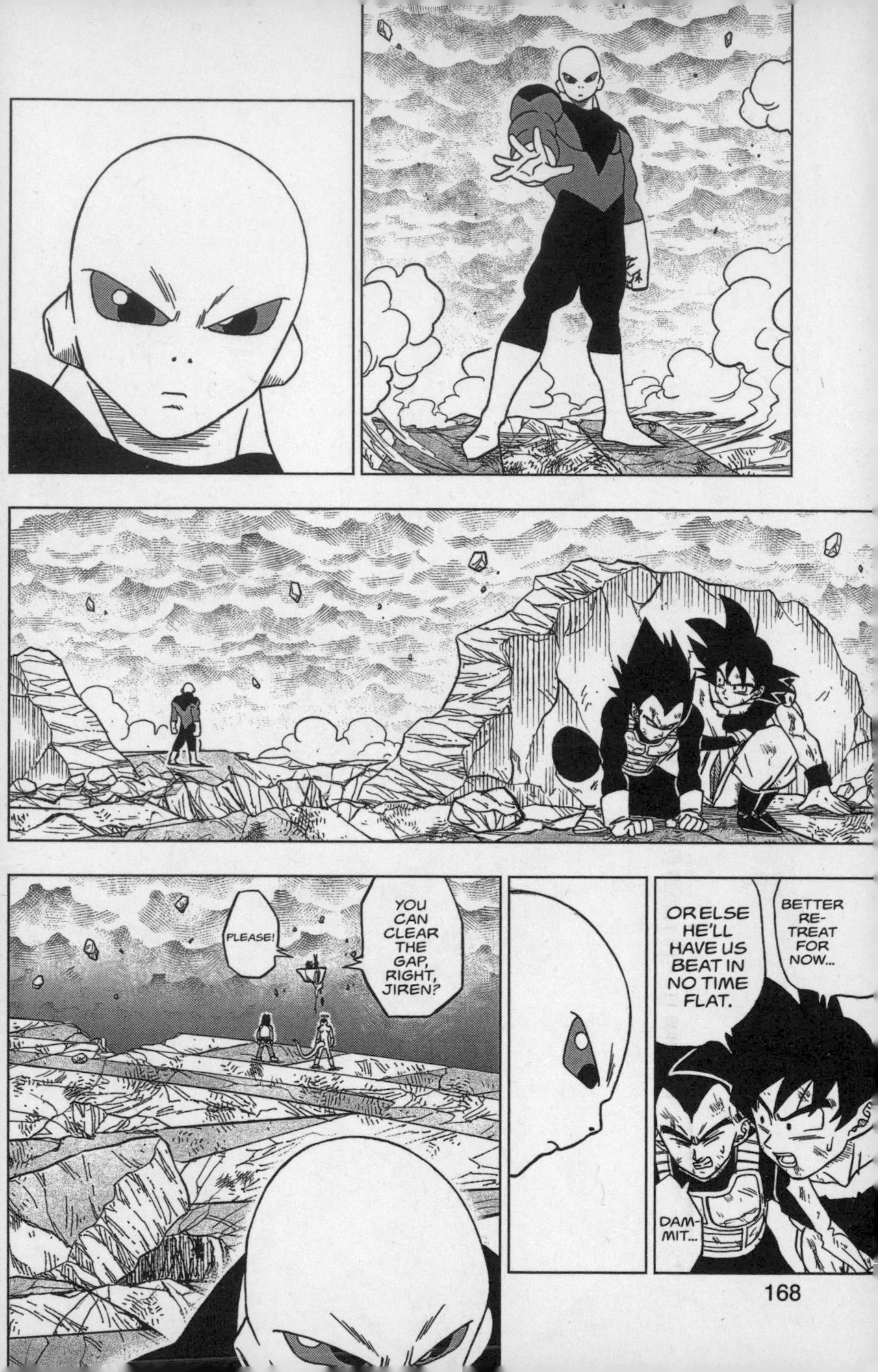
BETTER RE-TREAT FOR NOW...
OR ELSE HE'LL HAVE US BEAT IN NO TIME FLAT.
DAM-MIT...
YOU CAN CLEAR THE GAP, RIGHT, JIREN?
PLEASE!

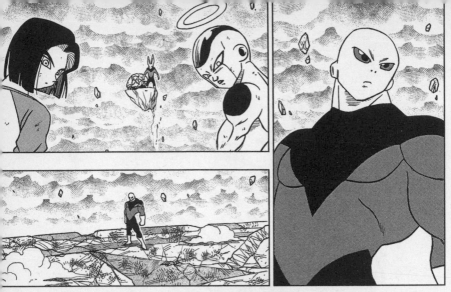

WHAT--

HUH?

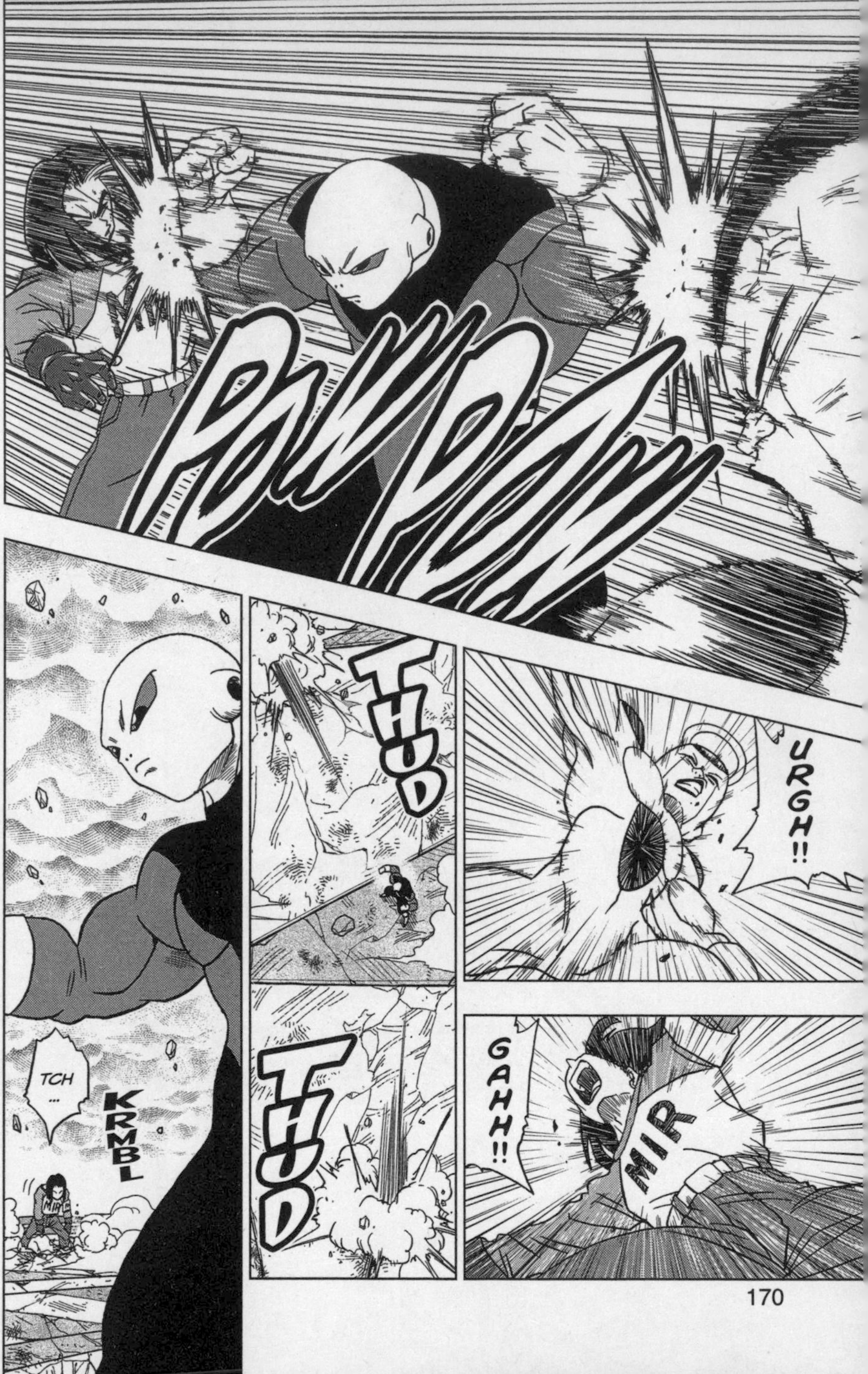
URGH!!
THUD
GAHH!!
MIR
THUD
TCH ...
KRMBL

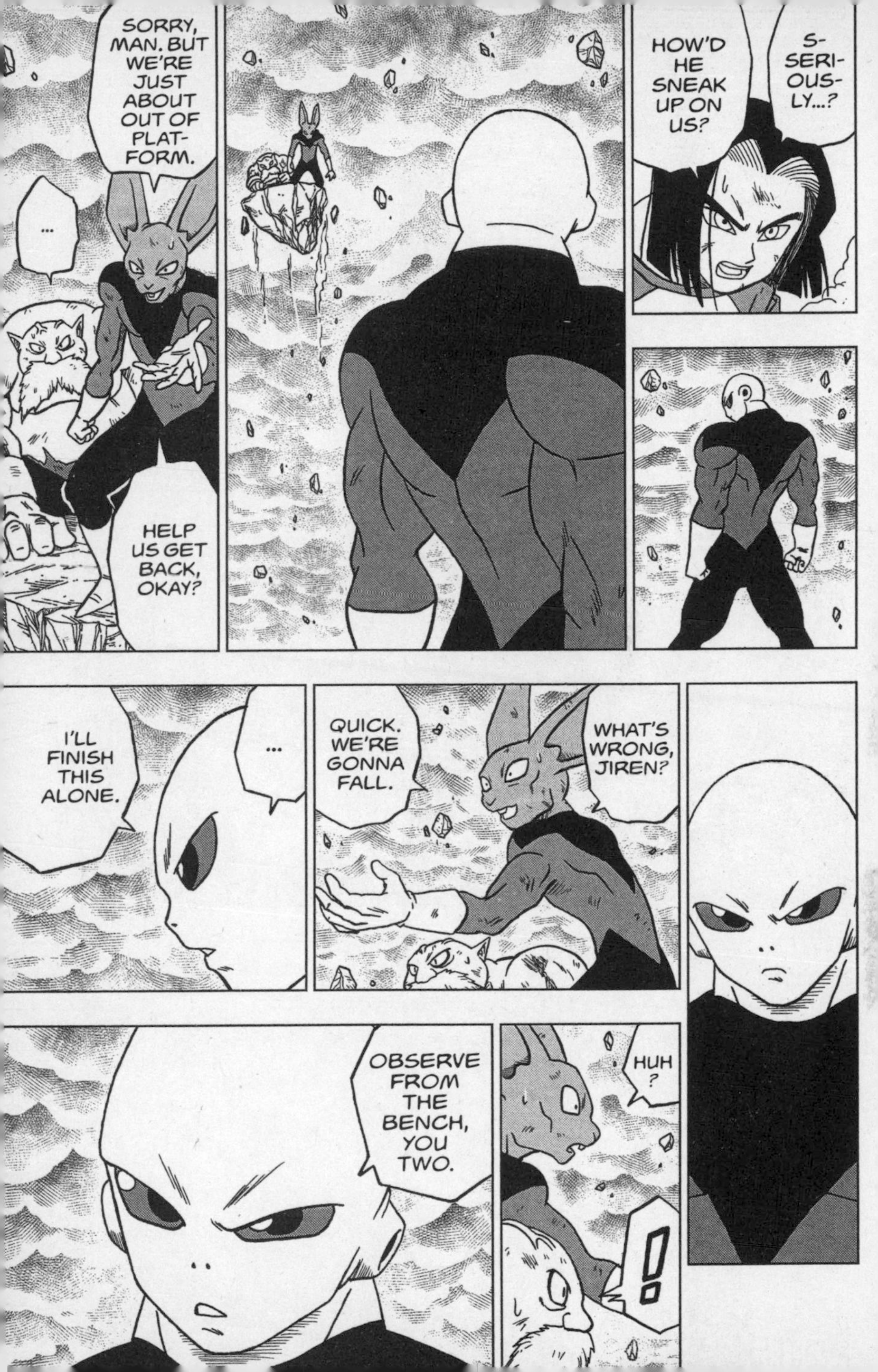
S-SERIOUSLY...?
HOW'D HE SNEAK UP ON US?
SORRY, MAN. BUT WE'RE JUST ABOUT OUT OF PLATFORM.
...
HELP US GET BACK, OKAY?
WHAT'S WRONG, JIREN?
QUICK. WE'RE GONNA FALL.
...
I'LL FINISH THIS ALONE.
HUH?
!
OBSERVE FROM THE BENCH, YOU TWO.

...!
W-WAIT...
!
KRAK
WHOA!
FSH
FSH

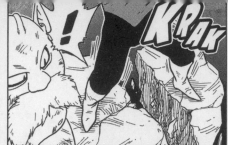

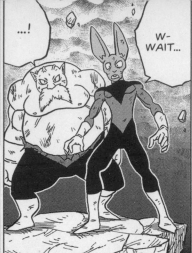

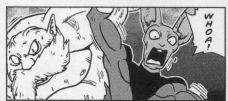

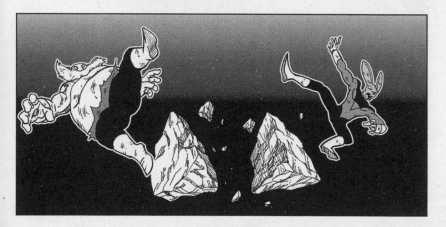

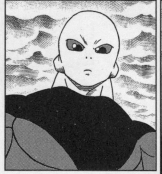

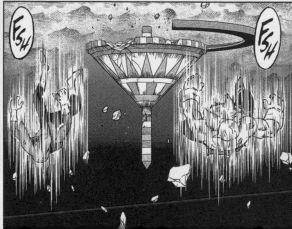

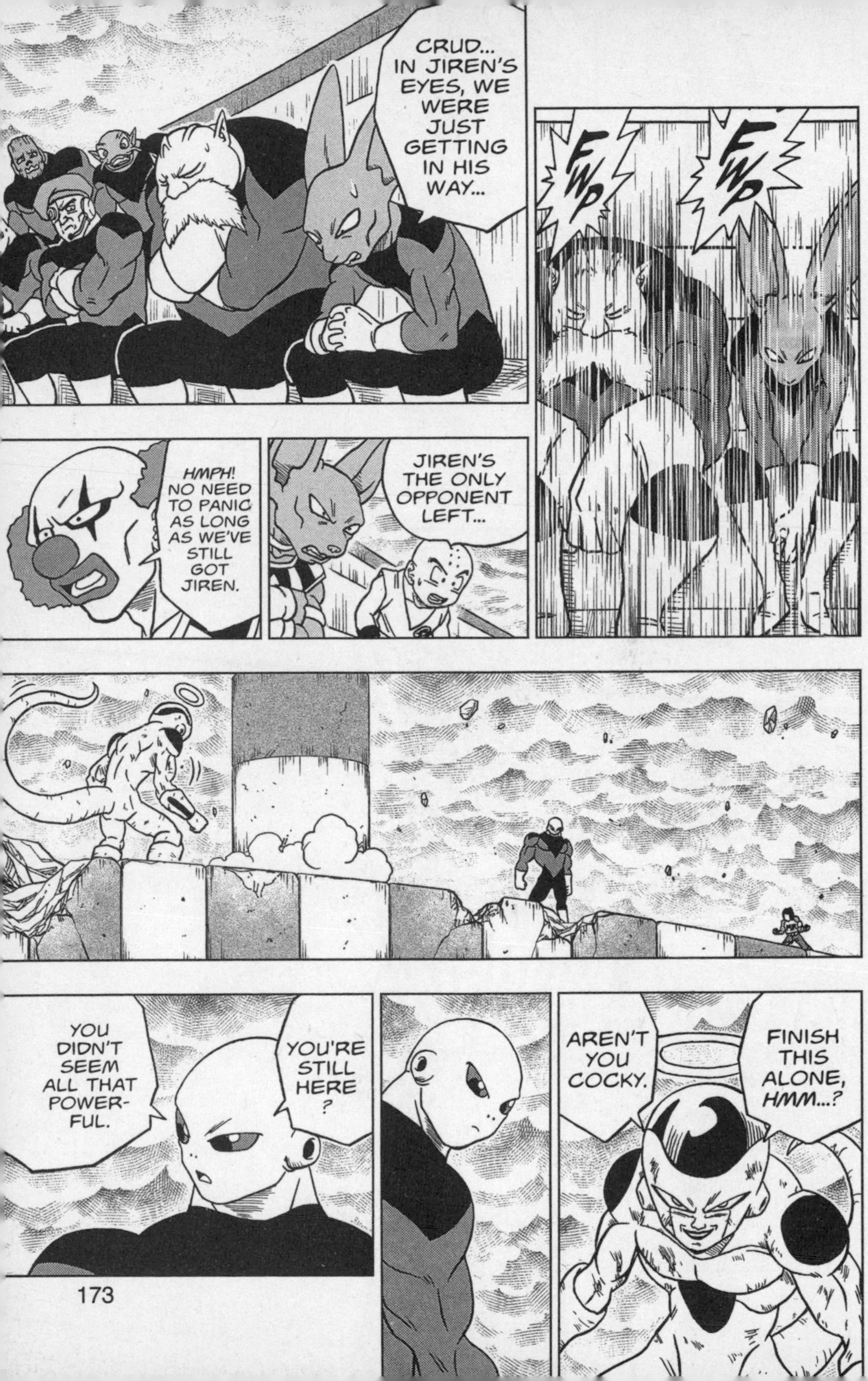
CRUD... IN JIREN'S EYES, WE WERE JUST GETTING IN HIS WAY...
FWP
FWP
JIREN'S THE ONLY OPPONENT LEFT...
HMPH! NO NEED TO PANIC AS LONG AS WE'VE STILL GOT JIREN.
FINISH THIS ALONE, *HMM...?*
AREN'T YOU COCKY.
YOU'RE STILL HERE?
YOU DIDN'T SEEM ALL THAT POWER-FUL.

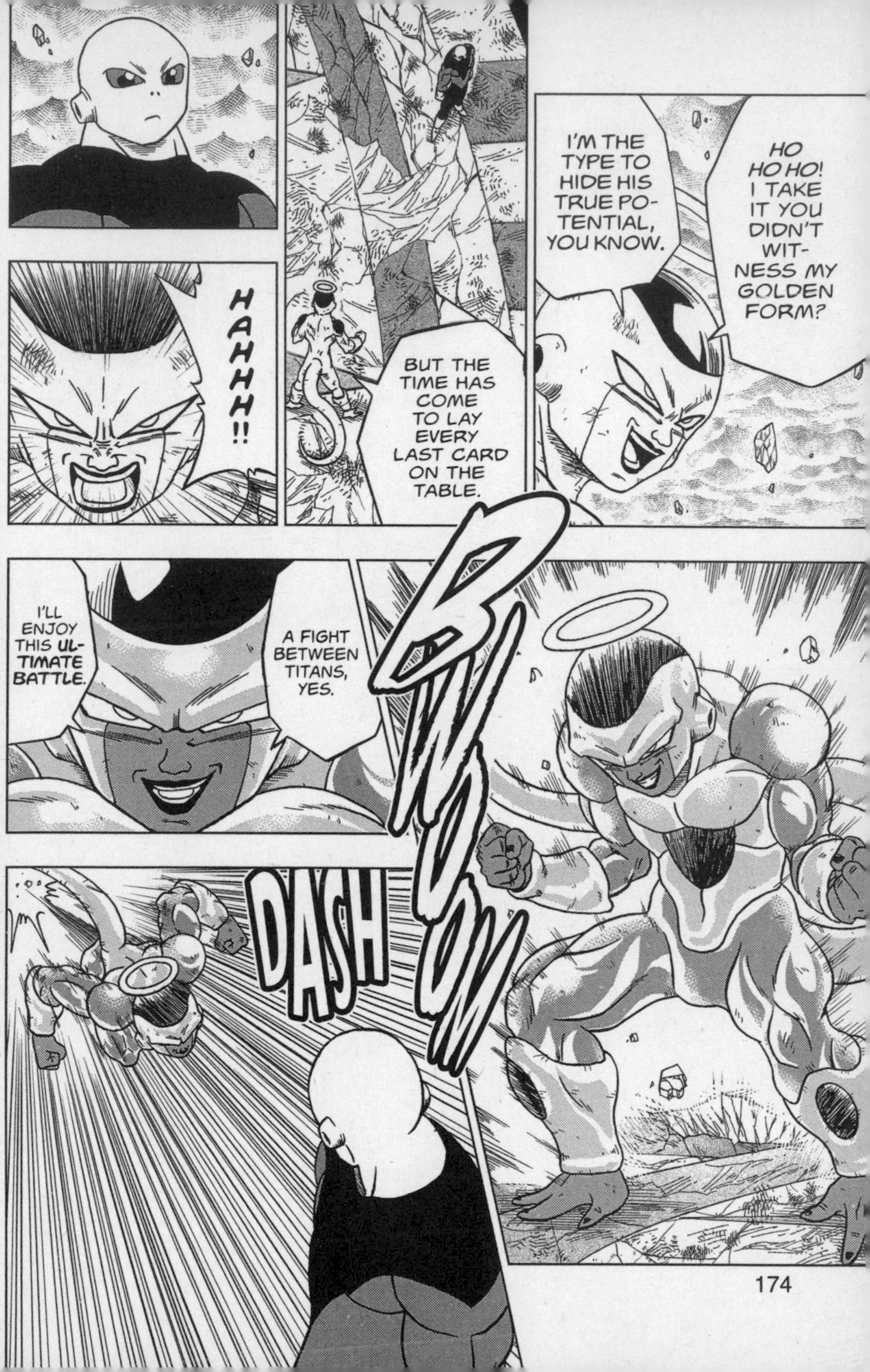
HO HO HO! I TAKE IT YOU DIDN'T WIT-NESS MY GOLDEN FORM?
I'M THE TYPE TO HIDE HIS TRUE PO-TENTIAL, YOU KNOW.
BUT THE TIME HAS COME TO LAY EVERY LAST CARD ON THE TABLE.
HAHHHH!!
A FIGHT BETWEEN TITANS, YES.
I'LL ENJOY THIS **ULTIMATE BATTLE**.
DASH

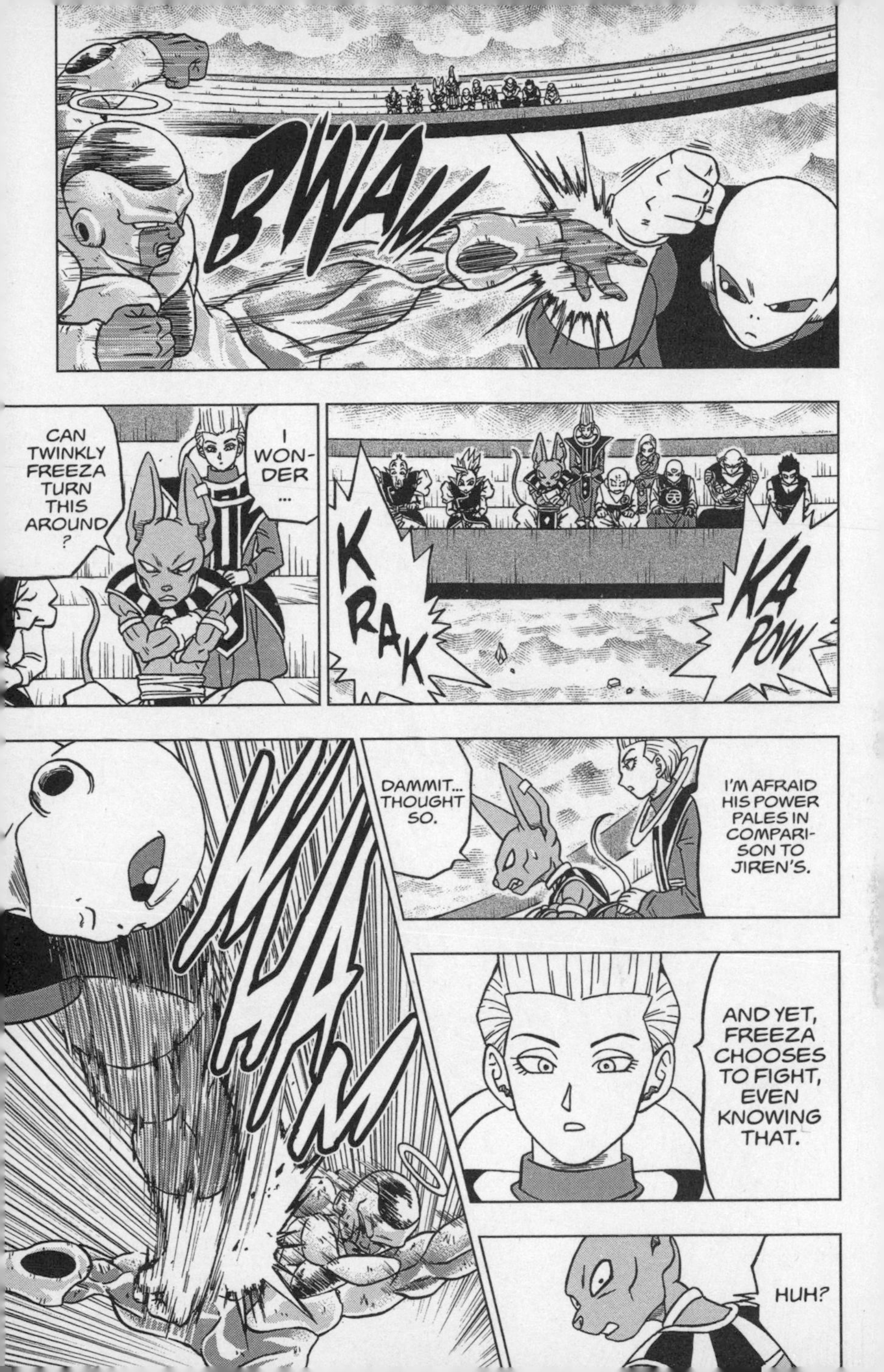
BWAM
KA POW
KRAK
I WONDER...
CAN TWINKLY FREEZA TURN THIS AROUND?
I'M AFRAID HIS POWER PALES IN COMPARISON TO JIREN'S.
DAMMIT... THOUGHT SO.
AND YET, FREEZA CHOOSES TO FIGHT, EVEN KNOWING THAT.
HUH?
WHAM

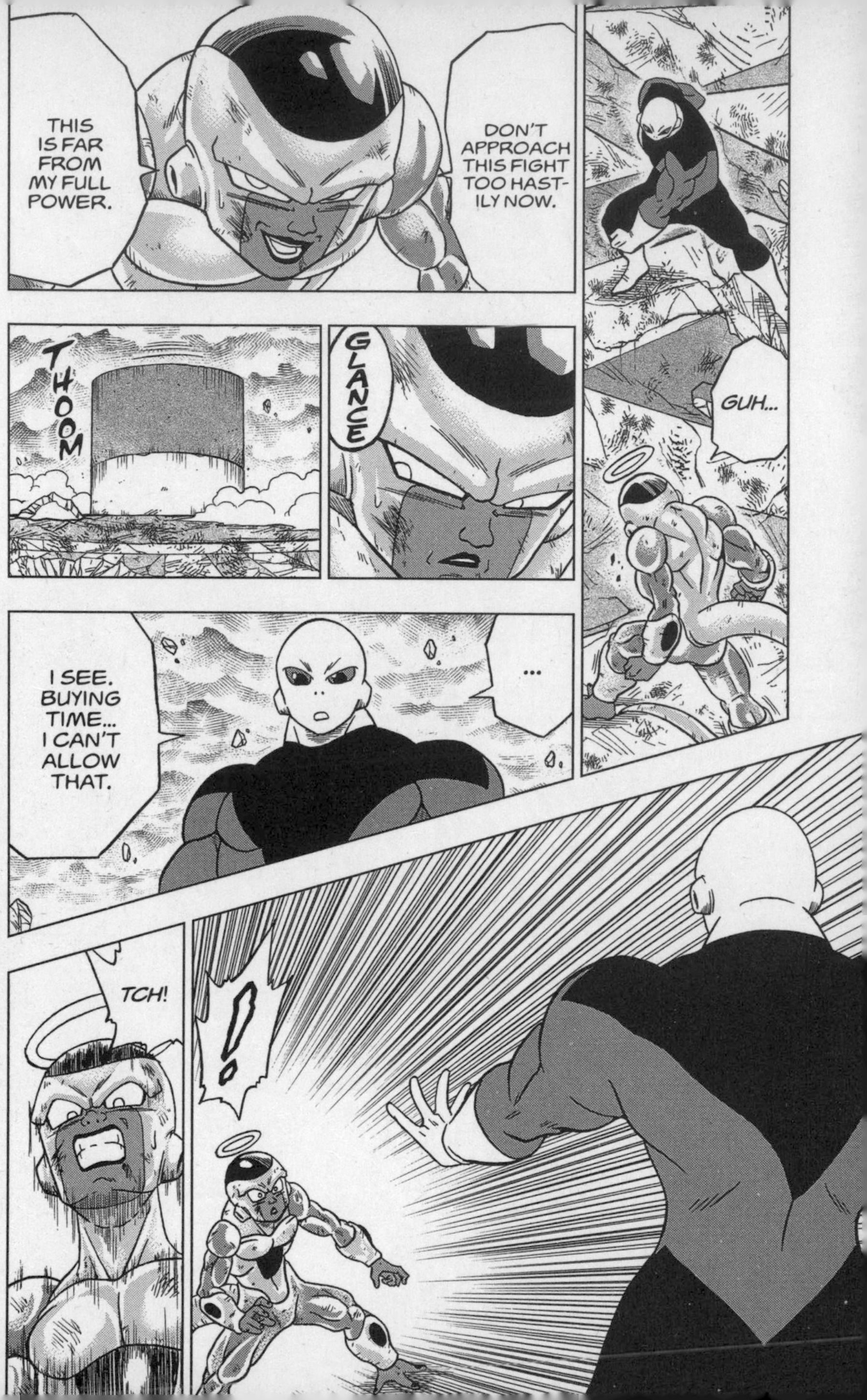
GUH...
DON'T APPROACH THIS FIGHT TOO HASTILY NOW.
THIS IS FAR FROM MY FULL POWER.
GLANCE
THOOM
...
I SEE. BUYING TIME... I CAN'T ALLOW THAT.
!
TCH!

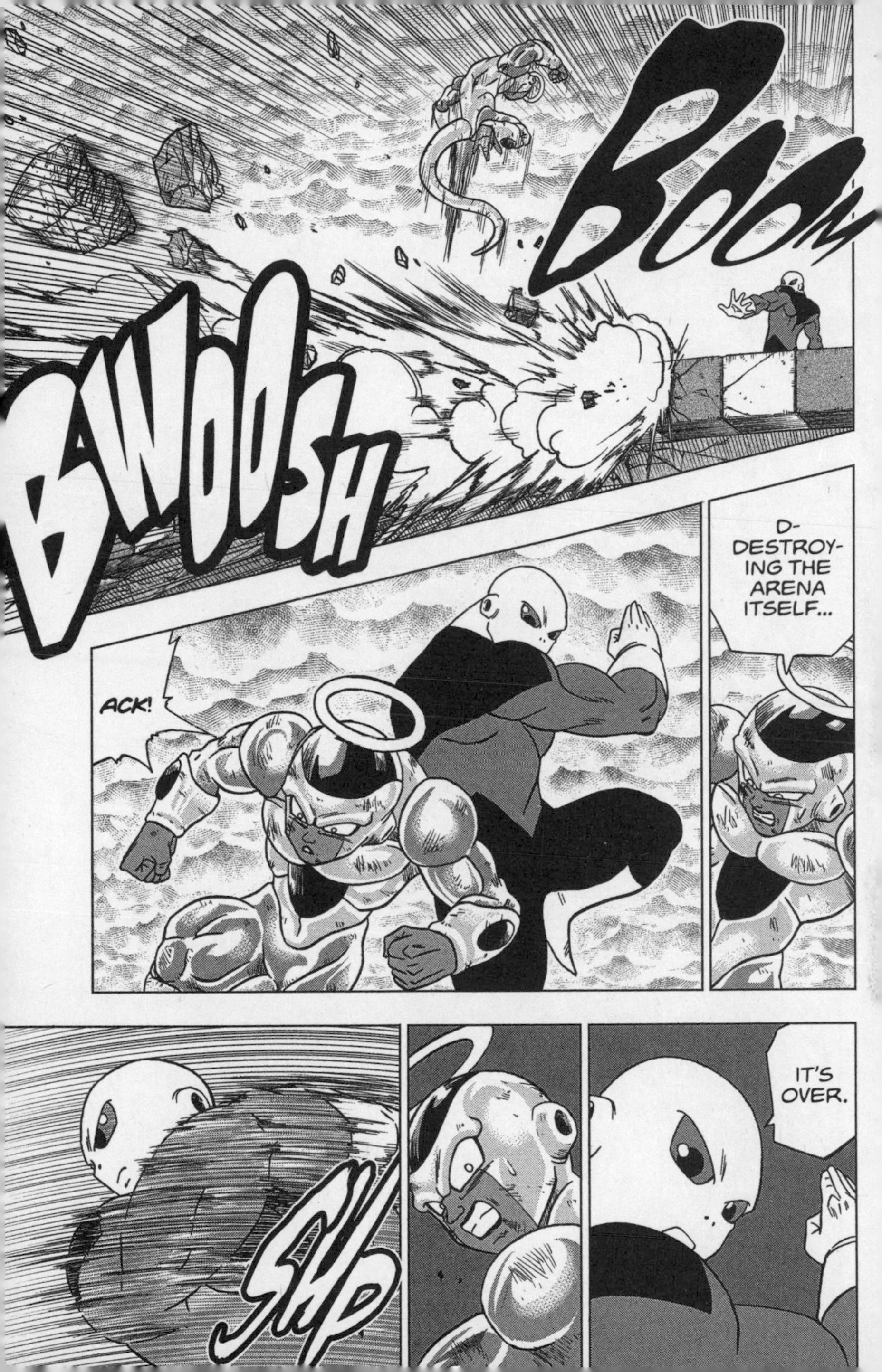
BOOM
BWOOSH
D-DESTROYING THE ARENA ITSELF...
ACK!
IT'S OVER.
SHUP

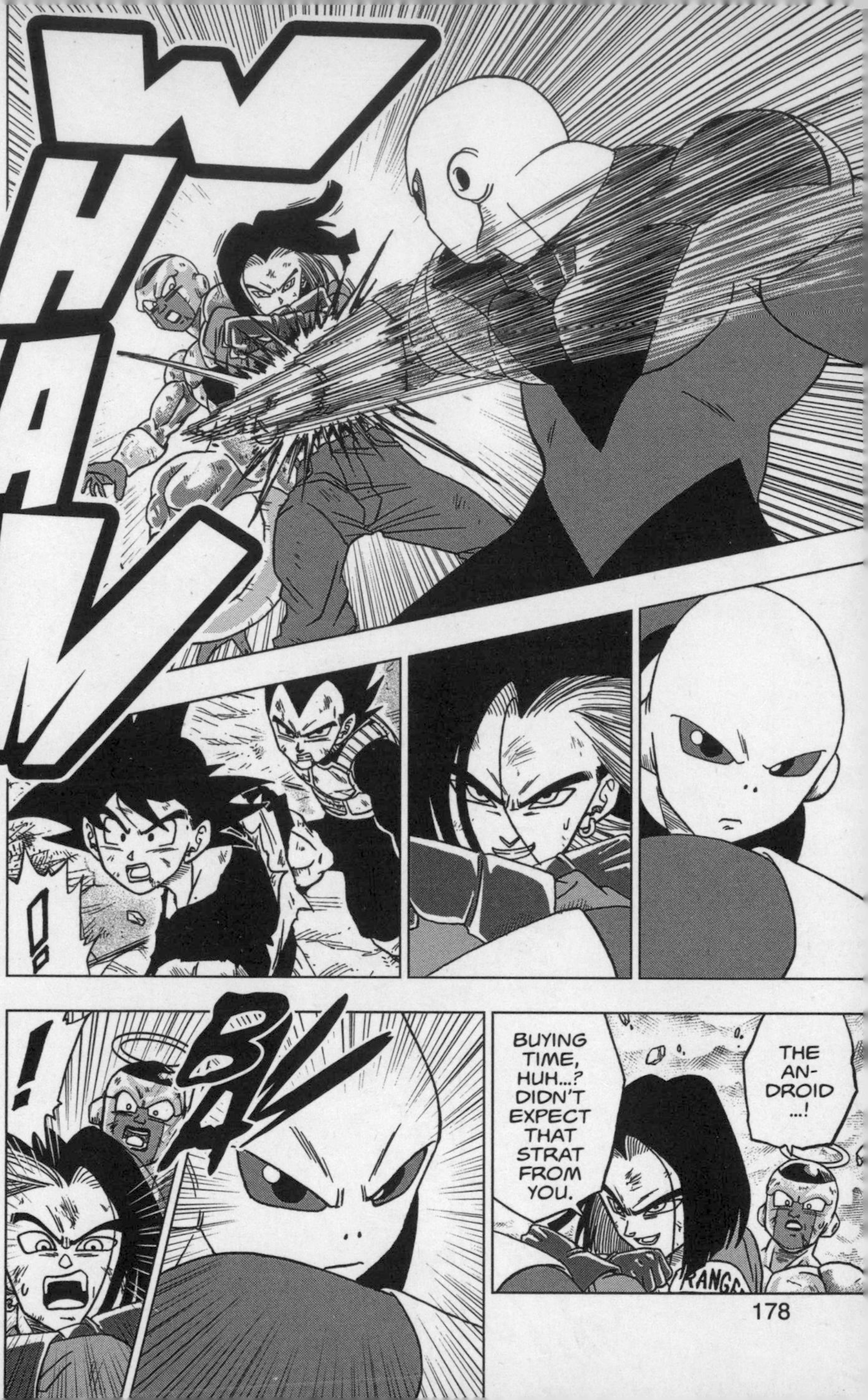
WHAM
!!
THE AN-DROID ...!
BUYING TIME, HUH...? DIDN'T EXPECT THAT STRAT FROM YOU.
BWA
!

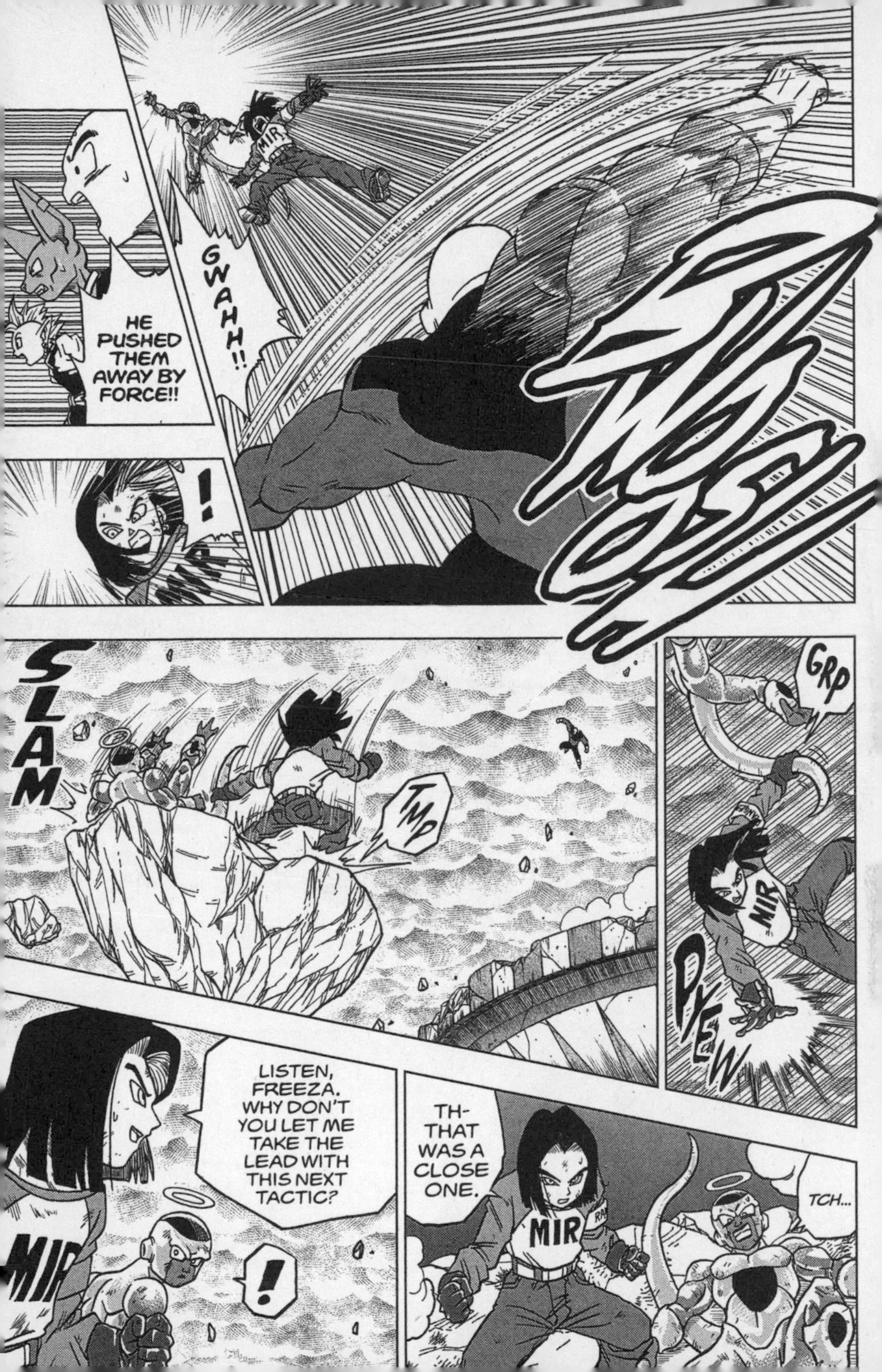
GWAHH!!
HE PUSHED THEM AWAY BY FORCE!!
!
GRP
PYEW
SLAM
TMP
TH- THAT WAS A CLOSE ONE.
TCH...
LISTEN, FREEZA. WHY DON'T YOU LET ME TAKE THE LEAD WITH THIS NEXT TACTIC?
!

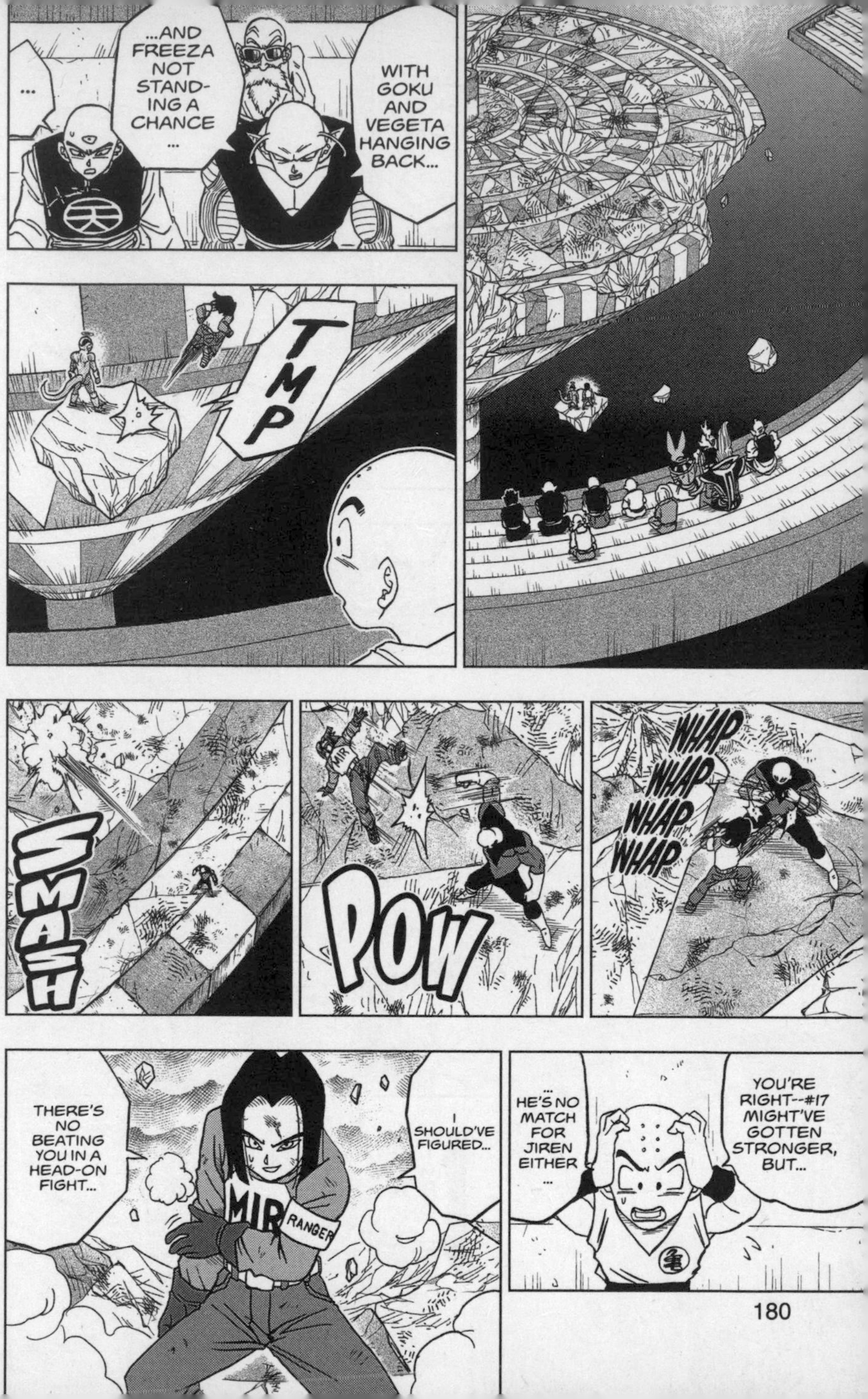

WITH GOKU AND VEGETA HANGING BACK...
...AND FREEZA NOT STANDING A CHANCE...
...
TMP
WHAP WHAP WHAP WHAP
MIR
POW
SMASH
YOU'RE RIGHT--#17 MIGHT'VE GOTTEN STRONGER, BUT...
...HE'S NO MATCH FOR JIREN EITHER...
I SHOULD'VE FIGURED...
THERE'S NO BEATING YOU IN A HEAD-ON FIGHT...
MIR
RANGER

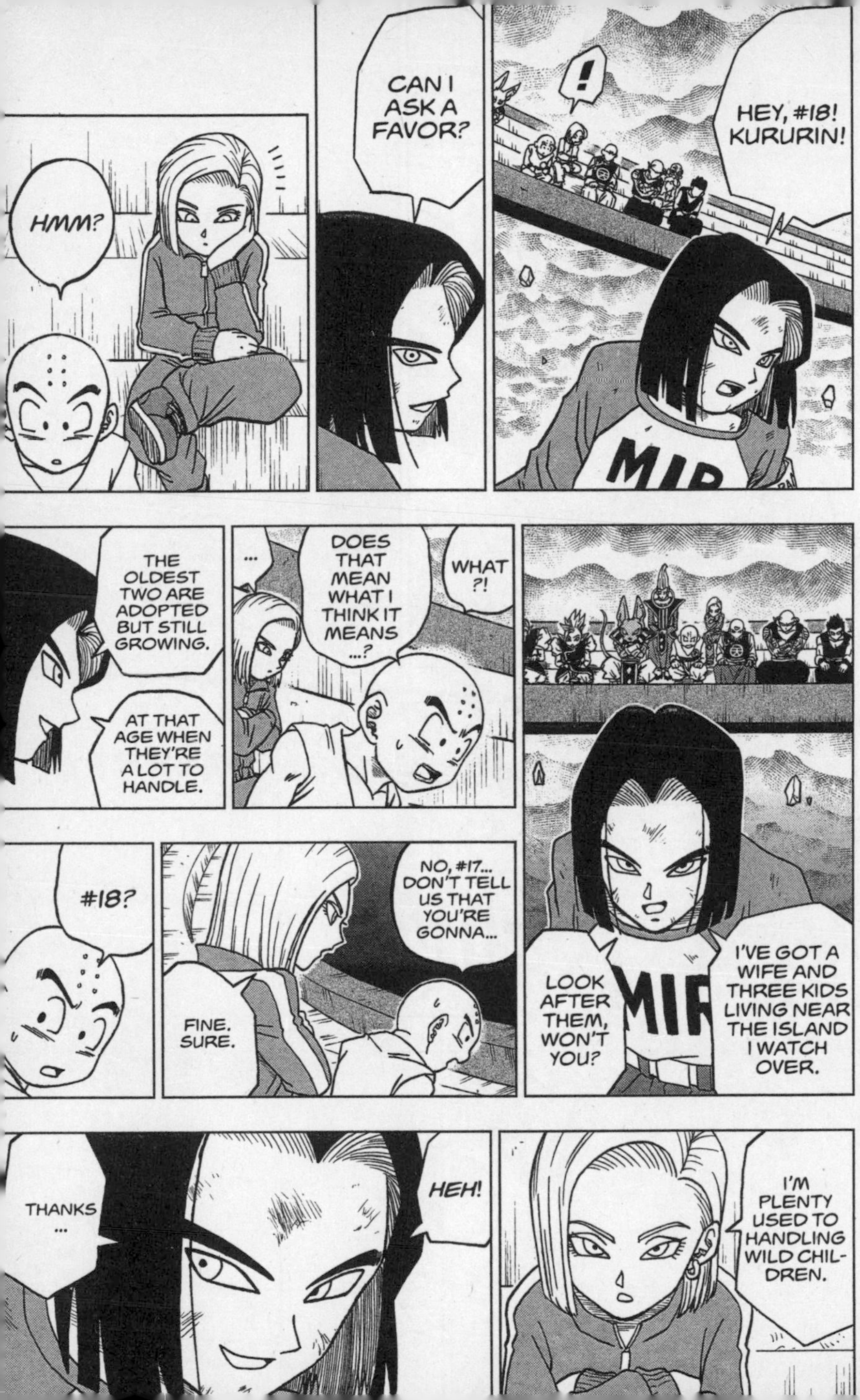
HEY, #18! KURURIN!
!
CAN I ASK A FAVOR?
HMM?
I'VE GOT A WIFE AND THREE KIDS LIVING NEAR THE ISLAND I WATCH OVER.
LOOK AFTER THEM, WON'T YOU?
WHAT ?!
DOES THAT MEAN WHAT I THINK IT MEANS ...?
...
THE OLDEST TWO ARE ADOPTED BUT STILL GROWING.
AT THAT AGE WHEN THEY'RE A LOT TO HANDLE.
NO, #17... DON'T TELL US THAT YOU'RE GONNA...
FINE. SURE.
#18?
I'M PLENTY USED TO HANDLING WILD CHIL-DREN.
HEH!
THANKS ...

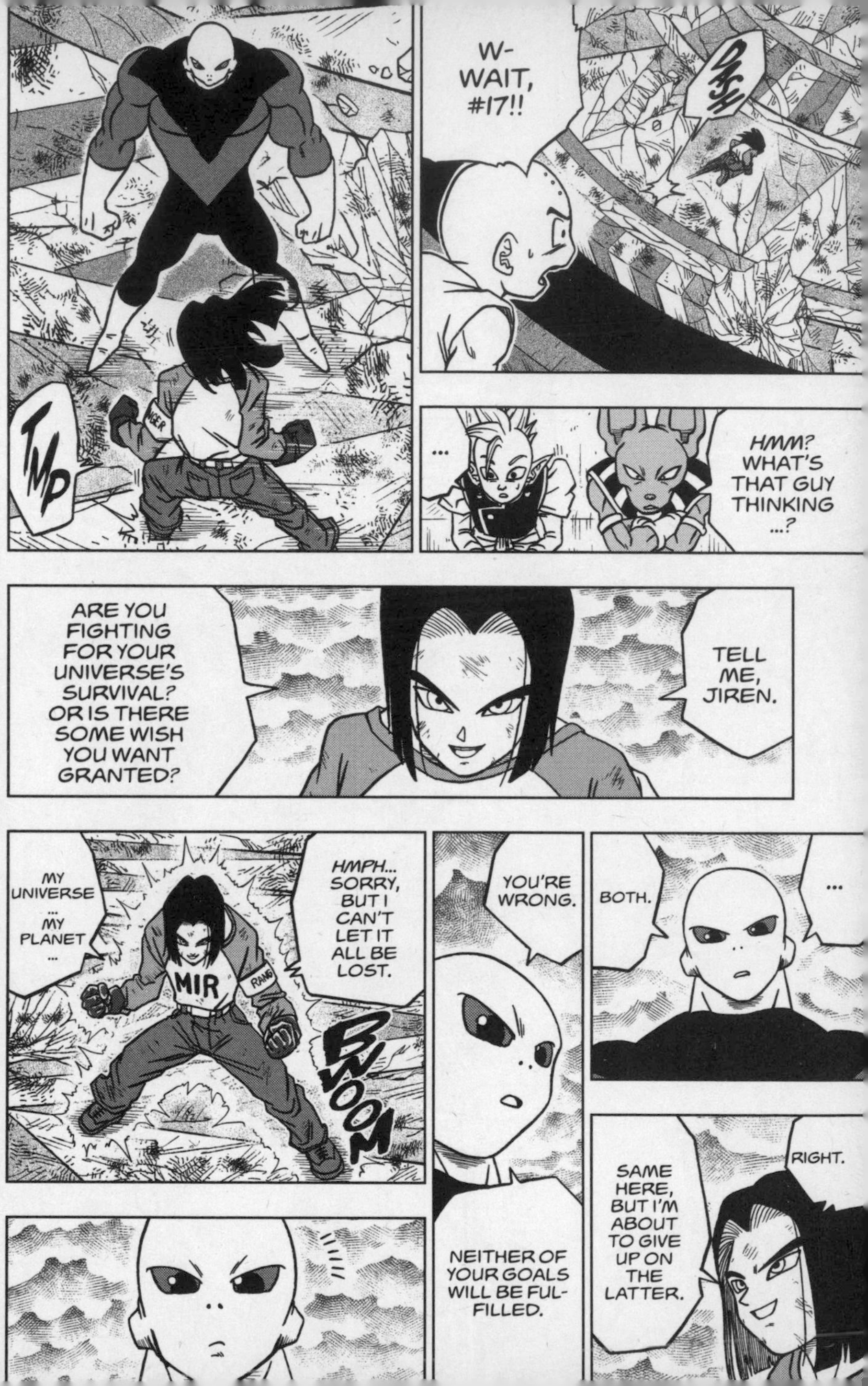
DASH
W-WAIT, #17!!
HMM? WHAT'S THAT GUY THINKING ...?
...
TMP
TELL ME, JIREN.
ARE YOU FIGHTING FOR YOUR UNIVERSE'S SURVIVAL? OR IS THERE SOME WISH YOU WANT GRANTED?
...
BOTH.
RIGHT.
SAME HERE, BUT I'M ABOUT TO GIVE UP ON THE LATTER.
YOU'RE WRONG.
NEITHER OF YOUR GOALS WILL BE FUL-FILLED.
HMPH... SORRY, BUT I CAN'T LET IT ALL BE LOST.
MY UNIVERSE ... MY PLANET ...
BWOOOM
MIR
RANG

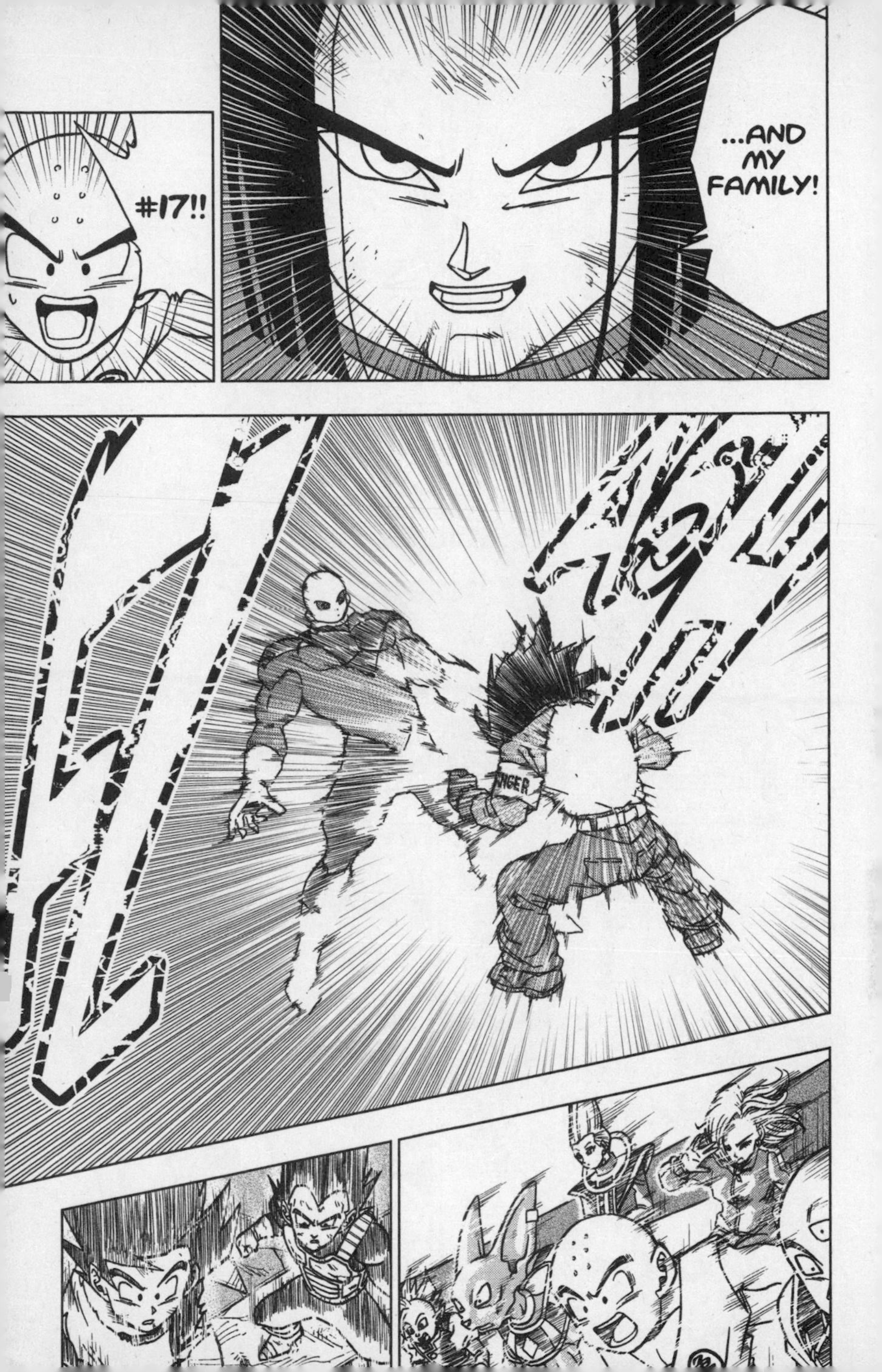
...AND MY FAMILY!
#17!!

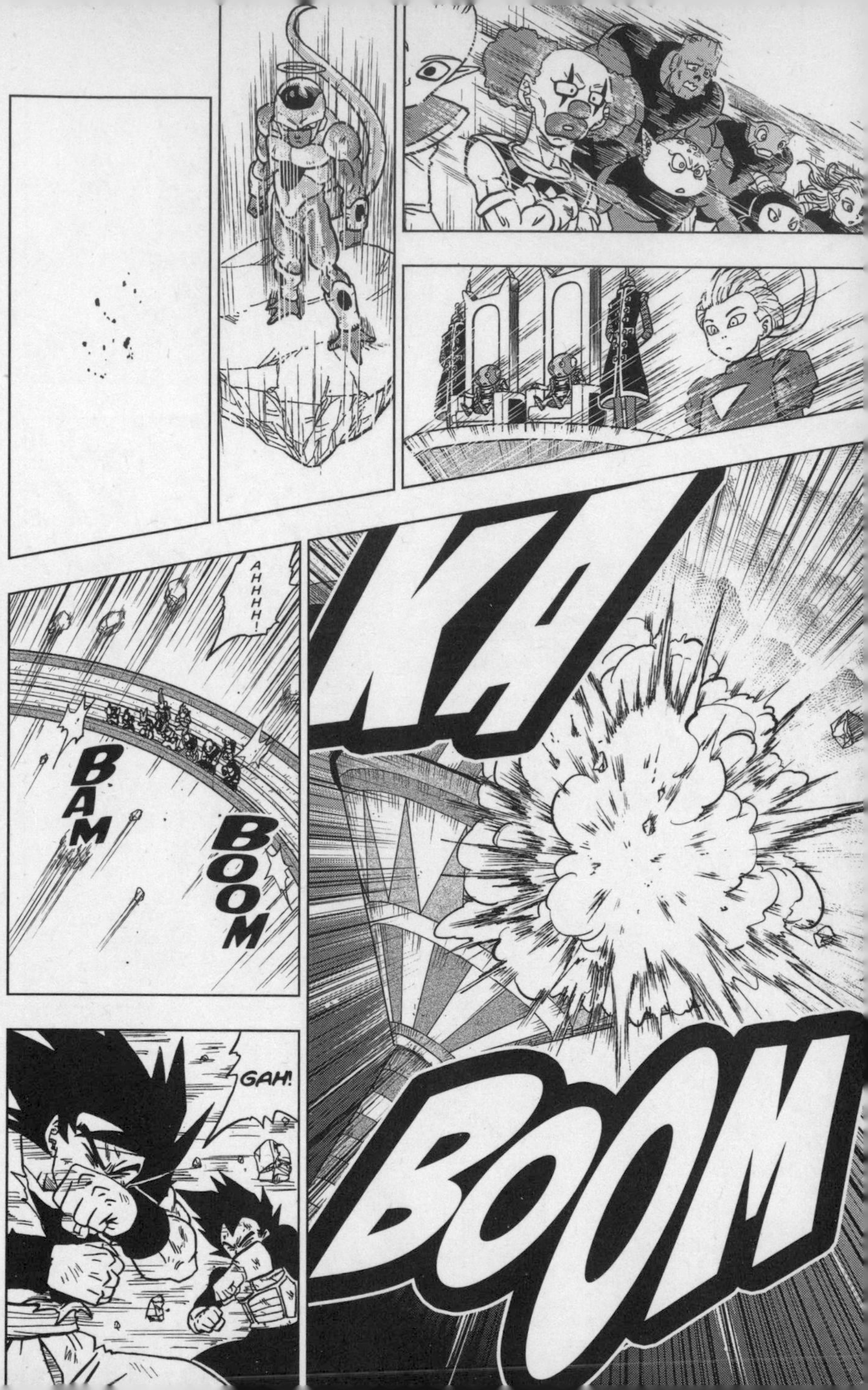
KA
BOOM
AHHHH!
BAM
BOOM
GAH!

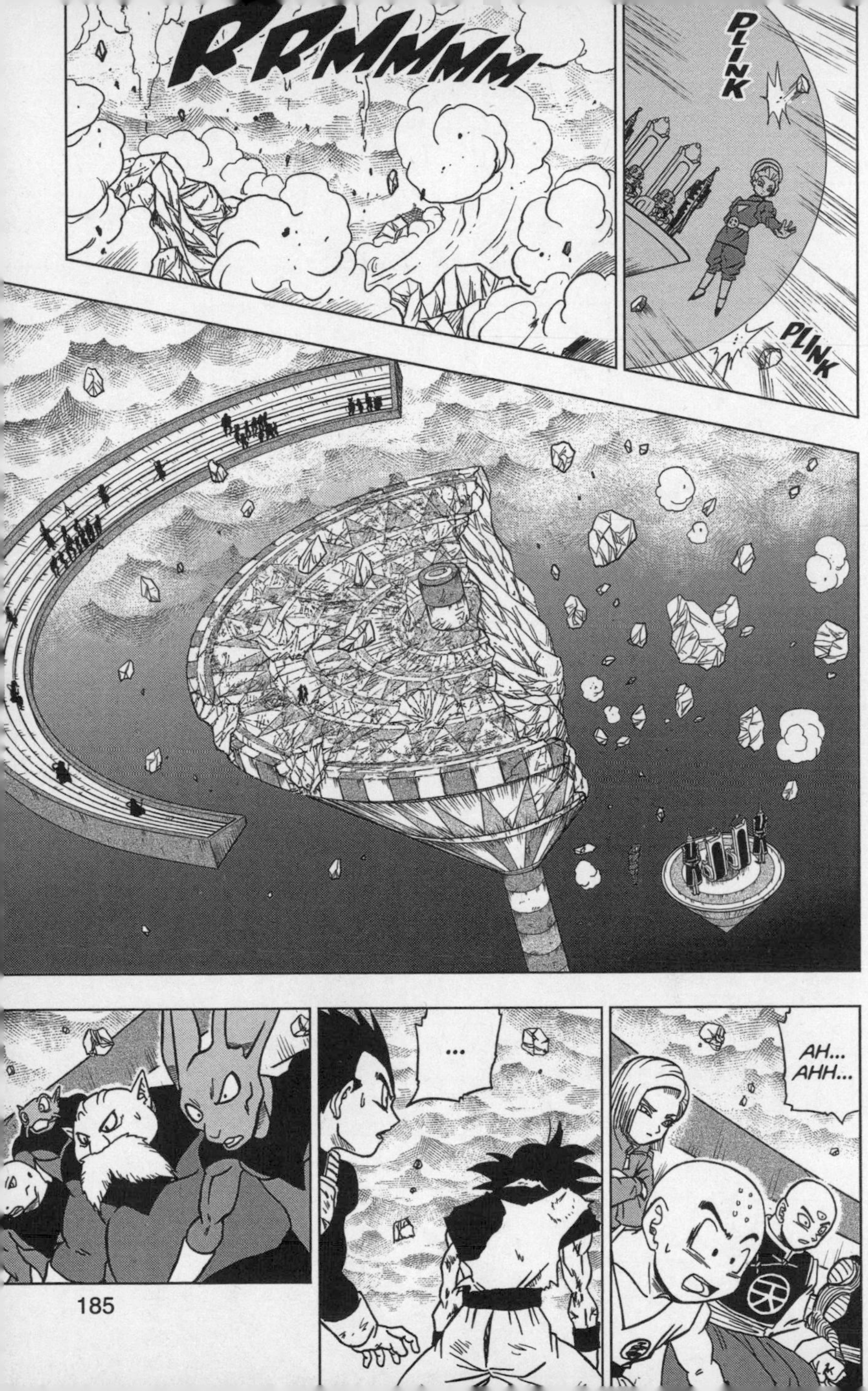
PLINK
PLINK
RRMMMM
AH... AHH...
...

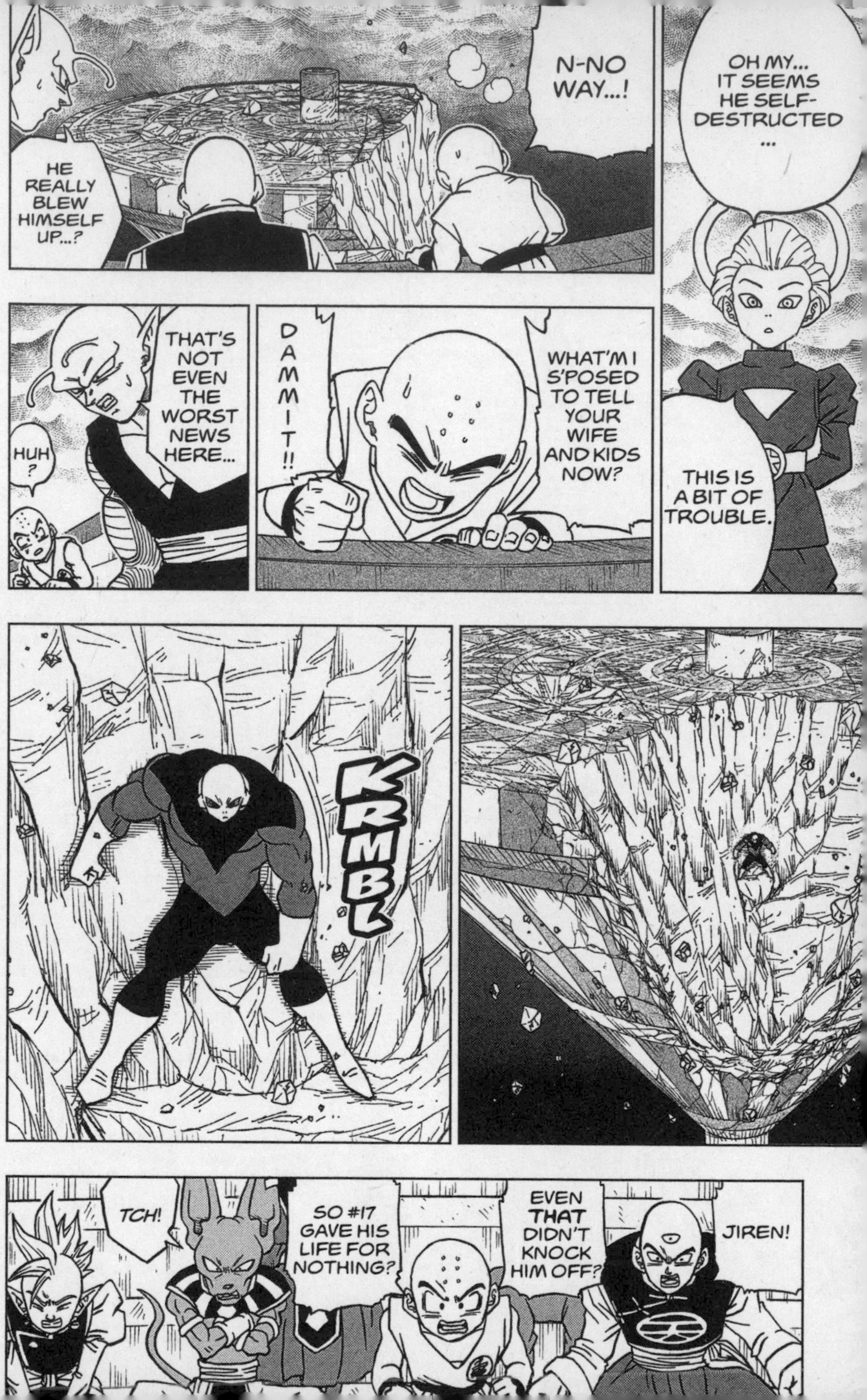
OH MY... IT SEEMS HE SELF-DESTRUCTED ...
THIS IS A BIT OF TROUBLE.
N-NO WAY...!
HE REALLY BLEW HIMSELF UP...?
WHAT'M I S'POSED TO TELL YOUR WIFE AND KIDS NOW?
DAMMIT!!
THAT'S NOT EVEN THE WORST NEWS HERE...
HUH?
KRMBL
JIREN!
EVEN **THAT** DIDN'T KNOCK HIM OFF?
SO #17 GAVE HIS LIFE FOR NOTHING?
TCH!

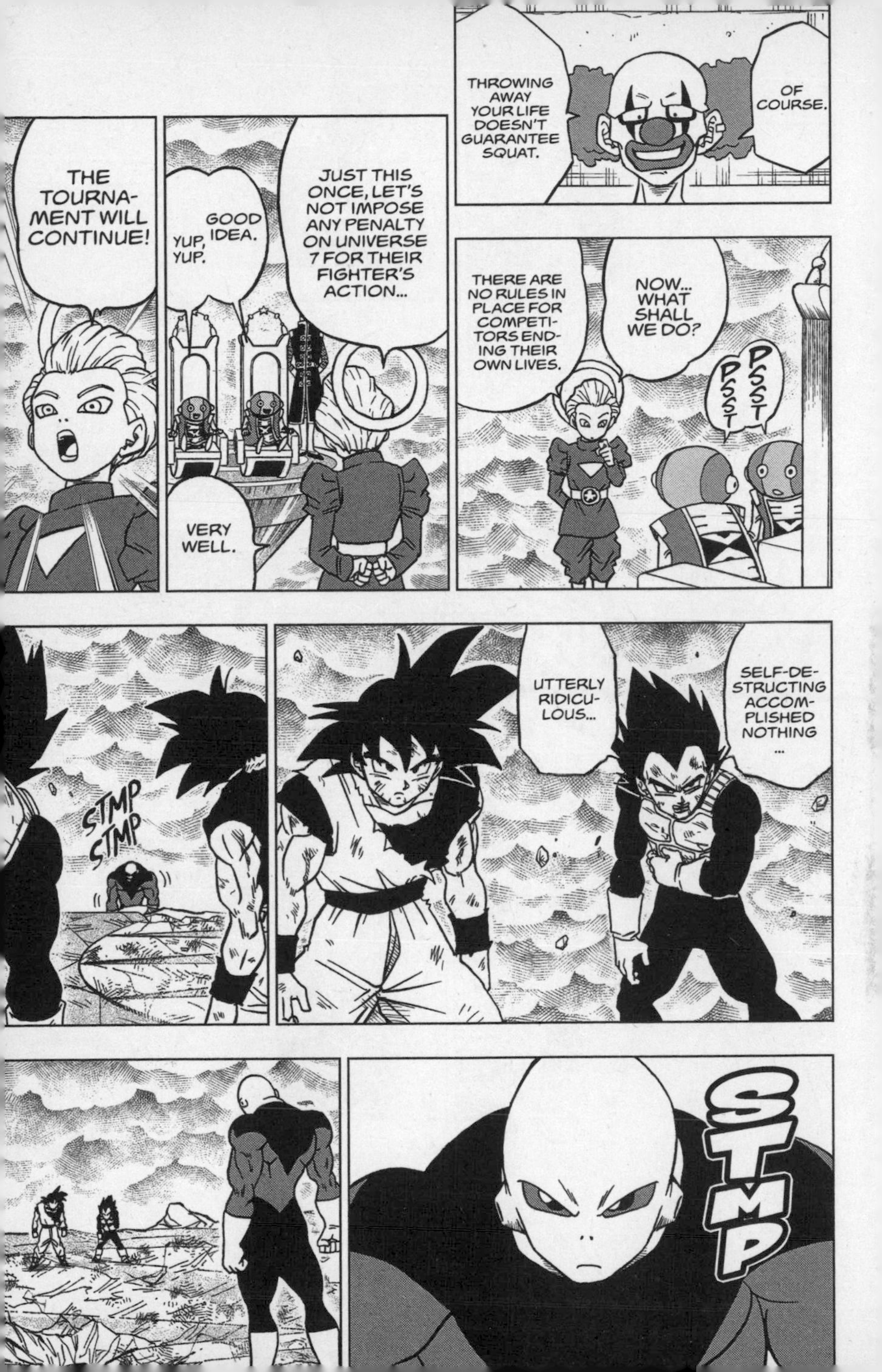
OF COURSE.
THROWING AWAY YOUR LIFE DOESN'T GUARANTEE SQUAT.
NOW... WHAT SHALL WE DO?
THERE ARE NO RULES IN PLACE FOR COMPETITORS ENDING THEIR OWN LIVES.
PSSST PSSST
JUST THIS ONCE, LET'S NOT IMPOSE ANY PENALTY ON UNIVERSE 7 FOR THEIR FIGHTER'S ACTION...
GOOD IDEA.
YUP, YUP.
VERY WELL.
THE TOURNAMENT WILL CONTINUE!
SELF-DESTRUCTING ACCOMPLISHED NOTHING ...
UTTERLY RIDICULOUS...
STMP STMP
STMP

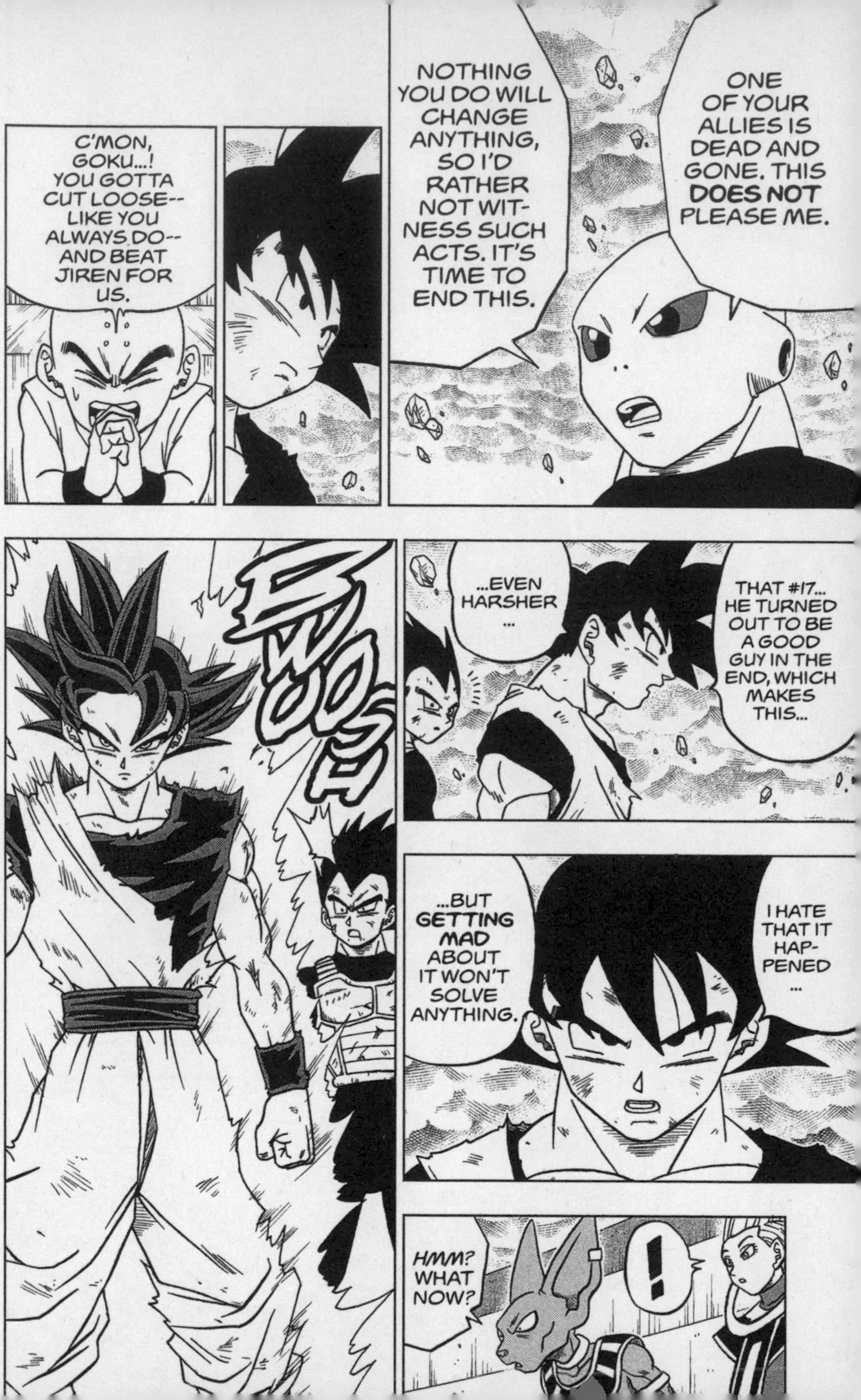
ONE OF YOUR ALLIES IS DEAD AND GONE. THIS DOES NOT PLEASE ME.
NOTHING YOU DO WILL CHANGE ANYTHING, SO I'D RATHER NOT WITNESS SUCH ACTS. IT'S TIME TO END THIS.
C'MON, GOKU...! YOU GOTTA CUT LOOSE-- LIKE YOU ALWAYS DO-- AND BEAT JIREN FOR US.
THAT #17... HE TURNED OUT TO BE A GOOD GUY IN THE END, WHICH MAKES THIS...
...EVEN HARSHER ...
I HATE THAT IT HAPPENED ...
...BUT GETTING MAD ABOUT IT WON'T SOLVE ANYTHING.
!
HMM? WHAT NOW?
WHOOSH

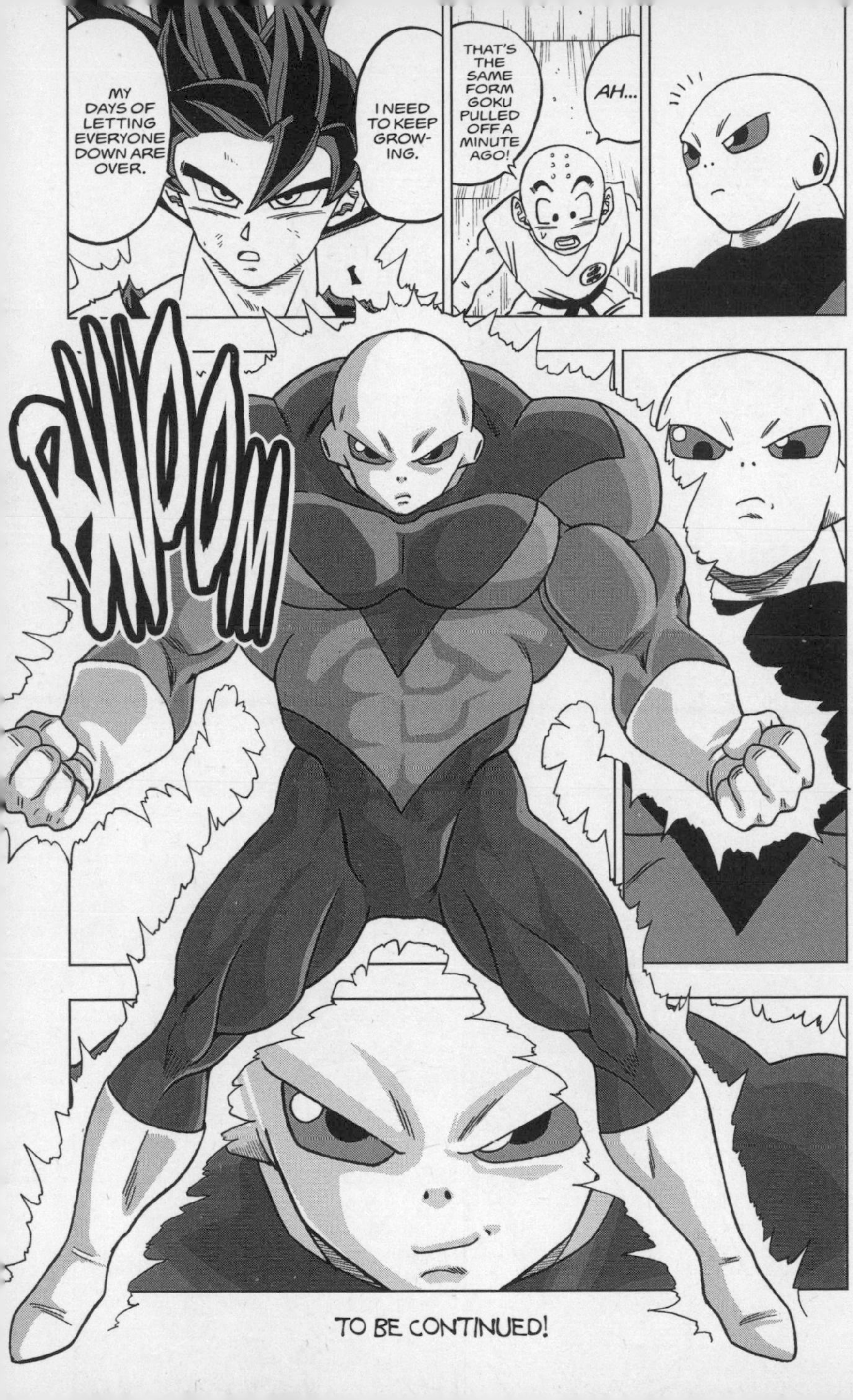
AH...
THAT'S THE SAME FORM GOKU PULLED OFF A MINUTE AGO!
I NEED TO KEEP GROWING.
MY DAYS OF LETTING EVERYONE DOWN ARE OVER.
TO BE CONTINUED!

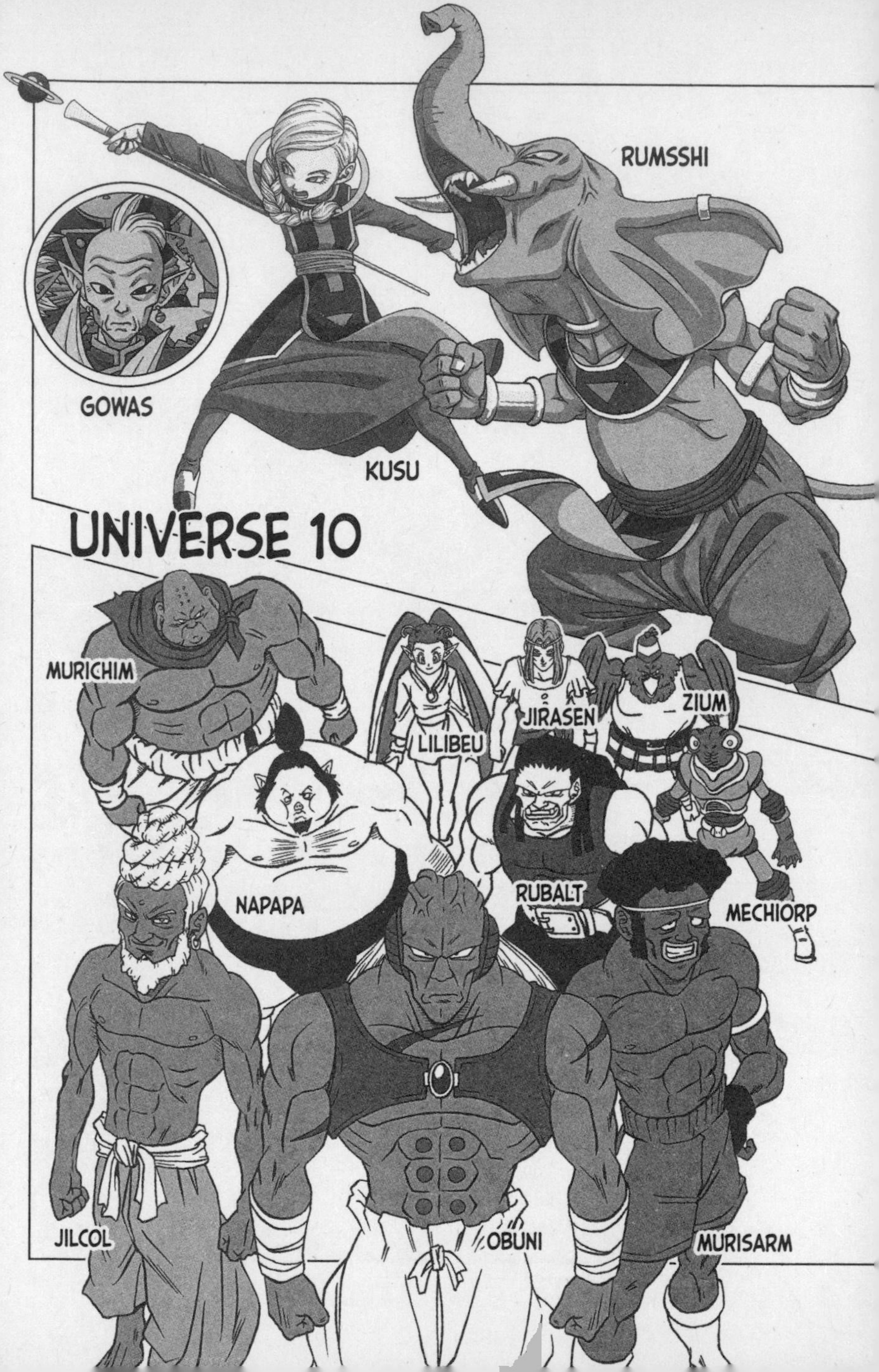
RUMSSHI
GOWAS
KUSU
UNIVERSE 10
MURICHIM
ZIUM
JIRASEN
LILIBEU
NAPAPA
RUBALT
MECHIORP
JILCOL
OBUNI
MURISARM

TORIYAMA SENSEI'S CORRECTIONS

※ I received some corrections on how to draw Jiren.

TOYOTAROU'S VERSION

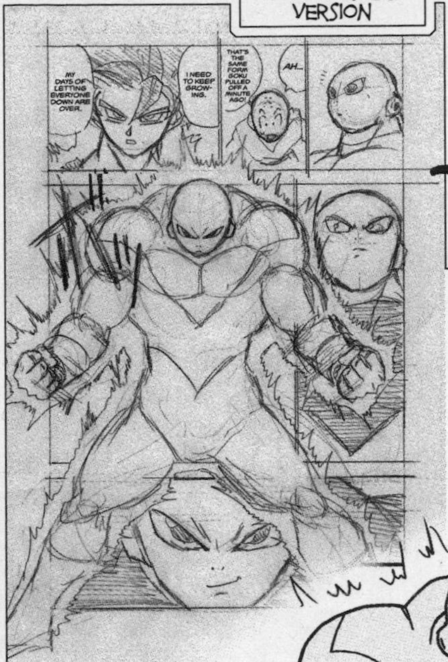
AH...
THAT'S THE SAME FORM GOKU PULLED OFF A MINUTE AGO!
I NEED TO KEEP GROW-ING.
MY DAYS OF LETTING EVERYONE DOWN ARE OVER.

TORIYAMA SENSEI'S VERSION

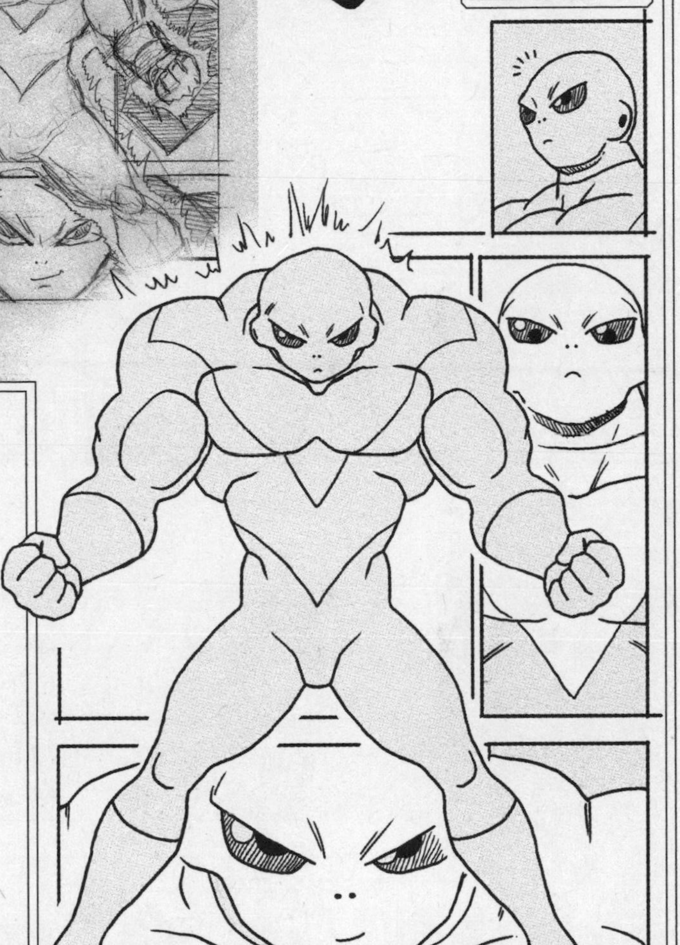

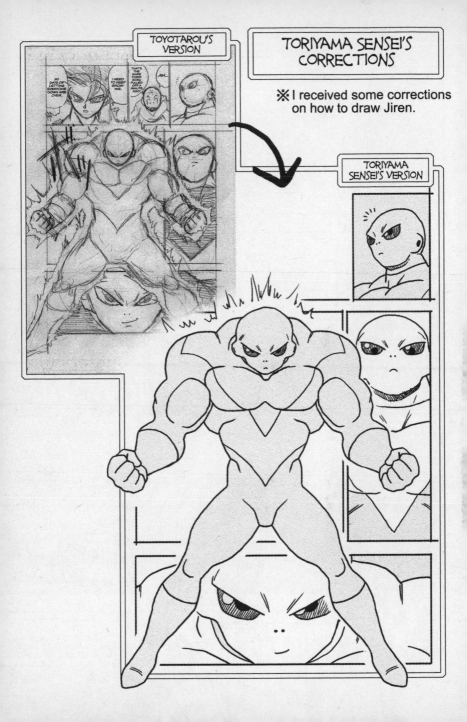

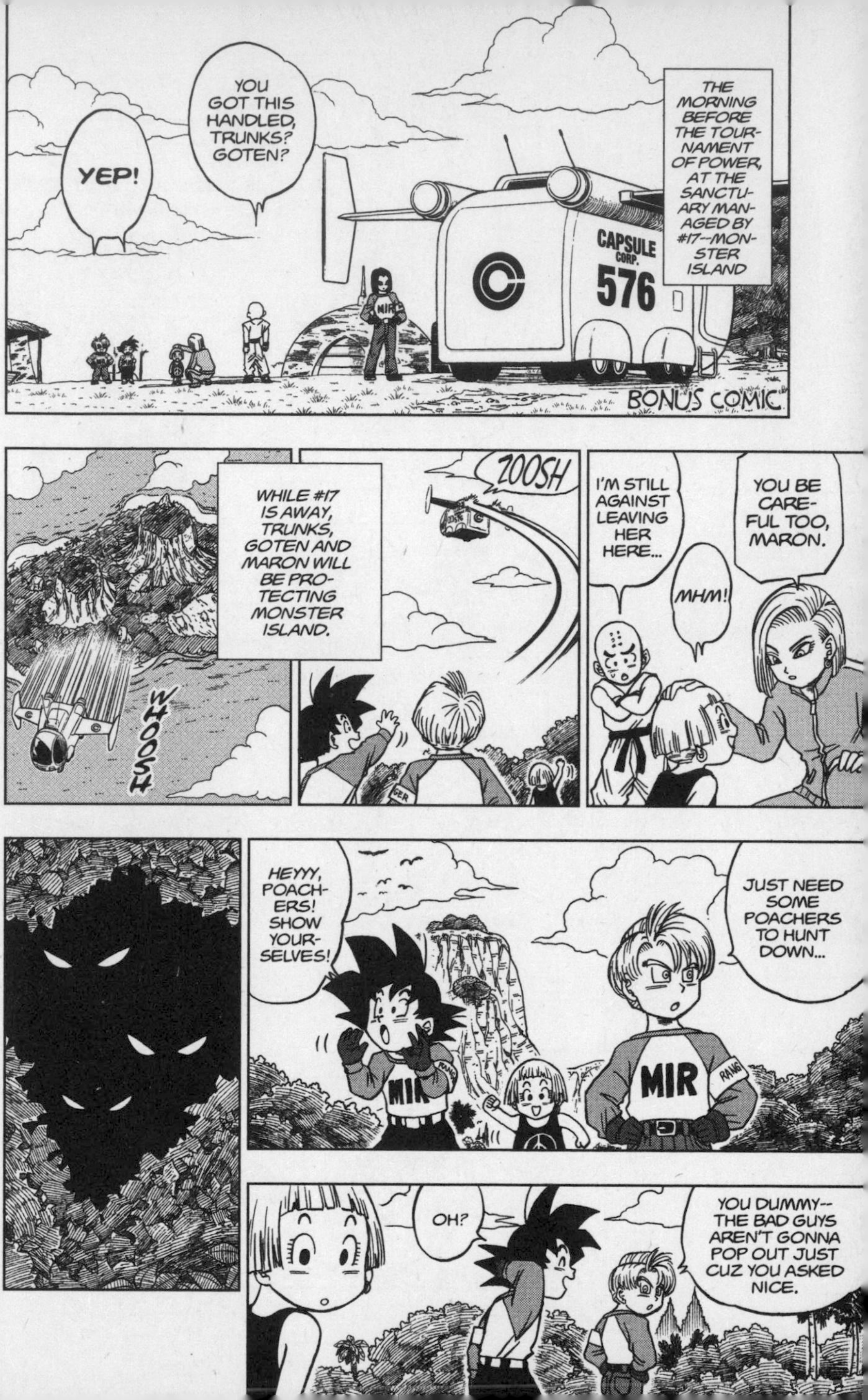
THE MORNING BEFORE THE TOURNAMENT OF POWER, AT THE SANCTUARY MANAGED BY #17--MONSTER ISLAND
YOU GOT THIS HANDLED, TRUNKS? GOTEN?
YEP!
CAPSULE CORP. 576
MIR
BONUS COMIC
YOU BE CAREFUL TOO, MARON.
I'M STILL AGAINST LEAVING HER HERE...
MHM!
ZOOSH
WHILE #17 IS AWAY, TRUNKS, GOTEN AND MARON WILL BE PROTECTING MONSTER ISLAND.
WHOOSH
JUST NEED SOME POACHERS TO HUNT DOWN...
HEYYY, POACHERS! SHOW YOURSELVES!
MIR
MIR
YOU DUMMY-- THE BAD GUYS AREN'T GONNA POP OUT JUST CUZ YOU ASKED NICE.
OH?

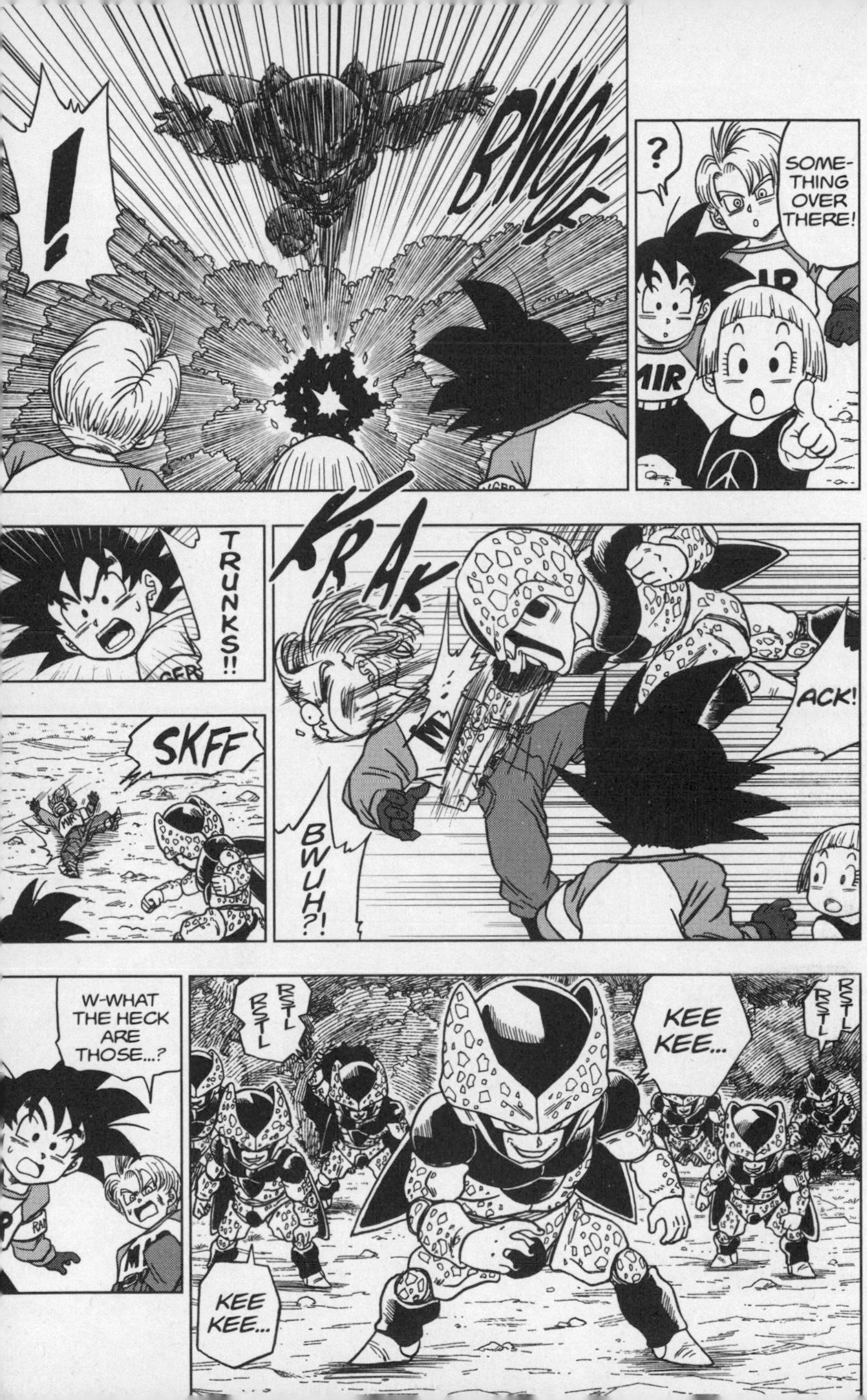
?
SOME-THING OVER THERE!
!
BWOOF
KRAK
ACK!
BWUH?!
TRUNKS!!
SKFF
RSTL RSTL
KEE KEE...
RSTL RSTL
KEE KEE...
W-WHAT THE HECK ARE THOSE...?

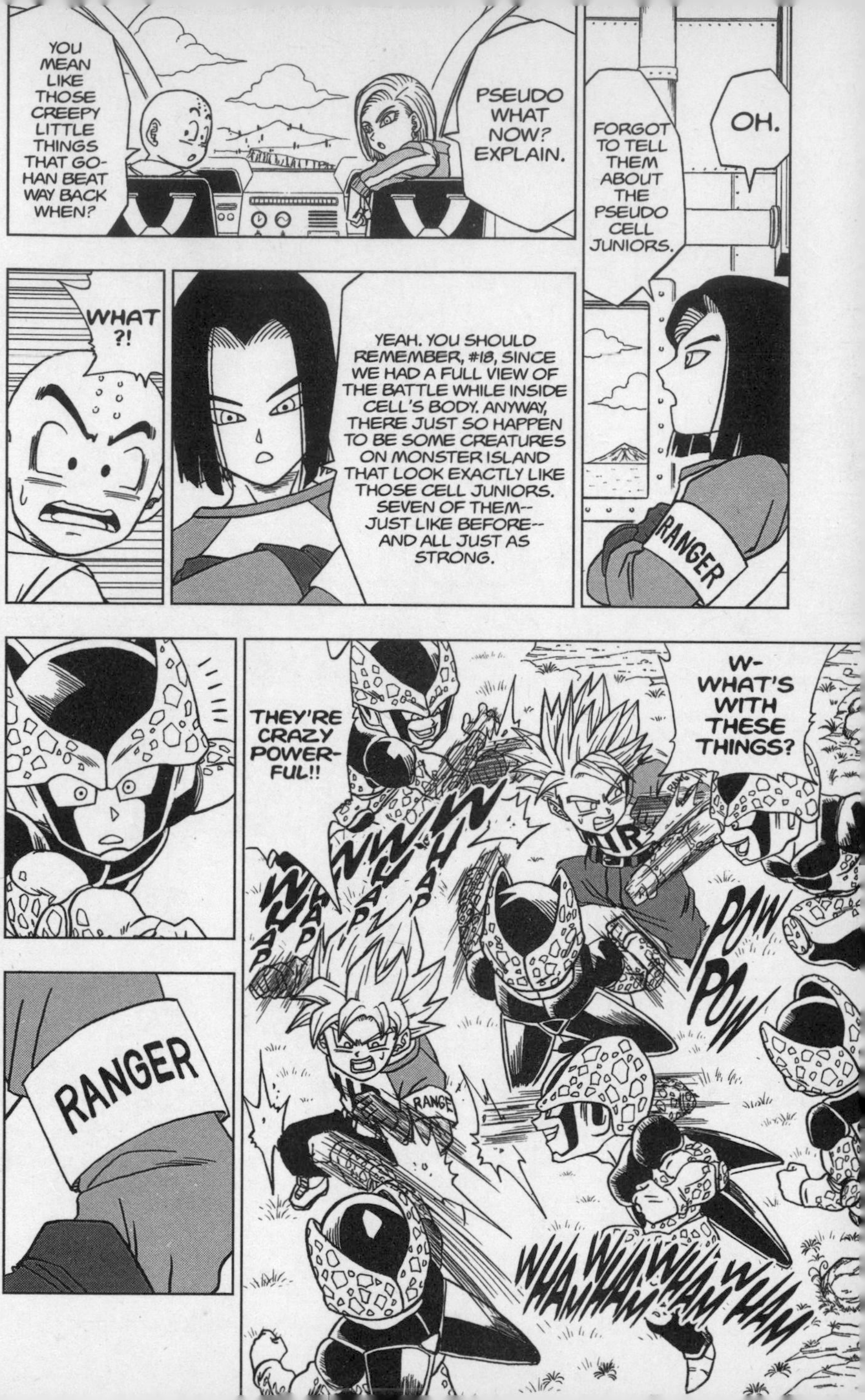
OH.
FORGOT TO TELL THEM ABOUT THE PSEUDO CELL JUNIORS.
PSEUDO WHAT NOW? EXPLAIN.
YOU MEAN LIKE THOSE CREEPY LITTLE THINGS THAT GO-HAN BEAT WAY BACK WHEN?
RANGER
YEAH. YOU SHOULD REMEMBER, #18, SINCE WE HAD A FULL VIEW OF THE BATTLE WHILE INSIDE CELL'S BODY. ANYWAY, THERE JUST SO HAPPEN TO BE SOME CREATURES ON MONSTER ISLAND THAT LOOK EXACTLY LIKE THOSE CELL JUNIORS. SEVEN OF THEM-- JUST LIKE BEFORE-- AND ALL JUST AS STRONG.
WHAT ?!
W-WHAT'S WITH THESE THINGS?
THEY'RE CRAZY POWER-FUL!!
POW POW
WHAM WHAM WHAM WHAM WHAM
RANGER

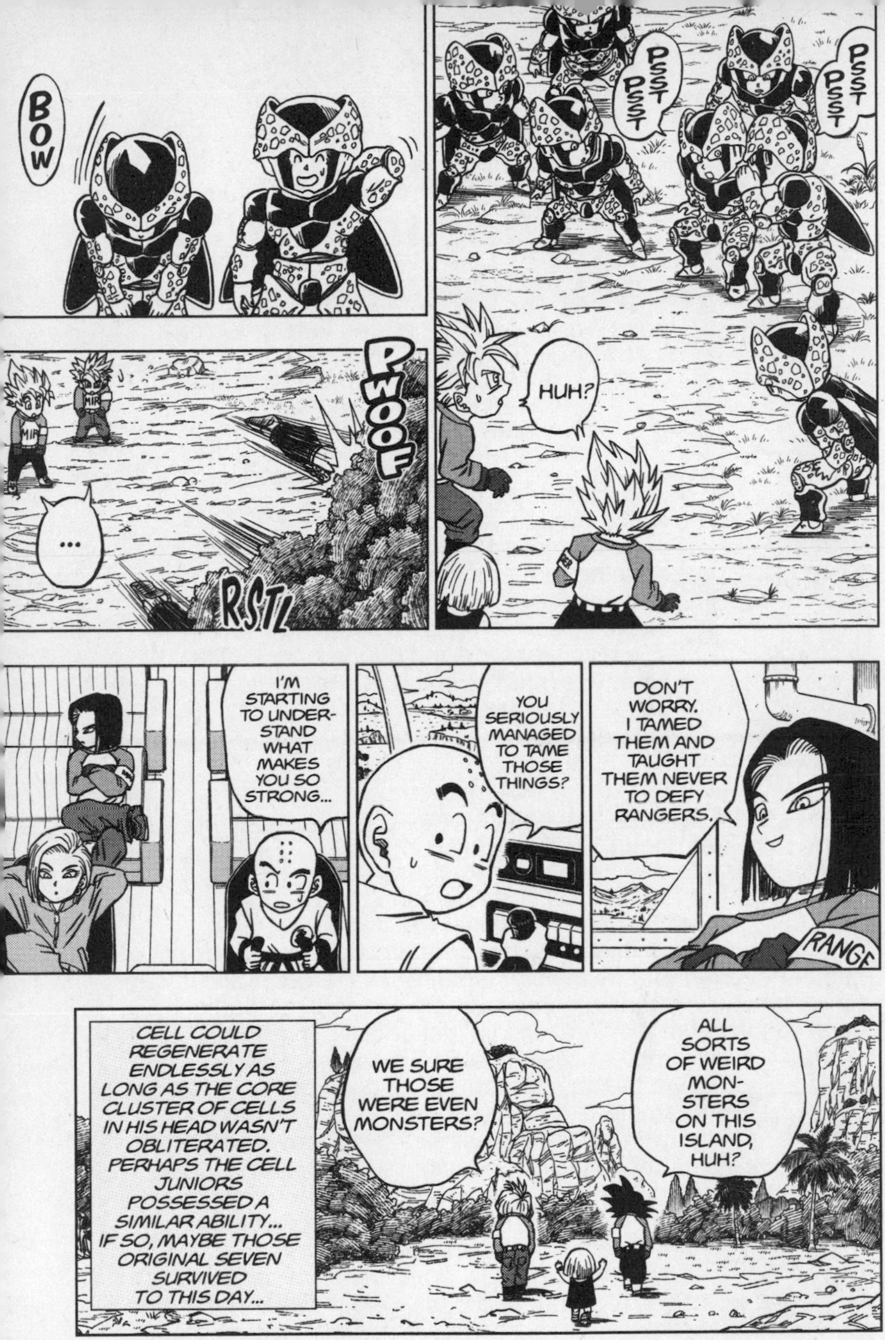
PSST PSST
PSST PSST
HUH?
BOW
PWOOF
RSTL
...
DON'T WORRY. I TAMED THEM AND TAUGHT THEM NEVER TO DEFY RANGERS.
YOU SERIOUSLY MANAGED TO TAME THOSE THINGS?
I'M STARTING TO UNDER-STAND WHAT MAKES YOU SO STRONG...
RANGE
ALL SORTS OF WEIRD MON-STERS ON THIS ISLAND, HUH?
WE SURE THOSE WERE EVEN MONSTERS?
CELL COULD REGENERATE ENDLESSLY AS LONG AS THE CORE CLUSTER OF CELLS IN HIS HEAD WASN'T OBLITERATED. PERHAPS THE CELL JUNIORS POSSESSED A SIMILAR ABILITY... IF SO, MAYBE THOSE ORIGINAL SEVEN SURVIVED TO THIS DAY...

ORIGINALLY PUBLISHED IN THE *JUMP VICTORY CARNIVAL OFFICIAL* 2018 GUIDEBOOK

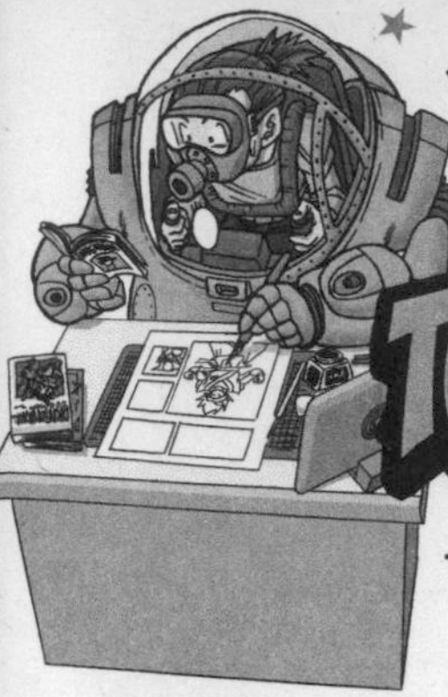

Toyotarou Asks!
TELL US, TORIYAMA SENSEI!!

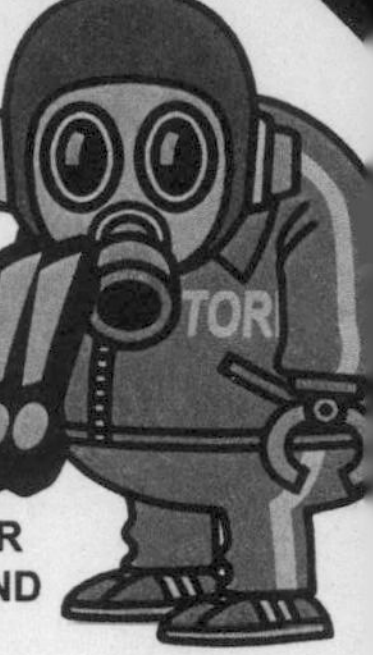

TOYOTAROU SENSEI ASKS ORIGINAL CREATOR TORIYAMA SENSEI ABOUT THE PROCESS BEHIND CHARACTER DESIGN AND STORY-CRAFTING. THOSE VALUABLE ANSWERS ARE HERE FOR EVERYONE!

Q.1 What's the most important thing when planning out the story?

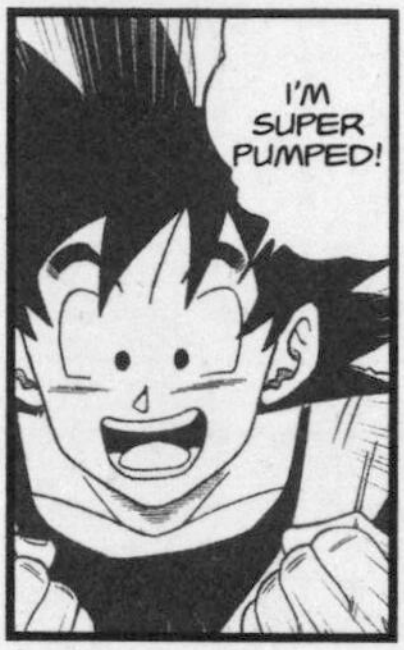
I'M SUPER PUMPED!

A The most important? That would probably be whether or not each new development can hold the readers' interest. It's key that you leave them wondering what exciting, new thing is about to happen. You also want to keep things novel, with elements that haven't been seen before, but at the same time simple and easy to understand.

Q.2 How do you come up with character designs and names?

A First I come up with their basic form. Naturally I go through trial and error to have these characters match the surrounding story elements, but I always prioritize designs that will take people by surprise. Take Freeza, for example. There's often this idea that big equals strong, so I subverted that by making him tiny. His second and third transformations are increasingly outlandish, leading one to think that his final form will follow suit, but then, nope--it's the simplest design yet. With names, I often want the sound of the word itself to match the character's overall image, but just as often I go with surprising names--like Piccolo--that I purposely pick because they don't seem to initially suit the character. When there are a whole bunch of new characters who need names, thinking up unique ones gets hard, so I'll pick a unified theme and do a series of parody names, like how the members of Freeza's army are based on foods you might find in the fridge or freezer. That's an easy approach, so it's one I use quite often.

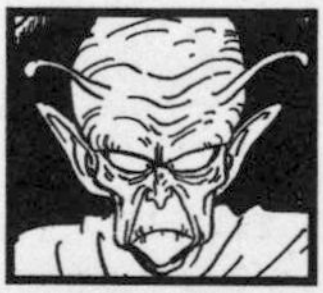

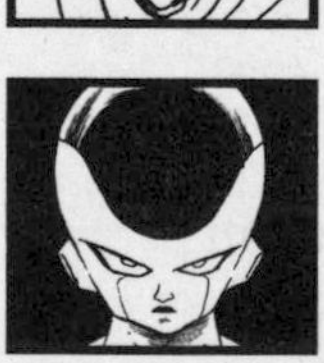

Q.3

Talk a little bit about how the characters in *Dragon Ball Super: Broly* came about.

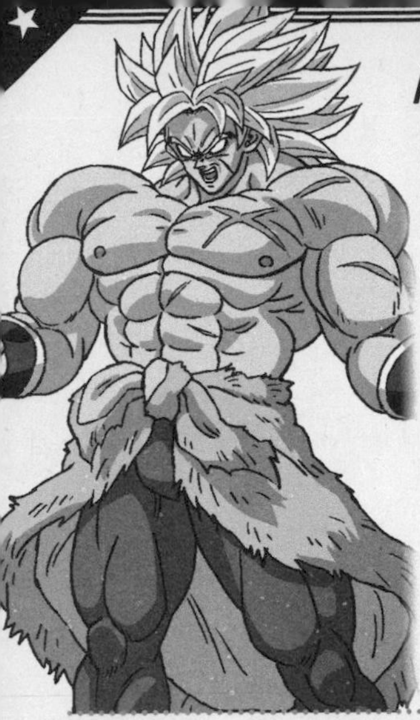

About Broly

A

Broly first appeared in those ancient animated movies. This was back when I was busy with the serialized manga, so when they asked me to create Broly, I came up with a basic design without knowing a thing about the stories he'd be involved in. In fact, I'd totally forgotten that I designed him. He was apparently a very popular character, so for the new movie, we tried to retain that original image while giving him something of a makeover.

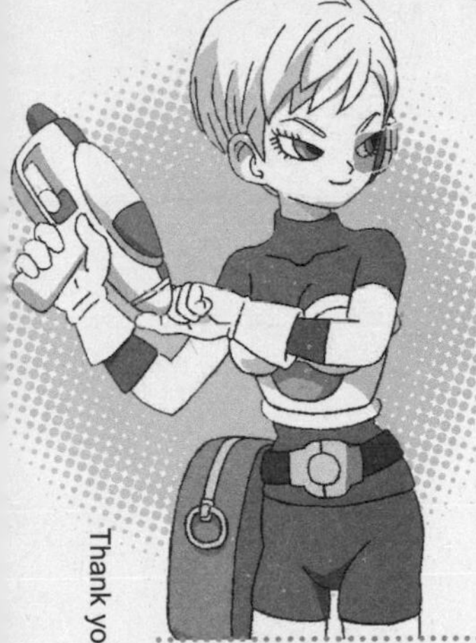

About Cheelai

A

Cheelai and Lemo are non-combatant members of Freeza's army. It sometimes got boring for me how *Dragon Ball* was full of nothing but fighters, and now and then I wished I could feature non-fighters like these guys. That's why these two in particular play important roles. When it came time to come up with their designs and stories, I got really excited and actually put in some effort. I realized I hadn't designed a "cute" female character in a long time, so I set out to make Cheelai the type of cutie pie I'm personally into. (^^)

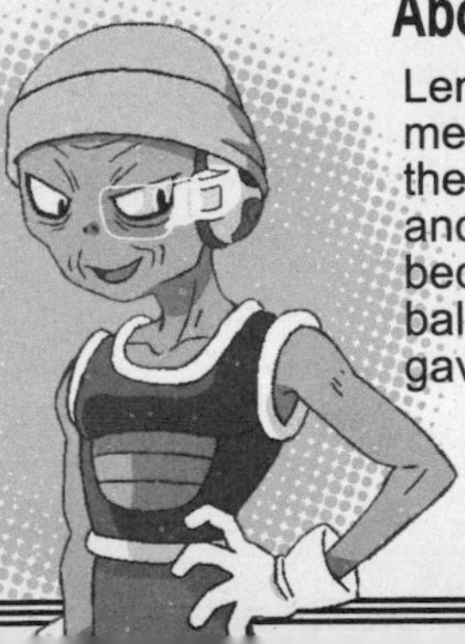

Thank you for this, Toriyama Sensei!
-Toyotarou

About Lemo

A

Lemo is an elderly, longtime member of the army. I actually love these sorts of subdued characters, and I went with a stereotypical alien look because I personally like it. There's a subtle balance to this guy design-wise that I think gave the animators some trouble. Beerus wasn't exactly easy to draw either, so as the original designer it's given me something to think about.

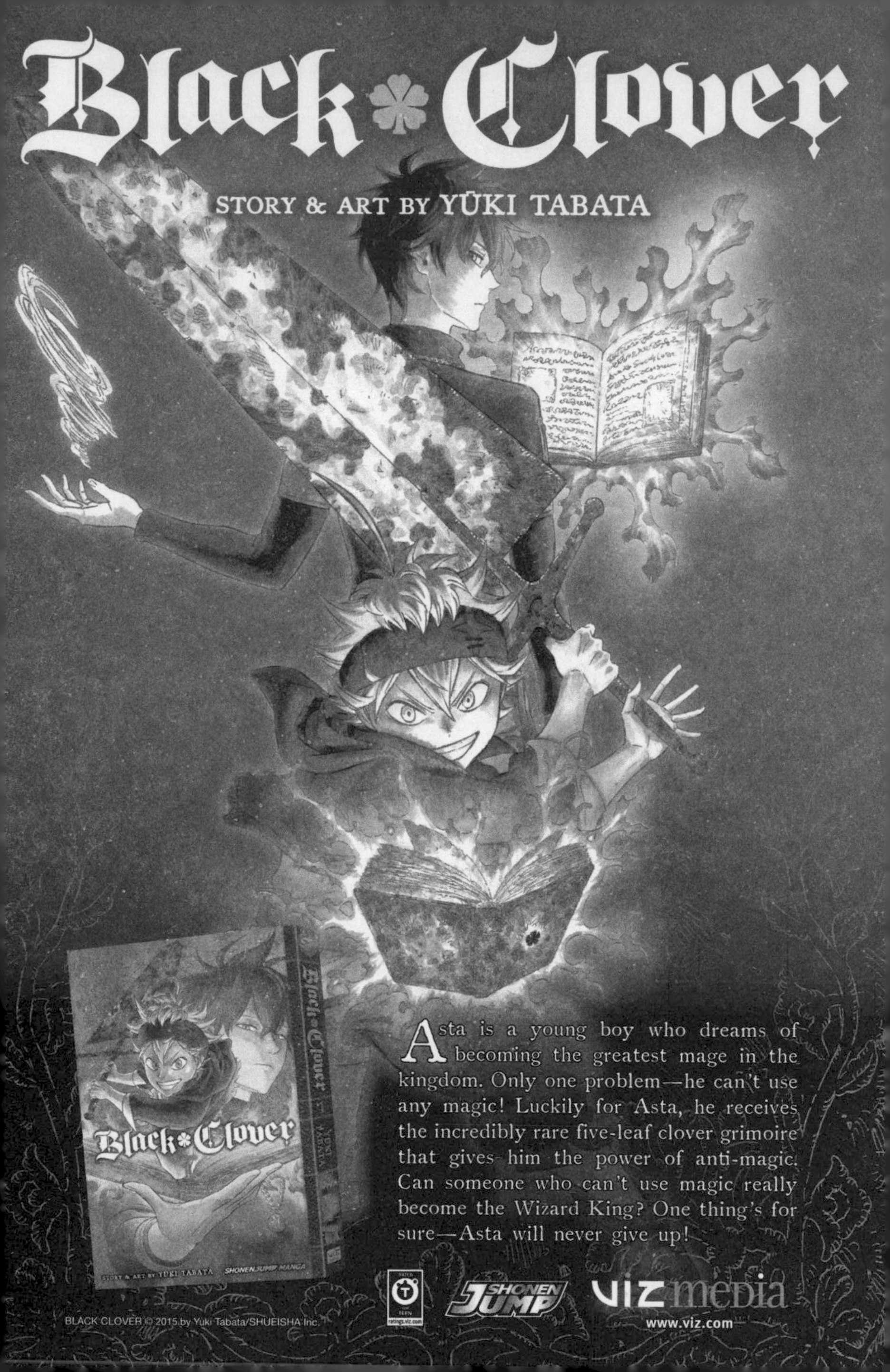
Black Clover
STORY & ART BY YŪKI TABATA
Asta is a young boy who dreams of becoming the greatest mage in the kingdom. Only one problem—he can't use any magic! Luckily for Asta, he receives the incredibly rare five-leaf clover grimoire that gives him the power of anti-magic. Can someone who can't use magic really become the Wizard King? One thing's for sure—Asta will never give up!
Black Clover
STORY & ART BY YŪKI TABATA
SHONEN JUMP MANGA
RATED T TEEN
ratings.viz.com
SHONEN JUMP
VIZ media
www.viz.com
BLACK CLOVER © 2015 by Yuki Tabata/SHUEISHA Inc.